SOURCES FOR THE STUDY
OF
HIGH MEDIEVAL CULTURE
1100-1300

The University of Michigan
Medieval and Renaissance Collegium
Publications

Nicholas H. Steneck, Editor

૭

The volumes in this series represent an effort by concerned teachers and scholars to make the process of publishing more responsive to the needs of their profession. Our objective is to produce inexpensive books that are of lasting quality, with regard to both content and material composition, by utilizing the advances of modern technology and assuming ourselves most of the work involved in preparing materials for publication. It is hoped that such an effort and objective, if combined with only a limited circulation, can result in an economically and intellectually justifiable venture.

SOURCES FOR THE STUDY
OF
HIGH MEDIEVAL CULTURE
1100-1300

Edited by Nicholas H. Steneck

with

Duncan Robertson and Harald Scholler

The University of Michigan Medieval and Renaissance Collegium

Ann Arbor, Michigan

To

the students of

MARC 201

CONTENTS

Preface   ix

1.   Historical Setting   1

     Chronicle of the Abbey of S. Werburg
       at Chester *1*
     Records from the Fourth Crusade *8*

2.   Socio-Economic Context   23

     The Account of the Daily Expenses of
       a Person of Rank in the Reign of
       King Edward I *23*
     On the Marvels of the City of Milan *29*

3.   The Institutions of Culture: Universities   37
     and Courts

     The Battle of the Seven Arts *37*
     Concerning the Trifles of the Court *48*

4.   Literature, Part I: The Epic Tradition   63

     The Song of Roland *63*
     Nibelungenlied *72*
     Nibelungenklage *87*

5.   Literature, Part II: Lyric Poetry   99

     Troubadours and Trouvères *99*
     Minnesong and *Spruchdichtung* *108*

6.   Literature, Part III: Saints' Lives   119

     The Life of Saint Alexis *119*
     The Life of Saint Mary the Egyptian *135*

7.   Literature, Part IV: Romance   155

     Tristan's Folly *155*
     Lanzelet *163*
     Parzival *170*

8. Architecture and Illumination 185

    On the Burning and Repair of the Church
      of Canterbury *185*
    The Technique of Manuscript Illumination
      201

9. The Twelfth Century: Currents of Debate 213

    A History of the Calamities of Abelard
      213
    Against Certain Heads of Abelard's Heresies
      229

10. Scholastic Philosophy and Theology 245

    Opus majus *245*
    Summa contra gentiles *259*

11. Two Views on the Human Condition 277

    The Mirror of Manslyfe. The First Booke
      277
    An Account of the Mind's Journey to God
      291

Preface

The selections that follow are designed to be read in conjunction with the study of high medieval culture, either through formal preparation by students enrolled in related courses or through informal reading and individual study by those with more than a passing interest in the richness and diversity of the high Middle Ages. The organization of the chapters follows roughly very traditional lines, although it is in no way exclusive; literature speaks to social concerns, artistic activities involve institutions and economics, manuscripts containing lyric poems can be used for the study of paleography, and so on. The brief introductions include only the barest of facts needed to place the selections into larger contexts and explain briefly their importance. If this leaves the task of reconstructing the past mostly in the hands of the reader, one objective of this book will have been met: to provide the materials that can be used for understanding the past and not the understandings themselves.

Funding for this book stems in part from the National Endowment for the Humanities, under whose auspices and guidance the general program in medieval and renaissance studies that led to this publication was begun at Michigan some three years ago, and in part by the University of Michigan College of Literature, Science, and the Arts. Numerous colleagues contributed suggestions regarding selections; three in particular took a special interest in the project since its inception and provided original translations when they were needed: Duncan Robertson of the Department of the Romance Languages and Literature at Michigan, Harald Scholler of the Department of Germanic Languages and Literature at Michigan, and Sarah White of the Department of French and Italian at Franklin and Marshall College. Ultimately, a project such as this cannot succeed without the gracious cooperation of many publishing houses and the use of earlier translations that are presently in the public domain. To these we are indebted as follows:

Chapter 1: *Annales Cestriensis: or, Chronicle of the Abbey of S. Werburg, at Chester,* edited with an introduction and notes by Richard Copley Christie, *The Record Society for the Publication of Original Documents relating to Lancashire and Cheshire* 14 (1886), London: The Record Society, 1887, abridged from pp. 17-121; "The Fourth Crusade," edited by Dana Carleton Monro, *Translations and Reprints from the Original Sources of European History* 3. no. 1, Philadelphia: Department of History of the University of Pennsylvania, 1896, pp. 2-20, reprinted by permission of the University of Pennsylvania Press.

Chapter 2: Joseph Hunter, "Travelling Expenses in the Thirteenth Century," *Retrospective Review and Historical and Antiquarian Magazine,* 2nd ser. 1 (1827): 269-276, 465-469; Bonvesin della Riva, *On the Marvels of the City of Milan,* from *Medieval Trade in the*

Mediterranean World, by Robert S. Lopez and Irving W. Raymond, New York: Columbia University Press, 1955, pp. 61-69, by permission of the publisher.

Chapter 3: Henri d'Andeli, *La Bataille des VII Ars,* translated by Louis J. Paetow, *The Battle of the Seven Arts,* 4, no. 1, History 1, no. 1, Berkeley: University of California Press, 1914, reprinted by permission of the publisher; Walter Map, *De Nugis Curialium,* translated by Montague R. James, *Walter Map's "De nugis curialium,"* London: Honourable Society of Cymmrodorion, 1923, pp. 1-8, 11-13, 17-20, 273-279.

Chapter 4: *La chanson de Roland,* from THE SONG OF ROLAND, translated by W.S. Merwin, Copyright © by W.S. Merwin, pp. 55-67, reprinted by permission of Random House, Inc.; *Nibelungenlied,* translated by Margaret Armour, *The Fall of the Nibelungs,* London: J.M. Dent, 1908, pp. 94-103, 210-221, 233-235; *Nibelungenklage,* translated by Harald Scholler, Thomas Kozak, and Philip Sweet from Karl Bartsch, ed., *Diu Klage, mit den Lesarten sämtlicher Handschriften,* Leipzig, 1875; reprint ed. Darmstadt: Wissenschaftliche Buchgesellschaft, 1964.

Chapter 5, Troubadours and Trouvères: A) Facsimile— *Le Manuscrit du Roi,* edited by Jean Beck, *Les Chansonniers des troubadours et des trouvères,* Philadelphia: University of Pennsylvania Press, 1938; French text—Raymond Hill and Thomas Bergin, eds., *Anthology of the Provençal Troubadours,* New Haven: Yale University Press, 1941, pp. 31-32; English translation— SONGS OF THE TROUBADOURS, edited and translated by Anthony Bonner, pp. 98-99, Copyright © 1972 by Schocken Books Inc., reprinted by permission of the publisher. B) Facsimile—*Le Manuscrit du Roi;* French text and English translation—from LYRICS OF THE TROUBADOURS AND TROUVÈRES as part of THE MEDIEVAL LYRIC (2 Vols.), Copyright © 1973 by Frederick Goldin, reprinted by permission of Doubleday & Company, Inc. C) Facsimile—*Le Chansonnier Cangé,* edited by Jean Beck, Philadelphia: University of Pennsylvania Press, 1927, fols. 28v-29r; French text—*Poètes et Romanciers du Moyen Age,* edited by Albert Pauphilet, Bibliothèque de la Pléiade, Paris: Galimard, 1952, pp. 919-920; English translation by Duncan Robertson. D) Facsimile—*Le Manscrit du Roi;* French text—*Chansons de Gace Brulé,* edited by Gédéon Huet, *Société des Ancienes Textes Français,* Paris: Firmin Didot, 1902, pp. 8-10; English translation by Duncan Robertson.

Chapter 5, Minnesong and *Spruchdichtung:* A) Facsimile— H. Tervooren and U. Müller, eds., *Die Jenaer Liederhandschrift, Litterae* no. 10, Göppingen: Alfred Kümmerle, 1972, fol. 29r; German text—Karl Lachmann et al., eds., *Des minnesangs Frühling,* Leipzig: S. Hirzel, 1888, 24.9; English translation—J.M. Thomas, *Medieval*

German Lyric Verse in English Translation, University of North Carolina Studies in the Germanic Languages and Literatures, No. 60, Chapel Hill: The University of North Carolina Press, 1968, p. 30, reprinted by permission of the publisher. B) Modern arrangement of melody with text—Friedrich Mauer, ed., *Die Lieder Walthers von der Vogelweide, Altdeutsche Textbibliothek,* no. 43, Tübingen: Max Niemeyer, 1960, p. 33; German text—Karl Lachmann, et al., eds., *Die Gedichte Walthers von der Vogelweide,* Berlin: W. de Gruyter, 1965, 104.7; English translation—J.W. Thomas, *Medieval German Lyric Verse in English Translation,* p. 121. C) Modern arrangement of melody with text—A.T. Hatto and R.J. Taylor, *The Songs of Neidhart von Reuental,* Manchester: Manchester University Press, 1958, p. 14; English translation—J.W. Thomas, *Medieval German Lyric Verse in English Translation,* pp. 131-133. D) Modern arrangement of melody with text—Ronald J. Taylor, *Die Melodien der weltlichen Lieder des Mittelalters,* Stuttgart: J.B. Metzler, 1964, p. 24; English translation—J.W. Thomas, *Tannhäuser: Poet and Legend. With Texts and Translations of his Works,* University of North Carolina Studies in the Germanic Languages and Literatures, No. 77, Chapel Hill: The University of North Carolina Press, 1974, pp. 151-155, reprinted by permission of the publisher. E) Facsimile— H. Tervooren and U. Müller, eds., *Die Jenaer Liederhandschrift,* fol. 80r-v; Music with German transcription—Georg Holz, ed., *Die Jenaer Liederhandschrift, Getreuer Abdruck des Textes* no. 1, Leipzig: C.L. Hirschfeld, 1901, pp. 134-135; Modern arrangement of melody with text and English translation—Wesley Thomas and Barbara Garvey Seagrave, *The Songs of the Minnesinger, Prince Wizlaw of Rügen,* University of North Carolina Studies in the Germanic Languages and Literatures, No. 59, Chapel Hill: The University of North Carolina Press, 1967, pp. 145-147, reprinted by permission of the publisher.

Chapter 6: *The Life of Saint Alexis,* translated by Sarah M. White from C. Storey, ed., *La Vie de Saint Alexis, Textes Littéraries Français,* Paris: Droz, 1968; *The Life of Saint Mary the Egyptian,* translated by William Kretschmar and Duncan Robertson from A. T. Baker, ed., *La Vie de Sainte Marie l'Egyptienne, Revue des Langues Romanes* 59 (1916-1917): 145-401.

Chapter 7: *Tristan's Folly,* translated by Duncan Robertson from Ernest Hoepffmer, ed., *La Folie Tristan de Berne,* Paris: Université de Strasbourg, 1949; Ulrich von Zatzikhoven, *Lanzelet,* from K.G.T. Webster (translator): *Ulrich von Zatzikoven, Lanzelet,* with revisions, additional notes, and introduction by R.S. Loomis, New York: Columbia University Press, 1951, pp. 30-33, 36-41, by permission of the publisher; PARZIVAL: A Romance of the Middle Ages, by Wolfram von Eschenbach, translated by Helen M. Mustard and Charles E. Passage, Copyright © 1961 by Helen M. Mustard and Charles E.

Passage, pp. 152-165, 214-220, reprinted by permission of Random House, Inc.

Chapter 8: Gervase of Canterbury, *On the Burning and Repair of the Church of Canterbury*, translated by Robert Willis, *The Architectural History of Canterbury Cathedral*, London: Longman and Co., 1845, pp. 32-62; *De arte illuminandi*, translated by D.V. Thompson, jr. and G.H. Hamilton, *An Anonymous Fourteenth-Century Treatise, De arte illuminandi, The Technique of Manuscript Illumination*, New Haven: Yale University Press, 1933.

Chapter 9: Peter Abelard, *Historia calamitatum*, from THE LETTERS OF ABELARD AND HELOISE, by Peter Abelard and Heloise, translated by C.K. Scott-Moncrieff, pp. 3-15, 23-33, Copyright 1926 and renewed 1954 by Alfred A. Knopf, Inc., reprinted by permission of Alfred A. Knopf, Inc.; Bernard of Clairvaux, "Against Certain Heads of Abelard's Heresies," translated by Samuel J. Eales, *Some Letters of Saint Bernard, Abbot of Clairvaux*, edited by F.A. Gasquet, London: John Hodges, 1904, pp. 259-266, 271-282, 286-293.

Chapter 10: Roger Bacon, *Opus majus*, translated by Robert G. Burke, Philadelphia: University of Pennsylvania Press, 1928, abridged from 1: 35-65, reprinted by permission of the publisher; Thomas Aquinas, *Summa contra gentiles*, translated by the English Dominican Fathers, London: Burns Oates and Washbourne, 1924, abridged from pp. 1-33.

Chapter 11: Innocent III, *De contemptu mundi*, translated by H. Kirton, *The Mirror of Man's Lyfe*, London: H. Bynneman, 1576; Bonaventura, *Itinerarium mentis in Deum*, translated by Thomas Davidson, "The Soul's Progress in God," *The Journal of Speculative Philosophy* 21 (1887): abridged from pp. 289-324.

1. HISTORICAL SETTING

Chronicle of the Abbey of S. Werburg at Chester

High medieval culture rests in part on a foundation of notable births and deaths, major military encounters, political confrontations, and ecclesiastical happenings. Such events were noted by comtemporaries, particularly among the clergy, in cummulative records called "chronicles" or "annals." In the excerpted sections of the *Annales Cestrienses* below, kings, dukes, and clergy make brief appearances, along with famines and other events of daily life, to provide a brief glance at the course of events of the day, as seen from the standpoint of brothers living in the Abbey of Saint Werburg, Cheshire, England.

1093 In this year the lord Anselm, abbot of the church of Bec, came to England, who before this had frequently been in England. On his coming to England this last time, Anselm was acclaimed by many as archbishop, but, humbly desiring to escape the burden of so great an honour, on the invitation of the noble prince, earl Hugh, he came to Chester, and there founded the abbey in honour of S. Werburg, and, having assembled the monks together, he appointed Richard, a monk of Bec, the first abbot. Having done this, in the same year, upon his return from Chester, he was made archbishop of Canterbury.

1094 At this time the great hall at Westminster was built.

1095 A council was held at Clermont.

1100 William [Rufus], king of the English, son of the great William, was killed in the New Forest.

1110 King Henry, son of William the bastard, gave [Matilda] his daughter in marriage to Udescalcus [Henry V.], emperor of Germany, who now lies buried at Chester.

1114 The Thames at London was completely dried up, and the sea overflowed its boundaries for a space of ten miles.

1118 Matilda II., queen of England, died.

1135 King Henry [I.] died.
      Hugh Malbanc died, Dec 29.

1144 A boy named William is crucified at Norwich, and there is a very great famine in the same year.

1149 The return of [Louis VII.], king of France, from Jerusalem.

1156 In this year Henry, king of England, first led his army into Wales against Owen.

1162 The most holy father Thomas [à Becket] was consecrated archbishop of Canterbury on June 3.

1164 Thomas, archbishop of Canterbury, departed out of England.

1168 Matilda, daughter of king Henry II., was given in marriage to the duke of Saxony.

1170 S. Thomas [à Becket] returned into England.

1178 The sea broke in, in Holland [Linconshire], on January 12, in the middle of the night. It drowned men and cattle, and wrought innumerable evils.

1179 A general council was held in the city of Rome, under pope Alexander III., at which three hundred and two bishops were present.

1180 Chester was almost entirely burnt down, that is to say, the greater part of the city, on Mid-Lent Sunday a 2 o'clock p.m.

1183 A great famine owing to the want of bread.

1185 In February, after the feast of the Purification of S. Mary, [Heraclius,] patriarch of Jerusalem, came to England to seek assistance against the Saracens.

   On the first day after Palm Sunday, that is on Monday, April 15, there was a great earthquake in very many places in England, and as some say particularly, in every region of the earth; it happened at the sixth hour of the day.

1187 In this year a great war began between Philip [Augustus] surnamed *Dieu donné,* king of France, son of Louis [VII.], and Henry, king of England; such a war, indeed, as that when the whole forces of each side were assembled together for the purpose of fighting, the standard is raised in the midst, but by the will of God, who looked with compassion on the effusion of so much blood, the two kings aforesaid [effected a truce].

   Pope Urban [III.] died on S. Luke the Evangelist's day [October 18], and in his place Gregory VIII. was elected, who died eight days before Christmas day, and Clement [III.] succeeded him.

   Also on May 1 the Saracens invaded the kingdom of Jerusalem in the Holy Land, and in the first battle killed the grand master of the Temple [Theodoric] by name, and two hundred horsemen and a thousand infantry. Afterwards, within the octave of the Apostles Peter and Paul, that is to say on July 9, came Saladin with a strong force into the Holy Land of Jerusalem and captured all the fortresses except four, and laid waste the whole territory. And the Holy Cross was also captured and carried away.

1188 Our Lord Jesus Christ in the triumph of the Cross appeared visibly in the air, from the twelfth hour of the day even until night, and was seen by all in Dunstable, and by an infinite number of people for a hundred miles round. There was also a star of wonderful brightness beyond the cross gradually preceding it to the highest point of the heavens, followed by the cross and the image of the Lord in the air.

1189 A great slaughter of the Jews throughout England.

1192 Richard, king of England, when he had heard a report that the king of France had devastated his territory, and had seized upon his castles in Normandy, made a three years' truce with Saladin and the Turks, and then undertook to return with very few followers—only six as they say. But when he had arrived in the territory of the duke of Austria, having been detected to be the king of England, and having been made prisoner by the duke of Austria, he was handed over to the emperor of Germany, and was detained in chains for a long time.

1193 On the promise of many thousand marks, Richard, king of England, was freed from his chains, but was not set at liberty. For whose ransom there was given the wool of the monks and canons throughout England, and also a fourth part of the income of other persons. But as this was not sufficient it was ordered that the rings of the bishops and abbots, and the golden vessels and silver cups wheresoever they could be found should be given up for the liberation of the king. The shrines were also stripped and the crosses and reliquaries, and so the money was got together.

1194 King Richard was set free by the emperor, or rather was ransomed for a hundred and sixty thousand marks, and having left certain hostages returned to England in Lent, and came to Nottingham on the Wednesday before Palm Sunday [April 1].

1195 A very great famine throughout all England, so that a load [or seam] of corn was sold for ten shillings.

1199 Richard, king of England, died, having been struck by an arrow. John Lackland succeeded him, and was crowned at London.

1203 King John lost much land and many castles beyond the sea.

1204 Two full moons were seen in a clear sky after vespers, but whilst it was still daylight.

King John gave his daughter, Joan, to Llewelin, prince of Wales, and with her the castle of Ellesmere.

Also king John, having assembled a noble and very large army at Portsmouth, put to sea, but soon returned, and dismissed his army, and every one returned to his own home.

In this year the council of Arles was held.

1208 The interdict began in England.

1212 London was burned down, and many persons were destroyed by the fire.

1213 John, king of England, did homage to our lord the pope, agreeing to pay every year a thousand marks of silver.

1214 The interdict ceased in England, and [men] began to celebrate divine service within the octave of the apostles Peter and Paul [June 29-July 6].

1219 The abbots of England of the black order [Benedictines], assembled at Oxford, concerning the monastic order of Preachers.

1230 About the feast of S. Hilary [January 13] Henry [III.], king of England, and the whole army of England, assembled at Portsmouth in order to cross the Channel. But, having taken counsel, they remained until the feast of S. Philip and S. James the Apostles, [May 1], when Henry, king of England, with his army, crossed to the parts beyond the seas [to S. Malo].

1235 Frederic [II.], emperor of the Romans, took to wife the sister of Henry III., king of England, Isabel by name.

1238 The clerks of Oxford attacked Otho the legate at Oseney.

1241 Great dissension between pope Gregory [IX.] and the emperor Frederic [II.].

Also Otho, the legate, departed from England, and was captured upon the sea by the emperor. There were captured with him the legate of France, and many archbishops, bishops, abbots, and clerks.

1245 The king and queen of England came together to Chester on Sunday, August 13, and with them an abundant army, that is to say, Richard, earl of Cornwall, brother of the king; Simon, earl of Leicester; Roger [de Quincy], earl of Winchester; William, earl of Albemarle; [Hugh], earl of Oxford, and almost all the nobles of the whole of England; and they stayed there until the Sunday following. And on the morrow of S. Philibert the king set out with his army for Wales [and stayed] the first night at Coleshill, the second and third at Witford, the fourth at Rhuddlan, the fifth at Abergele, the sixth at Gannoch, where he remained a long time encamped, until he had erected the fortifications of Gannoch; and whilst he was tarrying there, there came to him Richard, earl of Gloucester, and William de Vesci, with a great band of soldiers and armed men, and very soon after came Roger Bigod, earl of Norfolk, and William de Cantelupe and others, on their return from the council of Lyons, to confer with the king concerning the council. Afterwards, Maurice Fitz[-Gerald], justiciary of Ireland, with many horse and foot soldiers [arrived], and the king stayed there with his whole army until October 26, burning towns, laying waste cornfields, losing also his horse and foot soldiers, and very many horses, and making but little progress.

On the eve of the feast of the Apostles S. Simon [and S. Jude,

October 27], he returned thence to Chester, where the justiciary of Ireland was removed from his office, and John Lestrange, justiciary of Chester, from his, and the office of the former was committed to John Fitz Geoffry, and that of the second to John de Grey, and on the morrow of All Souls [November 3] the king departed from Chester.

Also new money was coined.

1247 On February 20, about noon [or the ninth hour of the day], there was a great earthquake at Holywell.

Also on the same day and hour, a great quantity of blood fell in two granges in Cheshire, so that the woodwork of the wall of one of the granges was dyed with blood. Many in Cheshire saw this.

1248 The king of France [S. Louis IX.] took his way towards the Holy Land.

1251 There came to Paris in great numbers the Shepherds who had assumed the cross, they were in number, as it is said, fifty thousand, by whom the University was much harassed, and the clerks killed, and many Christians were destroyed by them in France, Picardy, Flanders, and elsewhere.

1253 The holy Robert [Grosseteste], bishop of Lincoln, died.

1255 Pope Innocent IV. died, who had excessively oppressed the church of England, distributing ecclesiastical benefices to foreigners, and granting to Henry, king of England, for several years a tenth part of the ecclesiastical revenues. Alexander, who before his election was Rinaldo, bishop of Ostia, succeeded him.

1263 Dissensions again broke out between Henry [III.], king of England, and Edward, his eldest son, on the one part, and the chief men of England on the other, concerning the laws which had been renewed in the parliament of Oxford, but had not been observed by the king.

Concerning the clergy and the Jews.

At this time Henry [III.], king of England, expelled the university of the clergy from the town of Oxford. In the meantime the citizens of London who had joined the party of the barons, by the counsel of the lord Simon de Montfort, extorted much money from the Jews at London, converting some of them to the faith of Christ, and killing others who were unwilling to be converted.

1264   Bog lane.

William la Zouche, the justiciary, and the citizens of Chester, fearing that the city was about to be besieged by the barons or by the Welsh, at the suggestion of a certain cursed fellow named Robert Mercer, then sheriff of the city, the day before the Annunciation of Our Lady [March 24], pulled down the houses of S. Werburg that were in Bog lane, and, after totally destroying the gardens, they began to dig a ditch round the city, the justiciary himself and David Fitz-Griffin faithfully promising to the abbot that the lord Edward should restore an equivalent of land and rents to the church of S. Werburg.

At this time Simon de Montfort, earl of Leicester, and Gilbert de Clare, earl of Gloucester, and other barons and citizens of London, who maintained the Provisions of Oxford, on May 14, joined battle with Henry, king of England, at Lewes. Many were slain on both sides, and [the barons] captured the king himself, and Edward his eldest son, and Richard, earl of Cornwall the king's brother, together with many nobles of England, and having bound the said king Henry to the observance of the said Provisions [of Oxford], and having imprisoned the said Edward, they kept him in custody for seven months, and they also kept in prison Richard, the brother of king Henry, and others of the leaders who were captured at Lewes.

After the feast of All Saints [November 1], Henry, king of England, and Edward, his eldest son, granted to Simon de Montfort, earl of Leicester, and his heirs, Chester, with the whole county and the castle, Newcastle-under-Lyme, and the Peak castle [in Derbyshire] with all their honours and appurtenances, to be held in perpetuity for other lands in different parts of England, which the aforesaid earl Simon gave in exchange to the aforesaid Edward.

1269 The translation of the body of S. Edward, King [and Confessor, to a new shrine took place] October 12.

In the same year the twentieth penny was given to the king, and in this same year he demanded a tenth from all the clergy annually for three years.

1270 In this year, Henry of Germany, son of Richard [of Cornwall], king of Germany, was slain on the feast of pope S. Gregory [March 12] in the city which is called Viterbo. These notable verses were written on him:—

Henry, the illustrious offspring of Richard, the German king,
Is struck down as this picture shows,
As he is returning from Tripoli protected by the companionship of the kings
    [of France and Sicily],
As he is paying his allegiance to the Cross he suffers death at the hands of
    wicked men.
The sons of Guenelon rush into church after mass,
The sword of Simon and Guido pierces Henry.
God disposed it, that so great a man should be killed by these men,
Lest by their return to their own country the whole English race should perish.
A little before the year of our Lord one thousand
Two hundred and seventy, under the serene king [of Sicily] Charles,
In the city of Viterbo, the destruction of his body took place.
I pray, oh queen of Heaven, that you may be for a medicine [to his soul].

1275 Edward, king of England, in his general parliament after his coronation, made many statutes and obtained [as a subsidy a grant of] a tenth [of the goods] of the kingdom.

1276 In this year a mortality of cattle began.

1278 Almost the whole of Chester within the walls of the city was burned down on May 15. And Robert of Kilwarby was translated by pope Nicolas [III.] from being archbishop of Canterbury to be bishop of Porto [and cardinal]. And the Jews were seized throughout the whole of England, on the octave of S. Martin [November 18], by the order of king Edward, on the charge of clipping the coin, and very many were hanged, and in like manner many goldsmiths were seized and made to give security [not to clip the coin].

1279 New money was coined [namely] round halfpennies and farthings.

1284 In this year within twelve days of Christmas a great misfortune happened to the abbey of Strata Florida in Wales. The fire and lightning struck the belfry, and burned the whole of it with the bells, without the flames being seen, and then [the fire] devoured the whole church, which was completely covered with lead as far as the walls, except the presbytery which was seen to be miraculously preserved, inasmuch as the body of Our Lord was kept there on the great altar under lock (as elsewhere is the case according to universal custom). Whatever was there except [the walls of] the church was burned in that fire, including choral books and bells. This happened in the night.

1297 Twelve hundred and ninety seven. On August 22, king Edward crossed the sea into Flanders.

Records from the Fourth Crusade

Crusading, by the early thirteenth century, mixed economic, spiritual, and political motives together in ways that made the ultimate success of these attempts to win back the Holy Lands near to impossible. In the following accounts from the Fourth Crusade (1202-1204), drawn in part from Ville-Hardouin's *Conquête de Constantinople* and Robert de Clari's *La Prise de Constantinople*, popes and monks, emperors and kings, knights and merchants can be seen attempting to mount one such effort to defeat the infidel (or punish Christian sinners) and restore Christian control in the East.

1. The compact with the Venetians.

"Sire, we have come to you in behalf of the noble barons of France who have taken the cross, in order to avenge the shame of Jesus Christ and to reconquer Jerusalem, if God will permit. And because they know no people who are as able to assist them, as you and your people, they pray you, for God's sake, to pity the land of *Outre-mer* and the shame of Jesus Christ, and to endeavor to furnish them transports and ships of war."

"Under what conditions?" asked the doge.

"Under any conditions that you may propose or advise, if they are able to fulfill them," replied the messengers.

"Certainly," replied the doge, [to his associates] "it is a great undertaking that they have asked of us and they seem to be considering an important matter;" [to the messengers] "we will give you an answer in a week, and do not wonder if the time seems long, for such a great undertaking deserves much thought."

At the time fixed by the doge, they returned to the palace, I can tell not you all that was said, but the conclusion of the conference was as follows:

"My lords," said the doge, "we will tell you what we have decided, if we can get the Grand Council and the people of the country to agree to it; and you shall decide whether you can fulfill your part.

"We will furnish *huissiers*[1] for carrying 4,500 horses and 9,000 esquires, and vessels for 4,500 knights and 20,000 foot-soldiers. The agreement shall be to furnish food for nine months for all these horses and men. That is the least that we will do, on condition that we are paid four marks per horse and two marks per man.

1 *Huissiers* were vessels having a door, *huis,* in the stern, which could be opened so as to take in the horses. See Archer: Crusade of Richard I, p. 49, note and p. 57, note.

"And we will observe all these conditions which we explain to you, for one year beginning the day we leave the harbor of Venice to fight in the service of God and of Christianity, wherever we may go. The sum of these payments indicated above amounts to 85,000 marks.

"And we will do still more: we will add fifty armed galleys, for the love of God; on the condition that as long as our alliance shall last, of every conquest of land or money that we make, by sea or land, we shall have one half and you the other. Now deliberate whether you can fulfill these conditions."

The messengers went away, saying that they would talk it over and reply the next day. They consulted and discussed that night and then resolved to agree to it. The next day they went to the doge and said: "Sire, we are ready to make this agreement." The doge said that he would speak to his people and tell them the result. . . .

It was explained in council that they would go to Babylon [Cairo], because at Babylon they could do more injury to the Turks than anywhere else. And in public it was announced that they would go across the sea. It was then Lent [March, 1201], and on St. John's day the following year, the 1202nd year after the Incarnation of Jesus Christ, the barons and pilgrims were to be at Venice and the vessels were to be ready on their arrival.

2. Compact of the Venetians with the sultan of Babylon.

[Anno 1199?] After this he [the sultan of Babylon] summoned messengers and servants and sent them to Venice, loaded with great wealth and great riches. He sent them to the doge and gave beautiful presents to the Venetians, and commanded the latter, if they could avoid it, not to come to the land of Egypt; he would give them great treasures and many privileges in the port of Alexandria. The messengers went to Venice, did as they were commanded, and returned as quickly as possible.

3. The crusaders are unable to pay the Venetians.

. . . While the pilgrims were staying on the island of St. Nicholas, the doge of Venice and the Venetians went to speak to them and demanded the pay for the navy which had been prepared. And the doge said to them that they had acted wrongly in commanding through their messengers that vessels should be prepared for 4,000 knights and their equipment, and for 100,00 foot-soldiers. Of these 4,000 knights, there were not more than 1,000 present, for the others had gone to other ports. And of these 100,000 foot-soldiers there were not more than 50,000 or 60,000. "But," said the doge, "we want you to pay us the sum which you promised." When the crusaders heard this, they debated and arranged that each knight should pay four marks and four marks for each horse, and each esquire two marks; and those who paid less, should pay one mark. When they collected this money, they paid it to the Venetians. But 50,000 marks still remained due.

When the doge and the Venetians saw that the pilgrims had not paid more, they were all so incensed that the doge said to the pilgrims: "My lords, you have imposed upon us shamefully. For, as soon as your messengers had made the agreement with me and my people, I issued orders throughout my whole land that no merchant should undertake a voyage, but all were to aid in preparing this fleet. They have been waiting ever since and have gained nothing for the last year and a half; and, accordingly, they have lost much. Therefore my men and I want you to pay us the money which you owe us. If you do not pay us, you shall not leave this island before we get our money; and no one shall bring you anything to eat or drink." But the doge was a very excellent man and did not prevent the people from bringing enough food and drink.

When the count and the crusaders heard what the doge said, they were much troubled and grieved. They made another collection and borrowed all the money they could from those who were thought to have any. They paid it all to the Venetians, but after this payment 36,000 marks still remained due. They said to the Venetians that they had been imposed upon; that the army was greatly impoverished by this last collection; that they could not pay any more money at all, for they had hardly enough to support the army.

When the doge perceived that they could not pay all the money and that they were in sore straits, he said to his people: "Sirs, if we let these people go back to their own country, we shall always be considered base and tricky. Let us go to them and say that, if they are willing to pay us the 36,000 marks which they owe us, out of their part of the first conquests which we make, we will carry them across the sea." The Venetians were well pleased with the doge's proposition. Accordingly, they went to the camp of the pilgrims. When they came thither, the doge said to the crusaders: "Sires, we have agreed, I and my people, that if you are willing to guarantee faithfully to pay us the 36,000 marks, which you owe us, out of your share of the first conquests, we will carry you across the sea."

When the crusaders heard what the doge proposed they were very glad and fell at his feet for joy. They very willingly bound themselves faithfully to do what the doge had proposed. They were so joyous that night that there was no one so poor that he did not make a great illumination, and each one carried great torches made of candles on the end of his lance, both outside of the camp and inside, so that the whole army seemed intoxicated.

4. The new agreement with the Venetians.

Afterwards the doge came to the army and said: "Sirs, it is now winter, we cannot cross the sea, nor does this depend upon me. For I would have had you cross already, if it had not depended upon you. But let us do the best we can. There is a city near here, named Zara. The people of this city have done us much evil, and I and my men want to punish them, if we can. If you will take my advice, we will go there this winter and stay until Easter. Then we will make ready our navy and go to *Outre-mer* on Lady-day. The city of Zara is very rich and well supplied with all kinds of provisions." The barons and the nobles among the crusaders agreed to what the doge proposed. But no one in the army knew this plan, except the leaders.

5. The capture of Zara.

The day after the feast of St. Martin, some people from Zara came to speak to the doge of Venice, who was in his tent. They said to him that they would surrender the city and all their property to his mercy, if their lives were spared. The doge said that he would not accept these or any other conditions without the advise of the counts and barons, and that he would go and discuss the matter with them.

While he went to talk to the counts and barons, that party, of which I have already spoken, who wanted to break up the army, said to the messengers: "Why do you want to surrender your city? The pilgrims will not attack you and you have nothing to fear from them. If you can defend yourselves against the Venetians, you need have no anxiety." And they sent one of them, named Robert de Boves, who went to the walls of the city and announced the same thing. So the messengers returned to the city and the plan of surrender was given up.

The doge of Venice, when he came to the counts and barons, said to them: "Sirs, the people yonder want to surrender the city to my mercy, on condition that their lives are spared. But I will not make this agreement or any other without your advice." The barons replied: "Sire, we advise you to make this agreement and we pray you to do so." He said that he would, and they all went back together to the doge's tent to make this agreement. They found that the messengers had gone away, following the advice of those who wanted to break up the army.

Then the abbot of Vaux of the order of Citeaux rose and said to them: "Sirs, I forbid you, in the name of the pope of Rome, to attack this city; for the inhabitants are Christians and you are pilgrims." When the doge heard this he was much irritated and troubled. He said to the counts and barons: "Sirs, this city was practically in my power, and your people have taken it from me, you had promised that you would aid me in conquering it; now I require you to do so."

Then the counts and barons and those who belonged to their party held a conference and said: "Those who have prevented this agreement have committed a very great outrage, and it was not right for them to try to break up the army. Now we shall be disgraced, if we do not aid in capturing the city." They went to the doge and said to him: "Sire, we will aid you in capturing the city, in spite of those who wish to prevent it." . . .

Accordingly the city was surrendered to the mercy of the doge of Venice, on condition that the lives of the inhabitants should be spared. Then the doge went to the counts and barons and said to them: "Sirs, we have conquered this city, by the grace of God and through your aid. It is now winter and we can not leave here until Easter. For we should find no provisions elsewhere; and this city is very rich and very well supplied with everything needful. Let us divide it accordingly into two parts; we will take one half of it and you the other half."

6. The summons to Alexis.

In the meantime the crusaders and the Venetians remained at Zara during the winter. They considered how great the expense had been and said to one another that they could not go to Babylon or Alexandria or Syria; for they had neither provisions nor money for the journey. They had already used up everything they had, either during the sojourn that they had made or in the great price that they had paid for the vessels. They said that they could not go and, even if they should go, they would accomplish nothing; they had neither provisions nor money sufficient to support them.

The doge of Venice saw clearly that the pilgrims were ill at ease. He addressed them, saying: "Sirs, Greece is a very rich land and bountifully supplied with everything. If we can find a sufficient excuse for going there and taking food and other things, so as to recuperate ourselves, it would seem to me advisable, and then we could easily go across the sea." Then the marquis rose and said: "Sir, I was in Germany at the emperor's court last Christmas. There I saw a young man who was the emperor's brother-in-law. This young man was the son of the emperor *Kyrsac* of Constantinople, from whom his brother had taken the empire of Constantinople by treason. Whoever could get this young man," said the marquis, " could certainly go to the land of Constantinople and take provisions and other things; for this young man is the rightful heir."

7. The proposition made by king Philip.

"My lords, king Philip sends us to you and also sends the son of the emperor of Constantinople, who is his wife's brother.

"My lords, says the king, I shall send you my wife's brother; I place him in the hands of God (may He preserve him from death!), and in your hands. Since you are fighting for God, for the right and for justice, you ought, if it lies in your power, to restore to their inheritance those who have been wrongfully disposessed. He [Alexis] will make with you the best agreement which has ever been made by any one and he will give you the most powerful aid in conquering the land of *Outre-mer*.

"In the first place, if God permits you to restore him to his inheritance, he will put all the empire of Romania under the obedience of Rome, from which it has been separated for a long time. In the second place, he knows that you have spent your property and that you are poor; he will give you 200,000 marks of silver and provisions for all the members of the army, humble and noble. He will himself go with you to the land of Babylon or will send thither with you (if you think it better) 10,000 men at his expense. This service he will perform for you during one year. And so long as he lives, he will maintain at his own expense 500 knights in the land of *Outre-mer,* to guard the land.

"My lords, we have full power," said the messengers, "to make this agreement, if you wish to do so. And be sure that such a fine offer was never made to any one, and he who refuses this can have no great desire to conquer." The leaders said that they would discuss the matter and an assembly was appointed for the next day. When the host had assembled this offer was presented to them.

There it was hotly discussed, "pro and con." The abbot of Vaux of the order of Citeaux and the party that wanted to break up the army said that they would not agree to it; that it was fighting against Christians; that they had not set out for this purpose, but they wanted to go to Syria.

The other party replied: "Good sirs, in Syria you can do nothing, you can see that clearly from those who have left us and gone to other ports. You know that it is through the land of Babylon or through Greece that the land of *Outre-mer* will be reconquered, if it is ever recovered. If we refuse this offer, we shall always be ashamed."

The army was in discord just as you have heard. And do not wonder that the laymen could not agree; for the white monks of the order of Citeaux in the army were also in discord. The abbot of Loos, who was a very holy and excellent man, and the other abbots who agreed with him preached to the people and cried out to them to have mercy, saying that, for God's sake, they ought to keep the army together and to make this agreement; "for it is the best means of recovering the land of *Outre-mer.*" And the abbot of Vaux in his turn, and those who agreed with him, preached very frequently and said that that was all wrong; that they ought to go to the land of Syria and do what they could.

Then the marquis Boniface of Montferrat, Baldwin, count of Flanders and Hainaut, count Louis and count Hugh of St. Pol and those who belonged to their party, went and said that they would make this agreement; for they would be ashamed to refuse it. So they went to the doge's lodging and the messengers were summoned.

They concluded the agreement, just as you have heard it above, by their oaths and by sealed compacts.

And in regard to this matter, the book tells you that there were only twelve of the French who made the oaths; and they could not get any more. Of these, the first was the marquis of Montferrat, count Baldwin of Flanders, count Louis of Blois and Chartres, the count of St. Pol, and eight others who agreed with them. So the compact was made, the securities given, and the time fixed when the heir of Constantinople should come; it was to be a fortnight after Easter.

8. The discussion after the arrival of Alexis.

Then all the barons of the army and the Venetians were summoned. When they had all assembled, the doge of Venice rose and said to them: "My lords, we have now a sufficient excuse for going to Constantinople, if you think it wise, for we have the lawful heir." Now some who did not want to go to Constantinople, spoke thus: "Bah! what are we going to do at Constantinople? We have our pilgrimage to make and intend to go to Babylon of Alexandria. Our ships are only rented for one year and half the year is already over."

The others said in reply: "What are we going to do at Babylon or Alexandria, since we have neither provisions nor money enough to go? It is better to go where we have a sufficient excuse for obtaining money and provisions by conquest, than to go where we shall die of hunger. Then we can do it, and he offers to go with us and to pay for our ships and our navy another year at his own expense." And the marquis of Montferrat did all in his power to urge our going to Constantinople, because he wished to take vengeance for a wrong which the emperor of Constantinople had done him.

9. The first payment.

Afterwards all the barons assembled one day at the palace of the emperor and demanded of him their pay. He replied that he would pay them, but he wished first to be crowned. Accordingly they made preparations and set a day for the coronation. On that day he was crowned emperor with due ceremony, with the consent of his father, who willingly granted it. After he had been crowned the barons demanded their pay. He said he would very willingly pay what he could and at that time he paid 100,000 marks. Of this sum the Venetians received one-half; for they were to receive one-half of the conquests. Of the 50,000 which remained, 36,000, which the Franks still owed for the vessels, were paid to the Venetians. And all those who had advanced money to pay for the passage, were repaid out of the 14,000 marks which the pilgrims had left.

10. The public defiance.

They dismounted from their horses at the gate, entered the palace and found the emperor Alexis and the emperor Isaac, his father, seated upon two thrones, side by side. Near them was seated the empress, who was the father's wife, the son's step-mother, and the sister of the king of Hungary; a beautiful and good lady. A great number of nobles were with them; and it certainly seemed the court of a rich prince.

According to the agreement with the other messengers, Conon of Bethune, who was very rich and very eloquent, spoke: "Sire, we have been sent to you by the barons of the army and by the doge of Venice. Know that they reproach you because of the great service which they have done you, which everybody knows and which is apparent to you. You have sworn to them, you and your father, to keep the agreement that you have made with them; and they have your written compact. You have not kept your agreement with them, as you ought.

"They have summoned you many times, and we summon you in their name, before all your barons, to keep the agreement which you have made with them. If you do so, all will be well; if you do not keep it, know that in the future they will consider you neither as lord nor as friend; but they will try to get their rights in any way they can. They announce to you that they would injure neither you, nor anyone else, before the defiance; for they have never acted treasonably, and in their country it is not the custom to do so. You have heard what we have said to you and you can do as you please."

The Greeks marveled much at this defiance and great insult. They said that no one had ever been so bold before as to defy the emperor of Constantinople in his own halls. The emperor Alexis looked savagely at the messengers, and so did all the Greeks, though, they had on many occasions in the past looked very friendly.

11. The doge's threat.

At these words the barons left the palace and returned to their camp. After returning they deliberated upon the course to follow. Meanwhile they sent two knights to the emperor and demanded again that he should pay them. He replied to the messengers that he would pay nothing, that he had already paid too much, and that he was not afraid of anyone. He also commanded them to go away and leave his land; they were to understand that if they did not depart, he would injure them. Then the messengers went back and told the barons the emperor's reply. When the barons heard this, they deliberated as to what they should do. The doge said that he wanted to speak to the emperor.

He sent a messenger to demand that the emperor should come to the harbor to speak to him. The emperor went on horseback. The doge prepared four armed galleys; he went in one and took the other three for protection. When he was near the shore he saw the emperor who had come on horseback. He addressed the latter as follows: "Alexis, what do you think you are going to do? Remember we have raised you from a very humble estate. We have made you lord and crowned you emperor. Will you not keep your agreement with us and will you not do more?" "No," replied the emperor, "I will not do anything more." "No?" said the doge, "wretched boy, we have raised you from the mire, and we will throw you into the mire again; and be sure that I will do you all the injury that I can, from this time on."

12. The sermons before the final attack on Constantinople.

When the pilgrims saw this, they were very angry and grieved much; they went back from the other side of the harbor to their lodgings. When the barons had returned and gotten ashore, they assembled and were much amazed, and said that it was on account of their sins that they did not succeed in anything and could not capture the city. Meanwhile the bishops and the clergy in the army debated and decided that the war was a righteous one, and that they certainly ought to attack the Greeks. For formerly the inhabitants of the city had been obedient to the law of Rome and now they were disobedient, since they said that the law of Rome was of no account, and called all who believed in it "dogs." And the bishops said that for this reason one ought certainly to attack them, and that it was not a sin but an act of great charity.

Then it was announced to all the host that all the Venetians and everyone else should go and hear the sermons on Sunday morning; and they did so. Then the bishops preached to the army, the bishop of Soissons, the bishop of Troyes, the bishop of *Havestaist,* master Jean Faicette, and the abbot of Loos, and they showed to the pilgrims that the war was a righteous one; for the Greeks were traitors and murderers, and also disloyal, since they had murdered their rightful lord, and were worse than Jews. And the bishops said that, by the authority of God and in the name of the pope, they would absolve all who attacked the Greeks. And the bishops commanded the pilgrims to confess their sins and receive the communion devoutly; and said that they ought not to hesitate to attack the Greeks, for the latter were enemies of God. They also commanded that all the evil women should be sought out and sent away from the army to a distant place. This was done; the evil women were all put in a vessel and were sent very far away from the army.

13. The compact of division.

Then the members of the host debated and consulted upon the best course to pursue. The discussion was long and stormy; but the following was the result of the deliberation: If God granted that they should capture the city, all the booty that was taken should be brought together and divided fairly, as was fitting. And, if they captured the city, six men should be chosen from the Franks and six from the Venetians; these were to take oath upon relics that they would elect as emperor him whom they should judge to be the most useful for the good of the land. And he whom they chose as emperor, should have one quarter of all the conquests both in the city and outside; and in addition he should have the palace of the Lion's mouth and of Blachern. The other three quarters should be divided into two parts, one-half for the Venetians and one-half for the crusaders. Then twelve from the wisest of the army of the pilgrims and twelve of the Venetians should be chosen to divide the fiefs and the offices among the men and to define the feudal service which each one owed to the emperor.

This compact was guaranteed and sworn to both by the Franks and the Venetians, with the condition that any one who wished could go away within one year from the end of March. Those who remained in the country must perform the feudal service to the emperor, as it might be arranged. Then the compact was made and sworn to, and all who should not keep it, were excommunicated by the clergy.

14. Account of the sack.

How shall I begin to tell of the deeds wrought by these nefarious men! Alas, the images, which ought to have been adored, were trodden under foot! Alas, the relics of the holy martyrs were thrown into unclean places! Then was seen what one shudders to hear, namely, the divine body and blood of Christ was spilled upon the ground or thrown about. They snatched the precious reliquaries, thrust into their bosoms the ornaments which these contained, and used the broken remnants for pans and drinking-cups,—precursors of Anti-christ, authors and heralds of his nefarious deeds, which we momentarily expect. Manifestly, indeed, by that race then, just as formerly, Christ was robbed and insulted and His garments were divided by lot; only one thing was lacking, that His side, pierced by a spear, should pour rivers of divine blood on the ground.

Nor can the violation of the Great Church be listened to with equanimity. For the sacred altar, formed of all kinds of precious materials and admired by the whole world, was broken into bits and distributed among the soldiers, as was all the other sacred wealth of so great and infinite splendor.

When the sacred vases and utensils of unsurpassable art and grace and rare material, and the fine silver, wrought with gold, which encircled the screen of the tribunal and the ambo, of admirable workmanship, and the door and many other ornaments, were to be borne away as booty, mules and saddled horses were led to the very sanctuary of the temple. Some of these, which were unable to keep their footing on the splendid and slippery pavement, were stabbed when they fell, so that the sacred pavement was polluted with blood and filth.

Nay more, a certain harlot, a sharer in their guilt, a minister of the furies, a servant of the demons, a worker of incantations and poisonings, insulting Christ, sat in the patriarch's seat, singing an obscene song and dancing frequently. Nor, indeed, were these crimes committed and others left undone, on the ground that these were of lesser guilt, the others of greater. But with one consent all the most heinous sins and crimes were committed by all with equal zeal. Could those, who showed so great madness against God Himself, have spared the honorable matrons and maidens or the virgins consecrated to God?

Nothing was more difficult and laborious than to soften by prayers, to render benevolent, these wrathful barbarians, vomiting forth bile at every unpleasing word, so that nothing failed to inflame their fury. Whoever attempted it was derided as insane and a man of intemperate language. Often they drew their daggers against anyone who opposed them at all, or hindered their demands.

No one was without a share in the grief. In the alleys, in the streets, in the temples, complaints, weeping, lamentations, grief, the groaning of men, the shrieks of women, wounds, rape, captivity, the separation of those most closely united. Nobles wandered about ignominiously, those of venerable age in tears, the rich in poverty. Thus it was in the streets, on the corners, in the temple, in the dens, for no place remained unassailed or defended the suppliants. All places everywhere were filled full of all kinds of crime. Oh, immortal God, how great the afflictions of the men, how great the distress!

15. Abbot Martin's theft of relics.

While these victors were rapidly plundering the conquered city, which was theirs by right of conquest, the abbot Martin began to cogitate about his own share of the booty, and lest he alone should remain empty-handed, while all the others became rich, he resolved to seize upon plunder with his own sacred hands. But since he thought in not meet to handle any booty of worldly things with those sacred hands, he began to plan how he might secure some portion of the relics of the saints, of which he knew there was a great quantity in the city.

Accordingly, having a presentiment of some great result, he took with him one of his two chaplains and went to a church which was held in great reverence because in it the mother of the most famous emperor Manuel had a noble grave, which seemed of importance to the Greeks but ours held for naught. There a very great amount of money brought in from all the surrounding country was stored, and also precious relics, which the vain hope of security had

caused them to bring in from the neighboring churches and mona-
steries. Those, whom the Greeks had driven out, had told us of
this before the capture of the city. When many pilgrims broke into
this church and some were eagerly engaged in stealing gold and silver,
others precious stones, Martin, thinking it unbecoming to commit
sacrilege except in a holy cause, sought a more retired spot where the
very sanctity of the place seemed to promise that what he desired
might be found.

There he found an aged man of agreeable countenance, having a
long and hoary beard, a priest, but very unlike our priests in his
dress. Thinking him a layman, the abbot, though inwardly calm,
threatened him with a very ferocious voice, saying: "Come,
perfidious old man, show me the most powerful relics you have, or
you shall die immediately." The latter, terrified by the sound rather
than the words, since he heard but did not understand what was said,
and knowing that Martin could not speak Greek, began in the
Romana lingua, of which he knew a little, to entreat Martin and by
soft words to turn away the latter's wrath, which in truth did not
exist. In reply, the abbot succeeded in getting out a few words of the
same language, sufficient to make the old man understand what he
wanted. The latter, observing Martin's face and dress, and thinking it
more tolerable that a religious man should handle the sacred relics
with fear and reverence, than that worldly men should, perchance,
pollute them with their worldly hands, opened a chest bound with
iron and showed the desired treasure, which was more grateful and
pleasing to Martin than all the royal wealth of Greece. The abbot
hastily and eagerly thrust in both hands and working quickly, filled
with the fruits of the sacrilege both his own and his chaplain's
bosom. He wisely concealed what seemed the most valuable and
departed without oppositon.

Moreover what and how worthy of veneration those relics were,
is told more fully later. When he was hastening to his vessel, so
stuffed full, if I may use the expression, those who knew and loved
him, saw him from their ships as they were themselves hastening to
the booty, and inquired joyfully whether he had stolen anything, or
with what he was so loaded down as he walked. With a joyful
countenance, as always, and with pleasant words he said: "We have
done well." To which they replied: "Thanks be to God."

16. List of relics stolen by abbot Martin.

Therefore "Blessed be the Lord God, who only doeth wondrous
things," who in His unspeakable kindness and mercy has looked
upon and made glorious His church at Paris through certain gifts of
His grace, which He deigned to transmit to us through the venerable
man, already so frequently mentioned, abbot Martin. In the presence
of these the church exults and by their protection any soul faithful
to God is aided and assisted. In order that the readers' trust in these

may be strengthened, we have determined to give a partial list.

First, of the highest importance and worthy of all veneration, a trace of the blood of our Lord Jesus Christ, which was shed for the redemption of all mankind.

Second, a piece of the true cross on which the Son of the Father, the new Adam, sacrificed for us, paid the debt of the old Adam.

Third, a fair-sized piece of St. John, the fore-runner of our Lord.

Fourth, the arm of St. James, the Apostle, whose memory is venerated by the whole church.

There were also fragments of the following saints:

> Christopher, the martyr.
> George, the martyr.
> Theodore, the martyr.
> The foot of St. Cosmas, the martyr.
> Part of the head of Cyprian, the martyr.
> Pantaleon, the martyr.
> A tooth of St. Lawrence.
> Demetrius, the martyr.
> Stephen, the first martyr.
> Vincentius, Adjutus, Mauritius and his companion.
> Crisantius and Darius, the martyrs.
> Gervasius and Protasius, the martyrs.
> Primus, the martyr.
> Sergius and Bacchus, the martyrs.
> Protus, the martyr.
> John and Paul, the martyrs.

Also portions of the following: the place of the Nativity of our Lord; Calvary; our Lord's sepulchre; the stone rolled away; the place of our Lord's ascension; the stone on which John stood when he baptized the Lord; the spot where Christ raised Lazarus; the stone on which Christ was presented in the temple; the stone on which Jacob slept; the stone where Christ fasted; the stone where Christ prayed; the table on which Christ ate the supper; the place where he was captured; the place where the mother of our Lord died; her grave; the grave of St. Peter, the apostle; the relics of the holy apostles, Andrew and Philip; the place where the Lord gave the law to Moses; the holy patriarchs, Abraham, Isaac and Jacob; St. Nicholas, the bishop; Agricius, the bishop; John Chrysostom; John, the almsgiver; the Virgin's milk; Margaret, Perpetua, Agatha, Agnes, Lucia, Cecilia, Adelgundis and Euphemia, the virgins.

Written and sealed, in the year of our Lord's Incarnation, 1205, in the reign of Philip, king of the Romans, Innocent the pope, presiding over the holy Roman church, in the presence of Luthaldus of Basel and Henry of Strassburg.

17. Innocent commands crusaders to stay at Constantinople.

To all the clergy and people in the Christian army at Constantinople.

If the Lord had granted the desires of His humble servants sooner, and had transfered, as He has now done, the empire of Constantinople from the Greeks to the Latins before the fall of the Holy Land, perhaps Christianity would not be weeping today over the desolation of the land of Jerusalem. Since, therefore, through the wonderful transference of this empire God has deigned to open to you a way to recover that land, and the detention of this may lead to the restoration of that, we advise and exhort you all, and we enjoin upon you for the remission of your sins, to remain for a year in Romania, in order to strengthen the empire in its devotion to the Apostolic See and to us, and in order to retain it in the power of the Latins; and to give wise advise and efficient aid to Baldwin, our most beloved son in Christ, the illustrious emperor of Constantinople; unless, perchance, your presence in the Holy Land should be necessary before that time, in which case you ought to hasten to guard it before the year elapses.

Notes

2. SOCIO-ECONOMIC CONTEXT

The Account of the Daily Expenses of a Person of Rank in the Reign of King Edward I

Philip de Castro

A journey by a person of rank in the thirteenth century involved usually a large entourage and a variety of expenses that would be well beyond someone of lesser rank. The surviving account from one such journey, kept by Philip de Castro for an unknown traveller, possibly from the county of Pembroke, England, about the year 1289, presents an interesting view of the living standards of the nobility as well as the relative costs of some everyday items such as food, labor, and alms for the poor. The journey is being made in February and March, from Oxford to Canterbury with stops at London.

Memorandum, that Philip de Castro received of his Lord 30 shillings on the Thursday next after the feast of the Purification of the Blessed Mary, (February 2) at Oxford.

Item, on Friday next after the feast of the Purification of the Blessed Mary (Feb. 2) at Oxford. In bread 6d. Two gallons of wine, a gift of hospitality from the rector of Berton. Item in bread 6d. Two gallons of wine, a gift of hospitality from the rector of Mistern. Beer 6d. Herrings 3d. Stock-fish 4d. Porpoise and fish 4d. Perch and roach 7d. Large eels 7d. Vegetables ¾d. Figs and raisins 2d. Fuel 5d. A bed for 2 nights 2d. Hay for 7 horses 7d. 4 bushels of oats 20d. Apples ½d. Sum, 6s. 8¼d.

Item, on the Saturday next after the same. Bread from the store. Beer 3d. Wine 2¼d. Item in one flaggon of wine at Dadinton 4½d. Stock-fish 2d. Pike, roach, and butter 4½d. Fuel 1d. A sumpter saddle 3d. Shoeing the horses 1¾d. 2 pairs of shoes for my Lord 12d. Item delivered to John the clerk 4s. 9d. which I had before received at [?] and have reckoned in another roll. On the same day at supper at Dadinton. Bread 2¾d. Beer 4d. Eels 6d. Stock-fish 1d. Fuel 2d. Candles from the store. Bed 1d. Hay for seven horses 3½d. Straw ½d. 3½ bushels of oats 14d. Sum, 10s. 5¾d.

Item, on the Sunday next after the same, at breakfast 1d. Item delivered to John Houscard 7s. for his expenses towards Wales.

Delivered to Cole Le Tat on the same day 4d. for the players. Item at Adderbury in horse-bread for William Janitot 1d. In beer ½d. Sum, 7s. 6½d.

Item, on Monday next at Dadinton. Bread 2d. Beer 2d. A hen 3d. Eggs 1d. Fuel 1d. Candles ½d. Hay 2d. Straw ½d. 2 bushels of oats for 4 horses 8d. Sum, 1s. 8d.

Item, on Tuesday next after the same, at breakfast. Bread 1d. Beer 1¾d. Cooked meat 2d. Horse-bread ½d. Shoeing the horses ¼d. To a poor person ¼d. Item, on the same day, at supper, at Oxford. Bread 3d. Beer, 3 gallons 4½d. Wine, 1 bottle 2¼d. Cookery, in shambles meat 3½d. A capon and 2 [?] 5½d. Cheese ½d. Fuel 2d. Straw 2d. Candles 1d. A bed 1d. Hay for 4 horses 3d. 2 bushels of oats for 4 horses 10d. Sum, 3s. 8d.

Item, on Wednesday next following. Bread 4½d. Beer, 5 gallons, 8½d. 3 quarts of wine 3¾d. Shambles meat 6d. 2 hens 6½d. Vegetables ½d. Groats ½d. Fuel 3¼d. Candles ½d. A bed 1d. Hay for 4 horses 4d. 2 bushels of oats 10d. The ferry to Godstowe 2d. Bran ½d. Sum, 4s. 3½d.

Item, on Thursday next following, at dinner. Bread 2½d. 2 gallons of beer 3d. Wine 1¼d. Cooked meat 4¾d. Fuel 1d. Shoeing the horses 1d. Shoes for my Lord 6d. Ginger-comfeit, and blanchpowder, 12d. Of the debt of Thomas de la Roche 12d. Sum, 4s. 1½d.

Item, on Friday, one pound of ginger comfeits, and one pound of sugar in plate, 4s. 8d. Sum, 4s. 8d.

Item, on Sunday next I received of my Lord at Farnham, 20s., out of which, in expenses in the roll above, 12s. 2d., and delivered to the boy of Sir William Habsaundre 6d., about to go from Farnham towards Wales. Sum, 6d.

Memorandum, that Philip de Castro received of his Lord 12s. 8d., on Tuesday the vigil of St. Peter in Cathedra, (Feb. 22) at Brentford, out of which he delivered to his Lord 12d. on the same day.

Item, he received of his Lord 10s. on Thursday, the morrow of St. Peter, in Cathedra, (Feb. 22) at London.

Item, he received of his Lord 30s. at London, on Friday next before the feast of St. David, (March 1) and received of his Lord 10s., on Sunday the morrow of St. Oswald, (Feb. 28) at London.

Item, on Sunday next before the feast of St. Peter in Cathedra, at Abingdon, for the fare towards London, for 9 horses 5d. And at Dorchester at night, beer 1d. It was no more, because we were at supper with Sir Richard Simoun, Candles ¼d. Hay for 8 horses 2d. 2 bushels of oats 8d. Straw ½d. Sum, 16¾d.

Item, on Monday next, in the vigil of St. Peter in Cathedra, in expenses there in the morning, bread and beer 1d. And at Henley at dinner, Bread 5d. Beer 5d. Wine 1¼d. Shambles meat 2d. Bread and oats for the horses 5d. The same day at night, at Maidenhead, beer 1d. at my Lord's chamber. No more, because we were with Sir Richard Simoun. Candles ¼d. Hay for 4 horses 2d. 2 bushels of oats

8d. Straw 1d. Sum, 2s. 7½d.

Item, on Tuesday next, in the vigil of St. Peter in Cathedra, at Brentford, expended in Bread 4d. Beer 6d. Wine 5d. Fish 6d. Fuel 1½d. Hay and bread for 9 horses 6d. On the same day at supper at London, Bread 6d. Beer 8d. Wine 2d. Shambles meat 8d. A hen and a plover 7d. Birds 2½d. Candles 1½d. Fuel 2½d. Hay for 2 horses 2d. Oats 6d. Litter for 9 horses at night 7d. Sum, 6s. 10d.

Item, on Wednesday, in the feast of St. Peter in Cathedra, in ginger-comfeit, and other spicery bought in Cheapside 5d. In wine in Bread-street 1d. In hay for 3 horses 3d. A bushel and a half of oats 6d. In shoes for Tomkeyn 6d. Sum, 1s. 9d.

Item, on Thursday next, in expenses there. Bread 12¾d. Beer 12½d. Wine 6d. Shambles meat 13d. 2 hens 7d. Larks 5¼d. 3 [?] 3d. Honey 1½d. Groats, and salt, and apples ¾d. Wine in Bread-street 1d. Candles 1d. Fuel 4d. Hay for 3 horses 2d. Oats 5d. 2 pairs of gloves bought for my Lord 3d. Shoes for John Vatnel and John the clerk 10d. Sum, 7s. 3¾d.

Item, on Friday next before the feast of St. David, delivered to Tomkeyn, Yenan, Cole, and Maddoc Le Somer 2s. 7d. for four days, when my Lord went to Canterbury. Sum, 2s. 7½d.

Item, on Sunday next, at Canterbury, in the offering of my Lord xii d. Item, at Newenton, at supper. Bread 5¾d. Beer 7d. Wine 5d. Shambles meat 7d. Young doves 4d. Fuel 3d. Salt, vegetables, groats, and candles 1½d. Hay 6½d. Oats 11½d Horse-bread 3½d. Beds 3d. Sum, 6s. 2¾d.

Item, Monday next, at Rochester, at breakfast, Bread 4d. Beer 5¾d. Wine 3¼d. Shambles meat 6d. Rusks 4d. A hen 3½d. Hay there 1d. Horse-bread 7d. Fuel 1d. Item, the same day, at supper, at Dartford, Bread 4½d. Beer 6¼d. Wine 7½d. Shambles meat 9½d. A hen 3d. A plover 2d. Candles ¾d. Fuel 2½d. Vegetables ¼d. Hay 5½d. Oats 15d. Shoeing Morel 4½d. A poor person ½d. Sum, 8s. 2d.

Item, on Tuesday next, at Murlworth, Bread 1½d. Beer ¼d. Also the same day at London in ginger-comfeit, & blanchpowder 7d. Also in bread the same day at dinner and supper 11d. Beer 14½d. Shambles meat 9½d. Two rabbits 11d. Candles 2d. Coal 2d. Straw 3d. Oats 15½d. Sum, 6s. 5d.

Item, on Wednesday next, in Hay bought 10d. 5 bushels of oats 19d. Fare to Westminster 1d. Sum, 2s. 6d.

Item, on Friday next, Hay bought 12d. A bushel of oats 4d. Garters bought for my lord 16d. Wine in Cheapside 1¼d. Item, to see the leopard 1d. To a poor person ¼d. Sum, 2s. 10½d.

Item, on Saturday next, the feast of St. Oswald, at Westminster, at breakfast, Bread 1d. Wine 2½d. Stockfish and whiting 2½d. Dates and apples 2½d. Oats 8d. Sum, 1s. 4½d.

Item, on Sunday next, at Westminster, Bread 5d. Wine 15d. Eels and lamprouns 18d. Stockfish and salmon 13½d. Fare to Westminster 1d. Hay bought 5d. Oats 8d. Sum, 5s. 5½d.

Item, on Monday next, at Westminster, To the poor 1d. To the barber 1d. Oysters ½d. Fare to Lambeth and back 2d. Hay 3d. For 2 bushels of oats 8d. A brush 1d. Sum, 1s. 5d.

Item, on Tuesday next, at Westminster, Bread 3d. Wine 7½d. Eels and laumprouns 8d. Stockfish and whiting 4½d. Hay 6d. Oats 8d. Sum, 3s. 3d.

Item, on Wednesday next, Bread 4d. Beer 5½d. Wine 2½d. Stockfish 4d. Herring 2d. Haddock and melewell 4d. Eels and lamprouns 5d. A pike 4d. Roach 2d. Whelks 2d. Vegetables ½d. Groats and salt ½d. Candles ½d. Fare from Westminster 1¼d. Hay 2d. Oats 6d. Sum, 3s. 9¼d.

Sum, 5l. 3s. 11½d.

Memorandum, that Philip de Castro received of his Lord, on the Friday next before St. Gregory the Pope, 26s. 8d., of which he delivered to his lord 10s. for different affairs, and half a mark to a Serjeant in the church of St. Paul. Also received of the Lord 20s. 8d., on Wednesday next after the feast of St. Gregory the Pope.

Item, Thursday next before the feast of St. Gregory the Pope, in expenses. Bread 7d. Beer 8½d. Wine 2½d. The meat supplied from the store, particulars in another roll. On the same day, at breakfast, in Breadstrete, when Sir Nicholas de Bonevile, and Philip Columbers, and many others of the household of Sir William Martin, were there, 19d. At the same place, Wine 1¼d. Dates and apples 2d. Going to Westminster and back 2¾d. Candles and vinegar 1d. Hay 2d. Oats 6d. Fuel ½d. A bed for John Perot and Standdard 1d. Shoes for Philip de Castro 6d. Sum, 4s. 11½d.

Item, Friday next, in expenses. Bread 1½d. Beer 4¾d. Wine 1¼d. Fish 1¼d. On the same day, in expenses of my Lord in Breadstreet. Bread 2d. Beer ¾d. Wine 3¾d. Stockfish and merleyng 2½d. Eels and lamprouns 4d. Oysters ½d. Dates 1½d. Fare from Westminster to London 2d. Wine of Vernai in Cornhill 4d. Ginger-comfeit 3½d. To the poor 1d. Candles ½d. Hay for 3 horses 6d. A bushel and half of oats 6d. Sum, 3s. 10¾d.

Item, on Saturday next, in expenses. Bread 7½d. Beer 9d. Wine 7½d. Herring 2d. Stockfish 3½d. Salmon 6d. Whelks 2d. A pike 6d. 2 Eels and lamprouns 6d. Roaches and [?] 3d. Vegetables ½d. Candles ½d. Hay reckoned before. A bushel and half of oats for 3 horses, 6d. [   ] to wash my Lord's head 1d. Fuel 1½d. Groats ¼d. Sum, 5s. 3¼d.

Item, on Sunday next, in the vigil of St. Gregory the Pope, in expenses. Bread 4d. Beer 7½d. A Turbot bought 4d. Ginger-comfeit 2d. Greek wine 4d. On the same day, at Westminster. Wine 2½d. The poor ½d. On the same day, in Breadstreet. Ginger-comfeit 6d. Wine 5d. Groats and salt ½d. Fuel 1d. Dates and apples 2d. Candles ½d. Hay 5d. Oats 8d., being 2 bushels for 5 horses. Sum, 4s. 4½d.

Item, on Monday, the feast of St. Gregory the Pope, in expenses. Bread 3d. Beer 6½d. Stockfish 3d. Herrings ½d. Conger eel 4d. Salmon 3d. Eels and lamprouns 5d. Oil ½d. Vegetables ¼d. Groats

¼d. Candles ½d. Fuel ½d. Hay 3d. 2 Bushels of oats 8d., for 5 horses. Fare to Westminster and back 1¾d. To the poor ½d. Sum, 3s. 4¼d.
Sum of the sums above written, 21s. 10½d.

Item, Tuesday, the morrow of St. Gregory the Pope, in expenses. Bread 2d. Beer 5½d. Herrings 1d., with fish from store. Also, the same day, at Westminster, when Sir Nicholas de Bonvile, and many others of the household of the Earl of Pembroke, were there to breakfast. Bread 5d. Wine 13¾d. Stockfish 2d. Salmon, 10d. Eels and lamprouns 6d. Whelks 1d. On the same day, in Bread-street. Bread ½d. Wine 2½d. Dates 1d. Also wine in Lombard-street, 2½d. To the poor ½d. 2 Glasses 1d. Hay for 4 horses 4d. 2 Bushels of oats 8d. Candles ½d. Sum, 5s. 6¾d.
Item, on Wednesday next, in expenses. Bread 3d. Beer 3d. Wine 2½d. Stockfish 2d. Herrings 2d. Place 1d. Conger 3d. Whelks 2d. On the same day, at Westminster, in ginger-comfeits 1d. Wine 1¾d. Serjeant 6s. 8d. Hay for 3 horses 5½d. 2 Bushels of oats 8d. Wine in Bread-street 2½d., when Sir John de Hatton was there. Candles ½d. Sum, 9s. 9¼d.
Item, on Thursday next, in expenses. Bread 8d. Beer 6½d. A gallon of wine of the gift of the rector of Egliscovin. Herrings 2d. Stockfish from the store. Ray bought 1½d. Salmon and conger and whelks 6d. On the same day, in Friday-street, in ginger-comfets, and sugar in plate 4d. Wine there 3¼d. Candles ½d. Fuel 1d. Hay 3¼d. 2 Bushels of oats 8d. A seal for Philip de Castro, of the gift of his Lord 12d. A knife bought for his Lord 1d. A bodkin bought ½d. Sum, 4s. 10d.
Item, on Friday next, in expenses. Bread 5d. Beer 9½d. Wine from the store. Herrings 1½d. Stockfish 4d. A pike, eels, and lamprouns, 12d. Salmon 4d. Muscles 1d. Oil and vegetables 1d. Groats and salt ½d. Onions ¼d. Fuel ½d. Candles ½d. Hay 3½d. 2 Bushels of oats 8d. On the same day, in ginger-comfeits, and sugar in plate, in Cheapside, 4d. Wine 1¼d. To the poor 1¼d. Fare to Westminster and back 2d. A belt bought and given to Sir Thomas Wetheyr 12d. A bridle bought for [?] Somer 6d. Sum, 6s. 7d.
Item, on Saturday next, in expenses. Bread 5d. Beer 13½d. Herrings 1d. Stockfish from the store. Melewel 2d. Salmon 6d. Whelks 3d. Eels and lamprouns 3½d. Groats and oil ½d. Fuel ½d. Candles ½d. Hay for 5 horses 5d. 2 bushels of oats 8d. On the same day, at Westminster. Bread 3d. Wine 16¼d. Stockfish 4d. Eels and lamprouns 9d. Spices 1d. To the friars 1d. To the poor 1d. Sum, 6s. 11¾d.

Memorandum, that Philip de Castro received of his Lord 40s. on Sunday next after the feast of St. Gregory the Pope. Item, on the same Sunday, in expenses of my Lord at Westminster, when he held a breakfast there for knights, clerks, and esquires, at the house of William de Chauylu. Bread 2s. Beer 12d. Wine 3s. 8d. Half a salmon for the standard with the chine 3s. 8d. A fresh congor 3s. 3 fat pikes, 5 fat eels, and 27 fat roaches 12s. 4d. Half a hundred lamprouns 12d. Oysters 3d. Vegetables 2d. The hire of a boy to prepare the breakfast 1d. Fare to Westminster 1d. A basket 1¼d. On the same day at the inn. Bread 5½d. Beer from the store. 2 gallons of beer for the boys 2d. Fish from the store. Candles ½d. Fuel ½d. Hay bought 5¾d. Straw 6d. 2 bushels of oats 8d. 2 pair of shoes for my lord 12d. Sum, 30s. 3¼d.

Item, on Monday next, in expenses. Bread 5½d. Beer 9d. Stock-fish and herrings 3d. Other fish accounted for before. Candles ¼d. Fuel 1d. Hay 5d. 2 bushels of oats 8d. Apples and dates 1½d. Sum, 2s. 9¾d.

On the same day in spicery bought 5s. 7d. A pair of boots 2s. 1d.

On the Marvels of the City of Milan

Bonvesin della Riva

Much of the vitality of high medieval culture stems from the revival of city life in the Western World toward the end of the early Middle Ages. The complexity of the socio-economic context of the medieval city, and also its potential for varied forms of cultural activity, is succinctly captured by the thirteenth-century Milanese Friar, Bonvesin della Riva, in his survey, of one of Italy's most important cities, *De magnalibus urbis Mediolani.*

Milan, [1288]

In regard to housing. . . the truth is there before the eyes of those who see. The streets in this city are quite wide, the palaces quite beautiful, the houses packed in, not scattered but continuous, stately, adorned in a stately manner.

1. Dwellings with doors giving access to the public streets have been found to number about 12,500, and in their number are very many in which many families live together with crowds of dependents. And this indicates the astonishing density of population of citizens.

2. The roofed commons [open to all] neighbors in those squares which are popularly called *coperti* almost reach the record number of sixty.

3. The court of the Commune, befitting such a great city, spreads over an area of ten *pertiche* or thereabouts. And in order to make this more easily understandable perchance to some people, [I shall specify that it] measures 130 cubits from east to west and 136 from north to south. In the midst of it stands a wonderful palace, and in the court itself there is a tower, in which are the four bells of the Commune. On the eastern side is a palace in which are the rooms of the podestà and of the judges, and at its end on the northern side is the chapel of the podestà, built in honor of our patron, the Blessed Ambrose. And another palace prolongs the court on the north; so, similarly, on the west. To the south there is also the hall where the sentences of condemnation are publicly proclaimed.

4. The city itself is ringed as a circle, and its wonderful rounded

shape is a mark of its perfection. . . .

5. . . . Outside the wall of the moat there are so many suburban houses that they alone would be enough to constitute a city. . . .

6. The main gates of the city are also very strong, and they reach the number of six. The secondary gates, named *pusterle,* are ten. . . .

7. The sanctuaries of the saints . . . are about two hundred in the city alone, having 480 altars. . . .

8. [In honor of the Virgin Mary] thirty-six churches have been built in the city, and undoubtedly there are more than 260 in the county (*comitatus*). . . .

9. The steeples, built in the manner of towers, are about 120 in the city. . . .

10. In the county there are pleasant and delightful localities, even stately towns, fifty in number; and among them is Monza, ten miles distant from the city, worthier to be named a city than a town. Indeed, 150 villages with castles are subject to the jurisdiction of our Commune, and among them there are a great many, each of which has more than five hundred inhabitants able to bear arms. And in these very towns as well as in the villages not only farmers and craftsmen live but also very many magnates of high nobility. And there also are other isolated buildings, some of which are called mills and others, popularly, *cassine*—the infinite number of which I can hardly estimate. . . .

Milan, [1288]

When considered in regard to population, it seems to me that it outshines all the other cities in the world.

1. In fact, its natives of both sexes have the peculiarity of being rather tall, jovial in appearance, and quite friendly, not deceitful, still less malicious in dealing with people from outside their town, and because of this they also are more highly considered abroad than are others. . . . They live decently, orderly, and magnificently; they use clothing that does them honor; wherever they may be, at home or elsewhere, they are quite free in spending, esteemed, honorable, good humored in customs and way of life. . . .

2. The population, as numerous in the city as in the county or in its district, increases every day, and the city spreads out with the [erection of new] buildings. How could the people not thrive where it is so glorious to live? For this reason, if citizens are counted together with strangers of all kinds they are found in all to be many more than 200,000 men [in the entire county] —each of them to be regarded as an able man at war. And we have not counted in their number men of different kinds exempted [from military service]— monks, canons, and other clerics and religious, both those professed and those living in their own homes with their servants. . . .

3. In the city, indeed, there are ten canonries, excluding from this number the house of canons [located] where the cathedral church is. But in the county there are seventy, not including seven caononrics of the Order of the Humiliati, and the canons regular complete the number with twenty-one.

4. Then there are in the city ninety-four chapels. . . .

5. In the city there are six convents of monks, and the nunneries are eight. . . .

6. Again, in the city, including the suburbs, which are always to be regarded as included whenever the city is mentioned, there are ten hospitals for the sick, all properly endowed with sufficient temporal resources. The principal one of these is the Hospital of the Brolo, very rich in precious possessions; it was founded in 1145 by Goffredo de Bussero. In it, as its friars and deacons testify, at times and particularly in the days of dearth[?], when count is made, there are found more than five hundred poor bed patients and just as many more not lying down. All of these receive food at the expense of the hospital itself. Besides them, also, no less than 350 babies and more, placed with individual nurses after their birth, are under the hospital's care. Every sort of the poor people mentioned below, except the lepers, for whom another hospital is reserved, are received there; and they are kindly and bountifully restored to health, bed as well as food being provided. Also, all the poor needing surgical care are diligently cared for by three surgeons especially assigned to this task; the latter receive a salary from the Commune. In conclusion, the misery of no man who is in want meets refusal or rejection here. In the county, indeed, there are fifteen hospitals or thereabouts.

7. There are also houses of the Second Order of the Humiliati of each sex which in the city and the county reach the number of 220; inside them there is a copious number of persons leading the religious life while working with their own hands. . . .

8. The houses of the Order of St. Augustine of each sex undoubtedly are sixty. . . .

11. This, however, I affirm with certainty, that inside as well as outside the city, counting priests and other clerics of all orders . . . more than ten thousand religious are eating Ambrosian bread. . . .

12. What else can be said of the huge number of the multitude living in Milan and in the county? Silence; whoever can grasp it, let him grasp it. This, however, will be forgiven me: that I am by no means silent. For, as I roughly estimate—and many definitely assert the same—more than 700,000 mouths of the two sexes, including all infants as well as adults, obtain their sustenance from the surface of the Ambrosian earth. Every day—and it is wonderful in what manner —they receive, from the hand of God, Ambrosian food.

13. Why not, even if their number is so great, since in the city alone, with its dense population, there undoubtedly are 115 parishes, among which there certainly are some in each of which indeed more than five hundred families live, while in a few others about one thousand live?

14. Let therefore anyone who can count how many persons live in such a city. And if he is able to do it accurately, he will count up to the number of about 200,000, as I firmly believe. For it is certainly proved and supported by serious, careful investigation, that every day, taking into account the different seasons, 1,200 *modii* of grain and more are consumed in the city alone. That this is the truth of the matter, those who are wont to collect the tribute of the grain ground in the mills can certify.

15. Whoever wishes to know how many warriors there are in time of war should know that more than forty thousand—that is, counting each and all—live in this city who are able to fight the enemy with sword or lance or other weapon. . . .

16. In it and in its county more than ten thousand could easily maintain war horses [if] ordered by the Commune. . . .

17. There are in this city alone 120 doctors of both laws, and their college is believed to have no equal in the entire world, either in number or in learning. All these, ready to give [judicial] sentences, gladly take the money of the litigants.

18. The notaries are more than 1,500, among whom there are a great many who are excellent in drawing contracts.

19. The messengers of the Commune, popularly named *servitori* undoubtedly are six hundred.

20. Six, indeed, are the principal trumpeters of the Commune, honorable and distinguished men. . . .

21. The experts in medicine, who are popularly named physicians, are twenty-eight.

22. The surgeons of different specialties, indeed, are more than 150, among whom are a great many who, obviously being excellent physicians, have derived from the ancestors of their family the ancient traditions of surgery. They are beieved to have no equals in the other cities of Lombardy.

23. The professors of grammatical art are eight. They supervise crowds of pupils, each professor with his rod, and teach grammar with great industry and diligence, surpassing the doctors of other cities, as I have clearly determined after careful examination.

24. There are fourteen doctors in the Ambrosian chant, of so excellent renown that because of them this city is noted for its crowds of clerics.

25. The teachers of the elements of reading and writing indeed number more than seventy.

26. The copyists, although there is no university (*Studium generale*) in the city, surpass the number of forty, and by writing books with their hands every day they earn their bread and other expenses.

27. Indeed, there are three hundred bakeries in the city (as one learns from the books of the Commune) which bake bread for the use of the citizens. There are also very many other bakeries exempt [from taxation] which serve monks or religious of each sex; of these I think there are more than a hundred.

28. The shopkeepers, who sell at retail an amazing amount of goods of all kinds, doubtlessly are more than a thousand.

29. The butchers number more than 440, and excellent meat of quadrupeds of all kinds, as suits our customs, is sold in great quantity in their shops.

30. There are more than eighteen fishermen [who catch] all kinds of fish—trout, carp, large eels, tench, grayling, eels, lampreys, crabs—and who every day bring a supply of large and small fish of every species from the lakes of our county. Those who bring fish from the rivers number more than sixty, and those who bring fish from the numberless mountain streams state that they are far more than four hundred.

31. The hostelries giving hospitality to strangers for profit number about 150.

32. The smiths who outfit quadrupeds with iron shoes number about eighty, and this indicates the multitude of horsemen and horses. How many are the saddlers, how many the smiths of bridles and spurs and stirrups, I pass over in silence.

33. The makers of the sweet-sounding brass bells which are attached to the breasts of horses—and which we do not know are made anywhere else—are more than thirty, and each of them has under him many assistants in his craft. . . .

Milan, [1288]

When considered in regard to the fertility of territory and the abundance of all goods useful for human consumption, [its excellence] already is evident, but I shall explain it more plainly.

1. In fact, in our territories, fertile, fortunate, fruitful, all kinds of cereals are produced: wheat, rye, millet, panic from which bread is made, and all kinds of vegetables which can be cooked and are excellent to eat—beans, chickpeas, navy beans, small chick peas, lentils—in such an amazing quantity that after being distributed in different places they not only make good the deficiency of foodstuffs in the city of Como but also are transported and distributed to feed peoples beyond the Alps. Why not, since . . . more than thirty thousand yoke of oxen cultivate our territory? . . . Also, in our fields an infinite and unbelievable quantity of flax is produced. . . .

3. Sour and sweet cherries of all kinds, both cultivated and wild, grow in such great quantity that sometimes it happens that more than sixty carts of them are in one day brought through the gates of the city, and they are available for sale in the city at any hour from mid-May until almost mid-July. Plums, too, white, yellow, dark, damascene, likewise in almost infinite quantity, are distributed ripe from shortly before the Kalends of July until the month of October.

At the same time plums begin to appear, pears, summer apples, blackberries, and the figs named 'flowers' appear in abundance; then follow cultivated filberts; afterwards the cornel-berries, particularly appropriate for ladies; also jujubes and peaches amazingly abundant; likewise, figs and grapes of various kinds; also almonds, although few of them; wild filberts, nuts in unbelievable quantity, which all citizens who like them enjoy all the year round after all meals. Nuts can also be mixed, ground, with eggs and cheese and peper to stuff meat in winter. Also an oil is obtained from them which is liberally consumed among us. Then again, winter pears and apples and crab-apples grow, all of which abundantly supply our citizens throughout winter and beyond. Also pomegranates appear, most useful to the sick. Grapes of many kinds are abundant, and they appear ripe about the middle of July and are available for sale until the Kalends of December or thereabouts.

4. Also the common and the noble chestnuts—the latter named *marroni*—grow in infinite quantity and they are distributed all the year round in abundance to both citizens and foreigners. These, served in different ways, abundantly refresh our families. In fact, they may be cooked green in the open fire, and may be consumed after the other foods instead of dates and, in my opinion, they taste better than dates. Often they are boiled, and many eat them, cooked like this, with a spoon; then, very often, the water in which they were cooked is poured out and they are chewed without bread, indeed instead of bread. Also, when dried out by the slow heat of the sun, they are then recommended for the sick. Very many medlars, so displeasing to bankrupt gamblers, appear in the month of November. Olives grow in some parts of our county, although they are not very abundant, and laurel berries, which should be eaten with warm wine to cure pains in the stomach. Other kinds of fruit also grow, but what was said above about them will be enough for the present. No dates, pepper, or any of the very many spices from overseas are grown here—and I am not sorry for this, since they do not grow anywhere except in arid and extremely hot climates. . . .

6. . . . The monastery of Chiaravalle alone gathers in its own fields every year more than three thousand cartloads of hay, as the monks of that house tell me. . . .

8. . . . More than 150,000 cartloads [of firewood] are certainly burned every year in the city alone. . . .

11. . . . It is worth noting that in the city alone about seventy oxen are slaughtered every day—counting only the days in which the consumption of meat is permitted to Christians—as I investigated carefully from a few butchers.

12. . . . As the sellers of fish themselves, having investigated carefully the truth of the matter, plainly declare, counting all days from Quinquagesima Sunday to the feast of Saint Martin [November 12], more than seven *modii* of crabs are eaten every day in the city alone. And in order that no one may remain in doubt as to what quantity is understood by *modius*, let him know that the size of the *modius* with us is eight *sextaria*, and it weighs [as much] as a heavy

man. . . .

16. . . . It was learned after careful examination of those who collect the tribute of the salt for the Commune that 65,830 *sextaria* of salt or thereabouts are brought every year through the gates of the city. . . . But how much pepper is likely to be consumed within the city . . . I could not learn in any way.

17. Four general fairs are held in the city every year, that is, on the day of the ordination of the Blessed Ambrose, on the feast of the Blessed Lawrence, on the Ascension of the Blessed Mother of God, and on the feast of the Blessed Bartholomew. It is amazing to see almost innumerable merchants with their variety of wares and buyers flocking to all these fairs. Furthermore, ordinary markets are held in different parts of the city two days a week, that is, on Fridays and Saturdays. Indeed—and this is more [amazing]—practically anything that man may need is brought daily not only into special places but even into the [open] squares, and all that can be sold is loudly advertised for sale. Also, there are many fairs in the towns and villages of our county, being held every year on certain days. In many of them, indeed, there is a market every week, and merchants and buyers hasten to all of them in large numbers. It is evident, after [all] that has been said, that in our city it is a wonderful life for those who have money enough. Every convenience for human pleasure is known to be at hand here.

18. Also it is obvious that here any man, if he is healthy and not a good-for-nothing, may earn his living expenses and esteem according to his station. And it is worth noting that here the fecundity in offspring is just as prolific as the abundance of temporal goods. In fact, when on festive days one looks at the merry crowds of dignified men, both of the nobility and of the people, also at the bustling throngs of children incessantly scurrying here and there, and at the comely gatherings, comely groups of ladies and virgins going back and forth or standing on the doorsteps [of their homes], as dignified as if they were daughters of kings, who would say that he has ever met such a wonderful show of people this side or the other side of the sea? . . .

Notes

3. THE INSTITUTIONS OF CULTURE
UNIVERSITIES AND COURTS

The Battle of the Seven Arts

Henri d'Andeli

The little-known trouvere of the first half of the thirteenth century, Henri d'Andeli, left several accounts relating to academic life in his day: *Lai d'Aristote, La Bataille des Vins,* and *Le Dit du Chancelier Philippe.* His allegorical poem, *La Bataille des VII Ars,* gives insights into the personalities, authorities, and issues current during the crucial decades when universities were taking shape and scholastic debate was becoming the dominant form of intellectual activity.

Paris and Orleans are at odds.
It is a great loss and a great sorrow
That the two do not agree.
Do you know the reason for the discord?
It is because they differ about learning;   5
For Logic, who is always wrangling,
Calls the authors authorlings
And the students of Orleans mere grammar-boys.
Each, she says, is well worth four Homers,
For they drink huge bumpers   10
And are so skillful at versifying
That about a single leaf of a fig-tree
They will compose you fifty verses.
But they retort that verily
They call Dialectic,   15
In evil spite, a cock-a-doodle-doo.
As for those of Paris, the clerks of Plato,
They do not think them worth a button.
However, Logic has the students,
Whereas Grammar is reduced in numbers.   20
Grammar is much wrought up;
And has raised her banner
Outside of Orleans, in the midst of the grainfields;

There she assembled her army.
Homer and old Claudian,   25
Donatus, Persius, Priscian,
Those good author knights
And those good squires who serve them,
All set out with Grammar
When she went forth from her bookcase.   30
The knights of Orleans set out
Who were men-at-arms of the authors:
Master John of Saint Morisse,
Who knows his authors as well as one could wish,
Odo, Garnier and Balsamon,[1]   35
Who had inscribed a salmon
On his shield, between two dace,
With a hot pepper volant,
Blacker than charcoal,
A relish for the royal fish of the Loire   40
And for drinking the wines of Orleans
Which grow without the aid of fertilizers.
Then without jest or laughter,
They marched toward Paris.
Dame Logic heard of it;   45
She cried out full of wrath:
"Alas! I lost my support
"When Raoul de Builli died."[2]
She marshalled her forces near Tournai
Under Sir Pierre de Courtenai,[3]   50
A very learned logician.
There was master John the rustic[?],
And Pointlasne, he of Gamaches,[4]
Master Nicholas with the prominent buttocks.[5]
These three put the trivium and quadrivium   55
In a tub on a large cart;
The bedels drew the cart.
Robert the Dwarf in great derision

1 John of Saint Morisse, Odo, Garniers, and Balsamon were either contemporaries of Henri d'Andeli or older poets who had a reputation in or about Orleans.

2 Raoul de Builli, possibly the Radalphus mentioned as abbot of St. Victor of Paris in 1237, and again in 1248 as a ci-devant abbot of St. Victor.

3 Heron, 144, is sure that this Pierre de Courtenai was a canon of Paris and son of Pierre de Courtenai, who was emperor of Constantinople (d. 1219).

4 The family bearing the curious name Pointlasne was very famous in Paris during the thirteenth century. Pierre de Limoges tells of a certain Jean Poinlane who earned his living as a butcher's boy, carrying a large platter through the streets of Paris. Later, when he became a self-made captain of industry and one of the richest men in Paris, he had this old platter mounted in gold and silver, and guarded it as a relic of his previous poverty. About the middle of the thirtennth century, his son became a celebrated doctor in the University and was known as John of Paris, who became a Dominican, not to be confounded with the famous orator of the same name, called Quidort, who died in 1306.

5 In a document of the University of Paris, dated 1248, among the masters of canon law is mentioned a certain *magister Nicholaus de Pondearche* (Denifle et Chatelain, *Chart. Univ. Paris.*, I, 210. A note explains "i.e. Ponte Arche.") There is some reason for suspecting that this may be our Nicholas.

Pricked them all with a goad;
He pokes old Cheron in the bag.   60
Then they all set out.
There was many a pavilion of silk
On Montlhéry near Linas;[6]
There they gave one another cruel blows.
Civil Law rode gorgeously   65
And Canon Law rode haughtily
Ahead of all the other arts.
There was many a Lombard knight,
Marshalled by Rhetoric.
Darts they have of feathered tongues   70
To pierce the hearts of foolish people
Who come to attack their strongholds;
For they snatch up many a heritage
With the lances of their eloquence.
Augustine, Ambrose, Gregory,   75
Jerome, Bede, and Isidore,
They quoted to Divinity as authorities
That she might avoid their vanity.
Madam Exalted Science,
Who did not care a fig about their dispute,   80
Left the arts to fight it out together.
Methinks she went to Paris
To drink the wines of her cellar,
According to the advice of the chancellor,[7]
In whom she had the greatest confidence   85
For he was the best clerk in the Isle de France;
But in one trifle he considered her foolish,
That when she holds disputations in his schools
She abandons strict theological questions
And trumpets philosophy.   90
As for the arts students, they care for naught
Except to read the books of nature;
While the grammarians perverse
Have for their part forsaken Claudian and Persius,
Two very good old books,   95
The best belonging to the grammarians;
All are in opposition
To good antiquity.
Medicine, Hippocrates, Galen,
And those bold chirurgeons   100
He of the Rue Neuve, Robert,[8]
And he of Glatigny, Hubert[?],

6 Montlhéry, situated in the Arrondissement de Corbeil (Seine et Oise), not far from Paris, near the road to Orleans, was famous for its ancient strong castle, of which a tower is still standing.

7 In all probability this was Philippe de Grève who was chancellor of Paris 1218-1236.

8 This probably was Robert de Douai, canon of Senlis, physician to Louis IX, or to the queen Marguerite.

And master Peter the Lombard[9]
Who tricks Paris with his arts,
And Gerald[?] , another devil,   105
And master Henry of Venables[?] ,
And Raoul of the Charité[?] ,
Little Bridge and their vanity,
They all would turn to money making
If they saw in it no danger.   110
Villainous Chirurgy
Was seated near a bloody cemetery.
She loved discord much better
Than bringing about nice concord.
She carried boxes and ointments,   115
And a great plenty of instruments
To draw arrows from paunches.

It did not take her long to patch up
The bellies she saw pierced:
However, she is a science.   120
But she has such bold hands
That she spares no one
From whom she may be able to get money.
I would have had much respect for them
If they had cured my eyes;   125
But they dupe many people,
While with the copper and silver
Which they receive for their poisons
They build them fine houses in Paris.
From Toledo came and from Naples,   130
She who knew the carnage of battles,
At midnight, Necromancy,
Who clearly told them their evil destiny:
That everyone should arm his head,
Which destiny she had divined in the sword.   135
At a cross-road she made a fire,
Near a circle, at twilight.
There she had sacrificed two cats
And two stray pigeons
In the name of the malign deity   140
To search out the truth.
The daughter of Madam Astronomy,
Who was an accomplice in their evil deeds,
Told them very well that the battle
Would occur tomorrow without fail.   145
Arithmetic sat in the shade,
Where she says, where she figures,
That ten and two and one make thirteen,

9 A Peter Lombard was physician to King Louis IX; afterward he became canon and
sub-deacon of Chartres.

And three more make sixteen;
Four and three and nine to boot   150
Again make sixteen in their way;
Thirteen and twenty-seven make forty,
And three times twenty by themselves make sixty;
Five twenties make hundred, and ten hundreds a thousand.
Does counting involve anything further? No.   155
One can easily count a thousand thousands
In the foregoing manner
From the number which increases and diminishes,
And which in counting goes from one to hundred.
The dame makes form this her tale,   160
That usurer, prince, and count
Today love the counteress better
Than the chanting of high mass.
Arithmetic then mounted
Her horse and proceeded to count   165
All the knights of the army;
And she had at her side
Her companion Geometry
Who there again showed her skill.
In a spot between the combatants   170
She described a small circle,
And said that within thousand feet of ground
This was would be brought to a close.
Madam Music, she of the little bells
And her clerks full of songs   175
Carried fiddles and viols,
Psalteries and small flutes;
From the sound of the first *fa*
They ascended to *cc sol fa.*
The sweet tones diatessaron   180
Diapente, diapason,
Are struck in various combinations.
In groups of four and three,
Through the army they went singing,
They go enchanting them with their song.   185
These do not engage in battle;
But Donatus without delay
Dealt Plato such a blow
On the chin with a feathered verse
That he frightened him thoroughly;   190
And Sir Plato in great wrath
Struck back at him so hard with a sophism
Upon his shield, in the midst of a rhyme,
That he made him tumble in the mud
And completely covered him with blood.   195

Aristotle strikes Priscian
Our noble ancient authority
That he made him drop to the ground;
He wanted to trample him under his horse,
But Priscian had two nephews   200
Who were very handsome and brave,
Sir Graecismus and the Doctrinale;
They crippled him his horse,
And rendered the animal three-legged.
Aristotle, who was unhorsed,   205
Make Grammar tumble backwards.
Then pricked forward master Persius,
Sir Juvenal and Sir Horace,
Virgil, Lucan, and Statius,
And Sedulius, Propertius, Prudentius,   210
Arator, Homer, and Terence:
All smote Aristotle,
Who stood firm as a castle on a hill.
Priscian with his two nephews
Tried to beat out his eyes,   215
When Sophistical Refutations and the two Logics,
On Interpretation and the Topics,
The books of nature, Ethics,
Madam Necromancy, Medicine,
And Sir Boethius and Sir Macrobius   220
Dressed in a caitiff garb,
And Porphyry, came on a run
To bring aid to Aristotle.
The Lombards of dame Rhetoric
Rode hard after Dialectic,   225
Although they did not love her,
For they were but little acquainted with her;
But they wounded many an honest man
For the booty which they won there.
The Categories and the Six Principles,   230
Two good buyers of tripe,
Pricked after Sir Barbarismus
Who rode the fiftieth of the troop.
He was liege man of Grammar
One of the best men of her book case;   235
But he favored this war
Because he held land from Logic.
By treason he was alienated
Because he was a native of Poitou.
These bad, spiteful people   240
Attacked Grammar, their mother.
Ah! if you had seen them there throwing lances
To disembowel these good authors,

Shaking heads and beating hands,
And loosening the reins on tongues!   245
A thousand arrows flew at one time,
Worse than those made of willow or aspen,
For there is more venom in words
Than in a hundred thousand silly sticks.
The authors defended themselves   250
And struck them great wounds,
With penknives and styluses,
Long fables and lies.
Their castle would have been defensible enough
If it had not been so stocked with fables;   255
For they palm off their nonsense
As truth, by means of fine phrases.
Grammar strikes one of their disciples
In the body with a participle
Which felled him to the ground,   260
Then to him said: "Now go and learn something."
Then she stretched five more of them on the sod
At the point of her adverb;
But Sir Socrates made her hide,
For she could not answer all his questions.   265
She turned towards those of Orleans,
Who for a long time have exalted her.
From the depths of a valley
They brought forth her horse
Which was being held by Orthography,   270
The foundation of learning;
Then back with her authors
Dame Grammar retreated.
Ah! if you had seen the logicians
How they slew the authorlings   275
And caused such havoc
Among those fine constructions!
The sophists despised them
Because they did not understand each other;
For there was so much contention among them   280
That the one knew little of what the other said.
One knight, On Interpretation,
Killed my lord Architrenius,[10]
One of the barons of Normandy;
After that he also slew Tobit.[11]   285
Four of them he killed in one onset.
Both the *Gesta ducis Macedum*

10 The *Archetrenius* (The Arch-weeper) is a lugubrious Latin poem of some merit by the Norman John de Hauteville, who spent much time in England and flourished near the end of the twelfth century.

11 The *Tobias* (ed. Müldener, 1855) of Matthew of Vendôme (d. c. 1200) is a Latin epic poem relating the history of the two biblical Tobits, father and son, and their wives, with many digressions and frequent prayers put into the mouths of the characters.

And the versified Bible
He then cut to pieces with a huge battle-ax.
But when against the Patronymics   290
Advanced the family of the Topics,
They failed to force their way through,
So strong are the Patronymics.
Sirs *Juste* and *Praeterea*
For this reason killed   295
The good *Ego mei vel mis,*
Who was their great enemy,
Because they did not know whence he came
Nor how he was declined.
When Logic had shown her prowess,   300
She returned with great joy
To her standard, to her banner;
Then the army withdrew.
Astronomy and Rhetoric
Advised Dialectic,   305
That, before night-fall,
They had better enter Montlhéry.
The dames, who were very wise,
Entered Montlhéry,
And they did it not from fear,   310
But rather simply from the desire
To possess the castle;
And by this they made it known
That they love lofty things,
Whereas Grammar loves the fountains.   315
The authors were much troubled
When they assembled,
So they awaited the rear guard,
Which two knights were bringing up,
Primat of Orleans and Ovid. [12]   320
They brought to their aid,
With great impetuosity, ten thousand verses,
Inscribed on their banner,
Which Ovid wove with his hands
In the exile where he was in want: 325
Martial and Martianus Capella,
Seneca and Anticaudian [13]
And Sir Bernard Silvester, [14]
Who knew all the languages
Of the sciences and the arts;   330

12 Primat of Orleans was a teacher and poet of Orleans about the middle of the twelfth century. His real name was Hugo, and he was nicknamed "the Primat" (probably a title of distinction which meant "the chief"). This Primat was noted for his facility in improvising witty verses and also for the freedom with which he revealed contemporary manners and vices, especially those of the clergy.

13 The *Anti-Claudianus* is a famous poem by Alain de Lille (c. 1128-1202).

14 Bernard Silvester of Tours was an important humanistic Latin poet, who flourished 1145-53. He is not identical with Bernard of Chartres.

He did not come as a mere squire,
But he brought so large a band
That the whole place was full of them.
The Achilleis of Statius,
Strong in chest and back,   335
Bore before him the stakes.
There was the wise Cato,
Avianus and Pamphilus;
Sir Theodulus carried there
A banner bipartite;   340
In it was woven with great skill
Sir Pseustis with pierced shield
Vanquished by Alithia,
Who was pictured on the other half.
Like leopards, this whole crowd   345
Followed the banner;
So nimble they are and so quick
They almost flew,
They almost captured
Among the stakes, dame Logic,   350
Astronomy, and Rhetoric.
But they are lodged so high up
That they strike them with their whips
And with their tongues the air and the wind.
They often fatten their scholars on it,   355
Whence they themselves are altogether weak.
The dames have tiresome tongues;
Logic strikes in her hand so much
That she has torn her gown into shreds.
She makes us a knife without a blade,   360
Who wears a sleeve without the gown.
We see from the looks of her arms,
That on her body she has no substance.
Rhetoric goes to her aid,
She who earns money by pleading.   365
The Novels, Code, and Digest, 15
Make her hot potions for her head;
For she has so many quack lawyers,
Who of their tongues make clappers
To get the goods of the common herd,   370
That all the country is full of them.
One of the pupils of dame Logic
Was sent to Grammar;
He bore letters to make peace.
Now I simply cannot refrain from telling this,   375
That when he arrived at his destination
He did not know the sense

15 The Novels, Code, and Digest are parts of the *Corpus juris civilis* compiled at the command of the Emperor Justinian.

Of the presents nor the preterits;
And that there where he had been brought up,
He had dwelt on them but little.   380
He had not learned thoroughly
Irregular conjugations,
Which are most difficult to inflect,
Adverbs and parts of speech,
Articles and declensions,   385
Genders and nominatives,
Supines and imperatives,
Cases, figures, formations,
Singulars, plurals, a thousand terms;
For in the court of Grammar are more corners   390
Than in all of Logic's prattlings.
The boy did not know how to come to the point;
And came back in shame.
But Logic comforted him,
Carried him to her high tower,   395
And tried to make him fly
Before he was able to walk.
Astronomy, who soars high,
Has retained neither retreat nor school,
Neither in the city nor in the country;   400
In truth, she would have been entirely lost,
Had it not been for brave master Gautier,
Who out of little makes his living,
The Englishman who holds disputations on the Little Bridge,
Who hides himself for poverty.   405
Grammar withdrew
Into Egypt, where she was born.
But Logic is now in vogue,
Every boy runs her course
Ere he has passed his fifteenth year;   410
Logic is now for Children!
Logic is in a very bad situation
In the tower on Montlhéry;
There she practices her art;
But Grammar opposes her   415
With her authors and authorlings
Sententious and frivolous.
Echo answered in the tower
To the great blows given all around,
For there they all hurl their rhymes.   420
She defends herself with sophisms;
Often she makes them fall back
And they in turn hurl at her their verses,
So that the air is thick with them.
She defends herself with unsolvable questions,   425

With true and with false solutions.
The authorlings put in a great rage
All those assembled there
And so eager to get away,   430
Because, in truth, they will never raise the siege
Until the day that they surrender;
And if they [the besieged] fall into their hands,
They will drive them from better to worse.
All for naught they make their siege,
For Astronomy upon their tents,   435
From above, hurled her lightning;
All their pavilions she reduced to ashes;
And the authorlings fled,
And deserted Grammar.
The courtly Sir Versifier   440
Fled away between Orleans and Blois.
Henceforth he does not dare to go abroad in France,
Since he has no acquaintance there;
For students of arts and of canon law
No longer care for their [i.e., the vanquished] jurisdiction.   445
The Bretons and the Germans
Still do his bidding to some extent;
But if the Lombards got hold of him,
They (in a trice) would strangle him.
Sirs, the times are given to emptiness;   450
Soon they will go entirely to naught,
For thirty years this will continue,
Until a new generation will arise,
Who will go back to Grammar,
Just as it was the fashion   455
When Henri d'Andeli was born,
Who gives it us as his opinion
That one should destroy the glib student
Who cannot construe his lesson;
For in every science that master is an apprentice   460
Who has not mastered his parts of speech.

Here ends The Battle of the Seven Arts.

Concerning the Trifles of the Court

Walter Map

Walter Map's (d. ca. 1210) cynical view of court life grew from first-hand experience; he served in many capacities in the court of Henry II of England, prior to, at the latter's death, pursuing a career in the Church. His gossipy recounting of tales popular in the court, *De nugis curialium,* provides an insight into the literary tastes of the day—for stories like that of the King of Portugal—as well as the complex milieu within which court culture thrived and the attitudes of different classes toward learning and education.

1. A Comparison of the Court with the Infernal Regions.

"In time I exist, and of time I speak," says Augustine: and adds, "What time is I know not."[1] In a like spirit of perplexity I may say that in the Court I exist and of the Court I speak, and what the Court is, God knows, I know not. I do know however that the Court is not Time; temporal indeed it is, changeable and various, stationary and wandering, never continuing in one stay. When I leave it, I know it perfectly: when I come back to it I find nothing or but little of what I left there: I am become a stranger to it, and it to me. The Court is the same, its members are changed. I shall perhaps be within the bounds of truth if I describe it in the terms which Porphyry uses to define a *genus,*[2] and call it a number of objects bearing a certain relation to one principle. We courtiers are assuredly a number, and an infinite one, and all striving to please one individual. But today we are one number, tomorrow we shall be a different one: yet the Court is not changed; it remains always the same. It is a hundred-handed giant, who if he be all maimed, is yet all the same, and still hundred-handed; a hydra of many heads, that makes of none effect and despises the labours of Hercules, does not feel the force of that unconquered hero's hand, and—luckier than Antaeus—has of its mother earth, sea and air. It will not be crushed against the breast of Hercules; the whole world renews its strength. Yet when the supreme Hercules sees fit, His will be done.

If we apply to the Court Boethius' true definition of fortune, we find it in so far correct, that the Court is *constant only in inconstancy.*[3] To those alone is the Court satisfactory who obtain her grace. For she does confer grace, inasmuch as it is not the lovable or

1 Aug. *Conf.,* xi. 25.   2 Porph. *Isagoge,* 2.   3 Boethius, *Cons. Phil.,* ii., pr. I.

those worthy of love whom she affects, but to them that are unworthy to live she sheweth her grace. Grace of a truth it is that comes without reason, settles without desert, alights on the ignoble for no known cause. The mystic fan of the Lord separates to itself the wheat from the tares by a true judgement, a righteous winnowing. This of the Court with not less anxious care parts for itself the tares from the wheat. What the former in its wisdom chooses, the latter in its unwisdom casts away, and *vice versa,* as so often happens. Covetousness, the Lady of the Court, urges us on with so many prickings that our mirth gives way to anxiety. He that laughs is laughed at, he that sits in sadness is accounted wise. Nay, our judges set a penalty on joy and a premium on sorrow, wheras properly the good are happy in the consciousness of right, and the bad depressed in the consciousness of wrong, so that hypocrites should be always sad, and true worshippers of God cheerful. The judge who calls evil good and good evil is consistently enough, according to his own views, mild to the fierce and fierce to the mild. The indwelling of the Holy Spirit is a source of continual joy to the good, the upswelling of the scaly serpent a source of sadness to the evil. Trailing about the heart of the evil thinker he gathers a poisonous garlic, which pleases in the eating and thereafter does but stink. This garlic is most frequently offered to us here in this Court by him who envied us from the beginning. The man who is attracted by his snare is repelled by the Lord's correction.

Now how comes it that we men have degenerated from our original beauty, strength, and force, while other living creatures in no way go astray from the grace first given to them? Adam was created a giant in stature and muscle, and in mind, too, equalled the angels until he was overthrown: and, though his life was limited by time instead of being eternal, and was cut down from a whole to a fragment, it was yet lightened by the solace of a great longevity. This excellence of morals, strength, powers and life lasted long among his posterity; but about the time of David, the Lord's prophet, it is described by him as lasting fourscore years, whereas it had been eight hundred or more, before the time of labour and sorrow. We however now do not last out seventy years without loss of vigour: nay, as soon as we have attained discretion, we are driven either to death or dotage. The creatures of earth, sea and air—everything except man—rejoice in the life and powers with which they were created. They, it seems, have not fallen out of their Maker's favour. And what should this mean but that they still keep the obedience enjoined upon them, while we have spurned it from the beginning? Drearily indeed must we lament that while all else has kept its standing, we alone and the devils have fallen—that our deceivers are our companions in sorrow, that our own sin has condemned us to a short span of life and powers, and that because of our following of the first man we have fallen to be the worst.

Who was it that discovered how to melt metals and transmute one into another? that fused the hardest bodies into a fluid? that taught how solid marble could be cut with running lead? Who was it who found out that adamant would yield to the blood of a he-goat? Who melted flint into glass? Not we, assuredly. A course of three-score and ten years leaves no room for such discoveries. On the other hand, men who could spend seven or eight hundred years in the acquisition of wisdom, and were blessed with health and riches, these could well plumb the abyss of nature and bring deep things to light. It was they who, after the study of the stars, marked out the lives of beasts, birds and fishes, their tribes and alliances, the natures of plants and seeds; they who assigned a life of a hundred years to the crow, of a thousand to the raven (*or* stag), and to the stag (*or* raven) an age which can scarce be credited. Credited however they should be by us, particularly in what concerns wild creatures, since these lived with them unaffrighted before flesh-eating prevailed, just as dogs do with us, whose life and habits are open to our observation. Many of their discoveries they have left us in writing: many more have been handed down by the heads of generations from the first, and so our accomplishments are not our own, but have been trans-fused into us from them according to the measure of our receptivity.

Well, the Court was the subject with which I started, and see the point at which I have arrived! Such topics are always liable to emerge, perhaps not much to the purpose, yet refusing to be put aside; nor is it a very serious matter so long as they do not end in a black fish's tail, and the intrusive subject is one which fitly demands treatment. . . .

10. Of the Creatures of the Night.

There, too, are creatures of the night, the screech-owl, the night-crow, the vulture, and the owl, whose eyes love darkness and hate light. These are commissioned to go round about, to seek out diligently and to report accurately what of good happens that may concern Jupiter, what of harm falls to be condemned by Dis; and while they craftily lie in ambush here and there, they greedily follow up the odour of carrion. This they devour in secrecy, or conceal, and upon their return lay any accusations they please, besides what they gain for themselves in private by robbery. This Court, too, sends out beings whom it calls justices, sherffs, under-sheriffs and beadles, to make strict inquisition. These leave nothing untouched or untried and, bee-like, sting the unoffending—yet their stomach escapes uninjured. They alight on flowers to draw out of them what honey they can, and though when they take office they make oath before the Supreme Judge that they will faithfully and without damage serve their Lord and him, "rendering outo Cæsar the things that are Cæsar's, and unto God the things that be God's," yet gifts turn them aside; that the lambs may be stripped of their fleeces, the foxes go unharmed, for they have been approved by silver, knowing that "it is a clever thing to give."[4]

Now among such justices as I describe, the clerical officers are usually found more oppressive than the laymen; and I do not understand why this should be, unless my reply to the noble Ranulf de Glanville[5] gave the true answer. He asked this question, and I answered: "It is because the gentry of our land are too proud or too lazy to put their children to learning, whereas of right only free men are allowed to learn the arts, which for that very reason are called 'liberal.' The villeins on the other hand (or rustics, as we call them) vie with each other in bringing up their ignoble and degenerate offspring to those arts which are forbidden to them; not that they may shed vices, but that they may gather riches; and the more skill they attain, the more ill they do. The arts are as the swords of mighty men: their force varies with the method of him who holds them: in the hand of a merciful prince they bring peace, in that of a tyrant, death. The villein redeems his son from the lord, and on each side covetousness fights, and wins when freedom is conferred on freedom's foe. The famous poet points this out clearly where he says:

'Nothing is harsher than the ennobled clown,'

and what follows; and again:

'Nor any fiercer beast
Than a slave's vengeance on a freeman's back.' " [6]

The great man I mentioned approved my little discourse.

It happened of late that an Abbot procured himself to be made one of these justices, and he had the poor despoiled more savagely than any layman, hoping perhaps to gain a bishopric by the favour accruing from his prey; but vengeance met him after not many days, and caused him to turn his teeth upon himself and to die with his hands all be-gnawed. So have I seen crows hung up over the seed committed to the ground, that others might see them hanging, and fear and shun their fate: and they do shun it. Yet they whom the Lord calls the children of this world and describes as "wiser than the children of light"—adding the qualification "in their generation"—are not deterred, not afraid of becoming as this abbot, though they have before them the example of two other magnates whom one and the same circuit keeps helpless on their beds, smitten with palsy.

So far I bear witness concerning the Court of what I have seen. But, for the rolling flames, the blackness of darkness, the stench of the rivers, the loud gnashing of the fiends' teeth, the thin and piteous cries of the frightened ghosts, the foul trailings of vipers, serpents and all manner of creeping things, the blasphemous roarings, evil smell, mourning and horror—were I to allegorize upon all these, it is true that correspondences are not wanting among the things of the Court, but they would take up more time than I have at my disposal. Besides, to spare the Court seems only courteous; and it is enough to

---

4 Ov. *Am.*, i. 8, 62.   5 Ranulf de Glanville, Justiciar from 1180 to 1189.
6 Claudian, *in Eutrop.*, i. 181, 183.

conclude from the above, according to the reasons here set forth, that the Court is a place of punishment. I do not however say that it is Hell; that does not follow: only it is almost as much like Hell as a horse's shoe is like a mare's . . . .

Among this household I have some nephews who are completely masters of my property; no one can say them nay. They are the stoutest enemies I have; anything I spend on them they reckon as a due, and neither feel nor pay me any thanks for it. Were I to assign them the whole estate and keep back something which might be useful to them, they would think it nothing: they would even abuse me and be much annoyed, starting aside like a broken bow: their view being that I was born for their benefit and not my own, and that they are masters and I the servant, who have got together nothing for myself but everything for them. The father in Terence, who had similar saviours of his property, says: "My only possession is myself;"[7] and indeed many though not all fathers may say the same. Certainly my people have got the upper hand of me: 'Mine,' did I say? Rather their own, for they pay no attention to anybody but themselves. While they are fresh they exercise a good deal of care, but drop it later on. I know of a master of a house, who gets a new set of servants every year. A good many people consequently think him fickle, but to me he seems a wise and careful man, for he always finds his servants respectful and attentive.

Well, all this has been urged in defence of our king. How is he to keep in order thousands of thousands and govern them peaceably, when we small fathers of households cannot control the few we have? The truth is, that every house has one servant and many masters. The head serves every one; those by whom he is served are to be reckoned as masters. Our Court, I take it, lives in a more perilous whirl than other households, fluctuating and variable. Yet I dare not in any wise lay this to the charge of our king, for in a hall (palace) that holds many thousand diverse minds there must be much error and much confusion; neither he nor any other man can remember the name of each individual, much less know their hearts; and no one can entirely control a household whose thought and speech—I mean the speech of their hearts—he knows not. The Lord divides the waters from the waters, the peoples from the peoples: He is the searcher of hearts and the cleanser of them, sitting upon the waters and ruling them in power: but no one can prevent our giants murmuring beneath the waters.

You have heard that all courts are unquiet save that only to which we are bidden. That city alone which the Lord rules has peace, and it is promised to us as "an abiding city." And you, my dear Geoffrey,[8] would have me courtly (not to say witty: "I am a child, I know not how to speak."). Yet, I repeat, you bid me, me who am bound in and banished to this Court which I have here truly described, me who confess myself the Tantalus of this hell, to philo-

7 Terence, *Phorm.*, iv., 1, 20.   8 The person thus addressed has not been identified.

sophize. How can I, who thirst, give you to drink? Letters are the employment of a quiet and collected mind. What a poet needs is a permanent, safe, continuous abode; and not the most prosperous state of body or circumstances will avail if the mind be not tranquil within. You are asking an inexperienced and unskilled man to write, and to write from the Court: it is to demand no less a miracle than if you bade a fresh set of Hebrew children to sing out of the burning fiery furnace of a fresh Nebuchadnezzar. . . .

12. Of the King of Portugal.

The King of Portugal who yet lives, and still reigns after his manner, was once beset by many enemies, and almost forced to submission, when there came to his aid a youth of noble build and remarkable beauty. He remained with the King, and so distinguished himself in warlike deeds that his achievements seemed beyond the power of any individual. He re-established peace to the hearts' desire of the King and the kingdom, and was as of right received into the closest intimacy with his Sovereign, who showed him more favour—sending for him constantly, visiting him often, rewarding him richly—than tended to his prosperity. The nobles of the Court, seeing themselves less honoured than before by their lord, imagined that the favourite had by so much diverted favour from them, and the more highly they saw him exalted in the King's affection complained that they were defrauded by him to that extent. Maddened with envy, they used every effort to over-throw by malice him whom pre-eminence in virtue had raised to favour. They shrank from openly attacking one who was fore-armed or in any way prepared for it; so they sank to the lowest form of persecution, that is, accusation. They directed their aim to the spot in which they knew their lord to be bare and open to attack. They knew him to be madly prone to groundless jealousy, and sent to him two of their number, [commissioned] like the elders of Babylon, to accuse the queen—a second Susanna—of undue familiarity with the youth. The King, pierced to the heart, through that spot where the mail-coat of wisdom left him bare, was smitten with mortal anguish, and with blind rashness ordered the inventors of the crime to avenge him on the innocent man with the utmost savagery and secrecy. Thus was innocence delivered over to the snare. The traitors, warned to say nothing of the crime, ingratiated themselves with the youth by words, acts of courtesy, and every feigned appearance of affection, and climbed into his good graces by a false ladder of friendship. They took him away under cover of a hunting expedition to the depths of a forest in a distant lonely region; there they slew him, left him to the wolves and snakes, and divulged the murder only to the dupe whom they had made to order it. He (for his madness had not yet abated) hastened homeward, burst into the bed-chamber, an inner room which he scarcely ever entered, dismissed its other occupants, and furiously attacked the queen— now near her confinement—brutally setting upon her with feet and fists, and thus put an end to two lives by a single onslaught. He then privately summoned to him his villainous accomplices in crime, and in their presence proceeded to boast himself in exaggerated terms for his threefold offence, as having accomplished a righteous vengeance. They on their part extolled him with lavish praise for his spirit and valour, hoping to keep their dupe under a lasting delusion. For a time the conspiracy, kept within doors, made no sign; but, since, says the proverb, a secret murder cannot be long hid, at length it crept into the ears of the people, and the more firmly the fear of the tyrant repressed their voices, the more bloody did his infamy appear by the incessantly whispered reports. A forbidden tale, when it does break out, travels swifter than words which are licensed, and a wonder, passed from mouth to mouth, gains the wider publicity from the secrecy of its propagation. And why? Because every one who is told of a matter which he must not divulge always commits it to another for safe keeping. The King perceived that his Court was depressed, and kept an unwonted silence when he went abroad; the city was in evident sympathy with the Court. His conscience divined somewhat: he feared for his good name, and—how common a mistake it is with us!—after the deed was past, he saw what he had done. From many a mouth he learnt of the hateful scheme by which his betrayers had led him astray. His grief was inconsolable. He sated a wrath, now at last justified, upon the contrivers and accomplishers of that wickedness, whom he blinded and mutilated [*oculis privatos et genitalibus*] and so left them to a living death, in perpetual night, and deprived of all bodily enjoyment.

Such are the tricks of the Court, and such the deceits of devils that have place there; so, whoever enjoys beholding enormities, let him enter the courts of the mighty. And you would have me play the poet in the midst of these strifes, though our Court is stormy beyond all others, a mother of affliction and a nurse of wrath! It seems to me that you are using Balaam's spurs on me—the spurs with which he drove his ass to speak: for what other would avail to drive anyone into writing poetry? I am much afraid that my stupidity will cause our parts—mine of the ass, and yours of Balaam—to be reversed, so that when you try to make me speak I shall begin to bray—as the other spoke instead of braying—and you will have made an ass out of a man whom you wanted to make a poet. Well, as ass I will be, since you wish it: but beware, should the brainlessness of my braying make you ridiculous, lest the want of respect shown in your request prove to lack modesty. For myself, I have many fears: want of knowledge will accuse me, inaptness of speech will condemn me, the present generation will look down upon me because I am still living. The first two fears you put on one side by your orders to me: the third I do not care to abolish, for I wish to go on living. The subject you choose for me is so vast that no toil can master it, no effort cope with it: it is just the sayings and doings which have not yet been committed to writing, and anything I have heard that is more than ordinarily inspiring: all this to be set down, that the reading of it may amuse, and its teaching tend to moral improvement. My own purpose in the matter is to invent nothing new, and introduce nothing untrue, but to narrate as well as I can what having seen, I know, or what, having heard, I believe.

The present bishop of London, Gilbert Foliot[9] a man thoroughly at home in three tongues, Latin, French and English, in each of which he speaks with the greatest clearness and eloquence, in this his old age, when almost total blindness has come upon him, having already composed a few small but brilliant tractates, is now, as if atoning for a wasted leisure, unmooring his boats from the shore; he is to venture on the exploration of the open sea, and is hastening to redeem the time he has lost by compiling with a swift pen (thumb!) a work on the Old and New Testaments. Bartholomew, bishop of Exeter,[10] again, an old and accomplished man, is now engaged in writing; while Baldwin, bishop of Worcester,[11] a man of much learning, and wise in the things that belong to the Lord, grows weary if his pen be idle. These men are the philosophers of our day, who want for nothing, and have abodes filled with all manner of supplies, and tranquillity outside: they have begun well and will make a good ending. But whither, I would ask, am I to look for a harbour, who have barely leisure to live?

A recapitulation of the beginning of this Book, differing in Expression but not in Substance.

Augustine says: "In time I am and of time I speak, and what time is I know not." With like wonderment I may say that in the Court I am and of the Court I speak, and what it is I understand not. I know, however, that it is not time. Temporal indeed it is, unstable and various, stationary and wandering, and in the diversity of its composition often unlike itself. We withdraw from it often, and return, as the requirements of circumstances dictate either course. When we leave it we know it thoroughly; if we stand out of it for a year, a new face meets us on our return, and we ourselves are new. We find natives ousted by strangers and masters by their servants. The Court indeed is the same, but the members of it are changed. Porphyry says that a *genus* is a plurality standing in a certain relation to a single principle. The Court is certainly not a *genus,* though it be something of the kind: for we are a plurality standing in a certain relation to the lord king, inasmuch as it strives to please him alone. It is written of fortune that only in mobility is she stable. The Court is not fortune, yet it is unchangeably in movement.

Hell, they say, is a place of punishment. Whatever contains anything else within it is a place. So too the Court is a place; but is it one of punishment? Of a truth it is, and only in this respect milder than hell, in that those whom it torments are able to die. Macrobius asserts that it was the opinion of the most ancient *philosophers* that

9 Bishop of London from 1163 until his death on February 18th, 1187.
10 Died on December 15th, 1184.   11 Consecrated on August 10th, 1180.

hell was nothing else but the human body, whereinto the soul being cast suffers the foulness of darkness and the horror of filth; and of all the punishments which are reputed in fables to have been in hell, they tried to find a place for every one in the sepulchre of the human body.[12] But this, since it is lengthy to go through and may easily be found elsewhere, we leave aside. Yet if the human body can by any simile be called the prison and chaos of the soul, why should not the Court be called the prison of the body and soul alike?

Styx hate: heat Phlegethon: forgetfulness Lethe:

Cocytus wailing: Acheron standing for sadness:

All are in our Court. In these the outpourings of punishments are mingled together; in these are all manner of crimes chastised. There is no transgression for which in these rivers vengeance also does not meet its mate. Every wickedness finds here a hammer matched to it, so that Thy fury, O God, is seen in these rivers and Thine indignation in this sea. The Styx of the Court is the hatred inborn in us of our own or of others' fault: its Phlegethon is the heat of covetousness and wrath; its Lethe the forgetting of the goodness of our Maker, and of the promise given in baptism; its Cocytus the mourning inflicted on us by our excesses; it comes in many ways, along with that Evil One whom those excesses seem to invite, who is the source of dolours and the maker of idols in them that are his. Its Acheron is sadness, whether of penitence for deed or word, or because of things desired and not attained.

But the scourges of sins and the sufferings of punishments we can here distribute, if we are permitted. Charon, the ferryman of hell, carries none over in his boat but him who gives the coin from his mouth—from his mouth, it says, not from his hand, for our ferryman is obliging if you promise, but if you give will recognize you no more. So does it often happen in other cases: at the Court the shadow takes precedence of the body, doubt of certainty, promise of gift.

Tantalus there is mocked by the flying river. We here are deceived by the good things which we touch with the tips of our fingers and which start back from them, and the profit which seemed already grasped vanishes.

Sisyphus there carries a stone from the bottom of a valley to the top of a mountain, and when it rolls back thence follows it, to carry it back that it may fall again. Here too are those who gain the height of riches and think nothing has been attained, and follow their heart, fallen back into the valley of avarice, to bring it back to a mountain yet father off, wheron indeed it is not permitted to abide, because in hope of what is desired, what is obtained seems poor, and that heart is likened to a stone, for the Lord says: "I will take away their stony heart and give them a heart of flesh." May God so give and so do to them of the Court that they may be able to find rest on some one of the mountains.

Ixion there is rolled round on his wheel, often unlike himself, up,

12 Macrob. *in Somn. Scip.*, i. 10, 9, 10.

down, hither and thither. We too have our Ixions, whom rolling fortune torments with their lot. They climb to glory and fall to wretchedness, when down they hope, when up they exult; when at the bottom they mourn, when on the right hand they are in hope, when on the left they are in fear. And since on every side of the wheel there is room for fear, there is in it no place for any which is devoid of hope; and as it is shared by hope, fear, joy and grief, it is hope alone that makes and keeps together its occupants. It is all terrible, all in fight against conscience, but none the less for that is it sought after.

Tityus lusted after Juno at the first sight, and eagerly following his unlawful desire, did not bridle the heat of his foolish liver, wherefore he is rightly punished in that same liver, which grows again to its own loss: it feeds the greedy appetite of the vultures, and though it does not fail, it is condemned not to sate them. Am not I, and perhaps some other too, a Tityus at the Court; upon whose covetous heart vultures, that is, black passions, are set, which tear it because it has not striven, has not withstood a wrong desire? but I am not the Tityus who did not hide from Juno the anxieties of his lustful mind. His thoughts, his acts, his words, are clean contrary to the good man who hath not walked nor stood nor sat.

The daughters of Belus strive there to fill vessels with holes in them, without bottom, which let through all liquid, and lose the draughts continually drawn from the Lethean spring. Belus is interpreted to mean manly or virtuous: this is our Father, even God. We are not His sons, for we are not virtuous, nor staunch, but rather His daughters, for, effeminate to weakness, we labour to fill, with a sieve that parts the grain from the chaff—that is, with discretion—the pierced vessels, that is our insatiable souls, the bottom of which ambition has made unsound, which absorb like Charybdis what is poured into them, and without the appearance of being full, ever let go the useless draughts. This sieve does not strain off the troubled liquor from the clear, the thick from the bright, though it was created for that end; nor does it hold the water of a fountain springing up unto life eternal, not the water which whosoever drinketh shall not thirst again, but the water of Lethe, which the drinker remembers not, which deadens the throat, which makes one thirst again, which stealthily enters the very soul, mingles with it and forces it to go into the mud of the abyss.

Cerberus, the three-headed dog, is the porter there. He is tame to let men come in, in complete quiet, but when they would go out, attacks them in all his terrors with his three-fold voice. That porter enriches the hall of Dis with eager entries, and empties it not by withdrawals; he keeps, he does not spend. The Dis of this Court, too, has criminals whom he delivers to prison, and those who in feigned sympathy with them escort them into the pit; but when by the goodness of the prince they are free to go out, these bark against them with the three ravening alarms of demand and greed for food, drink and raiment, and compel men stripped bare and despoiled of all they have, to make promises: true Cerberi, for they devour the flesh of them that are in fetters, and very dogs, knowing how to fill their triple throats from them that are in trouble. These suffer hunger like dogs, and care not whose food they snatch, nor distinguish between meat and carrion, not parting fresh from stale, nor stench from odour, and taking no thought of what is lawful.

In the sooty palace of dark Dis, Minos, Rhadamanthus, and Æacus cast lots into an urn, and are set as judges and a tribunal over the wretched souls. Evil deeds they weigh at once. Good deeds they defer or annul. If a harsh lot comes out, they puhish the more harshly; if a mild one, they object and pervert it, that virtue may end in blame; if doubtful, they interpret it on the worser side. But they have earned praise for justice from their unjust lord, because they never remit aught of deserved harm. Yet it is said that if they be looked upon by those who pass by, their rigour fails as if under a spell; if not, they insist upon the crimes, they weigh evil deeds, and slaughter and destroy; good deeds they compel to slip by, and by offending God they appease the tyranny of Dis. Yet in some sort these judges are excusable, for they do but imitate the guile of their terrible prince. We too have censors under a most noble judge, and the justice of their lord reprehends their injustice, for though they are sworn before him to preserve fairness in trying men, yet, as in the case of those three clever judges of Pluto, if the guilty one look upon them he is righteous; if the righteous look not upon them, he is guilty. And this word "look upon" is to be glossed in the manner of the lord pope, who says: "Neither in his own person, nor by a messenger, hath he visited us nor looked upon us"—that is, "hath not given."

These, it seems, cast lots into an urn—that is, they conceal cases of causes in a wrapper, smothering the simple with charges, submitting accusations to a strict scrutiny; of which accusations none obtains pardon save that for which Mother Purse pleads with her wrinkled mouth. She is that lady of all, who pardons crimes, justifies the wicked and wills not the death of sinners, nor without cause casts out him that cometh to her and, abiding stable, she causes movement in all. Yet is there one place, the exchequer, in which she can do no miracles, for the glance of the just king seems ever to be fresh there. And thus it happened once that after I had heard a concise and just judgement given against a rich man in favour of a poor one, I said to Lord Randulf, the chief justice "Although the poor man's judgement might have been put off by many quirks, he has obtained it by a happy and quick decision." "Certainly," said Randulf, "we decide causes here much quicker than your bishops do in their churches." "True, " said I, "but if your king were as far off from you as the pope is from the bishops, I think you would be quite as slow as they." He laughed, and did not say no. I do not say that those whom the king has chosen to be the chiefs of all are purse-men, but those

whom covetousness and procurations have led to their own *rostra;*
nor is it surprising that those whom Simon has promoted to rule,
swear by Simon. It is the wont of merchants to sell what they buy.

A strong proof and argument of the justice of our king is, that
whoever has a good case is anxious to try it before him; whoever has
a bad one will not come to him unless he is dragged. I speak of King
Henry II, whom Spain chose to be the arbiter of an old and fierce
dispute that was waged between the kings of Toledo and Navarre,
whereas it was from old time the custom of all realms to choose the
Court of Rome and prefer it to all others; but now our Court, that of
our king, has been deservedly preferred to all, and the old cause was
neatly decided. And yet, though he is wellnigh alone in this vale of
misery in being an acceptable minister, buying and selling goes on
under his wings. But unjust officers pay more respect to him than to
God, for what they cannot hide from him they will do rightly against
their will, but what they know to be manifest to God, they do not
fear to pervert; for God is a late avenger, the king a swift one. I am
not speaking against all the judges but against the larger and insaner
part of them.

You have heard of Hell and of its allegories, but the rolling
flames, the clouds and stench, the hissings of serpents and vipers, the
groans and tears, the filth and horror—were it permitted to expound
each of these in allegory, matter would not be wanting. However,
one must spare the Court; for these things demand more space than I
see is open to me. Still, from what has been said it may be inferred
that the Court is a place of punishment. I do not call it Hell, but it is
almost as much like Hell as a horse's shoe is like a mare's.

Yet the king of this Court, if he knows it well, is not free of
blame, for he who is a rector is bound to be a corrector. But perhaps
they who are set over it with him will not accuse it lest it should be
made purer by him, because in muddy water they fish with more
profit, and they themselves do not know what goes on under them,
nor does the king himself know what they do. They that have power,
saith the Lord, are called benefactors—by their flatterers, be it understood. Certainly they that have power here are more properly called
venefactors (poisoners), since they oppress their inferiors and deceive
their superiors that from each side they may make gain anyway. But
all their villainies they hide from the king in order not to be
corrected and make less profit, and not to be pulled up themselves
and prevented from harming those below them. The king in his Court
is like a husband who is the last to learn of the unfaithfulness of his
wife. They craftily urge him out of doors to sport with hounds and
hawks, that he may not see what they are doing meanwhile indoors.
While they make him play, they concentrate on serious matters, they
seat themselves on the bench and decide equitable and unjust causes,
all to the same end. When the king returns from hunting or hawking
he shows them his bag and shares it with them, but they do not show
theirs to him. For the very thing which makes them praise him

openly, they condemn him in private. Is it surprising if he is deceived, who is so rich in enemies of his own household? Says Flaccus:

Poor is the house where there are not many things which the master knows not of, and by which thieves benefit.[13]

He gives us to understand that the larger the house, the more risk to persons and to substance is rife in it. And so in that large household of which I speak there is great confusion, and error above measure, which He only, when He sees occasion, will bring to calm, Who sitteth upon the throne and judgeth right.

13 Hor. *Ep.*, i. 6, 45.

Notes

4. LITERATURE, PART I: THE EPIC TRADITION

The Song of Roland

La Chanson de Roland (ca. 1100), the most famous of the old French epics, celebrates knighthood and the feudal military ideal: "Roland is brave and Oliver is wise." The two companions, together with a small contingent from Charlemagne's army, sustain the attack of a moslem horde and fight to the end.

145. When the pagans see how few of the French are left they feel proud; they take heart. They say to each other:
"The Emperor is in the wrong."
Marganice, mounted on a sorrel horse, digs in his golden spurs and strikes Oliver from behind, in the middle of his back. The shining hauberk parts, laying bare the body, and the spear passes through and out at the breast. Then the pagan says:
"You were hit hard that time! Charles the Great left you here in the pass to your sorrow! He has done us wrong, but he will have no reason to congratulate himself, for in your death alone I have avenged all of ours."

146. Oliver knows that he has been given a deadly wound, and he grips Halteclere and with its burnished blade strikes Marganice on the sharp-pointed golden helmet, smashes through its flowers and gems and cleaves the head from here down to the front teeth. He gives the sword a wrench and hurls down the corpse. And then he says:
"A curse on you, pagan! I cannot say that Charles has suffered no loss, but you at least will never go back to the kingdom from which you came and brag to any wife or woman that you left me the poorer by so much as a farthing, nor that you did me or anyone else any harm!"
Then he calls to Roland to come to his help.

147. Oliver knows that he has been dealt a mortal wound and his passion to avenge himself is insatiable. He charges into the thick of the pagans, striking out like a brave knight, shearing through the shafts of their spears, and their shields and their feet and their wrists and their saddles and their ribs. Any man who had seen him then

dismembering Saracens, flinging corpse upon corpse, would have
been able to remember a noble knight. He does not neglect to raise
Charles' battle cry, but shouts, "Mountjoy!" loud and clear. He calls
to his friend and his peer, Roland:

"My lord, companion, come to my side for today in bitter grief
we must separate."

148. Roland looks at Oliver's face and sees that it has turned
gray, livid, colorless, and pale, and he sees the bright blood streaking
down Oliver's body and falling in streams to the ground. The Count
says:

"Oh God, what can I do now! My lord, my companion, your
courage has been brought to grief, and no man will ever be your
equal. Ah sweet France, what a loss of noble knights you have
suffered today, and how stricken and wasted you are now! What a
heavy blow this will be to the Emperor!"

And with these words he faints on his horse.

149. Look now: Roland has fainted on his horse and Oliver has
been dealt a mortal wound and has lost so much blood that his sight
has become confused. He can no longer see anything clearly, whether
it is far away or near. He can no longer recognize any living man, and
finding his companion in front of him, he strikes with all his strength
at the helmet with its jewels set in gold, and he splits it down the
nose piece but does not touch the head. Roland, when the blow has
struck him, looks Oliver in the face and softly and gently asks him:

"My lord, companion, did you mean to strike me? It is I,
Roland, who have loved you dearly for so long. You never warned
me nor challenged me."

Oliver says: "Now I hear you speak, but I cannot see you. May
the Lord God keep you in His sight! I have struck you and I beg you
to forgive me!"

Roland answers: "I have suffered no harm. Here and before
God I forgive you."

With these words they bow to each other.

And look: it is thus, tenderly, that they part.

150. Oliver feels the pains of death encroaching upon him. His
eyes reel in his head. He loses his hearing. He can no longer see anything. He dismounts and reclines on the ground, and there in a loud
voice, with his hands clasped and lifted up toward heaven, he
confesses his sins and prays to God to receive him into Paradise, and
he blesses Charles and sweet France and above all other men his
companion Roland. His heart fails, his helmet sags, his whole body
slumps onto the earth. The Count is dead. He is there no longer.
Roland, that brave knight, weeps for him and gives way to his grief.
Never in this world will you hear a more sorrowful man.

151. Now Roland sees that his friend is dead and lying face
down on the ground, and with great tenderness he speaks his lament
and farewell:

"My lord, companion, your tempered courage has been brought to grief! We have been together for days and years and you never did me any wrong, and I never did you any, and now that you are dead it is a grief to me to be alive."

At this word Roland, the baron, faints, sitting on Veillantif his horse, and his stirrups of fine gold hold him up, so that whichever way he leans he cannot fall.

152. Before Roland returns to himself and recovers from his faint, terrible losses have been inflicted on his force, for the French are dead, they are all lost except the Archbishop and Gualter of Hum. Gualter has come down from the heights. He has fought hard against the Saracens of Spain; all his men are dead, overwhelmed by the pagans, and whether he wishes to or not he flees toward the valleys there and calls out to Roland to help him:

"Ah noble Count, man of courage, where are you? I was never afraid where you were. It is I, Gualter, who conquered Maelgut! It is I, the nephew of old white-haired Droun, and you used to love me for my courage. My lance is splintered, my shield is pierced, my hauberk is broken and rent, and as for my body . . . I will die in any case, but I have sold my life dearly."

Roland hears these words, and he spurs his horse and rides toward Gualter.

153. Roland, in his grief and his rage, strikes into the midst of the pagans and hurls down twenty of the Saracens of Spain, dead. And Gualter kills six, and the Archbishop five. The pagans say:

"These men are monstrous! Lords, take care that they do not get away alive! Any man who does not attack them now is a traitor, and he who lets them escape is a coward!"

Then they renew the hue and cry and ride to attack from all sides.

154. Count Roland is a noble warrior, Gualter of Hum is a superb knight, and the Archbishop is a brave and proven fighter. None of them would forsake the others on any account, and they charge into the midst of the pagans. A thousand Saracens dismount, and there are forty thousand on horses, and I swear it, they are afraid to approach. Instead they throw lances and spears, and bolts and javelins and arrows and sharp missiles and long darts. One of the first of these kills Gualter. Turpin of Reims has his shield pierced by another. And then another smashes his helmet and passes through to wound him in the head, and his hauberk is rent and broken, and four spears pass through his body. They kill his war horse under him. Now there is cause for grief, as the Archbishop falls.

155. Turpin of Reims knows that he has been mortally wounded. Four spears have passed through his body. That brave peer gets to his feet again, looks for Roland, runs to him, and says:

"I am not beaten! A good vassal never yields while there is still life in him."

He draws his sword Almace, with its burnished blade, and in the thick of the pagans he strikes a thousand blows and more. Charles said afterwards that Turpin of Reims spared none of the pagans, for he found four hundred of them lying around the Archbishop, some wounded, some cleft in two, some headless. That is what the Chronicle says, which was written by one who had seen the field: the worthy Gilie, for whom God performed wonders. He wrote the account in the monastery of Laon, and any man who does not know that is ignorant of the whole story.

156. Count Roland fights nobly, but his body is hot and running with sweat, and his head has been throbbing with fierce pains since he blew his horn and the veins burst on his temples. But he wants to know whether Charles is on his way, and he takes his ivory horn and blows it, feebly. The Emperor halts and listens.

"My lords," he says, "it is going badly for us! Today Roland, my nephew, is lost to us. From the sound of his horn I can tell that he does not have much longer to live. Any man who hopes to find him alive must ride fast. Now sound every trumpet in this host!"

Sixty thousand trumpets blare, and the sound crashes through the mountains, and the valleys echo. The pagans hear that note, and they are not moved to laughter. They say to each other:

"Charles is upon us!"

157. The pagans say: "The Emperor is returning! Listen: you can hear the trumpets of the French! If Charles comes our losses will be heavy, and Roland, if he survives, will renew the war, and our land of Spain will be lost to us."

Four hundred of them who pride themselves on being the best fighters in the field, mass together, helmet by helmet, to launch a single fierce, crushing attack on Roland.

This time the Count will have no leisure.

158. Count Roland sees them coming and his strength and pride and courage mount. He will never yield to them as long as there is life in him. Astride his horse whom men call Veillantif, he digs in his spurs of fine gold and charges into the thick of them, and Turpin, the Archbishop, with him.

The pagans say to each other: "Now let us go, friend! We have heard the horns of the knights of France, and Charles, the mighty King, is returning."

159. Count Roland never loved a coward, nor a proud man, nor a man of ill will, nor any knight who was not a brave fighter. He calls to Archbishop Turpin:

"My lord, you are on foot and I am mounted, and out of love for you I will stay beside you and together we will take what comes, good or evil, and no man made of flesh will force me from you. Let us go together to attack the pagans. Durendal still strikes hardest!"

The Archbishop says: "He who holds back now is a traitor! Charles is returning. He will avenge us."

160. The pagans say: "Woe to us that we were ever born! What an evil day has now risen above us! We have lost our lords and our peers. Charles the brave is returning with his great host and we can hear the clear trumpets of the knights of France, and the shout of 'Mountjoy' rings loud in our ears. Such is the fierce bravery of Count Roland that no man made of flesh will overcome him. Let us hurl our weapons at him and then leave him where he is."

And they throw javelins at him in great numbers, and spears and lances and feathered darts, and they have pierced Roland's shield and smashed it, and broken and rent his hauberk, but their weapons have not touched his body. But Veillantif is wounded in thirty places: they have killed the Count's horse under him. The pagans flee, leaving him on the field. Count Roland is left there, on foot.

161. Smarting with anger and rage, the pagans flee headlong toward Spain, and Count Roland, having lost Veillantif and been forced to dismount whether he likes it or not, cannot give chase. He goes to Archbishop Turpin to help him, unlaces the gold helmet from his head, draws the light, shining hauberk from his body, and cuts his tunic to pieces, which he stuffs into the gaping wounds. Then he draws the Archbishop to his breast and gently lays him down on the green grass. Then tenderly Roland begs a favor of him:

"Ah noble lord, give me leave to go from you! Our companions who were so dear to us are dead now, and we should not leave them where they are. Let me go and look for them and identify them, and bring them here before you and arrange them in a row."

The Archbishop says: "Go and return! The field is yours—I thank God—yours and mine."

162. Roland leaves him and goes off over the field alone, through the valleys, along the mountains, looking . . . There he finds Yvoerie and Ivun, and after him Engeler of Gascony. There he finds Gerin, and Gerer his companion, and Berenger and Otun. There he finds Anseis and Sansun, and after them Gerard the Old, from Roussillon. One by one he takes them up, that brave knight, and brings them all to the Archbishop, and sets them in a row before his knees, and the Archbishop cannot hold back the tears. He lifts up his hand and offers a benediction, and then he says:

"My lords, you were brought to grief, and now may God the Glorious receive your souls every one and lay them on the holy flowers in Paradise! Now the pains of my own death are upon me and I will never again see the Emperor in his might."

163. Roland leaves him and goes off over the field, looking. And he has found his companion, Oliver. He draws him to his breast, in his arms, and makes his way to the Archbishop as best he can, and lays Oliver on a shield beside the others, and the Archbishop absolves him and blesses him. Then sorrow and pity well up, and then Roland says:

"Fair companion, Oliver, you were the son of Duke Reiner who ruled the marches of the Valley of Runers. To shatter a lance and pierce a shield, to strike down the proud and fill them with terror, and to sustain the brave and give them counsel, and to strike down base and vile men and fill them with terror, there is no better knight in any country."

164. When Count Roland sees all the peers dead, and Oliver whom he had loved so dearly, tenderness wells up in him and he begins to weep. His face has grown pale, and his sorrow is so great that he cannot keep to his feet any longer, but his will forsakes him and he falls to the ground in a faint. The Archbishop says:
"Brave knight, I grieve for you!"

165. When the Archbishop sees Roland fall down in a faint his sorrow becomes even greater than it had been at any time before. He stretches out his hand and takes the ivory horn.

There is a stream at Roncesvalles, and the Archbishop wants to fetch some water to Roland. He walks away with little steps, swaying on his feet, so weak that he cannot go forward, having lost so much blood that all the strength has gone out of him, and after less time than it takes a man to cross an acre of ground his heart fails him, he falls forward, and the terrible agony of his death seizes him.

166. Count Roland recovers from his faint and gets to his feet, though in great pain, and looks around him, down along the valleys, up to the mountains, over the green grass, beyond his companions. And he sees on the ground that noble knight, the Archbishop, who had been ordained in the name of God. Gazing upwards, with his clasped hands lifted toward heaven, the Archbishop makes his confession and prays to God to receive him into Paradise. Now Turpin, Charles' warrior, is dead. In great battles and in beautiful sermons, all his life he was a champion of Christendom against the pagans. May God grant him His holy blessing!

167. Count Roland sees the Archbishop on the ground and the bowels sagging out of his body and the brain oozing over his forehead. On the breast, between the two collarbones, he crosses the white and shapely hands. Then, following the custom of his country, Roland speaks a lament over him:
"Ah noble sir, knight born of honored ancestors, today I commend you to the Glorious King of Heaven. No man ever served him with a better will. Never since the days of the saints was there such a man of God for maintaining the laws and drawing men to the faith. May your soul not suffer, and may the door of Paradise be open to you!"

168. Now Roland feels death near him. Hes brains have begun to seep out through his ears. He prays for the peers, asking God to summon them to His presence, and them for himself he calls upon the angel Gabriel. He takes his ivory horn, so that no one may be able to bring shame on him by showing it, and in the other hand he

takes his sword Durendal. A little farther away than a man might shoot with a crossbow, on the side toward Spain, there is a grassy place. Roland goes to it and climbs a little mound. There is a beautiful tree there and there are four great stones of marble under it. On the green grass he has fallen backward, and he has fainted there, for death is near him.

169. The mountains are high, and the trees are tall, and there are four great stones of marble there, shining. Count Roland faints on the green grass.

A Saracen has been watching him closely from among the corpses, where he has been lying with his body and face smeared with blood, pretending to be dead. He gets to his feet and begins to run. He is a man of handsome appearance and great courage. It is pride which spurs him on to this fatal folly. He seizes Roland by his arms and body and he says:

"Charles' nephew is beaten! I will take this sword to Arabia."
As he draws it the Count returns somewhat to his senses.

170. Roland feels the sword being taken away from him and he opens his eyes and says to the other:
"You do not look like one of ours."

He grips his ivory horn, which he had not wanted to leave behind, and with it he strikes the pagan on the helmet, which is covered with jewels set in gold, and smashes the steel and the head and the bone so that both the eyes burst from the face and the body falls dead at his feet. Then he says:

"Base pagan, what made you so rash as to seize me, whether by fair means or foul? Whoever hears the story will take you for a fool. But the mouth of my ivory horn is shattered, and the crystal has fallen from it, and the gold."

171. Now Roland feels the sight of his eyes forsaking him, and with a great effort he gets to his feet. All the color has left his face. He sees before him a gray stone. In sorrow and bitterness he strikes it ten blows with his sword, and the steel grates but will not break nor be blunted.

"Ah," says the Count, "Saint Mary help me! Ah Durendal, my good sword, you have fallen on sad days, for I am dying and you will no longer be in my keeping. With you I have won so many battles in the field and conquered so many broad lands which white-bearded Charles rules over! May you never fall into the hands of any man who will flee before another, for you have been owned by a brave knight for a long time, and holy France will never see another like you."

172 Next Roland strikes the great blood-red stone, and the steel grates but will not break nor be blunted. When he sees that he cannot break the sword, Roland begins to grieve over it:

"Ah Durendal, how beautiful you are, and how bright, and how dazzling, glittering and flashing in the sunlight! Charles was in the Valley of Moriane when God in heaven sent an angel to tell him to give you to a count, one of his captains, and it was then that you were girded upon me by that noble king, that great king.

"With this I conquered Anjou and Brittany for him, and for him I conquered Poitou and Maine. With this I conquered proud Normandy for him, and for him conquered Provence and Aquitaine and Lombardy and the whole of Romagna. With this I conquered Bavaria and all of Flanders for him, and Burgundy, and Poland from one end to the other, and Constantinople, from which he received homage, and in Saxony his command is obeyed. With this I conquered Scotland for him, and . . . and England, which he held as his own place. With this I have conquered so many lands for him, so many countries, and white-bearded Charles rules over them. And now I am full of grief and sorrow because of this sword, for I would rather die than let it fall into the hands of the pagans. God, Father, do not allow France to be thus dishonored!"

173. Roland, striking harder than I can say, brings the sword down on a gray stone, and it grates, but is neither chipped nor shattered. It rebounds toward heaven. When the Count sees that it will not be broken, very softly he grieves over it:

"Ah Durendal, how beautiful you are, and how blessed, with the holy relics in your golden hilt—there is a tooth of Saint Peter's there, and some of Saint Basil's blood, and several hairs of my lord Saint Denis, and a bit of a garment of Saint Mary's. It would not be right if you were to fall into the hands of pagans; you should be in the keeping of Christians. May no coward ever possess you! With you I have conquered many broad lands which Charles rules over. His beard is in flower. Because of you the emperor is venerable and mighty."

174. Now Roland feels death taking everything from him, descending from his head into his heart, and he runs under a pine tree and lies down with his face to the green grass. Underneath him he places his sword and ivory horn. He turns his head toward the pagans, so that Charles and all his knights may say:

"The noble knight died a conqueror."

He makes his confession, carefully, over and over, and he offers his glove, as a token of his sins, to God.

175. Now Roland feels that the end of his life has come. He has lain down on a steep hill with his face toward Spain and with one hand he beats his breast:

"God, I acknowledge my guilt and I beg for Thy mercy for all the sins, greater and lesser, which I have committed from the hour of my birth until this day when I lie here overcome by death!"

He has held out his right glove to God.

Angels descend out of heaven and come to him.

176. Count Roland has lain down under a pine tree, turning his face toward Spain. Many things come to his memory—so many

countries which he had conquered as a brave knight, and sweet France, the land of his ancestors and of Charlemagne, his lord, who had reared him. He cannot hold back the tears and the sighs.

But he does not wish to forget himself. He confesses his sins and prays to God for mercy:

"True Father, who never lied, who raised Saint Lazarus from the dead, and saved Daniel from the lions, save my soul in spite of all the perils which I have incurred with the sins of my life!"

He offers his right glove to God, and Saint Gabriel takes it from his hand. His head sinks onto his arm. With clasped hands he comes to the end of his life. God has sent His angels, Cherubim and Saint Michael of Peril, and Saint Gabriel with them, and they bear the soul of the Count to Paradise.

177. Roland is dead and God has taken his soul into heaven.

The Emperor reaches Roncesvalles. There is not a track nor a path, nor a yard nor even a foot of empty ground without a Frank or a pagan lying on it.

Charles calls out: "Where are you, fair nephew? Where is the Archbishop? and Count Oliver? Where is Gerin? And his companion Gerer? Where is Otun? And Count Berenger? Ivun and Yvoerie, who were so dear to me? What has become of Engeler of Gascony? And Duke Sansun? And the brave Anseis? Where is Gerard the Old, from Roussillon? Where are the twelve peers whom I left here?"

What good is it to call? Not one of them answers.

"Oh God!" the King says, "what reason I have now to lament that I was not here when the battle began!"

In his passion he tears at his beard. His brave knights weep. Twenty thousand of them faint to the ground. Duke Neimun is overcome with grief.

Nibelungenlied

Early Germanic folklore comes down to us in its best-known form in a work composed during the classical period of courtly literature, the *Nibelungenlied* (written between 1200 and 1205). The author, who was probably from the area east of Passau, is unknown. The version contained in manuscript B, the one read most today, consists of 2,379 strophes, each of which is made up of four long lines with end rhyme (*aabb*).

Adventure 16.
How Siegfried was slain.

. . . Then the others did off their clothes, till they stood in their white shirts, and they ran through the clover like two wild panthers; but bold Siegfried was seen there the first. Before all men he won the prize in everything. He loosed his sword straightway, and laid down his quiver. His good spear he leaned against the lime tree; then the noble guest stood and waited, for his courtesy was great. He laid down his shield by the stream. Albeit he was sore athirst, he drank not till that the king had finished, who gave him evil thanks.

The stream was cool, pure, and good. Gunther bent down to the water, and rose again when he had drunk. Siegfried had gladly done the like, but he suffered for his courtesy. Hagen carried his bow and his sword out of his reach, and sprang back and gripped the spear. Then he spied for the secret mark on his vesture; and while Siegfried drank from the stream, Hagen stabbed him where the cross was, that his heart's blood spurted out on the traitor's clothes. Never since hath knight done so wickedly. He left the spear sticking deep in his heart, and fled in grimmer haste than ever he had done from any man on this earth afore.

When stark Siegfried felt the deep wound, he sprang up maddened from the water, for the long boar spear stuck out from his heart. He thought to find bow or sword; if he had, Hagen had got his due. But the sore-wounded man saw no sword, and had nothing save his shield. He picked it up from the water's edge and ran at Hagen. King Gunther's man could not escape him. For all that he was wounded to the death, he smote so mightily that the shield well-nigh brake, and the precious stones flew out. The noble guest had fain taken vengeance.

Hagen fell beneath his stroke. The meadow rang loud with the noise of the blow. If he had had his sword to hand, Hagen had been a dead man. But the anguish of his wound constrained him. His colour was wan; he could not stand upright; and the strength of his body failed him, for he bare death's mark on his white cheek. Fair women enow made dole for him.

Then Kriemhild's husband fell among the flowers. The blood flowed fast from his wound, and in his great anguish he began to upbraid them that had falsely contrived his death. "False cowards!" cried the dying knight. "What availeth all my service to you, since ye have slain me? I was true to you, and pay the price for it. Ye have done ill by your friends. Cursed by this deed are your sons yet unborn. Ye have avenged your spite on my body all too bitterly. For your crime ye shall be shunned by good knights."

All the warriors ran where he lay stabbed. To many among them it was a woeful day. They that were true mourned for him, the which the hero had well deserved of all man.

The King of Burgundy, also, wept for his death, but the dying man said, "He needeth not to weep for the evil, by whom the evil cometh. Better had he left it undone, for mickle is his blame."

Then said grim Hagen, "I know not what ye rue. All is ended for us—care and trouble. Few are they now that will withstand us. Glad am I that, through me, his might is fallen."

"Lightly mayst thou boast now," said Siegfried; "if I had known thy murderous hate, it had been an easy thing to guard my body from thee. My bitterest dole is for Kriemhild, my wife. God pity me that ever I had a son. For all men will reproach him that he hath murderers to his kinsmen. I would grieve for that, had I the time."

He said to the king, "Never in this world was so foul a murder as thou hast done on me. In thy sore need I saved thy life and thine honour. Dear have I paid for that I did well by thee." With a groan the wounded man said further, "Yet if thou canst show truth to any on this earth, O King, show it to my dear wife, that I commend to thee. Let it advantage her to be thy sister. By all princely honour stand by her. Long must my father and my knights wait for my coming. Never hath woman won such woe through a dear one."

He writhed in his bitter anguish, and spake painfully, "Ye shall rue this foul deed in the days to come. Know this of a truth, that in slaying me ye have slain yourselves."

The flowers were all wet with blood. He strove with death, but not for long, for the weapon of death cut too deep. And the bold knight and good spake no more.

When the warriors saw that the hero was dead, they laid him on a shield of ruddy gold, and took counsel how they should conceal that Hagen had done it. Many of them said, "Evil hath befallen us. Ye shall all hide it, and hold to one tale—when Kriemhild's husband was riding alone in the forest, robbers slew him."

But Hagen of Trony said, "I will take him back to Burgundy.

If she that hath troubled Brunhild know it, I care not. It concerneth me little if she weep." . . .

Adventure 17.
How Siegfried was mourned and buried.

They tarried there that night, and then crossed the Rhine. Heroes never went to so woeful a hunt. For one thing that they slew, many women wept, and many a good knight's body paid for it. Of overweening pride ye shall hear now, and grim vengeance.

Hagen bade them bear dead Siegfried of the Nibelung land before the chamber where Kriemhild was, and charged them to lay him secretly outside the door, that she might find him there when she went forth to mass or it was day, the which she was wont to do.

The minster bell was rung as the custom was. Fair Kriemhild waked her maidens, and bade them bring her a light and her vesture.

Then a chamberlain came and found Siegfried. He saw him red with blood, and his garment all wet, but he knew not yet that he was his king. He carried the light into the room in his hand, and from him Kriemhild heard evil tidings.

When she would have gone with her women to the minster, the chamberlain said, "Lady, stop! A murdered knight lieth on the threshold."

"Woe is me!" cried Kriemhild. "What meanest thou by such news?"

Or she knew for certain that it was her husband, she began to think on Hagen's question, how he might guard him. From that moment her dole began; for, with his death, she took leave of all joy. She sank on the floor speechless; they saw the miserable woman lying there. Kriemhild's woe was great beyond measure, and after her swoon she cried out, that all the chamber rang.

Then said her attendants, "What if it be a stranger?"

But the blood burst from her mouth by reason of her heart's anguish, and she said, "Nay, it is Siegfried, my dear husband. Brunhild hath counselled it, and Hagen hath done it."

The lady bade them show her where the hero lay. She lifted his beautiful head with her white hands. Albeit he was red with blood, she knew him straightway. Pitifully the hero of the Netherland lay there.

The gentle, good queen wailed in anguish, "Woe is me for this wrong! Thy shield is unpierced by swords. Thou liest murdered. If I knew who had done this deed, I would not rest till he was dead."

All her attendants wailed and cried with their dear mistress, for they were woe for their noble master that they had lost. Foully had Hagen avenged Brunhild's anger.

The sorrowful one said, "Go and wake Siegfried's men quickly; and tell Siegmund also my dole, that he may help me to mourn for brave Siegfried."

Then a messenger ran in haste where Siegfried's heroes of the Nibelung land lay, and took from them their joy with heavy tidings. They believed it not, till they heard the wailing.

The messenger also came quickly where the king was. Siegmund slept not. I ween his heart told him what had happened, and that he would see his dear son never more.

"Arouse thee, Sir Siegmund! Kriemhild, my lady, hath sent me. For a wrong hath been done her, that lieth heavier on her heart than any other had done. Thou shalt help her to mourn, for it is thy sorrow also."

Up rose Sir Siegmund then, and said, "What is fair Kriemhild's grief, whereof thou tellest me?"

The messenger answered, weeping, "She mourneth with cause. Bold Siegfried of the Netherland is slain."

But Siegmund said, "Jest not with these evil tidings of my son, and say to none that he is slain; for never to my life's end could I mourn him enow."

"If thou believest not what I tell thee, hearken thyself to Kriemhild, how she maketh dole for Siegfried's death with all her maidens."

Then Siegmund feared and was sore affrighted. With an hundred of his men he sprang out of his bed; they grasped their long swords and keen, with their hands, and ran sorrowfully where they heard the sound of weeping. A thousand of Siegfried's knights came running. They thought not on their vesture till they were there, for they had lost their wits through grief. Mickle woe was buried in their hearts.

Then came Siegmund to Queen Kriemhild, and said, "Woe is me for our journey hither! Who, among such good friends, hath murderously robbed me of my child, and thee of thy husband?"

"If I knew that," answered the noble woman, "I were ever his foe with heart and with soul. Trust me, I would so contrive his hurt that all his friends, by reason of me, would yet weep for sorrow."

Siegmund took the prince in his arms; the grief of his friends was so great that, with their loud wailing and their weeping, palace and hall and the town of Worms rang again. None could comfort Siegfried's wife. They took the clothes off his beautiful body, and washed his wounds and laid him on a bier, and all his folk were heavy with great grief.

Then spake his knights of the Netherland, "Our hands are ready for vengeance. He that hath done it is in this house."

Siegfried's men armed them in haste; the valiant knights assembled to the number of eleven hundred. These had Siegmund, the mighty king, for his following; and, as his honour bade him, he had gladly avenged the death of his son. They knew not whom they should fall on, if it were not Gunther and his men, with whom Siegfried had gone hunting.

But when Kriemhild saw them armed, she was greatly grieved. For all her dole and her pain, she so feared the death of the Nibelungs at the hand of her brother's men that she forbade their vengeance, and warned them in love, as friend doth with dear friend.

The sorrowful queen said, "My lord, Siegmund, what wouldst thou do? Surely thou knowest not how many bold knights Gunther hath. If ye come to grips with them, ye must certainly perish."

They stood eager for strife with their shields dressed, but the queen begged and commanded them to forbear; that they would not, grieved her sore.

She said, "My lord Siegmund, let be, till more fitting season, and I will help thee to avenge my husband. Verily, I will show him that took him from me that he hath done it to his hurt. Here by the Rhine there are so many overweening men that I would have thee, for the present, forbear from battle; for thy one man they have at the least thirty. God do to them as they have done to us. Tarry here, brave knights, and mourn with me till it is day, and help me to lay my dear husband in his coffin."

The warriors answered, "Dear lady, be it so."

None might tell to the end the wailing that arose there from knights and women. It was so loud that they in the town heard it, and the noble burghers hasted thither, and mourned with the guests, for they were right sorrowful. They knew no fault in Siegfried for which he had lost his life, and the good burgesses' wives wept with the women of the court.

They bade the smiths go and make a coffin of silver and of gold, mickle and stark, and brace it strongly with good steel. Right heavy of their cheer were all the folk.

The night was ended. They told them it was day, and the queen gave order to bear the dead knight, her dear husband, to the minster; and all the friends he had there followed weeping.

When they came to the minster, how many a bell rang out! On all sides they sang requiems. Thither came King Gunther with his men, and also grim Hagen, that had better stayed away.

Gunther said, "Dear sister, woe is me for this grief of thine, and that this great misadventure hath befallen us. We must ever mourn Siegfried's death."

"Ye do wrongly," said the wailing queen. "If it grieved thee, it had never happed. I was clean forgotten by thee when thou didst part me from my dear husband. Would to God thou hadst done it to me instead!"

But they held to their lie, and Kriemhild went on, "Let him that is guiltless prove it. Let him go up to the bier before all the folk, and soon we shall know the truth."

It is a great marvel, and ofttimes seen even now, how that, when the murderer standeth by the dead, the wounds bleed again. And so it fell then, and Hagen's guilt was plain to all.

The wounds burst open and bled as they had done afore; and they that had wept already wept now much more. King Gunther said, "Hear the truth. He was slain by robbers. Hagen did it not."

"These robbers," she answered, "I know well. God grant that his kinsmen's hands may avenge it. By you, Gunther and Hagen, was it done." Siegfried's knights had fain fallen on them, but Kriemhild said, "Help me to bear my woe."

Gernot her brother, and Giselher the youth, both came and found Siegfried dead; they mourned for him truly, and their eyes were blind with tears. They wept for Kriemhild's husband from their hearts.

It was time to sing mass, and men and women flocked from all quarters. Even they that missed him little mourned with the rest.

Gernot and Giselher said, "Comfort thee, sister, for the dead, for so it must needs be now. We will make it good to thee while we live." But comfort her could none.

His coffin was ready by the middle of the day, and they lifted the dead man from the bier whereon he lay, but the queen would not let them bury him yet. All his folk must first toil sore.

They wound him in a rich cloth. Not one, I ween, was there that wept not. Uta the noble queen and all her women wailed bitterly for Siegfried.

When the folk heard they sang the requiem, and that Siegfried was in his chest, they crowded thither, and brought offerings for his soul. Amidst of his enemies, he had good friends enow.

Then poor Kriemhild said to her chamberlain, "For my sake, stint not thy labour. For Siegfried's soul, divide his wealth among them that were well minded to him, and are true to me."

The smallest child, if it understood at all, must go with its offering or he was buried. They sang at the least an hundred masses a day. And great was the press among Siegfried's friends.

When they had done singing, the folk rose and departed; but Kriemhild said, "Leave me not alone to watch the valiant knight. With his body lieth all my joy. Three days and three nights will I keep him here, till that I have had my fill of my dear husband. What if God let death take me too? So the sorrow of poor Kriemhild were ended."

The townsfolk went home; and priests, and monks, and all them that had served Siegfried, she bade tarry. Heavy were their nights and toilsome their days. Many a man neither ate nor drank, but they that desired it were bidden take their fill. Siegmund saw to that. No easy time had the Nibelungs. They say that all that could sing got no rest. What offerings were brought! The poorest was rich enow, for they that had naught were bidden bring an offering from the gold of Seigfried's own hoard. When he lived no more, they gave many thousand marks for his soul. Kriemhild bestowed lands and revenues over all, on cloisters and holy men. Silver and clothes in plenty they gave to the poor. She showed plain the love she bare Siegfried.

On the third morning, when mass was due, the great churchyard by the minster was full of weeping countryfolk; for they served him in death as dear friends should.

They say that, in these four days, thirty thousand marks, or more, were given to the poor for his soul's sake, when his beauty and his life were brought to nothing.

God had been served; the song was done. The folk were shaken with weeping. They bade carry him from the minster to the grave, and naught was heard but crying and mourning.

With loud wail the people followed after. None was joyful, neither woman nor man. They sang and read or they buried him. Ah, what good priests were at his funeral!

Or Siegfried's wife came to the grave, her faithful body was wrung with such grief that they ceased not from sprinkling her with water. None could measure her sorrow.

It was a wonder that she lived. Her weeping women helped her. Then said the queen, "Ye men of Siegfried, as ye love me, do me this grace. Give me, in my sorrow, this little joy: to see his dear head once more." She begged this so long, and with such bitter weeping, that they brake open the rich chest.

Then they brought the queen where he was. She lifted his lovely head with her white hand, and kissed him. Her bright eyes, for grief, wept blood. It was a pitiful parting.

Then they carried her thence, for she could not walk. And she lay in a swoon, as her fair body would have perished for sorrow.

When the noble knight was buried, they that were come with him from the land of the Nibelungs made measureless dole. Little joy was seen in Siegmund. For three whole days some neither ate nor drank for woe. Longer than that their bodies endured it not. And so they ate and got well of their grief, as many a one doth still. . . .

Adventure 36.
How the Queen had the hall burned down.

. . . The fire-flakes fell down on them in the hall, but they warded them off with their shields. Both the smoke and the fire tormented them. Never before suffered heroes such sore pain.

Then said Hagen of Trony, "Stand fast by the wall. Let not the brands fall on your helmets. Trample them with your feet deeper in the blood. A woeful hightide is the queen's."

The night ended at last. The bold gleeman, and Hagen, his comrade, stood before the house and leaned upon their shields. They waited for further hurt from Etzel's knights. It advantaged the strangers much that the roof was vaulted. By reason thereof more were left alive. Albeit they at the windows suffered scathe, they bare them valiantly, as their bold hearts bade them.

Then said the fiddler, "Go we now into the hall, that the Huns deem we be all dead from this torment, albeit some among them shall yet feel our might."

Giselher, the youth, of Burgundy, said, "It is daybreak, I ween. A cool wind bloweth. God grant we may see happier days. My sister

Kriemhild hath bidden us to a doleful hightide."

One of them spake, "I see the dawn. Since we can do no better, arm you, ye knights, for battle, that, come we never hence, we may die with honour."

Etzel deemed the guests were all dead of their travail and the stress of the fire. But six hundred bold men yet lived. Never king had better knights. They that kept ward over the strangers had seen that some were left, albeit the princes and their men had suffered loss and dole. They saw many that walked up and down in the house.

They told Kriemhild that many were left alive, but the queen answered, "It cannot be. None could live in that fire. I trow they all lie dead."

The kings and their men had still gladly asked for mercy, had there been any to show it. But there was none in the whole country of the Huns. Wherefore they avenged their death with willing hand.

They were greeted early in the morning with a fierce onslaught, and came in great scathe. Stark spears were hurled at them. Well the knights within stood on their defence.

Etzel's men were the bolder, that they might win Kriemhild's fee. Thereto, they obeyed the king gladly; but soon they looked on death.

One might tell marvels of her gifts and promises. She bade them bear forth red gold upon shields, and gave thereof to all that desired it, or would take it. So great treasure was never given against foemen.

The host of warriors came armed to the hall. The fiddler said, "We are here. I never was gladder to see any knights than those that have taken the king's gold to our hurt."

Not a few of them cried out, "Come nigher, ye heroes! Do your worst, and make an end quickly, for here are none but must die."

Soon their bucklers were filled full of darts. What shall I say more? Twelve hundred warriors strove once and again to win entrance. The guests cooled their hardihood with wounds. None could part the strife. The blood flowed from death-deep wounds. Many were slain. Each bewailed some friend. All Etzel's worthy knights perished. Their kinsmen sorrowed bitterly.

Adventure 37.
How Rudeger was slain.

The strangers did valiantly that morning. Gotelind's husband came into the courtyard and saw the heavy loss on both sides, whereat the true man wept inly.

"Woe is me," said the knight, "that ever I was born, since none can stop this strife! Fain would I have them at one again, but the king holdeth back, for he seeth alway more done to his hurt."

Good Rudeger sent to Dietrich, that they might seek to move the great king. But the knight of Bern sent back answer, "Who can hinder it? King Etzel letteth none intercede."

A knight of the Huns, that had oft seen Rudeger standing with
wet eyes, said to the queen, "look how he standeth yonder, that
Etzel hath raised above all others, and that hath land and folk at his
service. Why hath Rudeger so many castles from the king? He hath
struck no blow in this battle. I ween he careth little for our scathe,
so long as he has enow for himself. They say he is bolder than any
other. Ill hath he shown it in our need."

The faithful man, when he heard that word, looked angrily at
the knight. He thought, "Thou shalt pay for this. Thou callest me a
coward. Thou hast told thy tale too loud at court."

He clenched his fist, and ran at him, and smote the Hun so
fiercely that he fell down at his feet, dead. Whereat Etzel's grief waxed
anew.

"Away with thee, false babbler!" cried Rudeger. "I had trouble
and sorrow enow. What was it to thee that I fought not? Good cause
have I also to hate the strangers, and had done what I could against
them, but that I brought them hither. I was their escort into my
master's land, and may not lift my wretched hand against them."

Then said Etzel, the great king, to the Margrave, "How hast
thou helped us, most noble Rudeger? We had dead men enow in the
land, and needed no more. Evilly hast thou done."

But the knight answered, "He angered me, and twitted me with
the honour and the wealth thou hath bestowed on me so plenteously.
It hath cost the liar dear."

Then came the queen, that had seen the Hun perish by Rudeger's
wrath. She mourned for him with wet eyes, and said to Rudeger,
"What have we ever done to thee that thou shouldst add to our
sorrow? Thou hast oft times promised, noble Rudeger, that thou
wouldst risk, for our sake, both honour and life, and I have heard
many warriors praise thee for thy valour. Hast thou forgotten the
oath thou swearest to me with thy hand, good knight, when thou
didst woo me for King Etzel—how that thou wouldst serve me till
my life's end, or till thine? Never was my need greater than now."

"It is true, noble lady. I promised to risk for thee honour and
life, but I sware not to lose my soul. I brought the princes to this
hightide."

She said, "Remember, Rudeger, thy faith, and thine oath to
avenge all my hurt and my woe."

The Margrave answered, "I have never said thee nay."

Etzel began to entreat likewise. They fell at his feet. Sore
troubled was the good Margrave. Full of grief, he cried, "Woe is me
that ever I saw this hour, for God hath forsaken me. All my duty to
heaven, mine honour, my good faith, my knightliness, I must forego.
God above have pity, and let me die! Whether I do this thing, or do it
not, I sin. And if I take the part of neither, all the world will blame
me. Let Him that made me guide me."

Still the king and his wife implored him. Whence it fell that many valiant warriors lost their lives at his hand, and the hero himself was slain. Hear ye now the tale of his sorrow. Well he knew he could win naught but teen and scathe. Fain had he denied the prayer of the king and queen. He feared, if he slew but one man, that the world would loathe him evermore.

Then the bold man said to the king, "Take back what thou hast given me—castles and land. Leave me nothing at all. I will go forth afoot into exile. I will take my wife and my daughter by the hand, and I will quit thy country empty, rather than I will die dishonoured. I took thy red gold to my hurt."

King Etzel answered, "Who will help me then? Land and folk I gave to thee, Rudeger, that thou mightest avenge me on my foes. Thou shalt rule with Etzel as a great king."

But Rudeger said, "How can I do it? I bade them to my house and home; I set meat and drink before them, and gave them my gifts. Shall I also smite them dead? The folk may deem me a coward. But I have always served them well. Should I fight with them now, it were ill done. Deep must I rue past friendship. I gave my daughter to Giselher. None better in this world had she found, of so great lineage and honour, and faith, and wealth. Never saw I young king so virtuous."

But Kriemhild answered, "Most noble Rudeger, take pity on us both. Bethink thee that never host had guests like these."

Then said the Margrave, "What thou and my master have given me I must pay for, this day, with my life. I shall die, and that quickly. Well I know that, or nightfall, my lands and castles will return to your keeping. To your grace I commend my wife and my child, and the homeless ones that are at Bechlaren."

"God reward thee, Rudeger," cried the king. He and the queen were both glad. "Thy folk shall be well seen to; but thou thyself, I trow, will come off scatheless."

So he put his soul and body on the hazard. Etzel's wife began to weep. He said, "I must keep my vow to thee. Woe is me for my friends, that I must fall upon in mine own despite!"

They saw him turn heavily from the king. To his knights that stood close by, he said, "Arm ye, my men all. For I must fight the Burgundians, to my sorrow."

The heroes called for their harness, and the attendants brought helm and buckler. Soon the proud strangers heard the sad news.

Rudeger stood armed with five hundred men, and twelve knights that went with him, to win worship in the fray. They knew not that death was so near.

Rudeger went forth with his helmet on; his men carried sharp swords, and, thereto, broad shields and bright. The fiddler saw this, and was dismayed. But when Giselher beheld his father-in-law with his helmet on, he weened that he meant them well. The noble king was right glad. "Well for me that I have such friends," cried Giselher, "as these we won by the way! For my wife's sake he will save us. By my faith, I am glad to be wed."

"Thy trust is vain," said the fiddler. "When ever did ye see so many knights come in peace,with helmets laced on, and with swords? Rudeger cometh to serve for his castles and his lands."

Or the fiddler had made an end of speaking, Rudeger, the noble man, stood before the house. He laid his good shield before his feet. He must needs deny greeting to his friends.

Then the Margrave shouted into the hall, "Stand on your defence, ye bold Nibelungs. I would have helped you, but must slay you. Once we were friends, but I cannot keep my faith."

The sore-tried men were dismayed at this word. Their comfort was gone, for he that they loved was come against them. From their foemen they had suffered enow.

"God in Heaven forbid," said Gunther the knight, "that thou shouldst be false to the friendship and the faith wherein we trusted. It cannot be."

"I cannot help it," said Rudeger. "I must fight with you, for I have vowed it. As ye love your lives, bold warriors, ward you well. King Etzel's wife will have it so."

"Thou turnest too late," said the king. "God reward thee, noble Rudeger, for the truth and the love thou hast shown us, if it endure but to the end. We shall ever thank and serve thee for the rich gifts thou gavest to me and my kinsmen, when thou broughtest us with true heart into Etzel's land: so thou let us live. Think well thereon, noble Rudeger."

"Gladly would I grant it," said the knight. "Might I but give thee freely, as I would, with none to chide me!"

"Give that no thought," said Gernot. "Never host entreated guests so kindly as thou us; the which will advantage thee if we live."

"Would to God, noble Gernot," cried Rudeger, "that ye were at the Rhine, and I dead with honour, since I must fight with you! Never strangers were worse entreated by friends."

"God reward thee, Sir Rudeger," answered Gernot, "for thy rich gifts. I should rue thy death, for in thee a virtuous man would fall. Behold, good knight, the sword thou gavest, in my hand. It hath never failed me in my need. Its edge hath killed many a warrior. It is finely tempered and stark, and thereto bright and good. So goodly a gift, I ween, never knight will give more. If thou forbear not, but fall upon us, and slay any of my kinsmen here, thou shalt perish by thine own sword! Much I pity thee and thy wife."

"Would to God, Sir Gernot, thou hadst thy will, and thy friends were out of peril! To thee I would entrust wife and daughter."

Then said the youngest of fair Uta's sons, "How canst thou do this thing, Sir Rudeger? All that came hither with me are thy friends. A vile deed is this. Thou makest thy daughter too soon a widow. If thou and thy knights defy us, ill am I apayed, that I trusted thee before all other men, when I won thy daughter for my wife."

"Forget not thy troth, noble king, if God send thee hence,"

answered Rudeger. "Let not the maiden suffer for my sin. By thine own princely virtue, withdraw not thy favour from her."

"Fain would I promise it," said Giselher the youth. "Yet, if my high-born kinsmen perish here by thy hand, my love for thee and thy daughter must perish also."

"Then God have mercy!" cried the brave man; whereat he lifted his shield, and would have fallen upon the guests in Kriemhild's hall.

But Hagen called out to him from the stairhead, "Tarry awhile, noble Rudeger. Let me and my masters speak with thee yet awhile in our need. What shall it profit Etzel if we knights die in a strange land? I am in evil case," said Hagen. "The shield that Gotelind gave me to carry, the Huns have hewn from my hand. In good faith I bore it hither. Would to God I had such a shield as thou hast, noble Rudeger! A better I would not ask for in the battle."

"I would gladly give thee my shield, durst I offer it before Kriemhild. Yet take it, Hagen, and wear it. Ha! mightst thou but win with it to Burgundy!"

When they saw him give the shield so readily, there were eyes enow red with hot tears. It was the last gift that Rudeger of Bechlaren ever gave.

Albeit Hagen was grim and stern, he was melted by the gift that the good knight, so nigh to his end, had given him. And many a warrior mourned with him.

"Now God reward thee, noble Rudeger; there will never be thy like again for giving freely to homeless knights. May the fame of thy charity live for ever. Sad news hast thou brought me. We had trouble enow. God pity us if we must fight with friends."

The Margrave answered, "Thou grievest not more than I."

"I will requite thee for thy gift, brave Rudeger. Whatever betide thee from these knights, my hand will not touch thee—not if thou slewest every man of Burgundy."

Rudeger bowed, and thanked him. All the folk wept. Sore pity it was that none could stay the strife. The father of all virtue lay dead in Rudeger.

Then Folker the fiddler went to the door and said, "Since my comrade Hagen hath sworn peace, thou shalt have it also from my hand. Well didst thou earn it when we came first into this country. Noble Margrave, be my envoy. The Margravine gave me these red bracelets to wear at the hightide. See them now, and bear witness that I did it."

"Would to God that the Margravine might give thee more! Doubt not but I shall tell my dear one, if I ever see her alive."

When he had promised that, Rudeger lifted up his shield; he waxed fierce, and tarried no longer. Like a knight he fell upon the guests. Many a swift blow he smote. Folker and Hagen stood back, for they had vowed it. But so many bold men stood by the door that Rudeger came in great scathe.

Athirst for blood, Gunther and Gernot let him pass in. Certes, they were heroes. Giselher drew back sorrowing. He hoped to live yet awhile; wherefore he avoided Rudeger in the strife.

Then the Margrave's men ran at their foemen, and followed their master like good knights. They carried sharp weapons, wherewith they clove many a helmet and buckler. The weary ones answered the men of Bechlaren with swift blows that pierced deep and straight through their harness to their life's blood. They did wonderly in the battle.

All the warriors were now in the hall. Folker and Hagen fell on them, for they had sworn to spare none save the one man. Their hands struck blood from the helmets. Right grim was the clash of swords! Many a shield-plate sprang in sunder, and the precious stones were scattered among the blood. So fiercely none will fight again. The prince of Bechlaren hewed a path right and left, as one acquainted with battle. Well did Rudeger approve him that day a bold and blameless knight. Gunther and Gernot smote many heroes dead. Giselher and Dankwart laid about them, fearing naught, and sent many a man to his doom.

Rudeger approved him stark enow, bold and well armed. Ha! many a knight he slew! One of the Burgundians saw this, and was wroth; whereat Rudeger's death drew nigh.

Gernot cried out to the Margrave, "Noble Rudeger, thou leavest none of my men alive. It irketh me sore; I will bear it no longer. I will turn thy gift against thee, for thou hast taken many friends from me. Come hither, thou bold man. What thou gavest me I will earn to the uttermost."

Or the Margrave had fought his way to him, bright bucklers grew dim with blood. Then, greedy of fame, the men ran at each other, and began to ward off the deadly wounds. But their swords were so sharp that nothing could withstand them. Rudeger the knight smote Gernot through his flint-hard helmet, that the blood brake out. Soon the good warrior was avenged. He swung Rudeger's gift on high, and, albeit he was wounded to the death, he smote him through his good shield and his helmet, that Gotelind's husband died. So rich a gift was never worse requited. So they fell in the strife— Gernot and Rudeger—slain by each other's hand.

Thereat Hagen waxed grimmer than afore. The hero of Trony said, "Great woe is ours. None can ever make good to their folk and their land the loss of these two knights. Rudeger's men shall pay for it." They gave no quarter. Many were struck down unwounded that had come to, but that they were drowned in the blood.

"Woe is me for my brother, fallen dead! Each hour bringeth fresh dole. For my father-in-law, Rudeger, I grieve also. Twofold is my loss and my sorrow."

When Giselher saw his brother slain, they that were in the hall suffered for it. Death lagged not behind. Of the men of Bechlaren there was left not a living soul.

Gunther and Giselher, and eke Hagen, Dankwart and Folker,

the good knights, went where the two warriors lay, and there the heroes wept piteously.

"Death hath despoiled us sore," said Giselher the youth. "Stop your weeping, and go out to the air, that we strife-weary ones may cool our harness. God will not let us live longer, I ween."

They that were without saw them sitting, or leaning and taking their rest. Rudeger's men were all slain; the din was hushed. The silence endured so long that Etzel was angered, and the king's wife cried, "Woe is me for this treason. They speak too long. The bodies of our foemen are left unscathed by Rudeger's hand. He plotteth to guide them back to Burgundy. What doth it profit us, King Etzel, that we have shared all our wealth with him? The knight hath done falsely. He that should have avenged us cometh to terms with them."

But Folker, the valiant warrior, answered her, "Alack! it is not so, noble queen. If I might give the lie to one so high-born as thou art, thou hast foully slandered Rudeger. Sorry terms have he and his knights made with us. With such good will he did the king's bidding, that he and his men all lie dead. Look round thee for another, Kriemhild, to obey thee. Rudeger served thee till his death. If thou doubtest, thou mayest see for thyself."

To her grief they did it. They brought the mangled hero where Etzel saw him. Never were Etzel's knights so doleful. When the dead Margrave was held up before them, none could write or tell all the bitter wailing whereby women and men alike uttered their heart's dole. Etzel's woe was so great that the sound of his lamentation was as a lion's roar. Loud wept his wife. They mourned good Rudeger bitterly.

Adventure 39.
How Lord Dietrich did battle with Gunther and Hagen.

. . . Then said the prince of Bern, "Most high queen, there were never nobler captives than these I have delivered here into thy hands. Let the homeless knights live for my sake."

She promised him she would do it gladly, and good Dietrich went forth weeping. Yet soon Etzel's wife took grim vengeance, by reason whereof both the valiant men perished. She kept them in dungeons, apart, that neither saw the other again till she bore her brother's head to Hagen. Certes, Kriemhild's vengeance was bitter.

The queen went to Hagen, and spake angrily to the knight. "Give me back what thou hast taken from me, and ye may both win back alive to Burgundy."

But grim Hagen answered, "Thy words are wasted, noble queen. I have sworn to show the hoard to none. While one of my masters liveth, none other shall have it."

"I will end the matter," said the queen. Then she bade them slay her brother, and they smote off his head. She carried it by the hair to the knight of Trony. He was grieved enow.

When the sorrowful man saw his master's head, he cried to Kriemhild, "Thou hast wrought all thy will. It hath fallen out as I deemed it must. The noble King of Burgundy is dead, and Giselher the youth, and eke Gernot. None knoweth of the treasure now save God and me. Thou shalt never see it, devil that thou art."

She said, "I come off ill in the reckoning. I will keep Siegfried's sword at the least. My true love wore it when I saw him last. My bitterest heart's dole was for him."

She drew it from the sheath. He could not hinder it. She purposed to slay the knight. She lifted it high with both hands, and smote off his head.

King Etzel saw it, and sorrowed. "Alack!" cried the king, "The best warrior that ever rode to battle, or bore a shield, hath fallen by the hand of a woman! Albeit I was his foeman, I must grieve."

Then said Master Hildebrand, "His death shall not profit her. I care not what come of it. Though I came in scathe by him myself, I will avenge the death of the bold knight of Trony."

Hildebrand sprang fiercely at Kriemhild, and slew her with his sword. She suffered sore by his anger. Her loud cry helped her not.

Dead bodies lay stretched over all. The queen was hewn in pieces. Etzel and Dietrich began to weep. They wailed piteously for kinsmen and vassals. Mickle valour lay there slain. The folk were doleful and dreary.

The end of the king's hightide was woe, even as, at the last, all joy turneth to sorrow.

I know not what fell after. Christian and heathen, wife, man, and maid, were seen weeping and mourning for their friends.

I will tell you no more. Let the dead lie. However it fared after with the Huns, my tale is ended. This is the fall of the Nibelungs.

Nibelungenklage

In all of the complete manuscripts, the *Nibelungenlied* is followed imediately by *Die Klage (The Lament)*. Composed around 1220, *Die Klage* is the earliest detailed commentary on the great heroic epic and provides the audience with information concerning the survivors. The last chapter tells about Dietrich von Bern's and Hildebrand's return to their homeland. The edition of the B version has 4,360 short lines of rhyming couplets.

I
(Lines 1-586).

Here begins a tale which would be more pleasant to tell if not every listener had good reasons to lament it. For whoever understands it the way it is meant must be filled with sorrow.

I wish I could write so well that all who heard the tale would like it. The story has been handed down faithfully from the olden days. If it displeases anyone, let him put aside his prejudice and listen for a while.

A poet once had this ancient tale written down in a book. Thus it was bound to become known how the heroes of Burgundy acted with honor all the days of their lives. One of their kings was Dancrat. He left his wide lands to these proud princes and to the noble Lady Uote, who had shared the crown with him. And the heroes possessed everything that powerful princes would desire and rightly ought to have.

They had, as we know, a beautiful sister, who then was married. This was later the reason that many good men met misfortune, and that her husband himself found his death because of his pride. After some time she married again, taking a bold hero from Hunland. With him she now ruled again in great splendor, after long mourning.

The master of this tale has let it be recorded how powerful the Hunnish king was. All of us know it. Every day he had twelve kings who served him. I know it for true: he was honored far and wide. Seldom has a man of such nobility been heard of in Christendom and among the heathens. Many who knew it came riding to visit him in his realm. He was called Etzel.

His father, Botelung by name, left, at the hour of his death, vast power to Etzel his son. The story also tells us that Etzel had a wife, a woman unequalled in virtue by anyone, as long as she lived. Her name was Helche. Etzel took leave of her with great grief. Almighty Death had taken happiness from him. Years thereafter, his kin advised him to woo Lady Kriemhild, that generous and noble queen.

You have heard how Kriemhild ruled in Hunland, just as Helche had done before. And yet she grieved all the time; she was a foreigner there. Her great sorrow never left her for as little as even a day, because she could not forget how she had lost her happiness. Her closest kin had taken her dear husband from her. . . . Almost constantly people saw her eyes weeping.

After many more years, her position became so powerful that she secretly planned to seek revenge for the death of Siegfried, her beloved husband. He had been cruelly betrayed by her brother Gunther, by Gunther's wife, and by Hagen, who, as we know, killed him. . . . They reaped only suffering for the wrong they did her; she did her duty and took vengeance. No one should blame her for that. If a person capable of loyalty had to pay a penalty for it, he would soon give up trying to demonstrate his faithfulness. The essential quality of true faith is that it makes men worthy and honors fair women in such a way that they would never do anything shameful, neither in thought nor in deed. Thus it was with Lady Kriemhild. No man was ever justified in speaking ill of her. Anyone who really understands her story will consider her innocent, for he will say that this noble and worthy woman had wreaked vengeance out of faithfulness and in great distress.

The princes from the Rhine came, proud and magnificent. . . . Never before had so many excellent warriors gathered at the Hunnish court. Gunther, his brother Giselher and also Sir Gernot had led them from the Burgundian realm. But the red gold of Kriemhild had been left behind, on the Rhine. Cursed be the moment that they got hold of it. In my opinion, the penalty they now paid was no more than what was due for their past sins. . . . However much Etzel, the mighty King, would have liked to serve them (and they, in turn, should have offered their services to him), they were bound to fail because of their guilt. Hagen, the haughty, had earned her hatred to a degree that she now had no choice but to seek revenge for everything she had lost. In the end, few of those who carried weapons got out alive. Instead of Hagen being the only one slain, almost forty thousand men had to die. Although Kriemhild, the Queen, had often tried to single him out, it was of no avail. Then she let things take their course. There was no other solution for her. Bad reasoning was the cause of everything. . . . Thus they all lost their lives after the fighting had broken out: acquaintances and strangers, the evil and the good, Christian and heathen, friendly ones and trouble-makers, the lords and the vassals. The one from afar and the one from nearby, each of them joined the fighting when he saw his friend lying dead before him.

Let us curse the day on which the battle took place and let us lament that Kriemhild ever saw noble Siegfried. Because of that, many a fair woman was deprived of her love. The action of this one woman caused so much harm to so many, Christians and heathens alike, that both women and men believe the tale that she, through her deed, had earned the torments of Hell. They say she had done such wrong against God's forgiving love, that He, who is our Lord, did not want her soul. Well, if someone had to prove this he would have to visit Hell himself. However, I for one would not go there in order to find out the truth of the tale.

The author of this ancient story said that a loyal person suffers where there is disloyalty. And since Kriemhild died because she was loyal, she will live in Heaven, in God's grace, and for many days to come. Before God all men are equal; therefore, whoever dies as a loyal person will have earned a place in Heaven. Furthermore, we are told the following truth: Whoever judges another in anger has sinned against God. How can he know what God will do with him one day? Let no one think himself so good, and so free of sin, that he would have no need of God's mercy on the Last Day, when each of us will get his just reward.

II
(Lines 597-1760).

. . . Etzel who always was greatly honored found his day of splendor darkened. He had lost his joy. The sun just wouldn't shine for him any more. From now on he would have to get by without the joys that should have been in his heart; for he saw nothing but many a bloody stream flowing from grave wounds which in a few hours had taken away his joy. From his eyes was now gone much that he had loved to look on. Death was responsible for the fact that he found little of it there. He began to twist his hand and head more than any king before or since. He experienced suffering and discomfort; one could see much of it in him. We can say of Etzel that in truth no man would ever grieve so much. How loudly he began to cry out. As when one hears an ox-horn, so from the mouth of the well-born prince his voice sounded forth in the hour of his great lament, so that tower and palace shook at the sound. Though there had been little joy there before, there was much less now. He had lost his senses so that he could not know that it was shameful for him. Many a noble orphan helped him lament his sorrow. If you want to hear wonders, pay attention to their lack of moderation. All the laments the world had known were nothing to this. Never did so many a worthy mother's child take up the lament as at that time were crying at Etzel's court. Many a maiden's hand was broken with wringing. Little was spoken there besides "alack and alas." However loudly the King cried out, the women screamed with him. Even now it is still people's custom, that when one suffers in his heart the other gives up cheerfulness in his presence. There too joy was abandoned. The people made their lament greater, beyond all limits. The fingers cracked in many a maiden's hand whom one found grieving there.

The people, hurrying in, all ran crying to that place, when they had heard what had happened, to see and to lament. Some came because they had been asked, some to avenge dear ones. But there was no need there for blows and stabbing. They were dead without their efforts, both friend and foe. The people were then ordered to clear away the bodies without delay. Toward the hall they began to clear a path through the bodies they found outside, those whom Volker's hand and Hagen had struck dead. They ordered that they be carried far enough from the house so that everyone could enter the hall. Death had taken from them so much of their happiness, that if any relatives had survivied in that fight, they would rather be dead with them. One saw much bloody armor removed from the dead. From them was unfastened many a punctured helmet. Red, bloody and wet was all their clothing. One saw there many a glorious shield chopped to pieces. The mighty become the dead. So many of them were carried away that all who heard tell of it were wondering whether it was right for anyone in all the land to feel joy then. The good warriors took little heed of what one said. Many a maid tore her hair from her head in anguish. Many a man's sweetheart was screaming there, who got blood from wounds on the hem of her dress. The common men and the lords were lying together there so that the rain of blood had soaked them all. If any woman neglected to lament the wounds of the dead, that was unwomanly conduct.

Hildebrand the noble hero heard loud crying; he heard the servants clamorously wailing. One of Uote's children lay there before the hall. Truly, on account of her wounds many a tear fell down from fair eyes. That was the Queen whom in his madness Hildebrand had slain, because she had struck down Hagen of Burgundy. There always remains something to be said of that—how it came to pass that Hagen died by a woman's hand, since earlier with his strength he had done many wonders. People actually still say that this is a lie. The truth of it is that Lord Dietrich compelled him, that praiseworthy hero, to be taken prisoner. Then the King's wife with her own hand struck him a sword-blow. On that account she lost her life, needlessly, by Hildebrand. In truth, one mourns the Queen's death with good reason. Knights and squires did as they should. And everyone all over Etzel's land was just as full of sadness.

Now Lord Dietrich came in a sorrowful mood to where he found Kriemhild. He asked the people there to stop crying for God's sake. No matter how much they promised they did not obey him. So unbelievable was the event that had taken place before them and that they had witnessed, that no one there could be happy at that hour. Then Lord Dietrich spoke: "Yes, I have seen in my days many a rich prince's kin, but never did I hear tell of a more beautiful woman. Alas, that death should come so swiftly to you! Although your counsel and action took my dearest relatives from me, I must unhappily mourn for you too, and for myself. In truth I do so with such great grief that I shall not punish you for your loyalty. Rarely did you refuse me anything I asked. Now the time has come, Lady, that I must pay it back. Still, it will not make me happy, no matter what I do after your death." Then the brave man took action, and ordered the people there to place her on a bier at once.

After the prince had put her head to her body she was laid on the bier. Hildebrand was heard lamenting there, he who had killed her. Then came Etzel of Hunland, full of sorrows, looking like Sorrow itself, as it befit him. In their grief they couldn't keep from helping him mourn. He began to curse his great misfortune; for he had inherited now a wealth of sorrow. She who in her life had always told the truth, his worthy wife—he sank down upon her breast. He kissed her white hands, he mourned, filled with longing. Only then did Lord Dietrich tell the King the true story.

"Alas, my agony!" spoke well-born Etzel. "How have I, poor man, lost both wife and child? And in addition many a dear kinsman of my noble family, and the joy my eyes had at my wife's kinsmen who were much honored while they were alive. Why have I, miserable man that I am, been cast into such great sorrow? Had I better recognized the loyalty in her worthy person I would have fled all lands with her, rather than lose her. A more faithful woman was never born of any mother. Alas for the noble princes, Gunther and his brothers, and my noble warriors, my brother and my kinsmen, who have been struck down, appallingly, by Death's destruction. How can I ever cease to mourn for those bold warriors, whom I had here from many lands for my festival? And then for all my own men, from among Christians and heathens, too numerous for me to name, through whom my honor always increased." After this lament he sank down as if he had fainted.

Lord Dietrich was not idle, for he saw men lying about him as thick as the stones. But the Lord of Bern was not the only one to bear sorrow—the King was grieved to see how great his loss was. Blood flowed all about and down through the drainage holes. No matter where they went they found nothing but corpses. They saw the hall dyed red with the blood of the wounded. Even the healthiest and strongest grew weak from the great lament. Never at any time has there been such grieving. Now eight hundred or more of them had been carried out, when new suffering arose: Master Hildebrand cried out as he found Wolfhart.

When he saw his nephew he said to his lord: "Now see, most noble Dietrich, how Death has sown his seed far and wide about him! How could I ever have thought that a man as youthful and inexperienced as the warrior Giselher could slay this veteran fighter? Now both are lying here, the royal Giselher and my nephew. May God hear how I lament that these two found each other in the hour of battle!" Lord Dietrich looked upon his vassal and began to grieve deeply. He saw Wolfhart there with a reddish beard, fallen down in the blood; the good hero felt all his sorrows again. Both of them cried then in their anguish of grief. And Etzel could not offer any help or protection. That powerful King stood next to Dietrich, wringing his hands in grief.

Wolfhart the warrior had clenched the sword in his hand in the hard press of battle, so that even when he was dead Dietrich and Hildebrand could not break the sword from the hand of the fiercely-bold hero, until with tongs they pried it loose from his long fingers. When they had the weapon, Lord Dietrich spoke: "Alas, good sword, who now shall wield you in such a lordly way? You will never again strike such blows as when, before powerful kings, and in a praise-worthy way, Wolfhart swang you. Alas, that I was ever born! Now that my ally is taken from me, what will I come to, helpless as I am?" Wolfhart still lay in the blood, before the knights, with clenched teeth.

They ordered that the noble hero be lifted from the ashes. His lord had him washed and cleansed, his armor removed. Wolfhart had been a vassal of great promise to him. He stood there above the worthy knight, and his death brought him grief. How well he remembered all this vassal had done to serve him! He began to speak about it. "Alas," spoke Lord Dietrich, "I am full of sorrow that you, hero, will no more accompany me with such great honor into battle as you so often did before. God has not treated me well in letting you die. In the thick of battle you were always by my side. Now I will never be consoled for having lost you. Etzel the mighty king has received many a victory from you. But it has unfortunately come to pass that your help is lost to us. Your color is faded because of the wounds Giselher struck. If I knew now on whom I should avenge your death, how gladly would I serve you, noble vassal, as you so often served me! But alas, it cannot be. All my comfort lies here at its end. My long exile has become even more unbearable. May the day be cursed, that I ever left Bern! You all went with me gladly, my relatives and vassals. You helped me, all of you, in whatever I decided to do. Now I stand alone."

Then Master Hildebrand spoke: "Alas, most noble warrior. Why don't you let your mourning be? If we had any benefit from it I would mourn forever for this noble knight. He was my sister's son. Sir, you shouldn't grieve so; turn your heart from sorrow. Such mourning does no one any good."

III
(Lines 2807-3703).

(Dietrich von Bern suggests to King Etzel that the belongings of the fallen be brought to Bechlaren and Worms, and that the news of the fateful battle be told there. The Fiddler Swemmel and twelve men are to serve as messengers.)

Lady Gotelind had long known the road up along the Danube which the messengers now took into her land. She had often seen her husband ride happily away on it. Many a fair maid had stood with the Margravine at the battlement. Now they saw the messengers riding hard, coming close enough to the castle so that they could discern the dust rising in Rüdeger's land as it always had before. Many a fair maid spoke then: "Praise be to the Lord. Look there, my Lady. We see people riding back from the festival. Our lord is coming back." (But their protector and their hearts' desire had been struck down by Gernot's hand in the distant land of the Huns. Of all their countrymen only seven of the Margrave's vassals returned. They brought back his equipment.) Lady Gotelind had also heard these remarks. She had gone to her daughter, and both now imagined they would have joy without sorrow, as they often had before, coming from dear ones. But now they experienced sorrow and long-enduring grief. . . .

Then the tale was told how everything had happened. The servants could not be dissuaded from carrying forth Rüdeger's garments, everything that was his and had been sent home where it was to be kept. Whoever wanted to look upon them saw there a bloody splendor. Where formerly the mail was whole, now it was tattered and hewn asunder. Within it had been slain the consolation of Rüdeger's wife and of many others.

Now more than ever arose a great lamenting. Neither water nor wine were offered to the guests. "How long do we want to remain here?" asked the Fiddler. "The Margravine is in such despondency and mental torture that she is not able to offer the customary libations." The people there throughout the castle could not act differently. The building and the rock on which it stood resounded therewith. Also one could hear in the city of Bechlaren the people grieve as they were affected by the sorrow. The Margravine was indeed afflicted with great suffering. It is a wonder that she was able to live to the end of that day. She with her own hands shed her garments. Never had grief been as great as could be seen there. The news, at other places too, caused many eyes to well up with tears from the heart.

The noble lady in her sorrow bade Etzel's messengers to be comfortably lodged in the city. The wits of the noble Margravine were then so strained that she recognized no one, neither friend nor guest. Then the messengers wanted to leave her land for the Rhine. The young Margravine was still somewhat in control of her senses. She sent the noble and generous queen, Brunhild, her fondest devotion. She also sent a message to Lady Uote about loyal Giselher and how she had been betrothed to him, and about what woeful end everything had found. It couldn't have been worse. And she sent message that Gernot had slain her father.

The messengers took their leave from that place. Swemmel then began to ride in the direction where he found the way into the land of the Bavarians, for that's where his mission led him. Between the

Danube and the Inn an old fortification still stands. It has the name
Passau. There resided a mighty bishop. The repute of his rule and his
court was known far and wide. His name was Pilgrim. This news now
came to him. The proud Burgundians were the children of his sister.
Soon he learned all about how the warriors had fared in the land of
the Huns.

The messengers rode across the Inn. The people ran on ahead in
front of them and wanted to let it be known at court that the good
Bishop should receive his nephews. But they were not so close as he
thought; it was to be many a day that he would spend thereafter
without them. Then he spoke to the knights: "Now you should all
hurry and receive my friends. Let each of my officials who harbor
good thoughts of me receive my sister's children. And those who
have come with them, let them want for nothing." Indeed he wanted
to give his guests a comfortable night's lodging, not knowing that
their life had found an end in the land of the Huns. If only one of
his nephews had returned, even that would have been so much better.
Soon he was told that they had all been slain. There was no comfort
for him in these tidings. It seemed to him unbelievable. Yet in
thinking about it he had to believe it sooner or later. He arranged to
have quarters prepared for the messengers. Then with great sorrow
he spoke: "Now lies buried in the land of the Huns the joy that I
should have had with my kinsmen. Because of this I must always be
sad for as long as I may live, until the end of my days. I have thought
much about this. Cursed be the festival Etzel gave them because of
which so many a worthy man has found such a mournful death."
Then he spoke: "Oh Heavenly Warrior, how could you have done
this to me?" Then Swemmel the Fiddler came to him. After greetings
the Bishop began to ask him about the events. The Fiddler told him
how it all had happened, as he well could because he had seen it with
his very own eyes.

Then the Bishop began to weep. All through his court there was
a great commotion. Because of the mourning the priests had to
neglect their hours, for there were weeping both the laity and the
priesthood, one louder than the other. Then the good Bishop began
to see to it that their mourning ceased. "I can find my peace," he said.
"If I could get them back with weeping and with mourning, I would
never again be silent until my sister's children, who were along with
many a warrior so terribly slain in Etzel's land, are all returned to
me, all those whose deaths I will not cease to mourn." Then the lord
sent for the monks and priests, and he began to make arrangements
according to Christian customs. He had the priests sing a mass for
those who had died. One could hear the bells pealing all over the
town from the churches, just as he had instructed. There was a large
crowd at the sacrificial mass. The Bishop himself sang to honor the
Heavenly Father, to increase the blessing of Christians, and to intercede for the souls of the deceased. For sorrow the Bishop bore much
suffering.

After the worship service the messengers wanted to start riding on their journey right away. "You should wait yet a while," said a chaplain to them. "You should go to my lord; he asked me to tell you that. I believe he wants to send a message with you to the Rhine for his sister, Lady Uote, about her great misfortune." Then the Fiddler went forth to the good Bishop who spoke: "If Etzel's court has been devastated by such distress, then Kriemhild, my niece, has indeed received evilly her brother and his warriors. She would have done better had she spared Giselher and Gernot. If only those who were responsible for Siegfried's death had paid for it, she would be without blame. It was Hagen after all who slew him. Because of this we will always have much grief to bare for our friends. Alas, that his mother ever bore him! May it be manifest to God, that such long enduring suffering, such gruesome events, and so much despondency were caused by him far and wide throughout the lands. Swemmel, tell my sister to cease her mourning in time. Even there at home death would have come to them someday. If only they had steered clear of the Nibelungs' red gold, then they could perhaps have ridden back to their sister with her grace. They are to blame themselves, they and their superbia, that we have lost those brave fighters—all of them together—in Etzel's kingdom. And tell the Queen that I, in my opinion, cannot give her any better advice, for I wish her well, than for her to moderate her sorrowing. One must let those go whom death daily takes from us. For it is Death's task to let joy end in sorrow. That is the way of the world. And also tell Gunther's men to think about how the King bestowed great honors upon them on so many occasions, and to make their loyalty manifest by protecting and honoring his young son, who now inherits the land of the kingdom, and by rearing him to manhood. For this they in turn shall win honor. Swemmel, make me a promise upon my hand, if you ride through these lands again, concerning this I beseech you, friend, to come here again. It should not be left at this. I want to have written down the encounters and the great despair, or how they all found their death, how it began, and how it developed, and how it all took an end. Whatever true events you have seen in this matter, you should then relate this to me. Furthermore, I intend to question every relation be it man or woman, whoever can tell anything about it. For this reason I am sending now my messengers into the land of the Huns. There I will find out the true story; for it would be a bad thing if the story were not preserved. It is the most astounding story that ever happened in the world." Swemmel spoke thereupon: "Whatever you desire of me, my lord, that you shall see fulfilled."

The messengers rode away soon thereafter. The Bishop had his men accompany them on their way as far as he could attend to them with food and protection. Whoever rode past them in Bavaria, by them nothing was done to the messengers (this they had to forego for the sake of their lord), except that gifts were given to them.

Then Swemmel and his companions rode with this news through Swabia to the Rhine.

When Swemmel was riding through Bavaria, the news was also spread by him on the roads. How could he help but tell the sorrowful despair and how they were all slain there at the festival? These stories then were passed along to Lord Else. He spoke, "This ought to be a sorrow to me, but it is impossible. I will always mourn the fact before God that they ever crossed the Rhine. My brother was slain as a result of their expedition to court; that I never did deserve; that they must bare out themselves. Now my revenge has been wrought on them as the old proverb says: Whomever the wolf revenges, he is avenged so well that one should not revenge further." That's what the mighty Margrave said. Then spoke some: "Our Lord in Heaven be praised that Hagen's rage is spent. He could never get his fill of fighting. Now he has come to a place where his arrogance will do us little damage."

Now let us leave this sort of talk. When the messengers had come across the Rhine over to Worms, they were taken notice of right away. One could partly recognize them by their clothing. It was elegantly cut according to the Hunnish custom. This surprising news began to cause the citizens to wonder where the strangers had come from and where they had gotten Gunther's steed. Then some of the people became very sorrowful, even before they had heard the story. Then arrived at the court those who had been sent from afar. The steeds and their accoutrements were so familiar to the courtly following that they did not wait any longer but spread the news at court that the princes' weapons and steeds had come. The joy of Queen Brunhild was very great. She spoke winsomely: "Whoever tells me precisely where the messengers have left the lords on the roads, for him my reward is ready and waiting." As that happened the messengers dismounted in front of the Queen's palace. Her entourage rushed to ask about the news, where King Gunther, the mighty prince, might be. The Fiddler answered somewhat reluctantly: "I am not supposed to tell this story piecemeal. I am to refrain from telling it, except at the right place. Bring me (as it is proper for you to do) to where I am by right supposed to tell it. There I will not be silent." Then one of Gunther's men went immediately before the Queen and asked her whether she were inclined to have the messengers come before her, "those we have just received. None of them is known to us. However, they are bringing into the land the armor of our lords. Swemmel is standing with them, Etzel's minstrel." She spoke: "Tell them to come here. I would like now to hear when the lords shall come."

Swemmel the good, along with his traveling companions, quite depressed in spirits, went before the Queen. When she saw them coming before her, the Lady spoke cordially: "Sirs, welcome. I would like to hear from you where you have left my husband. How gladly do I offer you the reward that I am supposed to give for this information. My heart is full of worries: if you take them from me it will be your benefit and my happiness. And if you do it promptly, I will give you my compensation all the more gladly. Yet I will not get over wondering how it happened that he did not send me any of his men whom I could recognize. He has never done that to me before; that troubles me greatly."

Then the Fiddler spoke: "Permit me to tell you the story, mighty Queen. Then I will tell you without delay what I know of the details. But it is my hope that you will first grant me your protection." She spoke: "You shall be blameless and may rest assured that no one here will do anything to you. Neither does anyone have the right to harm the messengers." She spoke: "I fear that the joy of my eyes has slipped too far away from me." She could not help weeping before the news was told.

Then the Fiddler spoke: "The most exalted king of the Hunnish realm extends to you his affection and gifts. Lord Dietrich has also sent to you his loyalty. We have noticed that all your sorrow is to them a trial and tribulation. The good Bishop Pilgrim also extends his loyalty to you and bids us tell you, my lady, that one should temperately mourn every sorrow. He is completely at your disposal in this matter, with deeds and advice, so that succor and honor might come to you in this world. Also I have heard from him, that he bids all the King's vassals, who remain loyal to him, to shield you and your child. For your husband is dead. Giselher and Gernot can never wear a crown again. They have all three been slain. Hagen, Volker, and Dancwart, the noble warrior, have died in battle with them in the Hunnish lands. where they hoped to meet with joy. Not one of all their following has survived."

There rose up as loud a lament as anyone had heard in the land of the Huns. Blood from the heart never did flow so fast out of any mouth as it did from Brunhild then because of her great sorrow. Both of the margravinen who at Bechlaren also had cause to sorrow never mourned so greatly. Brunhild the mighty sorrowed indeed in her own measure. No one now asked any questions, no one spoke to the messengers. Swemmel could see nothing but sorrowing and wailing and wringing of hands by all. But King Gunther's wife was not the only one tormenting her body. There were many sorrowing ones. The noble Lady Uote was in her lodging at Lorsch, in a great cathedral that she had had built there, where she spent her time on her knees in prayer and reading in her psalter every day. When she heard about the news that spread around Worms, her sorrows caused her much anguish. The story about her dear children was not good news. There had never been heard such awful woe of womankind. Right away she wanted to come to where she could see Brunhild, however that might be arranged. She was quickly brought there. The people were crying loudly in a huge commotion. The lamentation of her and of the others could not be equalled.

Notes

5. LITERATURE, PART II: LYRIC POETRY

Troubadours and Trouvères

The troubadours and trouvères flourished, respectively, in the south and north of France during the twelfth and thirteenth centuries. Consummate poet-musicians, they created the poetic forms and the code of manners we associate with "courtly love"; their influence was felt not only by contemporaries, but also by Dante, Petrarch, and succeeding generations.

A. Bernart de Ventadorn

Amics Bernartz de Ventadorn,
com vos podetz de chant sofrir,
can aissi auzetz esbaudir
lo rossinholet noih e jorn?
   auyatz lo joi que demena!
tota noih chanta sotz la flor.
melhs s'enten que vos en amor.

My friend Bernart de Ventadorn,
how can you refrain from singing
when you hear the nightingale
rejoicing night and day?
   Listen to his joy!
All night he sings beneath the flowers,
he understands love better than you.

Peire, lo dormir e·l sojorn
am mais que·l rossinhol auvir;
ni ja tan no·m sabriatz dir
que mais en la folia torn.
    Deu lau, fors sui de chadena,
e vos e tuih l'autr' amador
etz remazut en la folor.

Bernartz, greu er pros ni cortes
qui ab amor no·s sap tener;
ni ja tan no·us fara doler
que mais no valha c'autre bes,
    car, si fai mal, pois abena.
greu a om gran be ses dolor;
mas ades vens lo jois lo plor.

Peire, si fos dos ans o tres
lo segles faihz al meu plazer,
de domnas vos dic eu lo ver:
non toran mais preyadas ges,
    ans sostengran tan greu pena
qu'elas nos feiran tan d'onor
c'ans nos prejaran que nos lor.

Bernartz, so non es d'avinen
que domnas preyon; ans cove
c'om las prec e lor clam merce;
et es plus fols, mon escien,
    que cel qui semn' en l'arena,
qui las blasma ni lor valor;
e mou de mal ensenhador.

Peire, mout ai lo cor dolen,
can d'una faussa me sove,
que m'a mort, e no sai per que,
mas car l'amava finamen.
    faih ai longa carantena,
e sai, si la fezes lonhor,
ades la trobara pejor.

    Bernartz, foudatz vos amena,
car aissi vos partetz d'amor,
per cui a om pretz e valor.

    Peire, qui ama, desena,
car las trichairitz entre lor
an tout joi e pretz e valor.

Peire, I prefer my sleep and peace
to hearing nightingales;
you'll never persuade me
to return to a state of madness.
    I am, thank God, free
of chains while you and all the other
lovers remain as mad as ever.

Bernart, it's scarcely proper or courtly
that a man be unable to deal with love;
nor will it ever cause you such pain
as not to be worth more than other
    pleasures,
    for it quickly gives good for ill.
There is little pleasure without its share
of pain, and joy soon conquers grief.

Peire, if for two or three years
the world were run according to my
    desires,
I'll tell you how women would be treated:
they'd never be asked for anything,
    but made to suffer,
and they would honor us, and ask
of us, rather than we of them.

Bernart, women shouldn't ask—
it isn't right; but rather, men
should ask of them and cry for mercy.
And it strikes me as madness,
    like sowing in sand,
to blame them or their worth—
it only shows bad breeding.

Peire, my heart fills with grief
when I remember one false lady
who killed me, I know not why,
except that I loved her faithfully.
    I have fasted long,
but I know that if I fasted even longer
I'd find her no better disposed towards me.

    Bernart, you're mad
thus to alienate love from which
men gain worth and valor.

    Peire, love is senseless,
for those traitresses have absconded
with all joy and worth and valor.

B. Bernart de Ventadorn

Can vei la lauzeta mover
de joi sas alas contral rai,
que s'oblid' e·s laissa chazer
per la doussor e'al cor li vai,
ai! tan grans enveya m'en ve
de cui qu'eu veya jauzion,
meravilhas ai, car desse
lo cor de dezirer no·m fon.

Ai, las! tan cuidava saber
d'amor, e tan petit en sai,
car eu d'amar no·m posc tener
celeis don ja pro non aurai.
Tout m'a mo cor, e tout ma me,
e se mezeis e tot lo mon;
e can se·m tolc, no·m laisset re
mas dezirer e cor volon.

When I see the lark moving
its wings in joy against the light,
rising up into forgetfulness letting go,
    and falling
for the sweetness that comes to its heart,
alas, what envy then comes over me
of everyone I see rejoicing,
it makes me wonder that my heart,
right then, does not melt with desire.

I, weary, how much I thought I knew
about love, and how little I know,
because I cannot keep myself from loving
one from whom I shall get no favor.
She has it all: she took my heart, and me,
and herself, and the whole world.
And when she took herself away from
    me, she left me nothing
but desire and a heart still wanting.

Anc non agui de me poder
ni no fui meus de l'or' en sai
que·m laisset en sos olhs vezer
en un miralh que mout me plai.
Miralhs, pus me mirei en te,
m'an mort li sospir de preon,
c'aissi·m perdei com perdet se
lo bels Narcisus en la fon.

I have never had the power of myself,
I have not been my own man since tha
    moment
when she let me look into her eyes,
into a mirror that gives great pleasure,
    even now.
Mirror, since I beheld myself in you,
the sighs from my depths have slain me
and I have lost myself, as fair Narcissus
lost himself in the fountain.

De las domnas me dezesper;
ja mais en lor no m·fiarai;
c'aissi com las solh chaptener,
enaissi las deschaptenrai.
Pois vei c'una pro no m'en te
vas leis que·m destrui e·m cofon,
totas las dopt' e las mescre,
car be sai c'atretals se son.

I give up all hope in women.
I shall not put my faith in them again;
as much as I used to hold them up,
now I shall let them fall,
because I do not see one who is of any
    use to me
with her, who destroys me and brings
    down.
I shall fear and distrust them all,
because they are all alike, I know it we

D'aisso's fa be femna parer
ma domna, per qu'e·lh o retrai,
car no vol so c'om voler,
e so c'om li deveda, fai.
Chazutz sui en mala merce,
et ai be faih co·l fols en pon;
e no sai per que m'esdeve,
mas car trop puyei contra mon.

This is how she shows herself a woman
    indeed,
my lady, and I reproach her for it:
she does not want what one ought to v
and what she is forbidden to do, she d
I have fallen in evil grace,
I have acted like the madman on the br
and how this came about I cannot say,
except that I climbed too high on the
    mountain.

Merces es perduda, per ver,
et eu non o saubi anc mai,
car cilh qui plus en degr'aver,
no·n a ges, et on la querrai?
A! can mal sembla, qui la ve,
qued aquest chaitiu deziron
que ja ses leis non aura be,
laisse morrir, que no l·aon.

In truth, kindness is lost from the wor
and I never knew it;
for she who ought to have the most o
has none, and where shall I look?
Ah, you would never guess, when you
    look at her,
that she would let this man, miserable
    with desire,
who can never be well without her,
just die, just let him die and not help

Pus ab midons no·m pot valer
precs ni merces ni·l dreihz qu'eu ai
ni a leis no ven a plazer
qu'eu l'am, ja mais no·lh o dirai.

Since these things do me no good with
    my lady,
prayer, pity, the rights I have,
and since it is no pleasure to her
that I love her, I shall not tell her agai

Aissi·m part de leis e·m recre;
mort m'a, e per mort li respon,
e vau m'en, pus ilh no·m rete,
chaitius, en issilh, no sai on.

Thus I part from her, and I give it all up.
She has given me death, and I will answer
    her with death,
and I am going away, because she does
    not retain me,
a broken man, in exile, I know not where.

Tristans, ges no·n auretz de me,
qu'eu m'en vau, chaitius, no sai
      on.
De chantar me gic e·m recre,
e de joi e d'amor m'escon.

Tristan, you will have nothing more from
    me,
for I go away, a broken man, I know not
    where;
I shall withdraw from singing, I renounce it,
far from joy and love, I hide myself away.

C. Gautier d'Epinal

Commencemens de dolce saison bele
   Que je voi revenir,
Remembrance d'amor qui me rapele,
   Dont ja ne quiers partir,
Et la malvis, qui comence a tentir,
Et li douz sons del ruissel sur gravele,
   Que je voi resclarcir,
   Me font resouvenir
De la ou tuit mi bon desir
Sont et seront jusqu'au morir.

Tos temz m'est plus s'amors fresche
    et novele,
   Quant recors a loisir
Ses yeux, son vis qui de joie sautele,
   Son aller, son venir,
Son bel parler et son gent contenir,
Son douz regart qui vient d'une
    estincele
   Mon cuer el cors ferir,
   Sanz garde de perir.
Et quant je plus plaing et sospir,
Plus suis joianz, quant plus m'aïr.

Leals amors et fine et droituriere
   M'a si a son voloir,
Que ne m'en puis partir ne traire
   arriere,
   Ne je n'en ai pouvoir.
N'est pas amors, dont on se puet
   movoir,
Ne cil amis, qui en nule maniere
   La bée a decevoir;
   Or sai je bien de voir
Qu'ensemble convient remanoir
Moi et amor par estovoir.

Se li anuis de la gent malparliere
   Ne me feïst doloir,
Bien peüsse avoir ma joie entiere
   D'esgarder, de vëoir;
Mais ce que n'os por eus rementevoir,
Conoissiez, bele, au vis et a la chiere,
   Que je n'os mon voloir
   Dire por percevoir,
Mais bone dame doit savoir
Conoissance et merci avoir.

The beginning of the sweet season
which I see returning,
the remembrance of love calling me
   back,
from which I will never depart,
and the songbird beginning to sing,
and the sound of the brook on the
   gravel
which I see clearing—
these make me remember
from where all my good desires
come and will come until I die.

Always her love is fresher and newer;
each time I think over at leisure
her eyes, her face sparkling with joy,
her going and her coming,
her fine speech and noble bearing,
her gentle look which strikes
a spark into my heart,
I have no fear of dying;
and though I sigh and wail,
I am most joyous when most I suffer.

True Love, faithful and honest
has me so at his mercy
that I cannot pull back or turn away,
and I have not the power.
That is no love, from which one can
   leave,
nor is he a lover who in any way
seeks to deceive.
Thus I know for certain
that together we are compelled,
Love and I, to remain.

If troubles with gossipy folk
did not vex me,
I could have my joy entire,
looking and seeing.
But things that because of them I
   dare not mention,
you shall know, lady, by my face
   and aspect—
for I dare not speak my mind
for fear of being observed by them—
but a true, good lady must know how
to acknowledge and have mercy.

Vos merci je, ma dolce dame chiere,   I thank you, my dear sweet lady
  Qu'ains vos daigna sëoir   because you deigned to listen
Et qu'il vos plaist a oïr ma priere,   and it pleased you to hear my prayer,
  Ainsi con je l'espoir;   according to my hope;
Mais se merci m'i peüst eschëoir,   but if ever mercy could fall to my lot,
Granz fust ma joie et ma peine legiere   my joy were great and my troubles
  Sanz point de meschëoir   light,
  Mais molt fait bien paroir   without fail.
Amors, qu'ele me trait a hoir   But it is very clear
De moi faire tot son voloir.   that Love makes me his heir
                                    in order to make me do his will.

(Envoi:)   Envoi:

  Chanconete, por voir   Little song, truly
A celui, qui tant set valoir   to him who knows worth,
Te feras en Flandres savoir.   make yourself known in Flanders—
  Phelipe, a mon pouvoir   Phillip, as best I can,
Pri amor que vos laist veoir   I pray to Love that he let you see
Ce que fins amanz doit avoir.   what a true lover deserves.

D. Gace Brulé

Cil qui d'amor me conseille,	He who counsels me from love
Que de li doie partir,	or tells me that I should leave her,
Ne set pas ki me resveille,	knows not who moves me
Ne quel sont mi grief souspir.	or how heavy are my sighs.
Petit a sens et voisdie,	He has little sense or cleverness
Cil qui m'en veut chastier,	who would try to school me—
N'onques n'ama en sa vie.	nor has he ever loved in his whole life.
Cil fait trop nice folie,	It is a very foolish thing
Qui s'entremet dou mestier	to undertake a trade
Dont il ne se set aidier.	in which one has no skill.
Hé blanche, clere et vermeille,	Ah, clear white and red—
De vos sont tuit mi desir;	for you are all my desires;
Car faites en tel merveille	you work such a marvel
Droiture et raison faillir.	that reason and honor quite fail.
Quant je vos vueill a amie	When I want you for a lover,
Droiz nel poroit otriier;	Honor would not grant it;
Se vostre grant cortoisie,	if your great courtesy
De gentil dousor garnie,	and sweet nobility
Ne me deigne conseillier;	will not deign to counsel me,
Mar vos oï tant prisier.	ill have I heard you praised!
Qui trop haut bée et teseille	Whoever strives too high
Maint desconfort puet oïr;	will gain much suffering;
Mes tres granz amors pareille	but a great love lifts to itself
Ce que li plaist a sesir;	whatever it is pleased to grasp;
Sa tres haute seignorie	that high and mighty lordship
Fait monter et abessier.	raises or lowers all things.
Douce dame, vostre aïe!	Fair Lady, so help me!
Celle qui m'a en baillie	She who has me in her power
Puet bien conduire et haucier	well can guide and lift up
Mon outrageus desirier.	my outrageous desire.
Povres cuers se desconseille	A poor heart grows disconsolate
Et let de paor morir;	and dies in fear;
Li viguereus s'apareille	a vigorous one prepares itself
En biau confort de guerir.	to grow well in good comfort.
Dame, mais rien que je die	Still, Lady, nothing I can say
Ne me vaut, car je sorquier;	helps me, for I seek too much.
S'un petit de vilainie,	If some little villany
Esprise de felonie,	bent on misdeeds
Vos fet pitié desvoier,	makes you turn away pity,
Mar vos vi et ma mort quier.	ill have I ever seen you, and I seek my own death.
Dedens mon cuer monte treille,	In my heart a vine grows
Toute preste de florir:	all ready to bloom:
Granz amor fine et feeille	a great love, true and faithful

Cui la daigneroit joïr
Mes amors qui n'est joïe
Ne puet cuer esleecier;
Bien voi se mort ne chastie
Ma volenté, m'anemie,
Ne puis mon biau tort laissier
Ne mon outrage changier.

Bels Lorenz, felon, d'envie,
Me firent joie esloignier.
Meinte douce compeignie
Ont a lor tort departie
A mentir et a trichier,
Et rien ne s'en puet vengier.

Odins, cil cui amors lie,
Est cheüz en tel baillie,
Que nus nel puet desliier,
Se pitiez ne vuet aidier.

to any who will receive it.
But love not accepted
cannot gladden the heart.
I see that if death does not school
my will, my enemy,
I cannot leave my fair wrong
or change my outrage.

Fair Lorenz, envious traitors
sent joy away from me.
Many a sweet company
have they wrongly separated
by lying and deceit,
and nothing can avenge it.

Odins, he whom love binds
has fallen into such power
from which none can loose him,
if Pity does not bring help.

Minnesong and *Spruchdichtung*

When, in the twelfth century, new ideas with respect to content and form appeared in Provençal courtly love-lyric, they found a ready audience and well-prepared poets among the members of the nobility in German-speaking lands. Chivalric-courtly love, with its narrow thematic concern, was practiced by both Provençal troubadours and German *Minnesänger,* in some cases to the exclusion of other lyrical subjects. But this *Minnesang* ([*hôhe*] *minne* = courtly love) became more than a fashion. It was practiced by so many gifted poets for so long, and cherished by the entire class of rulers and leaders of society, that it is better called a convention.

Not all German lyrical poetry was minnesong. Another important field of lyrical activity was the so-called *Spruchdichtung,* that is, gnomic poetry in the broad sense, including panegyric, invective, political poetry (often satire), and gnomic poetry proper. In the twelfth and thirteenth centuries, a *Spruch* usually consisted of one stanza only, and it was sung, as was the rest of lyric poetry.

The poet-composers whose works follow are representatives of four subsequent stages and styles of the twelfth and thirteenth centuies: 1) the knightly chivalric era that links that heroic past with the courtly future (Spervogel); 2) the courtly era that brings forth the classical poets of minnesong and during which one poet broadens his thematic range and perfects his art to such a degree that he inspires poets of different tastes for generations to come (Walther von der Vogelweide); 3) a new era—disillusionment and parody (Neidhart von Reuental, and Tannhäuser); and 4) an era of continuation and enrichment (Wizlaw von Rügen).

A. Spervogel (born ca. 1160?)

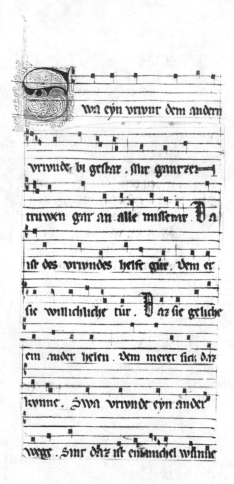

Swâ ein vriunt dem andern vriunde bî gestât
mit ganzen triuwen gar ân alle missetât,
dâ ist des vriundes helfe guot.
dem er si williclîche tuot,
daz si gehellent under in, dem mêret sich daz künne.
swâ vriunde ein ander waege sint, daz ist ein michel wünne.

When a friend will always stand beside his friend
with loyal hand and heart whenever woes descend,
then is his willing hand an aid
to him whose friendship is repaid,
and when they each support the other, then their strength increases.
When friends will help each other they have joy which never ceases.

B. Walther von der Vogelweide (ca. 1170-1230)

1 Mir hat her Ger-hart At-ze ein pfert er - schozzen zI-se-na - che;
5 Ez was wol dri - er mar-ke wert, nu hoerent fröm-de sa - - che:

daz klage ich dem den er be-stat:derst un - ser bei - der vo - get.
sit daz ez an ein gel-ten gat, wa mit er mich nu zo - get.

9 Er seit von gro- zer swae-re,wie daz min pfe - rit mae-re a-be
11 dem ros - se sip- pe wae-re,daz im den vin - ger

13 ge - biz-zen hat ze schan - den: ich swer mit bei-den han - den

daz si sich niht er - kan - den, ist ie-man der mir sta - be?

Mir hât hêr Gêrhart Atze ein pfert
erschozzen zIsenache.
daz klage ich dem den er bestât:
derst unser beider voget.
ez was wol drîer marke wert:
nû hoerent frömde sache,
sît daz ez an ein gelten gât,
wâ mit er mich nû zoget.
er seit von grôzer swaere,
wie mîn pferit maere
dem rosse sippe waere,
daz im den vinger abe
gebizzen hât ze schanden.
ich swer mit beiden handen,
daz si sich niht erkanden.
ist ieman der mir stabe?

Sir Gerhart Atze shot my horse
at Eisenache dead.
My grievances I now shall lay
before our mutual lord.
The beast was worth a lot, of course,
but just hear what he said
when it appeared he'd have to pay
the debt that he'd ignored.
He speaks of pain and need
and says my horse indeed
was brother to the steed
which bit his thumb in half
and caused him grief thereby.
I swear with both hands high
all that is just a lie.
Who here will hold my staff?

C. Neidhart von Reuental (ca. 1180-1240)

1. Blô - zen wir den an - ger li - gen sâ - hen, 2. end uns diu lie - be zît be - gun - de nâ - hen, 3. daz die bluo - men drun - gen durch den klê 4. ab'r als ê. 5. hei - de diust mit rô - sen nû be - van - gen: 6. den tuot der su - mer wol, niht wê.

Barren were the meadows and forsaken
until the summer came to warm and waken,
flowers pressed through grass and clover then.
Once again
summer now is opening the roses
and making lovely heath and glen.

Nightingale and thrush, we hear them singing,
with the sound the hills and vales are ringing.
They sing their songs of joyous summertime
as they climb.
May has brought us happiness and beauty:
the heath is blooming in its prime.

Spoke a maid, 'The dew is on the heather,
see the splendor summer brings together.
The trees that in the wintertime were bare
everywhere
wave their leafy branches in the breezes.
The nightingales are singing there.

'Losa, hear the songs of birds resounding,
they greet the May from all the trees surrounding.
I fancy, we are free of winter now.
Wierat, thou
must dance more spritely, wouldst thou gain my favor,
beneath the linden's leafy bough.

'Spring's the time for each to choose a lover,
Roses blossom 'neath the forest's cover
and I shall have a crown of roses red
on my head
when I'm dancing hand in hand so gaily
with such a handsome knight,' she said.

'Daughter, think no more of bold advances.
Should'st thou disturb the nobles at the dances,
who are not the sort for folk as we,
I forsee
thou willst have a lot of pain and trouble.
A sturdy farmer covets thee.'

'Let a heifer wed the worthy farmer!
My hope is for a stately knight in armor.
Why should I take a farmer as my man?
Never can
I be happy with a rustic lover.
A knight alone will suit my plan.'

'Daughter, don't despise his lowly station
to win a stupid noble's admiration.
This has caused your friends distress and pain.
All in vain
are thy promises, I tell thee truly,
thy wilfulness I never could restrain.'

'Mother mine, stop scolding, and believe me,
I would love him though my friends should leave me,
I never hid my wishes, I recall.
One and all
may the people know whom I have chosen,
for he's the knight of Reuenthal.'

D. Tannhäuser (ca. 1200-1266)

1. Mir tuot wol ein lie - ber wân, 2. den ich von der
5. al - lez des mîn her - ze gert, 6. des bin ich an

schoe - nen hân: 3. sô der Miu - se - berc zer - gê 4. sam der
ir ge - wert, 7. mî - nen wil - len tuot si gar, 8. bûw' ich

snê, sô lô - net mir diu rei - ne. 9. swâ si
ir ein hûs von hel - fen - bei - ne,

wil, ûf ei - me sê: 10. sô hab ich ir vriunt - schaft

unt ir hul - de. 11. bring' ich ir von Ga - li - lê

12. her ân al - le schul - de 13. ei - nen berc, ge -

vüeg' ich daz, 14. dâ her Â - dam û - fe saz, 15. hei - a

hei! 16. daz waer al - ler dienst' ein ü - ber - gul - de.

Constant service one should render
to the ladies, fair and tender,
just as I have done for mine:
salamanders she would have indeed.
She required one thing of me:
the Rhône, and this at once should be
from Provence brought to the land
of Nuremberg; then might my suit succeed—

the Danube is to take its place.
This done, she'll grant me all I have in mind.
I thank my lady for such grace;
that's why they call her kind.
I say "Yes!" and she says "No!"
We agree on all things so.
Hey-a-hey! She's been too long without my care, I find.
    "Yes," today and always, "Yes!"
    "Help me, help!" and still its "Yes!"
    Hearts, cry out in sore distress!
    How can the dear one act so coy,
    this perfect love of mine?
    Since she will not bring me joy,
    my heart must sadly pine.

This delights me even more—
a hope from her I so adore:
should Mouse Mountain melt away
with its snow, the dear will grant me all.
Whatsoever I prefer
I shall freely get from her,
she'll be glad to do my will
if I build for her an ivory hall
where she wants it, on a sea,
then I'll have her friendship and her pay.
Should I bring from Galilee,
unharmed in any way,
a mountain whereon Adam sat—
if I do for her all that—
hey-a-hey! All other deeds would be surpassed, I'd say.
    "Yes," today and always, "Yes!". . . .

A lofty tree in India stands
which she wishes from my hands.
She'll do anything I ask
if—but see just what she's thinking of:
I must bring her without fail
Parzival's mysterious grail
and the apple Paris gave
Lady Venus in exchange for love,
and the mantle which enclosed
only her whose virtue has no stain.
Other wonders she's proposed
which cause me bitter pain:
she must have the ark that bore
Noah in the days of yore.
Hey-a-hey! If I brought that what favors I would gain!
    "Yes," today and always, "Yes!" . . . .

E. Wizlaw von Rügen (1265?-1325)

*44. Loybere ri-sen. von dem[1]) boyme
hin tzů tal. des stan blot ir e-ste.
Blomen sich wi-sen. daz se sint
vůrtorben al. scone wast[1]) ir gle-ste
Sus twinghet de riphe. manigher
hande wrtzel sal. des bin ich ghar
se-re betrůbet. Nu ich tzů griphe.
sint der winder ist so kal. des wirt
nuwe vroyde ghe-v̌-bet.

45. Helphet mir scallen. hundert
tusent vroyden mer. wen
des meyien blůte kan bringhen.
Rosen de vallen. an mir vrowen
roter ler. davon wil ich singhen.
Tuwinct[1]) mich de kulde. al ir vůrt-
zel[1]) smaghes ger. de sint an ir libe
ghestrowet. Vvorbe ich ir hulde.
so bedrocht ich vroyden mer. sus
de mininglîche mich vrowet.[2])

Loy - be - re ri - sen.   yon dem boy - men
men sich wi - sen.   daz se sint vuor-

hin tzuo tal.   des stan blot ir es - te. Blo-
tor - ben al.   sco - ne wast ir gles -

te.   Sus twin - ghet de ri - phe. ma - ni - gher han - de

wuor-tzel sal.   des bin ich ghar se - re be - truo-bet.

Nu ich tzuo-gri - phe.   sint der win - der

ist so kal.   des wirt nu - we vroy-de ghe - uo - bet.

Helphet mir scallen.
hundert tusent vroyden mer.
wen des meyien bluote kan bringhen.
Rosen de vallen.
an mir vrowen roter ler.
da von will ich singhen.
Tuwinct mich de kulde.
al ir wuortzel smaghes ger.
de sint an ir libe ghestrowet.
Worbe ich ir hulde.
so bedrocht ich vroyden mer.
sus de minnighliche mich vrowet.

Leaves fall in shower
down from all the trees around,
limbs are bare and slender.
Look at the flowers
lying withered on the ground
where they bloomed in splendor.
Frost thus has blighted
all the blossoms that were here,
sad am I to lose these treasures.
You are invited,
since the winter is so drear,
now to join me in other pleasures.

Join in my praises
of the charm which far outstrips
joys which May can bring.
Roses she raises
on her lovely cheeks and lips,
and of them I sing.
Though frost may shake me,
from her body comes a scent,
fragrance of blooms and summer breezes.
If she will take me,
I'll lack naught to be content,
she is everything that pleases.

Notes

6. LITERATURE, PART III: SAINTS' LIVES

The Life of Saint Alexis

The *Lives* of Saint Alexis and Saint Mary the Egyptian were translated from Latin prose into Old French verse during the eleventh and twelfth centuries. Both poems express in legendary narrative the intensity of the contemporary spiritual renewal. *La Vie de saint Alexis* (ca. 1060) is particularly concerned with ascesis and apostolic renunciation of the world. The English rendition here follows the strophic form of the original.

The world was good in ancient times,
For there was faith, justice and charity;
There was belief, which is no longer prized;
All has changed and lost its color,
Never more will it be as it was for the forefathers.   5

In Noah's time and the time of Abraham
And of David whom God so dearly loved,
The world was good; it will never be as fine;
It is old and frail; all is declining;
It grows corrupt; all goodness passes away.   10

After that time in which God came to save us,
Our forefathers had the Christian faith;
There was a lord in Rome the city;
He was a rich man, of high nobility;
Thus, I want to tell you of his son.   15

Eufemian, for that was the father's name,
Was a Roman count, among the finest in his day;
Of all the peers, the Emperor loved him best.
The man took a virtuous, honorable wife,
One of the noblest in the land.   20

The two lived together a long time;
They were sorely grieved because they had no child;
They both appealed to God with whole hearts:
"O King of Heaven, by your own command,
Give us a child who shall be as You desire."   25

They prayed so much in deep humility
That God gave the wife fecundity;
He gave them a son, and they were very thankful;
They had him regenerated by holy baptism;
They gave him a good name in the Christian way.   30

He was baptized with the name Alexis;
She who bore him gladly nourished him;
Then the good father put him in school;
He learned so well that he became adept in letters;
Then he went to serve the Emperor.   35

When the father saw he would have no other child
(Only the one whom he so dearly loved),
He began to think about the times ahead;
He wished his son to marry in his own lifetime,
So he procured the daughter of a noble freedman.   40

The maiden was born of high parentage,
Daughter of a count in Rome
Who had no other child and wished to give her great honor;
The two fathers met and parleyed:
They wished their two children to marry.   45

They named a day for the marriage;
The time came, and it was done nobly:
Lord Alexis wed her properly,
But he wanted none of this;
His desire was wholly turned to God.   50

When the day had passed into evening,
The father said, "My son, now go to bed
With your bride, as the Lord of Heaven commands."
The youth did not wish to anger his father:
He went into the chamber where his wife waited.   55

When he saw the bed, he looked at the maiden,
And remembered his Heavenly Lord,
Whom he held dearer than any earthly thing:
"O God," he said, "sin presses me so hard!
If I do not flee, I fear it will make me lose You."   60

When they were left all alone in the chamber,
Lord Alexis addressed her:
He began to condemn all earthly life
And he showed her the truth of the heavenly one;
So impatient was he to be on his way.   65

"Hear me, Maiden! He is my spouse
Who redeemed us with His precious blood.
There is no perfect love in this world:
Life is frail, and has no lasting honor;
Happiness here turns to great sorrow."   70

When all his thoughts had been revealed to her,
He gave her the sashes of his sword
And a ring; he commended her to God.
Then he went out of his father's chamber;
In the dark of night he fled the country.   75

Then, he travelled straight to the ocean;
The ship was ready where he was to board it;
He paid his fare and was given a place inside;
They raised their sail and let the ship run at sea:
They came to shore where God had led them.   80

Straight to Laodicea—a most beautiful city—
The boat sailed in safety.
Then Lord Alexis disembarked;
I know not how long he remained there;
Wherever he was he did not cease to serve God.   85

From there he went to the city of Edessa,
Because he had heard of an image there
Made by angels at God's command
In honor of the Virgin who brought salvation,
Holy Mary, who bore the Lord God.   90

All the possessions he had brought with him
He distributed throughout the city Edessa;
Great alms, so that nothing was left to him,
He gave to the poor wherever he found them:
He wished not to be encumbered by any possessions.   95

When he had distributed all his goods,
Lord Alexis took his place among the beggars;
He received alms when God sent them:
He kept enough to sustain his body;
If any was left, he gave it to the poor.   100

Now I will return to the father and mother
And to the bride whom he had espoused;
When they knew that he had fled
Great was the grief they suffered
And great the mourning throughout the city.   105

The father said, "Son, how have I lost you!"
The mother echoed: "Alas! What has become of him?"
The bride said, "Sin has taken him from me,
Ah! Dear friend, I had you so little,
And now I am so wretched, I could not be more so."   110

Then the father chose some of his best servants;
He had them seek his son in many countries;
Two of them travelled all the way to Edessa;
And there they saw Lord Alexis seated
But did not know his face or his appearance.   115

The child's tender flesh was so much changed,
His father's two servants did not know him;
They put alms into his very hands;
He received it like the other brothers.
They did not know him; they returned right away.   120

They neither knew him nor singled him out,
And Lord Alexis praised the God of Heaven
For this his servant who now gave him alms;
He had been their lord, now he was their beggar.
I cannot say how happy it made him.   125

The men returned to Rome the city
And told his father they had not found him;
There's no need to ask if he was grieved;
The good mother went into mourning
And often lamented for her dear son.   130

"Alexis, son, why did your mother bear you?
You are gone from me and I am left sorrowing;
I do not know a place or a country
Where I may seek you, and I am all bewildered.
I will never be happy, dear child, nor will your father."   135

She came into the chamber full of woe,
She stripped it until nothing remained there:
No hanging was left nor any ornament.
She turned her whole mind to sorrow,
And from that day she had no happiness.   140

She spoke: "Chamber, you will never again be brightened,
And there will be no more happiness within you."
She laid it waste as if an army had plundered it.
She had it hung with sack-cloth and torn curtains,
She changed its great pomp into great mourning.   145

In her grief she sat down on the ground,
So indeed did Lord Alexis' wife:
"Lady," she said, "I have had such a great loss!
Form now on I will live like the turtle-dove:
I have lost your son; now I want to live with you."   150

The mother said, "If you want to stay with me
I will keep you for the love of Alexis,
You shall have no ill I cannot tend.
Let us mourn together for our loved one,
You for your lord, and I for my own son."   155

Since it had to be, they resigned themselves;
But they could not forget their pain.
Lord Alexis in Edessa the city
Served his Master with a good will:
The Enemy could not deceive him.   160

Ten and seven years, no less than that,
He mortified his body in the Lord God's service:
Not for the love of man or woman,
Nor for honors he might receive,
Would he turn from God as long as he lived.   165

When his whole heart had been so strengthened
That he would never, of his own will, leave the city,
God made the image speak for love of him
To the sacristan who served at the altar;
It commanded him: "Call the Man of God."   170

The image said, "Send for the Man of God;
For he has served God well and willingly,
And he is worthy to enter paradise."
He went, he sought, but could not single out
The holy man of whom the image spoke.   175

The sacristan returned to the image in church:
"Truly," he said, "I don't know which one to choose."
The image answered, "He is the one who sits near the door.
He is close to God and the kingdom of heaven;
He will never willingly stray from them."   180

The man went, inquired, and summoned him to the church:
Now the word went out all over the country
That the image had spoken for Alexis:
Everyone honored him, the great and humble,
And prayed that he have mercy on them.   185

When he saw how they wished to honor him,
He said, "Truly, I may not stay here;
I do not want these new honors to encumber me."
In the dark of night he fled the city,
And retraced his path straightway to Laodicea.   190

Lord Alexis boarded a ship:
They took the wind and let the ship run at sea;
He hoped to sail directly to Tarsus,
But this could not be; he was to travel to another place:
The seawinds carried them straight to Rome.   195

At one of the ports closest to Rome
The holy man's ship came to shore.
When he saw his own kingdom he was most fearful
That his parents, when they recognized him,
Would encumber him again with worldly honors.   200

"O God," he said, "Great King who governs all things,
If it had pleased You, I would not have come here.
When my parents, who live here, have once recognized me,
They will take me by plea or by force:
If I know the truth, they will drag me to damnation.   205

"Yet my father longs for me,
So does my mother, more than any woman living,
And my wife, whom I left with them.
But I will not allow them to place me in their power;
They will not know me; they have not seen me for so long."   210

He left the ship and travelled straight to Rome;
He walked through the streets he had once known so well,
One, then another, until he met his father
And with him a great crowd of his men;
He recognized him, and called him by his name: 215

"Eufemian, noble lord, rich man,
Lodge me, in God's name, in your house:
Under your stairway made me a cot
For your son's sake, whom you mourn.
I am so weak; feed me for love of him."   220

When the father heard the mention of his son,
He wept, he could not help it.
"For the love of God and for my dear one,
I give you all, good man, that you ask of me,
Bed and shelter, bread, meat and wine."   225

"O God," he said, "I wish I had a servant
Who might watch over the man; I would set him free for it."
One came forward right away:
"Here I am," he said, "and will watch him as you command;
I will bear the burden for your sake."   230

Then straightway he led the man under the stair,
And made him a bed where he could rest;
He provided him with all he needed.
He did not want to fail his master:
In no way can he be blamed for that.   235

Often the father and mother saw him
And the maiden he had married:
They never realized it in any way;
He did not tell them, and they never asked him
Who he was or where he came from.   240

Often he saw them show their great sorrow
And saw their tears flow most pitifully,
And all for him, for no other reason.
Lord Alexis resigned himself to it;
It was nothing to him; so fully were his thoughts turned to God. 245

Under the stair where he lay on his mat,
He fed on leavings from the table.
In deepest poverty he passed his noble life:
He did not want his mother to know it;
He loved God more than all his parentage.   250

Of the food which came to him from the house
He kept enough to sustain his body:
If any was left, he gave it to the poor;
He kept no stores to fatten his body
But gave them to poorer men to eat.   255

Gladly he frequented the holy church;
Every holy day he made communion;
Holy scripture was his counselor:
He wished to press himself hard in God's service:
He did not want to turn from it at all.   260

Under the stairs where he lay and lived,
There he delighted in his poverty.
His father's servants who waited on the household
Threw their wash-water on his head;
And he did not get angry or reproach them for it.   265

They all mocked him and took him for a fool;
They threw water and wet his cot;
This holiest of men was not angry at all.
He only prayed to God that He forgive them,
By his mercy, for they knew not what they were doing.   270

He lived there ten and seven years this way.
No one in his family recognized him,
Nor were his sufferings known by anyone
Except the cot where he lay so long;
There he could not help its being apparent.   275

Thirty-four years he had put his flesh to this torment;
God wanted to reward his service:
He made his infirmities grow much heavier;
Now he knew well that he would soon leave this life:
He called his serving man to him: 280

"Find me, good brother, some ink and parchment
And a pen; I ask this of your kindness."
The man brought them and Alexis received them;
He wrote the whole letter in his own hand,
How he had gone away and returned.   285

He kept it close to him, not wanting to reveal it;
No one knew it till after he was gone;
He commended himself perfectly to God.
His end approached; his body was oppressed:
Little by little, he lost his speech.   290

During the week he was to leave this life,
A voice was heard three times in the city
Out of the sanctuary, by God's command,
Who summoned all His faithful to come:
The glory He wished to send them drew near.   295

By another voice He made another summons,
That they seek the Man of God who was in Rome,
And beg him to keep the city from falling in ruins
And the people living there from being destroyed:
Those who heard it were left in terror.   300

Saint Innocent was the Pope at that time.
Rich people and poor came to him
And asked him for advice about this thing
Which they had heard and which deeply troubled them:
They knew not at what hour the earth would engulf them.   305

The Pope and the Emperors,
One named Arcadius, the other Honorius,
And all the people in a common prayer
Prayed to God to give them His counsel
About this holy man by whom they might be saved.   310

They prayed to Him that by His mercy
He would show them where he could be found.
A voice was heard which said to them,
"Inquire in the house of Eufemian,
For there he is; there you will find him."   315

Everyone turned on Lord Eufemian;
Some began to curse him loudly:
"You should have told us this thing
And told all the people who were distressed.
You have sinned greatly in concealing it."   320

He excused himself as one who did not know,
But they did not believe him; they set out for his house.
He went ahead to prepare the household;
Eagerly he questioned all his men;
They answered that none of them knew about the matter.   325

The Pope and the Emperors
Sat on their benches, pensive and tearful.
All the other lords watched them there
And prayed to God to give them counsel
About the holy man by whom they would be saved.   330

Then, while they were sitting there,
The soul of Saint Alexis parted from his body:
It went straightway to paradise
And to his Lord whom he had served so long.
O King of Heaven, summon us all there!   335

The good man who had willingly served him
Brought word to his father Eufemian;
Softly he called him and told him:
"Lord," he said, "your beggar lies dead,
And I know he was a good Christian man.   340

"I lived with him for a long time:
I can find no fault with him for anything;
It seems to me that this is the Man of God."
All alone Eufemian turned
And went to his son where he lay under the stair.   345

He drew aside the sheets which covered him:
He saw the holy man's face, clear and lovely;
God's servant held the letter in his hand
Where he had written his whole story:
Eufemian wished to read what it said.   350

He tried to take it, but the man would not release it.
He returned to the Pope all amazed:
"I have found what we have sought so long;
Under my stairs lies a dead pilgrim;
He holds a letter, but I cannot take it from him."   355

The Pope and the Emperors
Came forward and threw themselves into prayer;
They put their bodies in great torment:
"Pity, pity, pity, most holy man!
We did not know you, nor do we know you yet.   360

"Here before you stand two sinners,
Called Emperors by the grace of God;
By His mercy we are so honored.
We are judges over all this world;
We have great need of your counsel.   365

"This Pope must rule over souls:
That is the office he must serve;
Give him the letter, by your mercy.
He will tell us what he finds written there,
And God grant that it may heal us."   370

The Pope reached out toward the letter;
Saint Alexis' hand opened
And gave it to him who was Pope of Rome.
He did not read it or look inside:
First he gave it to a good, wise clerk.   375

The Chancellor, whose office it was,
Read the letter; the others listened.
Of that holy jewel which they had found there
He revealed the name, and those of his father and mother;
Thus they were told who his parents were.   380

He read them how he had fled by sea,
And gone to the city of Edessa,
How God had made the image speak for him,
And how, from the honors with which they would burden him,
He had fled back to the city of Rome.   385

When the father heard what the letter said,
He tore his white beard with both hands:
"Ah! My son," he said, "what sorrowful news!
I hoped you would return home to me,
By God's mercy, to be of comfort to me."   390

In a loud voice the father began to cry:
"Alexis, son, what sorrow has come to me!
I kept a poor watch on you under my stair.
Alas, I have been wretched and blind,
So often to see you and not to know it!   395

"Alexis, son, your sorrowing mother!
She has endured so much grief for you,
And so many hungers and privations,
And shed so many tears for your body!
This grief will be enough to break her heart.   400

"O son, who will have my large inheritance,
And all the wide lands I hold,
And my great palace in Rome the city?
And for you, my son, I have labored:
You would have been honored after my death.   405

"White is my hair, and my beard is gray.
I kept my noble rank
For you, but you did not care for it;
Such great grief has come upon me!
Son, may heaven forgive your soul for this.   410

"You should have worn the helmet and the breast-plate,
And girded on a sword as your peers have done:
You should have governed a great household,
And carried the banners of the Emperor
As your father did, and your ancestors.   415

"In such misery and such deep poverty
You lived, my son, and in strange countries!
And why, of the fortune which was to be yours,
Took you so little in your poor lodging?
Had it pleased God, you would have been its master."   420

The lamentations of the father
Made a loud noise, so the mother heard;
She came running out like a woman demented,
Beating her hands together, crying, dissheveled;
She saw her son dead, and fell on the ground, senseless.   425

Then whoever saw her make her lamentations,
Beating her breast, casting her body down,
Tearing her hair, gouging at her face,
Kissing and embracing her dead son,
Would have been a hard man had he not wept.   430

She tore her hair and struck her breast,
And put her own flesh in great pain:
"Ah, son," she said, "You must have hated me!
And I, so sorrowful, must have been blinded!
As often as I saw you I did not know you."   435

Her tears flowed down, and she uttered loud cries,
Mourning endlessly: "Dear son, I bore you for my woe!
Why did you nave no mercy on your mother?
Why did you see me wish for my own death?
It is a great wonder you did not feel pity.   440

"Woe! Alas! What a wretched fate for a mother!
Here I see my offspring dead.
My long wait has ended in great grief.
Why did I bear you, grieving, unfortunate?
It is a great wonder that my heart endures so long!   445

"Son Alexis, your heart was very hard
When you scorned your whole noble family!
If once you had spoken to me alone,
Your unfortunate mother, you would have comforted her
Who grieves so. Dear son, it would have been well done.   450

"Oh your tender flesh, son Alexis!
In what misery you spent your youth!
Why did you flee from me? I carried you in my womb;
And God knows how sorrowful I am:
Not for man of woman will I have joy again.   455

"Before I saw you I longed for you;
Before you were born I felt such anxiety;
When first I saw you born, I was happy and joyous;
Now I see you dead, and I am so sorrowful.
It grieves me that my death is so long in coming.   460

"Lords of Rome, mercy, for the love of God!
Help me to mourn the loss of my loved one;
Great is the woe which has come to me;
I can do nothing to solace my heart:
No wonder! I have no other son or daughter."   465

In the midst of the father's and mother's mourning
The maiden came whom he had married:
"My lord," she said, "You stayed away so long!
I waited in your father's house
Where you left me sorrowful and lost.   470

"Lord Alexis, I wished for you so long,
And shed so many tears for your body,
And so often watched for you afar off;
If you had returned to solace your bride
It would have been no shame or laxness.   475

"Alas, dear friend, for your lovely youth!
It grieves me that it will rot in the ground.
Ah! Noble one, how wretched can I be!
I waited for good news of you,
But instead I receive such hard, cruel tidings.   480

"O lovely mouth, lovely face, lovely body,
How changed is your lovely form!
I loved you more than any creature.
Such great sorrow has come upon me!
My friend, it would be better that I were dead.   485

"If I had known you were there under the stair,
Where you lay in your long illness,
No one could have dissuaded me
From living there beside you:
Had you allowed it, I would have cared for you.   490

"Now I am a widow, " said the maiden,
"Never more will I have joy, for that cannot be,
Nor will I have another man on this earth.
I will serve God, the King who governs all:
He will not fail me, when He sees me serving Him."   495

They wept so long, the father, the mother
And the maiden, that the people grew weary of it;
Meantime the holy body was prepared
By all the lords there; they clothed it beautifully:
How fortunate were the faithful who honored him!   500

"Lords, what are you doing?" said the Pope.
"What good are these cries, this grief and this noise?
To you it may be a grief, but to us it is a joy,
For in this man we have a good advocate:
Let us pray that he take away all our woes."   505

Those who could come took him up;
Singing, they bore the body of Saint Alexis,
And prayed to him that he have mercy on them.
Those who had heard the news needed no summons;
All came running, the great and the humble.   510

All the people of Rome were so moved,
Those who could run fastest were first to come.
Such a great crowd filled the streets
That neither king nor count could find a path through them,
Nor could they pass with the holy body.   515

The lords began to confer among themselves:
"The crowd is large; we cannot pass through.
Because of this holy body God has given us
The people are happy who have longed for him:
Everyone runs to him; no one wants to turn away."   520

The rulers of the empire answered them:
"Mercy, lords! We will seek a remedy:
Let us make a great distribution of our holdings
To the poor, who desire alms:
Though they crowd us, we will be free of them."   525

From their treasuries they took gold and silver,
And had it cast before the poor folk;
They thought their way would be disencumbered,
But it was not to be, for they wanted none of it:
All their desires were turned on the holy man.   530

With one voice the humble people cried:
"We care nothing at all for these offerings.
Such great joy has come to us
Because of this holy body we have in our keeping;
From him, God willing, we will have good help."   535

Never was there such happiness in Rome
As on that day for the rich and the poor
Because of the holy body which they had in their keeping;
It seemed to them that they held God Himself;
All the people praised God and gave thanks.   540

Saint Alexis had a good will:
For that he is still honored on that day.
His body lies in Rome the city,
And his soul has entered God's paradise:
Truly happy is he who dwells there.   545

He who has sinned may will remember this:
He can save himself by penitence.
This life is brief: look for a more lasting one.
Let us pray to God, the holy trinity,
That we may reign with God in paradise.   550

No deaf nor blind nor lame nor leprous man,
No mute nor unclean nor paralytic,
No a single sufferer,
Of all those who came sick
None carried his old pain away.   555

No one sick with any illness,
When he called upon him, was not cured.
Some came and some were carried there;
God showed them such true miracles,
Those who came weeping, went away singing.   560

The two lords who ruled the empire,
When they saw his powers so revealed,
Received him, wept for him, and honored him:
By prayers and especially by their great power
They went ahead, and broke through the crowd.   565

Saint Boniface, whom men call martyr,
Had a most beautiful church in Rome:
There they carried Saint Alexis,
And gently they set him on the ground;
Happy the place where the holy body dwells.   570

The people of Rome who had so long desired him
Kept him above ground for seven days in majesty.
There's no need to ask if the crowd was great;
From everywhere they so thronged around him
That it seemed no man could come near.   575

On the seventh day the resting place was made
For the holy man, for the heavenly jewel;
They pulled themselves away, the crowd cleared:
Willing or not, they let him be laid in the earth;
It grieved them, but it could not be prevented.   580

With censors and with golden candelabras,
Priests dressed in tunics and in mantles
Laid the body in a marble tomb.
Some were singing, most shed tears:
Never, of their own will, would they have left him.   585

The tomb was adorned with gold and jewels
For the holy body they must place in it;
Laboriously they set him in the ground.
The people of Rome the city wept:
No one under heaven could prevent it.   590

There's no need to speak of the father and mother
And bride, how they mourned;
Everyone's voice was so attuned
That all wept for him; all grieved for him:
A hundred thousand tears were shed that day.   595

They could no longer keep him above the ground:
Willing or not, they let him be buried;
They took leave of Saint Alexis' body
And prayed that he have mercy on them,
That he might plead for them before his Lord.   600

The people went away. The father and mother
And the maiden never parted;
They lived together until they returned to God.
Their company was good, and honorable:
By the holy man their souls were saved.   605

Saint Alexis is in heaven without a doubt
With God and the company of angels,
And with the maiden from whom he had been estranged;
He has her with him; their souls are together;
I cannot tell you how great is their happiness!   610

What good labors, O God, and what good sevice
Were done by the holy man in his mortal life!
For now his soul is replete with glory:
He has his desire, no less than that;
Above all, he looks on God Himself.   615

Alas! Wretched ones! How we are blinded!
We see how far we go astray.
We are so encumbered by our sins,
That we forget the right path completely;
Through this holy man may we recover our sight.   620

Let us hold, lords, this holy man in memory,
And pray that he take away all our ills
That, in this world, he find us peace and joy
And, in that other world, the most lasting glory!
So let us say, according to the Word, "Our Father."   625
                              AMEN.

The Life of Saint Mary the Egyptian

La Vie de Sainte Marie l'Egyptienne, from the second half of the twelfth century, dramatizes sexuality and repentance in a poetic form that is essentially that of courtly romance. The immensely popular legend that it presents contributed to the growing cult of the Virgin Mary and inspired the thirteenth-century elaboration of the legend of Mary Magdalene.

For the love of Jesus Christ, my Lords, listen to me for a little while, and then I will relate to you this story. You will find great profit in it since all of it is made from the truth—not a false word in it. Well do I believe that all those who wish to serve God will hear it gladly, though to those who pay no heed to Him his word is bitter and hard. All those who would hear this truth for the love of God, will hear the Life of St. Mary the Egyptian.

All sinners, who have transgressed against the Creator, know—that no sin is so heavy or so horrible or so great that God would not pardon it through faith and through confession; thus those who do penance rid themselves of misdeeds. When one abandons the mercy of God, this sin will never be pardoned because sin is definitely not a creation, but rather less than is in nature. God never created sin and nevertheless it has its place: in all men it has its house and makes them do evil. There is no man in this life but has his faults. The apolstles who served God often fell into sin. Because of this it does not surprise me when I see an unfortunate man sin, but there is a great marvel about the man who always sleeps and never rouses himself, and so remains in his sins until he feels death. When death comes and he feels it, then he says for the first time, "I repent". According to St. Augustine this is not at all a good end. When the wretch feels death, he can do neither right nor wrong; he abandons his iniquity when he no longer has power over himself. At the time when he still had health and life he acted foolishly. When his power for choice has left him, who can help him then? No one save only the God who had created him—but whatever he has done on earth he will now find again.

This woman about whom I wish to speak I have heard named Mary the Egyptian, called this because she was born in Egypt. She was born and baptized there, but became immoral and, in a word, promiscuous. She lost her honor and all sense of shame, and was so enflamed with debauchery that she had no care for anything else.

Because she was very comely and beautiful, she trusted in her youth
and did everything according to her pleasure, with no thought of
death. She took no heed of her two parents, but abandoned herself
to every man. There was no woman of such great lechery in this life,
certainly. Her father and mother lived for little save to be wounded
by grief. They wanted to bring her to rights, but she accepted not a
farthing of all that—she heeded warnings from her parents no more
than the murmuring of the wind.

"Daughter," so spoke her mother, "listen to the counsel of
your father. If you maintain this course for long we will have a
terrible reputation. In the name of God, Mary, stop this playing
around now. When you have thrown off this habit, we will give you
richly in marriage. It is not right that you should perish through the
lack of our help. Daughter, you are of grand parentage; it would be a
great pity if you should perish here because of your terrible vice.
Your father is enraged over your conduct (he will never be happy a
day in his life) and he curses his fate, that ever he sired such a child."

When Mary heard this, she was very annoyed, and had nothing
but scorn for all her mother said to her. Neither father nor mother
did she value a farthingworth. The better to carry out her desires, she
fled into another realm, abandoned her parents completely, and
never did they see her again. She stole away like a thief, without the
knowledge of father or mother. Mary took to the road, never asking
for any companion.

She arrived in Alexandria. At the head of the main street she
took lodging with the whores, and there she sold her body. She was
as white as a flower; she had the love of the young men, and they all
came to the bordello, possessed with passion for her. She received
them willingly. She had them with her all night long, not at all for
money, but for her own pleasure. Drinking, eating, and debauchery—
those were the sum total of her cares. Every hour the wretch was
attentive in her own delight. When she arose from eating she went off
to play with the boys. She loved her perversity so much, that her
only other thought was for fine clothes.

All the crowd was so taken with their passion for the girl that in
front of her house, in the entryway, they often fought. They dealt
each other great blows with pikes and swords; the blood that was
spilled there ran down the gutters. The wretch who saw this never
worried or feared: if one of her lovers died, she had four more to
make up for him. She saw all of those killed, yet never showed any
feeling. Those who were wounded because of her, by her were never
visited. She preferred to play with the healthy, rather than attend the
sick.

Mary was in Alexandria, where she led a wild, unruly life. The
wretch satisfied her lust for many days and years. The city was made
the worse by her presence, so was it led astray because of her—and
the countryside all around was in great jeopardy. I want to tell about
her beauty and her aspect briefly, as it is written down, before I go

any further. At that time there was no other woman quite so beautiful as she, for she was the pearl prized above all. Never did any
Countess or Queen have such a fine head of hair. She had round ears,
which were of a marvellous white. Her eyebrows were black and
comely, and her eyes clear and smiling. Her mouth was small, of
fitting proportion. Her face was tender and blushing, like the new
born rose; no defect at all could be perceived in either her nose or
chin. Above her neck, which was white like ermine, her blond hair
tumbled down in waves. The girl's breasts were no larger than apples.
There below her neck her bosom was white like the hawthorn flower.
Long arms she had, and white hands, round fingers, thin and even.
She had a beautiful, well-molded body, with sleek curves below her
shoulders, neither too large nor too small. The way she was will
never be described, nor her bearty written down well enough by any
man. She was so courteous of speech that she could not have been
better. It is to be lamented when such a creature pays no heed to her
Creator.

She received a great number of presents, and bought herself
clothes with them. She had becoming and beautiful dresses the better
to be pleasing to her lovers. She never needed to wear simple wool
any day of the week. Rather, she dressed in costly shawls and ermine
stoles. She wore well-colored shoes of Spanish leather all the days of
the year.

All those in the city loved her greatly for her beauty. The older
men and the wise said: "Alas, that she was ever born, how she wastes
her youth! Her whole life is a misfortune filled with such madness."
Everyone throughout the city was saying that she must be of noble
family, for she replied to everyone with reason, and she was so
beautiful to see that the son of an emperor could marry her with
great honor.

It was in May, a summer month, that she was at the city wall,
and was looking down toward the port area where she often went for
amusement. She saw a galley arrive that had come from Libya. It
was full of pilgrims, of older folk and young men who were going to
Jerusalem. In good faith they were making haste to be there at the
time of the feast of the Holy Cross which was soon to take place.
The most lively of these jumped down from the boat onto the beach,
and the young people walked hand in hand, laughing and sporting
along the river. When Mary saw them she could not help smiling. She
saw a man standing near them, and began to ask him questions:

"Sir," she said, "tell me, for the love of Christ I pray you,
where are these good people going, who have come out here from the
galley? May I go with them? I have no wish to remain here any
longer; I would go with them, that is my desire. I have been here too
long."

The gentleman answered her in this manner: "They are
travelling to Jerusalem. If you have anything to give them, well could
you go along."

"For God's sake, sir," said the poor girl, "I have beauty and youth; I will put my body at their disposal. I can make no other payment, nor give them any other compensation, for I do not have even a single penny."

When the gentleman heard this madness he could not help laughing. When he had heard this offer he left her, laughing as he went. The girl then turned away. She did not return to her house, but went down along the riverside at a great pace, as her adventure led her. She did not stop until she came to the ship where the gentleman stood, but spoke first to those who were playing on the beach. She spoke to them briefly enough, as sensibly as she could:

"Kind sirs," said she, "pilgrims, may God grant you a good end, and may He inspire you to be charitable with me. I am a poor woman here, and was born in another country. In the land of Egypt was I born, but I am stranded in this country. I have no parents or friends, so I live very poorly. I have no gold or silver with me; you can see before you all my treasure. I have no other possessions. But I prize your company greatly. If I may come aboard ship with you, very willingly would I serve you. I would like to go with you so much, if only you would take me. You won't arrive any the later for taking a poor woman with you." The youths answered, "Come along. It is all very well with us."

They had her come up aboard the boat, and soon after they weighed anchor. Quickly they left the shore, and the seamen rowed until they were on the high sea. At sea, they sailed all night by the stars. But they had no sleep; Mary kept them from it. First she began to caress them, then to embrace them, after embracing them to kiss them and to please them in every way. There was no one so quarrelsome be he a young man or an old husband, who could take respite until he had sinned with her that night. She was so accomplished in her skill that each one lay in sin with her. When she saw the high waves, marvelous and deep, and saw a great wind approaching, which brought with it a tremendous storm, her demeanor remained very happy; she feared her sins not at all. She comforted all the fearful and cajoled them to love. So much was she taken with lechery that she was in her shirt the whole night. She went that night through all the beds in order to satisfy their delight, and they embraced her willingly and fulfilled their desires. It was a marvel that one woman alone could serve such a great crowd; but there can be no doubt that the devil was with her, and would gladly have drowned her, if our Lord had let him. But He kept her safe from death, and then made the ship arrive in port.

When Mary landed she was sad and left to herself. She sighed and wept at the river's edge, not knowing what to do. She knew neither any man nor any woman there, and the country seemed very strange to her. Finally, she decided that she would go into the city and would keep to her same way of life. She had no desire to amend her ways.

She entered Jerusalem. Now you will hear about this unfortunate who did not delay at all in sinning; she began at once to become worse. Lord, what a great perdition! By the time if the Ascension of the Holy Cross, which is to be honored, she had so defiled the place that it would have been better for her to be burned in flames; for she deceived the youth with her beauty and charm, and the young men of the city were quite captivated.

It was only a little time thereafter that the great feast came, the high day of the Ascension, with the procession of pilgrims who have come from over the sea to hear mass at the cathedral. The pilgrims went to the cathedral in good faith, as wise men and honorable. When Mary saw them she quickly joined the company, went along with the procession, but not at all out of good intention. The pilgrims who saw her did not know in the least what she wanted to do, but if they had known about her life, she would never have had their company. They walked up the steps and entered the cathedral. The group entered, but by no means could Mary get in. When she wanted to proceed, she was forced to turn back. She put herself within the press of the crowd, but to no avail. It appeared to her fancy that she saw a great army, all of whom seemed to be knights. They had very fierce expressions on their faces, and each one brandished his sword at her, threatening her from the entry-way. When she wanted to go forward, the blades made her stand away.

When she saw that by no means could she enter, she turned away into a corner. Then she began to think about why it was that she was not able to enter. Finally she saw it, and understood that her sin was preventing her. She began to sigh from the heart and to weep bitterly. With her two hands she tore her hair. She beat her breast. She knew well that God was angry with her, and she dared not cry out for mercy.

"Alas, sinner that I am," she said, "I have been a harlot, I have committed shameful sins, for which God is angry with me. I have had evil counsel the whole time, when now I have lost my Creator. I am so full of vile filthiness, of evil and debauchery, that I cannot enter the cathedral, nor call the Lord God my father. What shall I do, miserable wretch? It's a grievous thing that I am even alive."

From her heart came heavy sighs: she would rather die than live henceforth. She looked to her right, and saw a statue of the Virgin Mary which had been carved into a niche. Very humbly she called out to it.

"Lady," she said, "kind mother, you who carried your father in your womb: holy Gabriel brought the message, and you answered him wisely when he said to you 'Hail Mary, full of grace, in you the Son of the Most High will take human form!' When he had spoken you answered, and called yourself the hand-maiden of the Lord; because of this you are now the queen of Heaven. From you alone do I seek my health; for my mortal wounds I seek no other cure. My Lady, only intercede for me with your Son and my wounds will be healed.

"Here I abandon the evil life; never more will I have companionship there. I put my faith in your Son. I give you my pledge and my faith, that for all time to come I will serve Him. Never will I leave Him. I give up this life totally, and all my horrible debauchery. There will never be a day when I do not feel the weight of it, and bitter will be my penance. Mother of pity, I well believe that there was never anything so hard or so difficult to pardon that, if ever you would ask it of your Son, He would not grant the pardon for your sake. Lady, have mercy on me now.

"I do believe that your Son was present at your birth: He placed in you virginity, and then engendered His godhead in you. It is a great miracle, the Father who created His mother from His daughter. From you He took humanity; you never lost virginity. He is your Son, and still your Father. You are His daughter, and yet you are His mother. That was a marvelous thing when from the thorn there grew the rose, and from the rose there grew the fruit by which the devil was destroyed.

"We have one name, *Mary,* but our lives are much different. You loved chastity at all times, and I lechery and evil. You had the devil as an enemy, and I served him always. Never was born in any kingdom a woman of your humility; I am poor and arrogant and lustful in my body. Our Lord loved you, and me, wretch, He refused; He refused me and He loved you. Lady, have mercy on me now.

"Lady, you carried the treasure that is worth more than silver or gold; from you the Son of the King took flesh, he whom St. John announced, 'Behold,' said he, 'the Lamb of God, who will take away the sins of the world.' But when the enemy saw this, he who threw us from paradise, that He would save the world, right away he thought to trick him as he had the first man, whom he had deceived by means of an apple. The thief tried three times, but he accomplished nothing. However, when he saw Him armed so powerfully, he contrived a death for Him by treason. Happy was the death from which life was recovered. If the Son of God had not been killed, then man would never enter paradise. Through death He found the power by which the devil was conquered. The murdered vanquished the murderer, and put him completely to shame; he broke down the gates of Hell, smashed the walls and set free the company which the devil had carried off. He led them to His Father, to the glory there where he was, and then miraculously returned to His body. He appeared to His apostles and was with them for forty days. He showed them the new law, and then kissed each one. He commended His gentle mother to them and then rose up to His Father in Heaven. From heaven he sent them such comfort that none of them feared death any longer. He sent them the Holy Spirit, who taught them all languages. Now He sits at the right hand of the Father, and you are with Him, His gentle mother. When it comes to the Judgment Day, to the time of His Second Coming, you will be in company with Him as His dear friend. He will judge both living and dead; the good will go into paradise, the bad into eternal fire where the devil will punish them. Virgin and crowned Queen, you who are so blessed, who carried in your womb the One whom the world cannot comprehend, as I believe and say, have mercy on me now."

At the end of her prayer Christ granted her pardon. Mary rose from her prayer confiding in her new Lord; she put all her faith in Him. She entered the cathedral without fear, went inside completely without hindrance, and then proceeded to hear the offices of God. With a marvelous fear she worshipped the Cross of the Saviour. When she had seen it she was inspired by the Lord in all her being.

When she had heard all of the divine office she then went outside of the church. Reflecting with good intentions, she went straight back to the statue: in Her she had all her faith, and sought from her wise counsel about what she should do and into what land she should go. There came a voice which she heard, speaking to her clearly: "Go from here to the monastery of Saint John, then go across the river Jordan. At this monastery you will take communion, then you will go into the wasteland where you will atone for your sins for all the days that you will live."

When she had heard the voice she made the sign of the cross and speedily set herself on the road. Before her she saw a pilgrim. He gave her three pence, with which she bought three small loaves. These made up all her sustenance during the time of her penance. Mary came to the river Jordan. She stopped that night close by the monastery of Saint John, on the bank of the Jordan. She lodged herself there without any shelter. She ate half of one of her loaves and drank from the holy water. She was much happier once she had drunk of it. As she washed her face in the pure water, she became cleansed of all her sins. She felt a little tired, for she had made a great journey, and made her bed on the hard earth. All night she lay there and slept, but only a little, for the hard bed kept her awake.

In the morning she went to the cloister to hear the service of the Lord, and she received Him with great love. When she had taken communion, she was indeed very happy; then she got into a little boat and passed over the river Jordan. When she had crossed over she went into the forest.

Mary went on through the wasteland. Often she prayed to the queen, from whom she had taken surety the preceding day before the statue, that through her mercy she would not abandon her, and would defend her from the devil. Therein did she place her faith.

She now began her penance. With no regrets, she would finally give herself up to death. She had only two and a half loaves of bread; now may Christ have mercy on her! She will not live very long on these if God does not grant her other aid. She went on through the wastes with great speed. She confided God, and was completely sure. When she had made each day's journey she leaned up against a tree, ate a little of her bread, and then slept until the next day. She arose very early in the morning, and set her face toward the east.

She went on so, both day and night, with hunger, thirst, and with hard beds. She stayed so deep within the forest that she became completely wild; but she never ever forgot to pray to the Virgin Mary. Often she remembered the statue from which she had taken her surety.

As time went on her clothing all wore out, and her shoes fell apart at the seams. When her clothes were ruined her body was left completely nude. Her flesh, which had been as white as any flower, changed color over the winters and summers. Her sides became completely black. Her hair changed and became as white as ermine. Her face was so burned by the sun and the cold that her mouth became pinched and blackened all around. She had a forehead so black that it was just like the charred end of a fire-brand. Her eyes grew squinty, dulled over; now she had no pride in them. If you saw her ears you would be greatly amazed, because they were black and deformed, and all shaggy with white hair. Her bosom was black and hairy, like thorny bark; she had no more flesh in her breasts than there is in a glove. Her arms, hands, and long fingers were blacker than any pitch. She had very long nails, which she cut with her teeth. Her stomach completely caved in, for she hardly ever ate. Her feet were torn, wounded in many places, because she did not watch for thorns as she walked through the forest; she thought and ever believed that one of her sins fell away whenever she suffered such a wound.

It is no wonder that she grew black, for she led a very bitter life. For more than forty years she went naked; it is no wonder that she grew shaggy. Few provisions had she with her—may Jesus have mercy on her now. She had two loaves of bread, hardly very large, upon which she lived for many years. Right from the first they became hard, as if they were made of stone. Each day Mary used up some of it, although only a little. When she had eaten all her bread, then she pulled up meadow herbs and ate them, like any wild animal. She was not discouraged by anything. She drank from the inside of a reed; she had no other vessel. How pitiful the sin for which her body was so chastised!

She lived on herbs and roots for eighteen years in the wasteland. Then for thirty years she did not eat at all unless an angel of God brought her something. The devil came to put her to the test; he tempted her. He made her recall all she had once loved, and the good dinners and the places where she was once wont to go for amusement. She felt happy then that it was all behind her. Never again in all her life did she recall her folly. Not once in all the forest did she ever see any wild beast, or any other living creature. She travelled through the forest completely safely, taking her rest in many places. Her life was completely spiritual.

Now let us leave Mary here, and let us speak of an abbey that was at the edge of the forest, just as the story tells it. Never did God make any men who served their Creator, as devotedly as did these.

They had no thought of evil, each one wore his hair shirt, and had no interest save only in bitter discipline. They wore hair shirts and went barefoot in order to expiate their sins. Neither during the day nor during the night were they ever found in bed; all day long they were in the church, excepting only at mealtimes. They lived very poorly, on barely bread and vegetables. On all the Fridays of the year they ate only walnuts and acorns. They drank brackish water because there was no spring there. Among them was no simony, nor any greed or envy. They had no desire for silver or gold, for in God they had their treasure. No one among them held any property; they were all of a common will. They led such a blessed life that there is no man who can tell you anything to their shame.

Whenever it came to the first day of the Lenten Season the abbot assembled them and gave them the Body of Christ. When he had given them communion he washed their feet for them one by one. After which they went to prayer and he gave them a sermon. He enjoined them to embrace one another, and then opened the portals of the church to send them out into the forest, commending them to the Lord God. The blessed monks departed, save only two who remained behind. It was not for fear of thieves that they might have at their house, but it was in order to perform the offices of the Lord that the two stayed in the church. For it is not right that the duties of the Lord be left undone in the holy church.

All of the others went out. Many then lived on fruit exclusively; for their great love of God they existed on herbs. When one monk saw another in the desert, quickly did he flee from the spot where the other stood. Each wandered in hiding, and one monk was not saluted by another. Each one rested wherever night found him, stretching out on the cold fields. On the next morning each got up and crossed himself with his right hand. He did not know where he would go, but commended himself to God. All of his companions had this same intention. They wept tenderly from the eyes when they remembered the Day of Doom, when all the angels will tremble with the great fear they will have; where they will see the Son of God in the throne of majesty, and before Him the eternal fire in which He will torment the devil and all the evil men whom He will torture in like manner; and then those will descend to Hell who will never leave it. For this reason the monks were in the forest in such hardship; in order to escape such great pain they remained in this exile.

When the forty days were passed, and it came to the day of the Last Supper, the time of the Easter lilies, they all repaired to the abbey. The blessed abbot was very happy when he saw them all come back. He had them enter the monastery, and closed the doors after them. Then they spent the entire year attending to the offices of the Lord.

There happened one year that they all went out according to custom. The abbot called each one in turn; first he had them embrace each other, then he opened the portals of the monastery;

and sent them out into the forest, commending each one to God.

One of their number who was of very blessed life, took the right hand direction. He was called Master Zosimas. He was dressed in very poor clothing, but he loved his poverty better than any count loved his great county. He travelled deep into the forest with such poor furnishings as he had. He hoped to find hermits there, with whom he wanted to talk about God. But when he had travelled twenty days, all of which were extremely long, and saw that he could fine no one, he had not the heart to go further. Around mid-day he began his prayer. He called out to God and beseeched him, and when he had finished his prayer he turned to his right and looked toward the east.

He thought he saw there a shadow which was either of a man or of a woman.

Lo, it was the shadow of the Egyptian; God had led her there. He no longer wished for her to be hidden: it was His purpose to reveal the treasure that was more precious than gold.

The saintly man was very frightened when he turned his head toward the shadow. He thought that it was an enchantment, and called out to God omnipotent to protect him from the Fiend and from evil temptation. When he had finished his prayer he saw the figure of Mary. He saw the outline of Mary, clearly without any covering. Around her was her hair, as white as ermine. The white and tattered hair fell down to her feet, and she had no other clothing. When the breeze lifted it up, flesh burned by the sun and cold appeared beneath. When Zosimas saw the figure he went towards it with great speed. When she saw him coming, the woman quickly began to flee. The holy man chased her, calling out to her as he went:

"Lady," he said, "if you have any faith in God, speak to me. I beseech you in the name of God to go no further."

When the woman heard him speak of God she began to weep for joy:

"Lord," she said, "I believe in you the Creator, and I worship you. For forty six years I have heard no word spoken of you. Now you have sent a holy man to me. I do not dare turn my face to him. I dare not show myself to him because I am a naked creature."

The lady stopped at this point; she did not dare go forward. She did not want to hide any longer. She began to speak to the old man:

"You sir!" she said, "Zosimas, throw me one of your cloaks. I dare not turn toward you for shame. Afterwards you may speak with me."

When Zosimas heard his name he knew well that God had made her speak, for she would not have known him if not by means of the Holy Spirit. He then threw her a cloak, and the lady approached; she ran to the cloak and covered part of her body with it. When she was dressed she turned toward the holy man.

"Sir," she said, "dear gentle friend, tell me what you seek here. You can see before you a poor woman who weeps and laments in this wasteland, for her sins and evil deeds. They are so horrible and ugly that there is no man who, if he knew of them, would not be agrieved. Now I am doing penance here."

When the holy man heard her say these things he began to weep for pity. He threw himself at her feet, and sought her blessing. The lady in turn fell down at his feet, for she feared greatly her sins; she called out repeatedly for mercy from him, then he in turn called out to her. Zosimas, who lay prostrate in the place, with great sighs and great sorrow wept very tenderly; from his eyes a stream of tears ran down his face. He suffered such anguish that the sweat ran down his white beard. Out of love the lady wanted him to say a prayer for the people and to give her his blessing.

"Sir," she said, "dear friend, you have requested a blessing of me. I do not understand what the reason may be that I should give you a blessing. You are a priest, one who sings masses; for this reason it is more fitting that you now give one to me rather than I to you. For God looks upon you so well that you have leave to sing mass. Anything at all would be well sanctified if it had the sign of the cross made over it by your hand. I do believe that when you give the sign, God works a miracle upon the altar in that bread becomes His body and wine the blood which sprang forth from it.

"God well knows your sacrifice; He has taught me all about your life. You have served him from infancy; you are able to have great faith in Him; you will have from Him a great reward. But now I beg of you a blessing."

"My lady," so answered Zosimas, "you will never have my blessing if first you do not grant yours to me. I will not rise from here, neither for hunger nor for any other suffering, until you grant it to me."

Then Mary saw well and understood that the holy man would never rise and would be in prayer for all time to come, if he did not receive her blessing. She turned toward the east and prayed to God omnipotent:

"God," said she, "gentle Creator, I praise you and adore you. Lord, may you be honored, in all your power. May you grant us pardon from our sins, and then may we have your blessing."

Master Zosimas then arose, sighing, for he was weary; but Mary comforted him. They often gazed at each other. She began to sigh, and then began to ask him about kings, about the courts of the land; if they had peace or if there was war; and about the shepherds that maintained the law, and how they kept themselves. Zosimas answered her in this way:

"God has made peace throughout the world. There is no man who may go so far in the land that he may hear any word of war. But the Holy Church is in dire need of your prayers, so may God grant it eternal peace and defend it from the devil."

Mary responded this to him: "May God keep it in His mercy," and turned toward the east, raised up her hands, and stretched them

toward the sky. She prayed to God, her Creator, devotedly in great
love, her mouth moving but no voice coming out. Immediately she
was taken up from the ground; she did not touch it at all. Zosimas
was greatly afraid, for God held her up thus safely. There were two
and a half feet between her and the ground, while she made her
prayer. Indeed, the Lord held her dear.

From the fright that he had Zosimas began to run away apace;
he thought he had discovered a phantom. When Mary saw him flee
she called to him gently:

"Now, Zosimas!" said she, "dear good father, what are you
afraid of? Why do you run from a woman? Don't worry, I am a
Christian! I was baptized as a child, and I have all my faith in God.
He is my love and my desire. I will serve him until I die."

She raised up her right hand and made the sign of the cross
upon her forehead. The holy hermit saw this clearly, and fell at the
feet of the lady. She made him arise immediately. He began to weep:

"Mercy," he said, "most saintly lady, where do you come from,
and from what kingdom? Reveal your life to me. In the name of God
do not hide it: tell it to me in confession so that God may grant you
true pardon."

"Sir," answered Mary, "I will not conceal anything from you.
Since you have seen me here naked, I will not hide my life from you.
To you I will uncover it all."

Now Mary began to tell her story. She held nothing back, but
recounted all her life from the hour she was born. You can imagine
her shame in the telling, and when she had finished she fell to his feet
and begged mercy of him. Zosimas heard her life, and glorified his
Creator for it. He gave thanks to the Creator, and then said to her
with great love:

"My lady, why do you fall at my feet? In the name of God I
pray you, stop this, I am not worthy, nor do I hold any such
authority. Having heard your tale, I scarcely dare raise my eyes to
look at you. Never have I seen your peer. Lady, have mercy on me
now. In charity tell if I may remain here with you."

"No, good father Zosimas," answered Mary, "rather you will go
from here. But do no venture to speak of my life until it shall be
finished. Although God has revealed me to you, by you I would like
to be hidden. You will speak to the abbot John; you will give him
this message: that he should take care of his flock, for there are those
that are too sure of themselves, and he should take care to watch out
for them for there is much to be amended. But when this time
comes next year, you will fall ill, I perceive. When your companions
go forth from their house, as the days of Lent arrive (each one on his
way), you will have to take to your bed. Not at all will you be able
to go out with them. When the day of the Lord's Supper comes, and
the forty days will have passed, you will be cured. Then, I pray you
may come to me. Bring me the Body of our Lord in a vessel, (let it
be very clean). Bring the Holy Blood in another vessel, but take care

that it be a beautiful one. Good father, when you bring it, you will find me very near to you. For you sake I will approach; when I see you I will be very happy. You will find me next year across from you at the river Jordan, for I will wish to take communion. Since I crossed the Jordan River near the house of Saint John, I have not received the Body of my Lord, with whom is all my joy; nor have I seen any man save only you. I must go now. Pray for me."

She turned from him onto a path and entered the great desert.

When the holy man saw her go away, he could hardly stand still; he followed her into the desert with his eyes; greatly sorry to lose her. He knelt down on the earth at the place where she had stood and kissed the ground often and often. Then he praised omnipotent God:

"Lord," he said, "praise be to you who have shown me such great virtue. May I thank you Lord, for allowing me to find her."

Then he remembered his monastery, from which he had originally come. He repaired then to the house, he and all his companions.

The abbot John was very happy to see everyone returned; but each of them was quite silent about what he had seen. No one needed to talk of it, for they would not want to boast of anything. The abbot John cherished them greatly. Now when the year had passed, the first day of Lent came, and each one went his way, but Zosimas lay ill in his bed, and did not go. He had to rest at the house, for he was taken sick and could not venture out. He knew well that this was the prophecy that he had heard from Mary.

The forty days all passed, and when the Thursday of the last Supper came Zosimas felt himself cured. He had obtained the Body of Christ, and likewise the precious blood, to fulfill the request that the lady had made of him when she took her leave. Zosimas set out on his journey; he took with him some peas and lentils, and did not worry about provision.

Zosimas came to the river Jordan. When he arrived there the evening was quite well along. He thought he would find Mary, but she was not there yet at all. He feared that what he most desired to see, would be taken from him because of his sins; or else that she had already been there and, because he had delayed too long, had become tired of waiting and had gone back for that reason.

"God of Majesty," said he, "do not leave me here abandoned. Let me see again the woman who has no peer in all the realm. May I live no longer, if I may not see her again, if she does not come to speak to me. But how will I be able to cross to her, to pass over the river Jordan, when I have here neither boat nor barge? Father of every creature, may you find the way. So great is your power that everything works according to your will."

When he had finished his prayer he saw Mary across the river. He saw her standing on the shore. Immediately he began to call to her.

"Lady," so spoke Zosimas, "dear mother, how will you do?

How will you cross over to me, when I cannot pass over to you? How will you cross the river Jordan when there is no boat or ferry?"

When Mary heard him speak she began to weep for pity. She commended herself to God, and started into the river. Without fear she went along on top of the river. So great was her faith that she was able to walk firmly on the water.

Zosimas was greatly amazed. The holy man wanted to worship her, but she chided him for that. The blessed one passed over quickly; she never had even wet the sole of her foot. When she had come to the shore she went to the saintly man and greeted him. After that she fell to his feet and cried out her sins. She prostrated herself at his feet and sought his blessing. The holy man wanted her to rise again, and he began to weep for pity. He did not dare make the sign of the cross over her when God had granted such a miracle for her sake; for he had just allowed her to walk on the waves, right over the deep river.

When he had raised her from the ground he kissed her in great love. Then she requested that he might say the Credo for her, in charity; and the Our Father as well; the lady answered after him. Each of them gazed at the other. When they had finished their responses he presented to her the Body of our Lord, by whom sinners will be saved. Zosimas held the host in his hand:

"Lady," he said, "this seems to be bread, but it is the Body of Jesus Christ, who was killed by evil people. He was put on the cross and murdered. A man will never attain holy paradise unless he believes it during his life."

"I well believe it," answered Mary, "and also I hold in my belief that he was struck with a lance; He makes a reconcilliation for us with His Father by means of the blood which sprang from the wound. By this He makes friends of those who were once His enemies through the sin of the first man, who ate the apple in spite of His prohibition. He left this holy blood for us; those who despise it are greatly mistaken. If you have brought it with you, in the name of God I pray you, give it to me."

The holy man heard her thus pleading, he marvelled at it greatly. He showed to her the sacrifice; she worshipped it. He gave it to her, and she received it; she ate the Body and drank the Blood.

When she had taken communion, she had never been so happy about anything.

"God," she said, "Gentle Creator, Father, I praise you and I adore you. Good Lord, now hear my prayer, and then grant to me my reward. I have served you for forty-six years; have mercy on me now. Do your pleasure with your daughter; now I would like to die. And if it please you that I should live further, dear good Father, I would not refuse. I would not renounce this life, for wish what you will. But if it please you, Lord, now I would like to die. Now would I receive the wages you have prepared for me. O Mary, Virgin, pray to your Son, that He place me among His company. If once I could be with You, I would never leave, this much I trust. With your hand-maidens, in your beautiful chambers, I will sing the New Song with the sweet sound, as Soloman sang it. I may not sing it here, for it would make me weep tenderly to hear it. In this life all joy turns to folly."

When she had finished her prayer she bowed humbly before the holy man.

"Sir," she said, "Master Zosimas, dear good father, now go from here. You have fulfilled my desire. Return to your monastery. Do not forget me next year, but come to speak to me. You will cross over the river Jordan, and then you will find me, either alive or dead, at the place where you first found me."

"This I will do," said Zosimas, "but if you do as I desire, you will eat some of our fruit."

He took some lentils out of his little bag; he had no other provision there. He offered them in his two hands, and the lady ate three grains. Thirty years had passed in which she had not eaten once. She drank some water without being thirsty, and then said to him, "Pray for me."

With this word she turned, and in a little time was back in the same place, which was very dear to her, where Zosimas had first seen her. The journey was long, but God carried her straight there. When she arrived at the spot where Zosimas had found her naked, a place which had a scent better and sweeter than ever any balm or spice, she fell to the earth and commended herself to God.

"Good Lord," she said, "who made me and who placed a soul in my body, may I deliver myself up to you, concede myself to you, commend myself to you. Now I know well that you hold me dear, for you have heard my prayer. I want to cut myself off from this life, then I wish to come into your company. I believe that they are coming for me; my body and my soul I commend to you."

Then she stretched herself out on the ground first as she was, completely nude. She crossed her hands on her chest, and enveloped herself in her hair, closed her eyes, her nose and her mouth. Her spirit went up to eternal heaven where the devil dares not come. The soul of Mary went up into the company of angels. Her body remained completely naked, save for a little, tattered cloak, which covered a part of her. In poverty her life thus ended. The lady thus gives us an example which the powerful of the realm should know: they who are not poor at death have done great wrong to our lord. The poor will be blessed, for they will have the kingdom of God, there where the rich will not enter if once they were not poor.

The body of Mary lay on the earth all the year without company. There was nothing in the desert so fierce that it once dared to approach there. No bird dared fly over her, so much did God wish to honor her. He granted such a great miracle on her behalf that her flesh was never tainted; neither in cold nor in heat did any bad odor come from it. The body lay above ground until the year passed by completely.

Zosimas did not forget his duty, but returned to his abbey. But he was greatly grieved, the holy man, when he thought that he had spoken with the lady and had not asked her her name, nor had he inquired in all the time they had spent together.

But when it happened that the whole year had passed, and he had permission to go out from the abbey, very quickly he crossed over the river Jordan. He came into the desert for the sake of the woman, out of a marvelous desire. He searched through the desert until he came to the place where the body was; but before he found it, he seemed lost. He grieved greatly, and wept, and cried out. He was near the body, but could not see it at all.

"Good Father who made me," said he, "show me that which I have sought. You know that I will never stray from this spot, not go away, until I see this woman, who never had a peer in all of this kingdom. Lord, show this woman to me, for this is all my desire. I will not live, if I do not see her alive or dead.

"Let me see the body of my love—for I think that she must be dead. If she were alive, she would come to me now, as I believe she would not let me be lost if she knew me to be in this wasteland. Lord, if you have a care for me, let me make her sepulchre. Good Father, King of Majesty, do not let me wander astray."

When he had finished his prayer God showed him the body of Mary. He looked toward the right; he saw an aura nearby. He saw a brilliance in that place, and thought that it was fire. He drew near the light and found the body; he was extremely happy for it. It lay stretched out on the ground, all but completely naked. Her face was turned toward the east, and her eyes were closed. The hair she had on her head was her only shroud.

Zosimas drew near to the body, and put over it one of his cloaks. Immediately he began to kiss her feet; he dared not approach any other part of the body. He looked up above her head and saw characters there, just as in a letter. In the characters that the holy man saw was written this commendation:

"Zosimas, take the body of Mary and inter it with the aid of God. When you have buried her with God's help, pray for her."

The characters were of such a turn as if they had been drawn that very day in the earth.

Zosimas read them aloud, but when he found her name he thanked God for it and was very pleased. The name he holds most dear. Then he began the service for the dead. But when he had finished the offices, and had said the psalms from the psalter, then he grew troubled. For he had brought nothing with him with which he could break the ground and bury the most saintly body.

By chance he found a piece of wood. He wanted to dig with it in the hard earth. He wanted to prepare the grave, but he could not break through the ground. He was all covered with sweat under his hair shirt, but could accomplish nothing. He was in great need of assistance. He had such trouble that he was drenched in sweat, and nevertheless, for all his trouble he would not succeed in all that year if God did not grant him aid, for Mary's sake.

God sent him a good companion, none other than a lion.

A lion came out of the desert; he came straight to where the body was. He began to lick her feet; he did not know how to kiss them in any other way. He made signs of humility, and that he would serve him willingly. When the holy man saw the lion (he had never had such a helper), he would not have cared for his company, if God had given him any other. At first, when he saw the beast come to the body, he wanted to flee, but when he saw him so friendly, and of such great humility, and as gentle as an angel, he was very pleased. He knew well that God had sent him to him. Then he said to him:

"Good dear friend, this woman, who was named Mary and who led a very saintly life, has shown me, in this letter that I found here at her head, that she wants to be buried here. But I am in great need of assistance. If you would help me at all, I wish to bury this holy body."

The lion seemed happy, joyous, at the command, in so far as he knew how to obey it. He began to dig in the earth; the lion broke the hard ground. The saint showed him the measure; the lion dug with his forepaws, and threw away the earth with those behind. The strength of the lion was great; he made the hard earth of the wood fly high and clear. If four men were put there, who had spades and good picks, they would have worn themselves out before the pit had been dug. The grave was prepared quickly and quite emptied of earth.

Zosimas, who watched this, was happy. He took up the body near the head, and the lion took it by the feet. Between the two of them they placed it in the grave; they put the body down into the ground. Zosimas climbed outside of it and gave the commendation for her (without the help of the lion). Here the beast could not help, for he was mute, but when he came to the interment he needed no encouragement at all. He piled up all the earth, then, and put it back on the holy body. But when the burial was finished his duty was fulfilled. He knelt down to the ground and made a sign that he bade farewell. Then he turned around and entered the great desert.

When Zosimas saw him turn he began to praise God.

"God," he said, "praise be to you, so great is your virtue. You have shown me well, through Mary, that he who forgets You is in the wrong. I will see and completely believe, without doubt, that penitence is a powerful thing. I will never do anything until I die but serve You. I will atone for all my sins, without care for my body."

In great devotion the holy man repaired to his house. The great penance of Mary, her poverty, her hard life, her labor, and the great love that she held towards her Creator, the good and true repentance that she had after her great folly, how our Lord held her dear through the entreaty of His gentle mother, and how she came into her glory, all have I described according to the story. May Jesus Christ, the celestial King, who deigned to be born of the Virgin, who was willing to suffer penitence, and repentance from out sins. May those who honor the Egyptian enjoy celestial joy.

AMEN.

Notes

7. LITERATURE, PART IV: ROMANCE

Tristan's Folly

The legend of Tristan and Iseut, immensely popular throughout the Middle Ages, surives in many different texts in all European languages. The *Folie Tristan* (Berne ms.) is a complete, narrative poem which evokes in a single, dramatic incident the major themes of the twelfth-century romance tradition. Contemporary readers were familiar with the story of two lovers bound by a love-potion to each other and to a life of deception at the court of King Mark, who is both Iseut's husband and Tristan's uncle. Finally caught in adultery, Tristan and Iseut escape into the Morois forest, where they live until the potion wears off. At this point they agree to return Iseut to her husband: Tristan gives to Iseut his hunting-dog, Husdent; she gives him her ring; and they separate. Tristan wanders in exile, and even marries "Iseut of the White Hands," the sister of a companion, Kaherdin, but now returns to visit his original lover.

Tristan is disgraced at court; he does not know where to go or turn. . . . He is in mortal dread of Mark, the king. Mark threatens him in dire earnest, and Tristan had better understand that if he is caught, kinship will not save him from death at the king's hands. Tristan has wronged him with his wife; Mark has denounced before his barons the shame and the outrage which his nephew, Tristan, has committed against him. It is Mark who bears the shame for what Tristan has done, and he can no longer continue to conceal it. He convokes all his barons and reveals the matter to them; he discloses to them Tristan's misdeed.

"My Lords," says he, "What can I do? It works very much against me that I did not take vengeance on Tristan; people think it childish weakness on my part. He has fled from this country, and I have no idea where to search; for ill shall I always have spared him, if that turns to my grief, by Saint Odé! . . . If any of you can catch sight of him, let me know it without fail, by Saint Samson of Cornwall! Whoever would bring him back to me would have my gratitude, and I would hold that man always the dearer for it." No man there fails to promise Mark that he will do his best to capture him.

Dinas the seneschal[1] heaves a sigh; in his heart he is sorely

1 Tristan's childhood tutor.

vexed for Tristan's sake, and deeply grieved in spirit. Quickly he has sent a messenger and informed Tristan how he has unknowingly lost the love of the king, who hates him mortally. Alas that Tristan ever laid eyes on his Good Pleasure! He is spied upon by the envious, and has quite often been injured by them. When Tristan heard the news, be assured it was not to his liking. He dares not return to the country from which he so often has fled; he sighs continually and bitterly grieves that he does not have Iseut with him. Iseut he has—but not the one who first was his beloved. He considers what he could do to bring her to him, for he dares not go into her country.

"Oh God," says he, "What a fate is mine! How I have suffered in such a love! Never have I reproached her, nor do I complain of my distress; why am I so assaulted? Why does it wound me so? God, what is to be done? What to think? Am I not doing what I should? No, not when I have left the lady who suffers such torment for my sake, such pain, shame and trouble. Alas!" he exclaims, "How wretched I am, woe that I was ever born! . . . suffered and had such pain! Never was seen so beautiful a lady. May whoever holds back from loving her never be loved at all, but rather always be called a coward! May Love who conquers all things grant that I might hold her in my arms again at will! And may God let me live long enough to see her safe and free! I would dearly prize the chance to even approach her. God give her joy and health, if it be His will, in His great goodness—and may He give me honor and joy, and guide my steps so that I might set eyes upon her once again, see her and meet with her. God, how beaten and confounded am I, and how little respected on earth! Alas, what shall I do if I do not see her? On her account I live in alarm, night and day and all the time; from not seeing her I am all but going mad. Alas! What should I do? I do not know; I am completely preoccupied with her, and shall continue so, truly, God willing! To God I pray that he not let me die before I have her! Most gently she healed my wound, which I got in Cornwall in the battle with the Morholt;[2] it was on the island to which I was rowed, where I fought to redeem the tribute due from the people of the land; my sword ended that war. She might think very ill of me if I let any threat keep me from going there under cover, or else in the garb of a timid fool. For her sake I will be shaved and shorn, since there is no other way to hide myself; I am too well known in the country, and would be quickly thwarted if I could not change at will my dress and appearance. This journey of mine I will end only when I can no longer walk."

So saying, he delays no longer, but sets out immediately; he left his domain and kingdom behind, taking with him neither hauberk nor helmet. Night and day he travels without stopping; he did not rest until he reached the sea. He came there through great hardship, and still I can tell you that he has long suffered such pain for her, and has been very much the fool, believe me. He changes his name, calling himself Tantris.[3] When he had crossed the sea, he went over

2 An Irish champion, Iseut's uncle, who came to Cornwall to demand a tribute due yearly from Cornwall to Ireland.
3 Anagram of Tristan.

on the shore. He would not be thought sane; he tears his clothes and scratches his face, and strikes out at everyone he sees. He has shaved his blond hair, and there is no one by the sea who does not think he is raving—but they do not know his intent. In his hand he carries a club, and goes on his way as a fool. People jeer at him and throw stones at his head. Tristan goes onward, stopping no more, and thus he travelled for a long time through the land—all for the love of Iseut. He was well content with what he was doing, and nothing troubled him except that he was not with Iseut: she is what he desires. He has not yet reached the court, but he will go there now, come what may, and he will try to pass for a fool—for he would speak to Iseut. He has come straight to the court, and nary a door was barred against him.

When Tristan came before the king, he was rather poorly dressed: with his head shaved close, he had a long neck and looked truly the perfect fool. He has really gone to great lengths for love. Mark calls him over and asks him: "Fool, what is your name?"

"I am called Picous."[4]

"Who sired you?"

"A Walrus!"

"On what did he beget you?"

"On a whale! I have a sister whom I shall bring you. The girl is called Bruneheut—you will have her and I shall have Iseut!"

"If we exchange, what will you do with her?"

Said Tristan, "Now pay attention! Between the clouds and the sky, with flowers and roses—no ice—there I will build a house, where she and I will take our pleasure. God shame these Welshmen here! I have not yet finished my tale. King Mark, the maid Brangien[5] drew— I swear to you—the drink which she gave to Tristan, from which he later suffered dire distress. Iseut, whom I see here, and I both drank of it—ask her! She now calls it a lie, and so I will just say that it was a dream, for I have dreamed it every night. King, you are still being misled! Look me right in the face: Do I not look like Tantris? I have jumped and thrown reeds, and held up cut sticks, lived on roots in the wilds, and in my arms I have held a queen! And I could tell more if I set out to."

"Take it easy, now, Picolet! It truly pains me that you have done so much. Enough of your jokes for now!"

"What do I care if it bothers you? I would not give a lump of clay for that!" (Now all the knights are saying: "Neither heed nor scold a fool!")

"King, remember a great fear, when you found us lying stretched out inside the leaf hut with my naked sword between us![6] I pretended then to be asleep, for I dared not run. It was hot, as in the month of May; in the middle of the hut I saw a ray of sunlight gleaming on her face. God's will was done: You put your glove into the opening in the branches, and went away. Nothing more took place; nor do I want to tell more—for he probably remembers it all too well!"

---

4 This name is a reference to King John of England's fool, William Picol.

5 Iseut's maidservant and confidante.

6 The King discovered them by accident one day in the Morois Forest, but told it to no one at court.

At these words Mark looks to the queen; she held her head low, and covered her face with her cloak: "Fool, cursed be the sailors who brought you over here, since they did not throw you in the sea!"

Then Tristan spoke: "Lady, ill befall this neck of mine, but if you were sure of me, if you knew my secret, and if you knew who I really am, neither doors nor windows would stop you, nor the command of the king. I still have with me the ring which you gave me as we parted, after that meeting of hateful memory! Cursed be that assembly! Many a painful day have I had and suffered since then. Restore to me, Lady, my loss in sweet kisses of true love, or in embraces under covers; you will have greatly comforted me, indeed, or otherwise I die. Not even Yder, who killed the bear, ever had such grief and pain for Guenevere, Arthur's wife, as I have had for you, for I am dying of it. I left Britain completely, and went alone to Spain; my friends never knew it, and neither did Kaherdin's sister. So far have I travelled by sea and land, that I have come back to seek you—and if I just leave now without showing it to you, then I will have lost my joy! Let none believe in augury!"

In the hall many confer about it, and murmur in each other's ears: "I believe my lord might almost believe this fool!"

The king has called for horses. He wishes to go out to watch his birds flying for cranes; it has been quite some time since they were out of the mews. All leave; the hall is empty, and Tristan rests on a bench. The queen entered into her chamber paved with marble, and there she called her maid: "By Saint Estretine, did you hear about that astonishing fool? May evil sickness take his ears! He has told much today about my doings and Tristan's, whom I have loved so much—and still love, believe me! Alas! He scorns me, and still I can hardly bear to be without him. Go get the fool and bring him to me!" Immediately she goes; Tristan sees her, and is very pleased.

"Sir Fool! My lady asks for you. You have gone to great trouble to tell us about your life today. You are full of melancholy? God help me, whoever hanged you would do a good thing, I think!"

"Surely he would do ill, Brangien. There are madder folk than I who ride horseback."

"What dusky, winged devils have told you my name, then?"

"Fair one, I have known it for a long time. By my head, which once was blond, reason has departed. It is gone because of you—and today I ask you to redeem it: do for me only enough to make the queen requite the fourth part of my service or the half of my travail." He heaved a deep sigh. Brangien looked him over closely: he has well-shaped arms, and exceedingly fine hands and feet, as she can see, and he is right trim at the waist. In her heart she thinks him sane, and suffering from something better than madness.

"Sir knight: God honor you and give you joy. But let it not turn to the queen's dishonor, nor to mine—I who am in her confidence! Forgive me what I said to you, I am very sorry."

"I forgive you, I am not offended." Then Brangien said a

courteous thing:

"By your leave, pursue your undertaking, but cover yourself with some other name than Tristan!"

"Oh, I would be right willing to do that! But the drink[7] from the medicine chest so completely took my heart and wits that I have no other purpose than to serve in love. God grant me good success! For ill was that business prepared! My reason has turned to folly— and you, Brangien, who brought it to me, surely you did very ill. That drink was made for misfortune, from many different herbs: I die for her, and she does not even feel it! There's unequal division here, for I am Tristan, the ill-fated."

At these words she recognized him; she falls to his feet to beg his mercy, that he should pardon her rudeness. He raises her by the hands, and kissed her more than a thousand times; now he begs her concerning her task, that she do the best she can without delay—she will be well able to manage. Brangien leads him by the hand; walking close to each other, they come into the chamber together. Iseut sees him and her heart trembles. She hates him bitterly for the outrageous things he said this morning. Simply and without flattery he greeted her, whatever might come of it.

"God save the queen," says he, "and with her Brangien, her maid! She would soon have cured me, only by calling me 'Lover.' I am a lover, and she beloved—but love is not shared equally. I am doubly in travail, while she has no pity at all. With hunger and thirst, on hard beds, pining, pensive in mind and heart, I have suffered much distress—and have done no wrong through negligence. But may God who reigns without end—He who at the wedding of Archedeclin[8] was so courteous a wine steward that He turned water into wine— may God put her in mind to bring me out of this madness!"

She is speechless and says not a word. Brangien observes her and speaks: "Lady, what a welcome are you giving to the most loyal lover who ever was or ever could be! Your love torments him too much—now put your arms around his neck! It is for your sake that he has shaved his head like a fool. Lady, hear what I am saying: this is Tristan, by my faith."

"Maid, you are wrong! You should have seen him at the port where he came in this morning. This is a very cunning lad indeed! If this were he, he would not have made such ugly jokes about me today in front of all the people in that hall. He would rather be lost and forlorn!"

"Lady, I did that to cover us—and to make fools of them all! I never knew anything about divining! Loving you torments me all too much. Little do you remember Gamarien,[9] who demanded nothing less than you yourself, whom he led away—who was it who delivered you?"

"It was Tristan, certainly, the king's nephew, who was very well equipped." Tristan looks at her, and is glad: he knows well that he will get his due—her love—and more he does not ask of her. He has

7 The love potion. 8 The marriage at Cana. 9 An unknown reference.

often gone to great lengths for her sake.

"Do I not at all resemble the man who came all alone and unaided to help you in that need, he who cut off Guimarant's hand?"

"Yes, you do—only in that you are a man! I do not know you, that is all there is to it!"

"Really, lady, that is a shame. I was your harper once. You watched me in the chamber, from the door, one time when I was very unhappy; and so, at that time were you. You cured the wound I bore, which he had given me in the shoulder, and that was how I came out of the affair: you made me safe and sound.[10] No one but you laid a hand on it. From the venom of the vicious serpent—may I be hanged if I lie—you cured me completely, and when I had stepped into the bath, you drew out my steel sword, and found the nick as you wiped it. Then you called Perenis[11] to bring the dark cloth band with the piece wrapped in it, you fit the steel fragment into the sword, and when you had joined the one metal to the other, then you did not love me at all! In great anger and meaning to strike, you went to seize it with both hands. You came toward me in fury, but I soon appeased you with the story of the hair[12]—from which I have had much grief since! You were then entrusted to my care, and the boat was well fitted out. When we had left the harbor, on the third day, the wind failed us, and we all had to row with the oars; I myself put my hands to it. It was very hot, and we were thirsty. Brangien, who stands here before you, ran in haste to the coffer; unwittingly she blundered: she filled up the cup with the brew. It was very clear and unclouded. She handed it to me; I took it. You were not ill before—nor the worse for it afterward! You know the story all too well. Alas, that ever I laid eyes on you, maiden!"

"You have studied with a very good teacher! If you had your way, you would be taken for Tristan, God preserve him! But you shall be turned away. Have you any other tale to tell us?"

"Yes— the leap from the chapel! When you were sentenced to be burned, and then given to the lepers, they started arguing and quarreling loudly among themselves; one was named to choose which of them should have you in the woods. The only ambush I made was with Gorvenal[13] alone—and you knew me very well when I broke them up! Still, not one was hurt by me, but Gorvenal, God help him, beat them soundly with the very sticks their limbs leaned on. We were in the forest for a while, where we wept many a tear. Is not the hermit Ugrin[14] still living? God give his soul a good end!"

"You might as well leave this be, there is no point in talking about him—you don't resemble him at all! He is a worthy knight and you are a beggar! It is a very strange thing you are trying to do. You can fool many with your beggary; I would soon have you hanged, and tell your doings to the king."

10 Another allusion to the battle with the Morholt (see note 2).   11 Iseut's valet.

12 Supposedly, a swallow carried off a hair of Iseut's to Cornwall, where King Mark saw it and so conceived his plan to marry the lady to whom the hair belonged.

13 Tristan's manservant and confidant. The events described occurred when they were taken in adultery.

14 The hermit Ugrin arranged the reconciliation of Iseut with her husband.

"Surely, lady, if he knew, I think you might regret it. It is said that he who has served in love is fully rewarded all in one day; this is very wrong in my case, in all that I see happening here. Once I had a lover—and now, I believe, I have lost her."

"Sir, who was it who troubled you?"

"She who has loved me for so long, and who will love me once again, God willing. There is no need for her to leave me yet. But now I will tell you something else, about the strange nature that there is in a dog. Say, what has become of Husdent? When they had held him for three days, he would neither drink nor eat, and was going rabid for my sake. Finally they took off his chain and opened the door—and he did not stop until he came to me."[15]

"By my faith, indeed I am keeping him, for one whom I hope we will welcome together."

"For me he would leave Iseut the blond! Show him to me right now, and see if he recognizes me!"

"Recognize! You are talking nonsense. He would have little regard for your distress, for since Tristan left no man has ever approached him whom he did not try to tear to pieces. He moans in the room in there. Maid, bring him in here." Brangien quickly goes and unties him; hearing Tristan's voice, the dog pulls the leash out the hands of the girl who leads him, and bounds eagerly to Tristan. He runs over to him, raising his head; never did a beast give such a welcome, pawing and pushing with his muzzle; it was truly a pity to see. He licks Tristan's hands and barks for joy. Iseut sees this and is very frightened; she fears he might be a sorcerer or some crafty charlatan, Tristan was so shabbily dressed. He spoke to the dog:

"May the training I put into you be blessed! You have not taken your love from me. You have shown me a far better face than she has, whom I loved so much. She thinks I am practicing a deception—but she will see the true emblem which she gave me with a kiss, when we parted in tears. This little ring of pure gold has been very close to me. Many a time have I talked to it and begged counsel, and when it could not answer me, I thought I should melt away. With love I have kissed the emerald, and my eyes have been wet with hot tears."

Iseut recognized the ring, and saw how the dog welcomed him, nearly going wild—and now she realizes in her heart that this is Tristan to whom she is speaking.

"Alas!" says she, "I am the one who is mad! Evil heart of mine, how do you not melt, not knowing the one being in this world who suffers the most for my sake? My Lord, have mercy, I repent!" She falls in a swoon, but he catches her, and now Brangien sees what she wanted to see: when Iseut revived, she clasps his thighs, and kisses his face and eyes and nose more than a thousand times.

"Ah, Tristan, my lord, what a pity that you suffer such pain for me! I am no true king's daughter if I do not reward you right now! Say, Brangien, what shall we do for him?"

"Lady, do not take it lightly, go bring him clothes. He is Tristan,

15 When the lovers escaped, Husdent was left behind. Released by King Mark, he tracked the lovers into the forest.

and you are Iseut; it is clear to see that whoever now complains any
more has very little reason to do so!"

"What pleasure shall we give him?" she asks.

"While you have the chance, take pains to serve him until Mark
comes back from the river."

"May he find it so plentiful that he not return for eight days!"

At these words, without great noise, and you have heard here,
Tristan gets under the covers, and in his arms he holds the queen.

Lanzelet

Ulrich von Zatzikhoven

The version of the Lancelot story abridged below, although written later (ca. 1195), is more archaic than the well-know *Chevalier a la Charrette* (ca. 1170) of Chrétien de Troyes. Its author, Ulrich von Zatzikhoven, was a priest of the Thurgau, now a district in the northeast part of Switzerland. His source for the story was a French tale, which he seems to have followed quite faithfully. The entire poem, which is 9,444 lines long, was written in rhyming couplets.

Lines 389-623.

The adventure tells us that a mermaid was his steersman. The queen too made the journey with him, accompanied by a fair retinue. She admonished and taught him to treat everybody honorably, to be steadfast, and always to do the best that he could. Thereupon in a short time they disembarked. The warrior took his leave—graciously he did it—and mounted his horse. Now hear something odd: the youth, not knowing how to hold his reins, just trusted to luck and hung on by the saddlebow! The horse began to rear wildly, because he touched it with his spurs, and the ladies could have sworn that he was sure to crash into many a great tree.

But luck was his guide, and the horse turned into the road which lay near the lake. So he rode all day, and little it distressed him, thanks to his happy spirits, which kept him from feeling tired.

Early the next morning he saw standing near the road a lofty, well-built castle. Moderating its pace, the steed turned toward the castle gate. In front of it was a dwarf, waiting on a white horse and carrying a long whip. He was a base creature and struck the noble hero's steed under the eyes. The youth—I will not deceive you— thought that that was the proper thing to do, and the steadfast warrior took the insult lightly until he himself got a whipcut from the goblin. Even then he took no vengeance on the wretch, for he deemed him too low of station, but he was intensely angered with the castle where this had occurred. He could not help going with his horse wherever it ran, were it by dry land or deep water, but he made inquiry who might be host at the place where this insult had happened to him. "The castle is called Pluris," said a bystander, "but what the name of the host may be, I really do not know."

Thence he turned at once on to a broad heath with pretty bushes, and presently he came to a place where a stream flowed that was neither very small nor very large and that ran gently. Beside it there was good hawking and a reedy marsh, rich in wildfowl. The horse did not want to go in that direction; the reins were lying about its ears, and its master was paying very little attention to it, except that he kept spurring it, so that it galloped downhill a little way, not very far. Now he saw riding toward him rapidly a young gentleman on a fine horse whose mane and tail reached to the ground. On his hand he carried a well-mewed hawk. The good lad's steed began to neigh and prance and whinny as soon as it spied the horse.

The falconer noticed his childish riding and said, "I shall be eternally grateful to you if in your courtesy you will ride more warily and not knock me down. In return I offer you my service, if it can be of any use to you, and besides I bid you also right heartily welcome." He thanked him for that.

"So help you God, why do you ride that way?" Said Johfrit de Liez (that, I understand, was the young man's name). "Is this a penance that has been laid upon you? It is certainly a remarkable way to behave, whoever the lady may be who has chosen you for her own. You carry your shield at random and you let your reins dangle. With your long legs you sit all hunched up; your horse goes jumping and galloping here and there. Besides, you handle your spear in a way that bothers you. Yet your surcoat is rich and well decorated; you are appareled like a real warrior. I'll wager that you are not despised by whatever lady has sent you forth. If you would not consider it rude, I should like to say in friendly fashion that since I was born I have not seen a man in this country whom I should be so glad to know. And so I beg with right good will that you will tell me who you are. Let me know your name, and if you will take me as your comrade, I shall gladly pay for it with service. It is not right for me to refuse, no matter what you might desire of me. For the sake of the lady that you love, you must not keep secret from me whatever you can properly tell me."

"I will conceal nothing from you," replied the warrior, "if you will truly assure me that I commit no fault in doing so. My name I cannot reveal, since I have never found it out myself. Who my relatives are is unknown to me; and so I have remained entirely ignorant of who I am and where I am going. If you will believe me, though I had pledged my head and were to lose it unless I told you where I was born, even then I should know nothing about it. That you see me riding like a fool means that I have never done much riding. Today is only the third day since I departed from a country where no one ever knew a man; only women live there. Now I long to behold knights and their manly deeds, and if someone could tell of fighting anywhere, I am not so slothful but that I dare risk my life either for honor or for the ladies, no matter whether I lose or win. I should like to gain fame and honor if I only knew how to go about it. But if I am doomed to failure, may God postpone it for many a day! There is nothing else I can tell you, except that I must ever be your servant for your courteous greeting. You seem to me of such high breeding that, if all the world were as perfect in fine sensibility and honor, I should be greatly surprised if anybody ever carried weapons in order to harm someone else."

At this speech the courteous Johfrit began to laugh. He judged his companion shrewd, and he swore that he had never seen any boyish warrior who knew how to speak so beautifully and yet rode so clownishly. "Grant me what I beg of you," said he to the warrior from the lake, "for you are making plenty of trouble for yourself and your good steed. By my advice you should always keep hold of the reins. Stop your bobbing about, pay more attention to what you are doing, and ride along as I do the rest of the day. I shall always be grateful if you will. If I find my house as I left it, I can offer you love and honor. My castle is not far from here. Consent to stay there and pay court to the ladies; they will afford you pastime. It is not half a mile distant," said the good knight. "My mother, who has always liked to meet worthy people, is still with me and will offer you every comfort that she can manage to provide."

Then the callow youth agreed—and it was a good thing for him later. He took the reins in his hand and rode so well that one would readily have sworn he had been riding badly on purpose before, with such skill did he follow the path. Shortly they came to a place from which they could see the fortress. The host began to hurry and considerately rode on ahead. On his arrival he found handsome ladies faultlessly arrayed.

"A wonderfully charming guest is coming to us," he told them all, "who is sure to please you well, young ladies and mother mine. Grant him a good reception."

As he bade, so was it done. The ladies obediently rose in stately manner and received the unknown knight with kind greeting. On this occasion the host's affection for his companion was manifest. The youth had to kiss all the ladies in the better group, those who were the noblest; he knew how to bear himself toward these so that they thought it praiseworthy.

When he had got acquainted, the hostess seated him next to her, close by her side. Then he proved a real courtier.

Lines 776-1183.

They were well received and greeted as they should be. Toward them ran many a servant, who took from them horse and shield. Now the host had been gaming and had met with good luck— fortunately for them all. Therefore they were joyously greeted, and they overcame their first anxiety. The host bade them make themselves at home; and then appeared their glittering armor white as tin. When they had laid that by, there was no one who could affirm that he had ever seen three such handsome knights. Their courteous carriage was noted, for each showed his breeding.

Then Galagandreiz said: "Whichever one you accord the honor shall walk beside me, and I will let you see my daughter and her ladies."

There was not a word of dissent, and their good manners prompted the two to put forward the youth. So the host led them to the door of the apartment where his daughter sat. Never were knights better greeted nor more lovingly; the lordly host ordered it thus.

The host's daughter welcomed the lad who had always lived with ladies and seated him by her side. Better fortune than that in courtly affairs he was not likely soon to enjoy. He talked to her about love in its manifold aspects. In whatever vein she addressed him, he replied in seemly wise, both in earnest and in game—and that with entire propriety. His companions were also merry. The young knight had the fortunate gift that everybody liked him. After he had sat there thus a while, the meal was ready. No matter how much one spoke of entertainment and of varied dishes, one could never tell all that was provided for them. They had a merry time till the hour arrived for sleep; then they had to meet a new experience. As befitted welcome guests, good beds were prepared for them, each by himself. The host escorted them and had good wine poured for them. He arranged the pillows for all with his own hand. Then he spoke: "Heros, take care to rest with propriety. May God, who guards all the world, protect you well with His power and grant you now good night." And they also prayed God to keep him.

Then the young warrior said, "Unless we are mad, we ought ever to praise this host."

Then, just as they were expecting repose, the lady, the host's daughter, came quietly walking in. Now it was her desire to have two great tapers burning there: she wanted to find out what the manners of the heroes were and how discreetly they slept, for she was on fire with strong love. She had got herself up well and fashionably enough. She wore a gorgeous mantle; the outside was of Saracen fabric, the best ever seen or heard of as far as Morzi in heathen land; the sable and feathers were rich. She had no hat, because she wished to look young, but she wore a chaplet that she had plaited with her own hands, well wrought of pretty flowers. She could not have been more fascinating. Her smock was of silk, and in it she looked charming, so I am informed. Her mind was bent upon nothing but that which occupies the thoughts of one filled with love-longing. She had eluded the chaperonage that all women detest. Love so tormented her and constrained her so powerfully that she had to be daring. Yet she was not alone; two pretty maids in two robes of green samite preceded her into the hall. The little girls carried two golden candlesticks—the candles gave a great light—and these they at once placed, according to the lady's orders, with the lights which they found. Then she said good-by to them; they bowed courteously to her and with graceful

demeanor went to their rest and left the mighty forester's child with
the guests. She wished to have it thus, that it might be a little better
with her.

She sat down beside Orphilet, for he lay sleeping nearest to her;
and this is how she addressed him: "Lord God, bless me! How silent
these knights who travel abroad this way and take pains to behave
courteously should converse somewhat about women and while away
the time in most pleasant conversation. I know not whom to believe.
I have been told a great deal about love and its sweetness: 'It is better
than mere goodness; through it one becomes happy.' They declare
that these are its weapons—'much thought and little sleep.' But now I
have had a taste of its treachery and am reminded of my father's
words, who says, 'Love is a longing sorrow, the image of many an
error, the neglect of everything that is profitable, the troubler of
men's spirits, to the timid a heavy load, to the feeble-hearted an
unwelcome guest. It parches the world like an oven. It is a source of
cowardly idleness. Love is the cause of dire distress, a false measure
of faithfulness.' So talks my father, and withal he is determined that
I shall ever be without a husband. Upon my life, I might be willing to
do that, were it not that I long to live like other women, who have
set their fancy on the love of good men and live for those who give
them great joy."

When she had said all this, Orphilet looked at her and asked
what she wished. Immediately she offered him a gold finger ring. He
dared not take it, for he was afraid of being made the butt of a joke,
as often happens. "I have not merited it by courtly service," he said,
"that I should want it at all."

"Say not so, dear friend. For the honor of all knights, release
me from suffering, from the tyrannous watch people keep over me.
I am speaking in all earnestness. Take this ring for friendship's sake
and thereafter all that is mine, whatsoever I can bring to you."

Orphilet was frightened by this offer and reasoned that the old
man would make him pay for disloyalty with battle—that was his
custom. "Lady, do as I ask you. Now that I understand your words I
will soon come here again. If you deign to love me, I will gladly carry
you away. For you I will not hesitate to risk life and honor as far as
ever I can. But just now I do not care to do anything about it."

Then the good maid replied: "Oh no, valiant knight. Think of
all that ever was courtly and lovable, upright and well-bred, of
unspoiled beauty of mind. Look at my lovely person. I am a woman
fit for a knight, and I make just one request, such as never woman
made before, that you will turn your mind to love of me, for you are
so very handsome. I declare in entire good faith that, so far as I can
distinguish, I never laid eyes on a man for whom a fortunate woman
should more gladly risk both her honor and her life. None of my kin
should I like so well as you, if it could only come to pass that you
will release me this time from the pain that cumbers me so. If ever
woman showed you favor, O knight, you should not timidly refuse,

nor deny me your body. One finds many a warrior wandering in strange lands for the sake of beautiful ladies not one of whom can compare with me in either wealth or looks. Make up your mind, hero, and kiss me lovingly—I will always repay you for it—and tell me your desire."

Then answered Orphilet at once: "I fear for my knightly honor. Dismiss this notion from your mind, for I mean to keep my good faith. Even if I dared to make bold with you, unless I killed your father, I might suffer such punishment for it as to be imprisoned for a year."

The lady replied: "The truth is that nobody ever achieved real manhood who did not at some time or other act indiscreetly for the sake of a woman."

The hero said: "By my life, I am not inclined to die on your account!"

Angrily she left him, her love-longing still unrelieved. Now Kuraus lay close by, between his two companions; and here let me tell you a strange thing. The lady, since love pained her sore, made up her mind to woo him also so ardently that no man was ever subjected to such earnest entreaties from a woman. She spoke: "A knight who wishes to live up the highest standards should never be fainthearted with a woman. I will tell you truly that I have been well informed how perfect you are in your manhood. Prove you mettle on me, and in me love a beauteous maid. If you find pleasure in a woman who is good to her lover, I shall be well rewarded by you, as I can discern. My father has forbidden me any husband: he thinks he cannot live without me. But now I will dispense with obedience to that command. I would rather myself woo a man who has sense and honor than wait for one who will prove quarrelsome. Accordingly I have chosen you: you are constant and wellborn, and surely dare to undertake all things. But if my hope should be deceived, I will never be gracious to a man again."

Then Kuraus replied: "You should be gracious to good knights. If it were not that I honor your father for the good will that he has shown me, nothing so pleasant could happen to me as that I should love you. Yet I would rather incur your ill will than destroy my luck. However, I will always complain to God that I have had to give you up. Therefore dismiss me from your mind." The hero covered his head and took the proposal as a joke. At that the lady began to feel humiliated. To be repulsed so emphatically seemed to the winsome maid an extraordinary thing.

Meanwhile the youth lay there and thought to himself, "Good Lord God! if it is ever my good fortune that the lady goes through with this, I shall be joyful for ever." She came along immediately, for love was tormenting her. Up jumped the young knight and spoke: "My lady, may you stand in high favor with the great God and myself! Gladly will I serve you; you have no need to woo me, for I would rather die on the spot than let you go hence. Whatever trouble

I get into thereby, I will disregard it all. Nothing pleasanter could happen to me—that will be made plain to you." He laid her on his arm and kissed her a thousand times at least. They knew the best love that ever came to two lovers. His comrades did not like it, but he paid no attention to all that and took possession of the lady right lovingly. These two were filled with joy and had a plenitude of bliss, and the very finest night that any woman ever experienced with a young amn. However, he never could forget that she came to him last. He concealed this feeling from her then, but she paid for it another time.

As this hero lay couched so softly, the unwished day appeared and the sweet night was over. Then their resolute host pounded angrily on the door. The guests were terrified at the sight of him, because he carried two sharp knives, pointed and very long, and two bucklers. His heart was troubled. The knives were double-edged. He spoke (it would have been better if he had not done so): "I am going either to lose my life or to present the morning gift, for which no one will thank me: it is sadness and sorrow and everlasting rue, for you have forfeited your loyalty and your honor. Never since I was born have I treated a man better than you; what has that profited me? I was so disposed then; but now, all lie still, as you value your lives, and tell me who has the woman, my child, the faithless baggage?"

The girl concealed herself under her lover, the youthful champion, and would gladly have lain dead there. Her father, perceiving it, ran thither swiftly and savagely threatened them. "Whoever robs me of my honor," he said, "will not enjoy it much! I will challenge you to a game. Take this shield in your hand and stay here by this wall, and I will go to the other side; and I will give you your choice. I will deprive you of your honor, or you me of mine. One of us must throw first. Whoever hits the mark, he wins the game; the other bears the loss."

The youth approved the plan: "Since I am on the defensive, it seems to me proper that you should throw before I do. May God give you bad luck, my hateful opponent! Please God you miss me!"

Then he relied upon his own skill, and kept a sharp eye on his father-in-law, always holding his shield in front of him. For this game no board was needed! Kuraus and Orphilet would have much preferred to be elsewhere. The host played first and hurled his knife with full force through the young warrior's sleeve into the wall. He fleshed him a little, so that he made the blood flow. Then the wounded one considered how he could make up for his injury. Instead of throwing and hurling, he rushed upon the wretch and gave him a frightful stab with his knife, so that he fell on the floor and never spoke again.

Parzival

Wolfram von Eschenbach

Wolfram von Eschenbach (ca. 1170-1220), a knight and poet of the first order, was born near Ansbach (southwest of Nürnberg). His famous poem, *Parzival,* which in its entirety is almost 25,000 lines long, was composed between 1200 and 1210. It was written in rhyming couplets and divided into sixteen books, each of which is further subdivided into groups of thirty lines.

Book VI (280.1-305.8).

Would you like to hear now why Arthur left his country and his castle at Karidoel? He had followed the counsel of his retinue and, with noble knights of his own and of other lands, so the story says, he was now riding for the eighth day in search of him who called himself the Red Knight, that same knight who had done him the honor of delivering him from great distress by slaying King Ither and by sending Clamidê and Kingrun, each one singly, to the Britons and to his court. He wished to invite him to become one of the company of the Round Table, and for this reason rode in search of him.

He had made the following decree: All those who belonged to the profession of knighthood, both the lowly and the powerful, had to pledge in Arthur's hand that whatever knightly deeds they might see, they would, by virtue of this oath, refrain from any joust unless they asked him for his permission to fight.

"We must ride into many a land," he said, "where knightly deeds may well challenge us. Upraised spears we shall certainly see. If you then vie with each other and rush out like wild mastiffs whose master slips their leash, that I do not wish. I shall prevent such turbulence. But I will help you when there is no other way. You may rely on my valor."

This was the oath, as you have heard it. Now will you hear where his journey has taken Parzival the Waleis? That night fresh snow had fallen thick upon him. Yet it was not the time for snow, if it was the way I heard it. Arthur is the man of May, and whatever has been told about him took place at Pentecost or in the flowering time of May. What fragrance, they say, is in the air around him! But *here* this tale is cut of double fabric and turns to the color of snow.

Arthur's falconers from Karidoel had ridden out in the evening for hawking along the Plimizoel and had suffered the misfortune of losing their best falcon. It had suddenly taken flight and remained in the woods all night. This came of overfeeding, for it spurned the food put out to lure it. All night it stayed near Parzival, for the forest was strange to both, and they very nearly froze.

When Parzival saw the daylight, he found his pathway covered over with snow and rode then at random over fallen tree trunks and stones. The day steadily shone brighter, and the forest began to thin out into a meadow, level except for one fallen tree toward which he slowly rode, Arthur's falcon following along. Resting there were perhaps a thousand geese, and a great cackling went up. Like a flash the falcon darted among them and struck at one so fiercely that it barely managed to escape under the branches of the fallen tree. Pain no longer let it fly.

From its wounds there fell upon the snow three red drops of blood. These brought Parzival great distress, from the trueness of his love. When he saw the blood-drops on the snow which was so white, he thought, "Who created this color so pure? Condwiramurs, this color does in truth resemble you. God must wish to give me fullness of bliss, since I have found here something which resembles you. Honor be to the hand of God and to all His creatures! Condwiramurs, here lies your image, for the snow offered the blood its whiteness, and the blood reddens the snow. Condwiramurs, your *beau corps* is like these colors. That you must confess."

From the way the drops lay on the snow, the hero's eyes fancied two as her cheeks and the third as her chin. His love for her was true and knew no wavering. And thus he mused, lost in thought, until his senses deserted him. Mighty Love held him in thrall. Such distress did his own wife bring him, for she had the very same colors, the Queen of Pelrapeire. She it was who robbed him of his senses.

So he remained still as if he were sleeping. And who came running up to him there? A squire of Cunneware's had been sent out on an errand to Lalant. Just then he saw a helmet with many wounds and a much-battered shield. And there was a warrior in armor—in the service of the squire's lady—with spear erect, as if he were waiting to do combat. The squire quickly retraced his steps. If he had recognized him as his lady's knight, he would not have raised such a hue and cry. He urged the people out to attack him as if he were and outlaw. He wanted to do him harm, but he lost thereby his name for courtesy. Never mind, his lady was also thoughtless.

"Fie upon you, fie, you cowards," cried the squire. "Do Gawan and the rest of this company of knights deserve knightly honor, and Arthur the Briton?" So cried the lad. "The Round Table is disgaced. Someone has ridden your tent ropes down."

Then there was a great clamor among the knights. They all began to ask whether a battle were going on. When they heard that a single man was there ready for combat, many a one regretted the oath he had given to Arthur. Quick as a flash, not walking, up leaped

Segramors, always eager for a fight, and broke into a run. Whenever he suspected a fight, they had to tie him hand and foot or he would be in the midst of it. Nowhere is the Rhine so wide but if he saw combat on the opposite shore there was no feeling if the bath were warm or cold—in he plunged, the reckless warrior.

Speedily the youth arrived at court in Arthur's circle of tents. The worthy King was fast asleep. Segramors ran in among the tent ropes, burst through the doorway of the tent, and snatched off the sable cover from the King and Queen as they lay there sleeping sweetly. They were awakened, yet they could not help laughing at his impudence.

"Ginover, my lady the Queen," he said to his mother's sister, "everyone knows we are kin, and far and wide it is known that I can count on your favor. Now help me, Lady, speak to Arthur your husband and say he must grant me this—there is an adventure nearby —that I be the first to the joust."

Arthur replied to Segramors, "You promised me on your oath that you would abide by my will and hold your folly in check. If you engage in a joust here, then many another man will ask me to let him ride out to combat and seek for fame in battle, and my own defense will be weakened. We are nearing the host of Anfortas which rides out from Munsalvaesche to defend the forest in combat. Since we do not know where the castle lies, things might well go hard with us."

But Ginover pleaded with Arthur so well that Segramors' wish was granted. When she won him this adventure, he would have done anything in return—except perhaps die for joy. Not for the world would he have given anyone a share in the adventure and his coming glory, that proud youth, still beardless.

Both he and his horse were armed, and away rode Segramors *le roi*. Galloping *par le jeune bois*, his horse leaped over tall underbrush, and many a golden bell rang on the horse's trappings and on the man. One could have thrown him into the briars like a falcon to start the pheasant. If you wanted to look for him in a hurry, you would find him by the loud jingling of the bells.

So the reckless hero rode toward him who was so completely in thrall to love, but refrained from blow or thrust until he had given him his challenge. Parzival remained rooted to the spot, lost to all around. Such was the power of the three blood drops and of that relentless love—which often robs me also of my senses and disquiets my heart. O, the grief one woman is causing me! If she wants to vanquish me thus and seldom give me succor, then she may take the blame and I shall flee from any solace she may offer.

Now hear about those two knights, how they met and how they parted. This was what Segramors said, "You behave, Sir, as though you were pleased that a king with his following is encamped so near. For all that you take it so lightly, you will have to pay him dearly for that, or I shall lose my life. In your search for combat you have ridden too close to us. Yet for courtesy's sake will I beg you to give yourself into my power, else you will make me such swift restitution that your fall will make the snow fly. You would do better to make an honorable peace before."

Parzival made no response in spite of the threat. Lady Love was speaking to him of other cares. The bold Segramors wheeled his horse around to gain the proper distance for the charge. At that Parzival's Castilian also turned, and the eyes of the fair Parzival, who had been sitting there in a trance, staring at the blood, were turned away from the drops. Whereby his honor was restored. When he saw the drops no longer, Lady Reason gave him his senses back again.

Here came Segramors *le roi.* Parzival lowered his spear, the spear from Troyes, firm and tough and gaily colored, which he had found outside the chapel. He received one thrust through his shield, but his return thrust was so aimed that Segramors, the noble warrior, was forced to quit the saddle. But the spear which taught him what falling was remained whole. Without a word Parzival rode back to where the blood drops lay, and when his eyes found them, Lady Love drew her chains tightly about him and he spoke no word at all, for he had parted again from his senses.

Segramors' Castilian set off for its stall, while he himself had to stand up to rest, that is, if he wanted to go and rest at all. Most people lie down to rest, you have heard that often enough. But what rest could he get in the snow? —I, for one, would find it very uncomfortable. It has always been thus—the reward for the loser is scorn, for the victor the help of God.

The army was encamped so near that they saw Parzival halt and stay motionless as before. He had to acknowledge the triumph of Love, which vanquished even Solomon. It was not long before Segramors returned to camp, as amicable to those who hated him as to those who wished him well—he rewarded them all with abuse.

"You know very well," he said, "that fighting is a game of chance and that a man can fall in a joust. A ship can sink, too, in the sea. I tell you there is no doubt he would never have dared to face me if he had recognized my shield. But then he was too much for me, he who is still waiting there for combat. Well, even he is worthy of praise."

The brave Keie straightway brought this news to the King, how Segramors had been unhorsed and how a sturdy youth was waiting out there, still intent on combat. "Sir," he said, "I shall always regret it if he gets away without being punished. If you think me worthy, let me attempt what he wants, since there he waits with spear erect, and that in the presence of your wife. I can remain no longer in your service, and the Round Table will be dishonored, if he is not checked in time. His challenge is a threat to our fame. Give me leave to fight. If we were all blind or deaf, you would have to defy him yourself— and that very soon."

Arthur gave Keie permission to fight, and the seneschal was

armed. He meant to use up the forest for spears against the unbidden guest. Yet the stranger already bore the heavy burden of love; snow and blood had laid it upon him. It is sinful to harass him further now. And Love gains but little fame thereby, for she had long since set her mighty seal upon him.

Lady Love, why do you so? Why do you make the unhappy man glad with a joy so briefly enduring and then leave him all but dead?

Is it fitting for you, Lady Love, to cause manly spirits and courage bold and high to be so humiliated?

Whatever on earth opposes you in any way, be it contemptible or noble, you have always quickly vanquished.

In all truth, without deception, we must grant that your power is great.

Lady Love, you can claim but one honor, and little else beside: Lady Affection is your companion, else your power would be riddled for fair.

Lady Love, you are disloyal in ways that are old, yet ever new. You rob many a woman of her good name, you urge upon them lovers blood kindred to them. And it is by your power that many a lord has wronged his vassal, friend has wronged friend, and the vassal has wronged his lord. Your ways can lead to Hell. Lady Love, you should be troubled that you pervert the body to lust, wherefore the soul must suffer. Lady Love, since you have the power to make the young old, whose years are yet so few, your works are insidious treachery.

Such words would be seemly only for one who never received consolation from you. Had you been of more help to *me,* I would not be so slow to praise you. To me you have allotted privation, and have thrown me such luckless dice that I have no trust in you. Yet you are far too highly born that my puny wrath should bring a charge against you. Your thrust has so sharp a point, and on the heart you lay a heavy burden.

Heinrich von Veldeke, with true artistry, fitted his tree to your nature. If he had only taught us more of how to keep you! He had given us only a splinter from the tree—how one can win you. From ignorance many a fool must lose his precious find. If that was my lot in the past and is still to be my lot in the future, I blame you, Lady Love, for you keep Reason under lock and key.

Neither shield nor sword avails against you, nor swift horse, nor high fortress with stately towers—your power transcends any defense. What can escape your attack, by land or by sea, swimming or flying? Lady Love, you proved your power when Parzival, the warrior bold, took leave of his wits because of you, as his fidelity directed

him. His noble, sweet, and lovely wife, the Queen of
Pelrapeire, sent you as messenger to him. And Kardeiz,
le fils de Tampenteire, her brother, you killed. If one must
pay you such a price, it is well for me that I have nothing
from you—unless you gave me something more pleasant.
I have spoken for all of us.

Now hear what was happening there. The mighty Keie came
riding out in knightly armor, as if he would do battle. And battle, I
think, the son of King Gahmuret gave him. All ladies who know how
to vanquish men should wish him safekeeping now, for a woman
brought him to such a pass that love chopped away his wits.

Keie withheld his charge, first saying to the Waleis, "Sir, since it
has so happened that you have insulted the King, if you will take my
advice, I think your best course is to put a hound's leash about your
neck and let yourself be led like that before him. You cannot escape
me, I shall take you there by force in any case, and then they will
deal with you in a rather unpleasant fashion."

The power of love held the Waleis silent. Keie raised his spear
shaft and gave him such a blow on the head that his helmet rang.
"Wake up!" he said. "You shall sleep, but not between sheets. I am
aiming at something quite different—on the snow you shall find your
bed. Even the beast that carries the sack from the mill would rue his
indolence if he got such a beating as I have given you now."

Lady Love, look here, this is an insult to you. Only a peasant
would speak so about what has been done to my lord. And Parzival
would also protest if he could speak. Lady Love, let him seek revenge,
the noble Waleis. If you set him free from your harshness and the
bitter burden of your torment, this stranger would defend himself
well, I think.

Keie charged hard against him and in so doing forced his horse
to turn around so that the Waleis lost sight of his bitter-sweet distress,
the image of his wife the Queen of Pelrapeire—I mean the red against
the snow. Then Lady Reason came to him as before and gave him his
senses back. Keie set his horse at a gallop, and the other came on for
the joust. Both knights lowered their spears as they charged. Keie
aimed his thrust as his eyes directed and drove a wide breach in the
Waleis' shield. This blow was repaid. At the countercharge Arthur's
seneschal Keie was thrown right over the fallen tree where the goose
had taken refuge, so that horse and man both suffered harm. The
man was wounded, his horse lay dead. Caught between the saddlebow and a stone, Keie's right arm and left leg were broken in this fall.
Saddlegirth, bells, and saddle were shattered by the crash. Thus did
the stranger avenge two beatings; the one a maiden had suffered for
his sake, the other he had endured himself.

Once more Parzival, the uprooter of falseness, was shown by his
fidelity where to find the three snowy drops of blood that set him
free of his wits. His thoughts about the Grail and the Queen's likeness

here—each was a painful burden, but heavier lay on him the leaden weight of love. Sorrow and love can break the strongest spirit. Can these be called adventure? They both should better be called pain.

Courageous men should lament Keie's misfortune. His manly spirit sent him bravely into many a fight. Far and wide it is said that Arthur's seneschal Keie was a rogue. *My* tale acquits him of this charge and calls him honor's companion. Though few may agree with me—Keie was a brave and loyal man—this I do maintain.

I will tell you more about him. Many strangers came to Arthur's court, seeking it as their goal, worthy and worthless alike. By those of dapper manners who practiced trickery Keie was not impressed. But the man of courtesy who was an honest friend, him Keie could respect and was always ready to serve. I grant you, he was a carper. Yet the harshness which he displayed was for the protection of his lord. Tricksters and hypocrites he separated from the noble folk, and on them he descended like harsh hail, sharper than the sting of a bee's tail. You see, these are the ones who defamed Keie's name. He always practiced manly loyalty, yet from them he got only hate.

Herman, Prince of Thuringia, some of those I have seen residing *in* your house should better be residing *out*. You too could use a Keie, for your true generosity has brought you a motley following, in part a mean and worthless band, in part a noble throng. This is why Sir Walther sings, "I greet you one and all, the base and the good." Where such a song is sung, there false men are too highly honored. Keie would not have allowed this, nor Sir Heinrich of Rispach either.

Now listen to more of the strange things that happened on the field of the Plimizoel. Keie was carried away and brought into Arthur's pavilion. His friends began to bewail him—many ladies and many men as well.

Then came Sir Gawan too and bent over Keie where he lay. "Unhappy day," he said. "Alas that this joust was ever fought, in which I have lost a friend." And grievously he mourned for him.

But the angry Keie spoke out, "Sir, are you pitying me? Let old wives make such laments. You are the son of my lord's sister. Would that I could still serve you as you wished! When by God's grace my limbs were whole, my hand never shirked from fighting often for you. I would do so still if I could. Now lament no longer and leave the pain to me. Your uncle, the noble King, will never find such a Keie again. You are too highly born to take revenge for me. But if *you* had lost even a finger there I would risk my head to avenge it. Believe me or not, as you please. Far be it from me to urge you. He can hit hard, the one who waits out there, and he is not fleeing, either at a gallop or a trot. As for you, a single hair of a woman, be it ever so thin and fine, would be a chain strong enough to stay your hand from a fight. A man of such gentle demeanor is an honor to his mother indeed; bravery comes from the father's side. Follow your mother, Sir Gawan, then you will turn pale at the flash of a sword and your manly strength will become soft."

Thus was this well-respected man attacked where he had no defense, with words. He could not respond in kind. Shame seals the mouth of a man of breeding, while the shameless know no restraint.

In answer to Keie, Gawan said, "Where blows of sword and thrusts of lance were aimed at me in battle, no one, I think, has ever seen my color pale from either thrust or blow. You have no cause to be angry with me. I have always been ready to serve you."

With that Sir Gawan left the tent and bade his horse be brought. Without a spur and without a sword the noble warrior mounted and rode out to where he found the Waleis, whose wits were still in pawn to Love. His shield showed three punctures, made by the hands of heroes, for Orilus too had pierced it. Gawan came riding up to him, but not galloping his horse nor poising his lance for a thrust. He wanted to come in peace and discover who it was who had done this fighting.

He gave greeting to Parzival, but Parzival scarcely heard. So it had to be—Lady Love showed her power over him whom Herzeloyde bore. The heritage of suffering from father and from mother and from uncounted ancestors bereft him of his senses. So the Waleis heard little of the words Sir Gawan's mouth was uttering.

"Sir," the son of King Lot said, "you must want to do combat, since you refuse to greet me. But I am not so timid that I dare not question you further. You have brought dishonor to the King's men and his kin, even to the King himself, and have heaped disgrace upon us. Yet if you will follow my counsel and come with me to the King, I can move him to show you mercy and pardon you your offense."

For the son of King Gahmuret threats and pleas alike were as a mere breath. But Gawan, the pride of the Round Table, was well versed in such pangs from his own painful experience when he had driven the knife right through his hand. To this the power of love had forced him and the favor of a noble woman. A queen had saved him from death when the bold Lehelin in a splendid joust had vanquished him so completely. The sweet and gentle lady offered her head as ransom for him. *La reine* Inguse de Bahtarliez was the name of that loyal woman.

And Sir Gawan reflected, "What if love holds this man enslaved as it enslaved me then, and what if his faithful memories force him to yield the victory to love?" He observed how the Waleis was staring, and followed the direction of his gaze. Then taking a scarf of faille from Syria, lined with yellow sendal-silk, he flung it over the drops of blood.

Once the faille had covered the drops so that Parzival could no longer see them, the Queen of Pelrapeire gave him his wits again. But not his heart, that she kept with her.

Hear now the words which he spoke, "Alas, my lady and my wife," he said, "who has taken you from me? Did this hand of mine really win with knightly service your noble love, a crown and country? Am I the one who delivered you from Clamidê? I found distress and misery among those who were serving you, and many a brave heart heavy with sighs. And here in bright sunlight a mist before my eyes has taken you from me, I know not how. Alas," he said, "what has become of my spear, which I brought here with me?"

Then Sir Gawan said, "It was broken in jousting, my lord."

"With whom?" asked the noble warrior. "You have neither shield nor sword. What honor could I gain in fighting you? Yet though I must bear your mockery now, you will perhaps speak better of me in time. I too have often jousted and I kept my seat. If I cannot fight with you, the lands around are large enough for me to find honor and travail there and suffer both joy and affliction."

Sir Gawan then replied, "The words I spoke to you just now are clear and kindly meant; they are not dark with hidden meanings. What I ask of you I shall earn by my service. A king is encamped nearby with many knights and many a lady fair. I will bear you company there if you will allow me to ride with you, and I will protect you from any attack."

"I thank you, Sir. Your friendly words I would gladly repay with my service. Since you offer me your escort, tell me, who is your lord, and who are you?"

"I call a man my lord from whom I have received much wealth. A part of it I will tell you here. He was always kindly disposed toward me and showed me true knightly courtesy. His sister was given King Lot as wife, and it was she who brought me into the world. Such as God made me, I am pledged in service to him. King Arthur is his name. My name is also not unknown, and nowhere is it concealed. Those who know me call me Gawan. I and this name are at your service if you do not shame me by refusing."

"Are you Gawan?" said Parzival. "Small honor can I take to myself that you show me such kindness now, for I have always heard it said of you that you treat everyone with kindness. Still I accept your service, but only if I can repay it in kind. Now tell me, to whom do all the tents belong which are set up over there? If that is Arthur's camp, I do regret that I cannot with honor see him or the Queen. I must first avenge a beating I saw, which has grieved me since the day I left them. The reason is this: A noble maiden laughed when she saw me, and because of me the seneschal beat her so that splinters flew as at the felling of a forest."

"That has been avenged already," said Gawan, "in a most ungentle manner. His right arm and left leg are broken. Ride over here and look at the horse and the stone too. And here on the snow lie splinters of your spear which you asked about before."

When Parzival saw this proof, he questioned further and then said, "I trust to you, Gawan, that this was the same man who insulted me then. If that is so, I shall ride with you wherever you like."

"I am not lying to you," Gawan said. "Here Segramors also fell in the joust, a hero in combat, ever famous for his knightly prowess.

You vanquished him before Keie was felled, and from both you have gained renown."

They rode on together then, the Waleis and Gawan. . . .

Book VIII (398.7-407.30).

Gawan had honor and good fortune, both in full share. But now his battle hour approaches.

Long and broad was the forest through which he had to make his way if he was not to shun the battle to which, through no fault of his, he had been summoned. Moreover, Ingliart was lost, his horse with the short ears—never was a better horse jumped by Moors in Tabronit. Now the forest became intermittent, with here a wooded stretch and there an open field, some of the latter of a breadth that a tent would scarcely stand on them. Gazing, he perceived cultivated land, and that was Ascalun. From people he encountered he inquired for Schanpfanzun. High mountains and many a marshy moor he had traversed on his way there, but now he caught sight of a castle, and oh! how nobly it shone! Toward it the stranger to that country made his way.

Now listen to adventures, and amid them help me lament Gawan's great distress. My wise man and my foolish man, by your friendliness, do so and grieve with me for him.

Alas! I should now be silent. No, let him sink lower yet, who often enough had his luck to thank and who was now sinking toward misery.

This castle was so splendid that never did Aeneas find Carthage so magnificent when Lady Dido's death was the pledge of love. How many halls did it have? And how many towers were there? There were enough of them for Acraton, which, aside from Babylon, encompassed the greatest breadth according to the arguments of the heathens. All around, it was so high—and moreover it fronted on the sea—that it feared no assault nor any great violent hostility. Before it lay a mile-wide plain, across which Sir Gawan rode. Five hundred knights or more, with a commander over them, came riding toward him attired in colored garments of trim cut. As the adventure told me, their trained fowl were hunting there for cranes or for whatever they could start. On a tall Arabian horse from Spain rode King Vergulaht, and his splendor was like day, even in the midst of night. His family issued from Mazadan out of the mountain in Famorgan, and his race was of the fairy. To see this king's beauty, you would think you were seeing the Maytime adorned at proper season with flowers. Gawan thought, as the king's brightness flashed toward him, that it was a second Parzival and that he had the features of Gahmuret the way this story portrayed him as he rode into Kanvoleis.

A heron in flight escaped to a swamp-like pond, brought down by falcon swoops. To help the falcons, the king got into a deceptive fording place and was drenched, losing his horse thereby and his clothes as well—but he rescued the falcons from their distress. Horse and garments were taken by the falconers. Did they have any right to them? Yes, they did have a right, they properly claimed them, and they had to be allowed their rightful claims. Another horse was furnished him and he relinquished his own. Different garments were placed upon him, for the others now belonged to the falconers.

At this point up rode Gawan. Ah! then it could not be otherwise but that he was better received than Erec was at Karidoel when he came to Arthur after his battle, and when Lady Enite was safe-conduct to his joy, after the time when the dwarf Maliclisier rudely slashed his skin with the whip in the sight of Ginover, and after the fight took place in the broad ring at Tulmeyn for the prize of the sparrow hawk. Ider, *le fils de* Noyt, famed in story, gave him his oath of surrender there, forced to do so or face death. —But let us leave that topic and listen to this: never, I think, have you heard of so noble a reception and greeting as here. Alas! this child of noble Lot will pay most unkindly for it.

If you would rather, I will stop here and tell you no more about it. For very grief I will turn back. And yet, by your kindness, hear how a pure nature was troubled by the falsity of others. If I carry this story on for you with true report, you will come to sadness from it, along with me.

Then said King Vergulaht, "Sir, I have considered, and you shall ride inside over there. If it may be with your gracious pleasure, I shall not bear you company. If, however, my continuing my ride offends you, I shall leave whatever I have to do."

Then the noble Gawan said, "Sir, whatever you bid, you do so properly. It is quite without offense to me and readily pardoned."

To which the King of Ascalun replied, "Sir, you see Schanpfanzun: up there is my sister, a maiden, and whatever lips may have said about beauty, she has her full share of it. If you would consider it any pleasure, she will take pains to entertain you till I return. I will come to you sooner than I was planning to. But you will gladly wait for me once you have seen my sister, and you won't be sorry if I am away still longer."

"I shall be glad to see you, as I shall her. However, grown ladies have always spared me their hospitality." So spoke proud Gawan.

The king despatched a knight and instructed the maiden that she was to entertain him in such a way that he would think a long stay was a hastening away. Gawan rode to where the king had indicated.

If you want me to, I can still keep silent about the great unhappinesss. —No, I will go on with the story.

The road and a horse took Gawan to the gateway at one end of the great hall. Anyone who has ever built anything can tell you better than I can about the solidness of this building. There stood a castle, the best that was ever called an earthly construction, and immensely vast was its expanse.

Praise of the castle we shall pass over here, because I have a great deal to tell you about the king's sister, a maiden—enough has been said here about buildings—and I shall describe her as I properly should. If she was beautiful, it became her well; and if she had a good disposition besides, that was a help in her nobleness. Thus her manners and her nature were like those of the Margravine who radiated beauty down from the Heitstein across all the marches. A lucky fellow is he who might privately know her charms! Believe me, he found better entertainment there than elsewhere. —Of women I can speak what my eyes are able to see, and wherever I bestow a good word it must have the guarantee of good breeding.

Now let the true-hearted and the well-wishing listen to this adventure! About the untrue-hearted I do not care. With their contrition full of holes, they have all lost their salvation anyway, and their souls will certainly suffer wrath on that account.

To the courtyard there before the great hall rode Gawan in search of entertainment just as he had been sent to do by the king—who presently behaved dishonorably toward him. If womanly honor may be considered a commodity, she had driven a good bargain in it, rejecting all that was not genuine, and thus her purity had won renown. A pity that the wise gentleman from Veldeke should have died so young! He could better have sung her praises.

As Gawan came in sight of the maiden, the messenger approached her and delivered all that the king had bidden him to say.

Whereupon the queen without hesitation said, "Come nearer, Sir. You are the preceptor of my behavior. Command me and instruct me. If entertainment is to be provided for you, such must be indicated in your orders. Since my brother has recommended you so warmly to me, I shall kiss you—if you wish me to. Command me, according to your standard of propriety, what I am to do and not to do."

Very graciously she stood there before him, and Gawan answered, "Lady, your mouth is so kissable that I shall have your kiss of greeting." Her mouth was hot, full, and red; upon it Gawan pressed his own, and there ensued a nongreeting-like kiss. Beside the maiden rich in courtesy the highborn guest sat down.

Sweet converse did not fail either party, and they spoke openly to each other. They could only reiterate, he his plea, she her refusal. Whereat he complained bitterly. Yet he kept right on asking for her favor.

Then the maiden replied as I am about to tell you: "Sir, if you are otherwise discreet, you will consider that you have gone far enough. At my brother's request I am treating you no less kindly than Ampflise treated my uncle Gahmuret, without going to bed together. My kindness would in the long run outweigh hers, if anyone were to weigh us properly. And besides, Sir, I don't know who you are, and yet in such a short space of time you want to have my love."

Then the noble Gawan said, "Knowledge of my kin informs me, and I can inform you, Lady, that I am my aunt's brother's son. If you want to do me a favor, don't let my ancestry keep you from it. Compared to yours, it is well enough vouched for that they can both stand on a par and keep step with one another."

A serving maid poured them drink and immediately disappeared again. Other ladies were, however, sitting there, but they too did not forget to go and find something to do. The knight who had escorted him was also out of the way. Now that they had all gone out, Gawan reflected that weak eaglet will often catch the large ostrich. He slipped his hand under her mantle, and I think he touched her thigh. This only increased his anguish. Love drove both maid and man to such distress that something came very near happening, if malevolent eyes had not caught sight of it. They were both eager for it.

But see, their hearts' sorrow now approaches. In through the door came a white knight, that is to say a grey-haired one. On recognizing Gawan he named his name in a call to arms and set up a loud shouting: "Alas! and hey-hey! for my master whom you murdered, and, as if that weren't enough, here you are about to rape his daughter!"

At a call to arms men always come, and so did it happen here.

To the maiden Gawan said, "Lady, let's have your advice, for neither of us has much in the way of weapons of defense." And he added, "If I only had my sword!"

Then said the noble maiden, "Let's go to some place of defense, let's flee up into that tower over there, the one that stands next to my chambers. Maybe it will all turn out favorably."

Notes

8. ARCHITECTURE AND ILLUMINATION

On the Burning and Repair of the Church of Canterbury

Gervase of Canterbury

Architectural activity in the high Middle Ages was spurred on by the tastes of patrons, competition between religious centers, and in some cases unforeseen tragedies, such as fire and collapse. One such tragedy and the building program that followed is described by Gervase of Canterbury (1141-1210), who, as a resident of the convent of Christ Church, Canterbury, was witness to the conflagration of 1174 as well as an equally destructive event of the period, the conflict between Henry II and Thomas à Becket. In his account, or *Chronica,* Gervase describes the steps by which the cathedral was rebuilt, giving in the process insights into the motives of and methods used by those involved in the project.

1. The Conflagration.

In the year of grace one thousand one hundred and seventy-four, by the just but occult judgment of God, the church of Christ at Canterbury was consumed by fire, in the forty-fourth year from its dedication, that glorious choir, to wit, which had been so magnificently completed by the care and industry of Prior Conrad.

Now the manner of the burning and repair was as follows. In the aforesaid year [A.D. 1174. Sept. 5, between 3 and 4 p.m.], on the nones of September, at about the ninth hour, and during an extraordinarily violent south wind, a fire broke out before the gate of the church, and outside the walls of the monastery, by which three cottages were half destroyed. From thence, while the citizens were assembling and subduing the fire, cinders and sparks carried aloft by the high wind, were deposited upon the church, and being driven by the fury of the wind between the joints of the lead, remained there amongst the half rotten planks, and shortly glowing with increasing heat, set fire to the rotten rafters; from these the fire was communicated to the larger beams and their braces, no one yet perceiving or helping. For the well-painted ceiling below, and the sheet-lead covering above, concealed between them the fire that had arisen within.

Meantime the three cottages, whence the mishief had arisen,

being destroyed, and the popular excitement having subsided, everybody went home again, while the neglected church was consuming with internal fire unknown to all. But beams and braces burning, the flames rose to the slopes of the roof; and the sheets of lead yielded to the increasing heat and began to melt. Thus the raging wind, finding a freer entrance, increased the fury of the fire; and the flames beginning to shew themselves, a cry arose in the church-yard: "See! see! the church is on fire."

Then the people and the monks assemble in haste, they draw water, they brandish their hatchets, they run up the stairs, full of eagerness to save the church, already, alas! beyond their help. But when they reach the roof and perceive the black smoke and scorching flames that pervade it throughout, they abandon the attempt in despair, and thinking only of their own safety, make all haste to descend.

And now that the fire had loosened the beams from the pegs that bound them together, the half-burnt timbers fell into the choir below upon the seats of the monks; the seats, consisting of a great mass of wood-work, caught fire, and thus the mischief grew worse and worse, And it was marvellous, though sad, to behold how that glorious choir itself fed and assisted the fire that was destroying it. For the flames multiplied by this mass of timber, and extending upwards full fifteen cubits, scorched and burnt the walls, and more especially injured the columns of the church.

And now the people ran to the ornaments of the church, and began to tear down the pallia and curtains, some that they might save, but some to steal them. The reliquary chests were thrown down from the high beam and thus broken, and their contents scattered, but the monks collected them and carefully preserved them from the fire. Some there were, who inflamed with a wicked and diabolical cupidity, feared not to appropriate to themselves the things of the church, which they had saved from the fire.

In this manner the house of God, hitherto delightful as a paradise of pleasures, was now made a despicable heap of ashes, reduced to a dreary wilderness, and laid open to all the injuries of the weather.

The people were astonished that the Almighty should suffer such things, and maddened with excess of grief and perplexity, they tore their hair and beat the walls and pavement of the church with their heads and hands, blaspheming the Lord and His saints, the patrons of the church; and many, both of laity and monks, would rather have laid down their lives than that the church should have so miserably perished.

For not only was the choir consumed in the fire, but also the infirmary, with the chapel of St. Mary, and several other offices in the court; moreover many ornaments and goods of the church were reduced to ashes.

2. The Operations of the first year.

Bethink thee now what mighty grief oppressed the hearts of the sons of the Church under this great tribulation; I verily believe the afflictions of Canterbury were no less than those of Jerusalem of old, and their wailings were as the lamentations of Jeremiah; neither can mind conceive, or words express, or writing teach, their grief and anguish. Truly that they might alleviate their miseries with a little consolation, they put together as well as they could, an altar and station in the nave of the church, where they might wail and howl, rather than sing, the diurnal and nocturnal services. Meanwhile the patron saints of the church, St. Dunstan and St. Elfege, had their resting-place in that wilderness. Lest, therefore, they should suffer even the slightest injury from the rains and storms, the monks, weeping and lamenting with incredible grief and anguish, opened the tombs of the saints and extricated them in their coffins from the choir, but with the greatest difficulty and labour, as if the saints themselves resisted the change.

They disposed them as decently as they could at the altar of the Holy Cross in the nave. Thus, like as the children of Israel were ejected from the land of promise, yea, even from a paradise of delight, that it might be like people, like priest, and that the stones of the sanctuary might be poured out at the corners of the streets; so the brethren remained in grief and sorrow for five years in the nave of the church, separated from the people only by a low wall.

Meantime the brotherhood sought counsel as to how and in what manner the burnt church might be repaired, but without success; for the columns of the church, commonly termed the *pillars,* were exceedingly weakened by the heat of the fire, and were scaling in pieces and hardly able to stand, so that they frightened even the wisest out of their wits.

French and English artificers were therefore summoned, but even these differed in opinion. On the one hand, some undertook to repair the aforsaid columns without mischief to the walls above. On the other hand, there were some who asserted that the whole church must be pulled down if the monks wished to exist in safety. This opinion, true as it was, excruciated the monks with grief, and no wonder, for how could they hope that so great a work should be completed in their days by any human ingenuity.

However, amongst the other workmen there had come a certain William of Sens, a man active and ready, and as a workman most skilful both in wood and stone. Him, therefore, they retained, on account of his lively genius and good reputation, and dismissed the others. And to him, and to the providence of God was the execution of the work committed.

And he, residing many days with the monks and carefully surveying the burnt walls in their upper and lower parts, within and without, did yet for some time conceal what he found necessary to be done, lest the truth should kill them in their present state of pusillanimity.

But he went on preparing all things that were needful for the work, either of himself or by the agency of others. And when he found that the monks began to be somewhat comforted, he ventured to confess that the pillars rent with the fire and all that they supported must be destroyed if the monks wished to have a safe and excellent building. At length they agreed, being convinced by reason and wishing to have the work as good as he promised, and above all things to live in security; thus they consented patiently, if not willingly, to the destruction of the choir.

And now he addressed himself to the procuring of stone from beyond the sea. He constructed ingenious machines for loading and unloading ships, and for drawing cement and stones. He delivered molds for shaping the stones to the sculptors who were assembled, and diligently prepared other things of the same kind. The choir thus condemned to destruction was pulled down, and nothing else was done in this year.

As the new work is of a different fashion from the old, it may be well to describe the old work first and then the new. Edmer, the venerable singer, in his Opuscula, describes the ancient church built in the Roman manner, which Archbishop Lanfranc, when he came to the see, utterly destroyed, finding it in ashes. For Christ Church is recorded to have suffered thrice from fire; first, when the blessed martyr Elfege was captured by the Danes and received the crown of martyrdom; secondly, when Lanfranc, abbot of Caen, took the rule of the church of Canterbury; thirdly, in the days of Archbishop Richard and Prior Odo. Of this last conflagration, unhappily, we have not read, but have seen it with our own eyes. . . .

3. Of the Church of Lanfranc.

I will first describe the work of Lanfranc; beginning from the great tower, not because the whole of this church has been destroyed, but because part of it has been altered. The tower, raised upon great pillars (*AAAA*, see fig.), is placed in the midst of the church, like the centre in the middle of a circle. It had on its apex (*pinna*) a gilt cherub. On the west of the tower is the nave or *aula* of the church, supported on either side upon eight pillars. Two lofty towers (*BC*) with gilded pinnacles terminate this nave or aula. A gilded *corona* hangs in the midst of the church. A screen with a loft (*pulpitum*) (*DD*), separated in a manner the aforesaid tower from the nave, and had in the middle, and on the side towards the nave, the altar of the holy cross (*E*). Above the *pulpitum,* and placed across the church, was the beam, which sustained a great cross, two cherubim, and the images of St. Mary, and St. John the Apostle. In the north aisle (*ala*) was the oratory and altar of St. Mary (*F*). In this nave, as above related, we for five years endured banishment. The

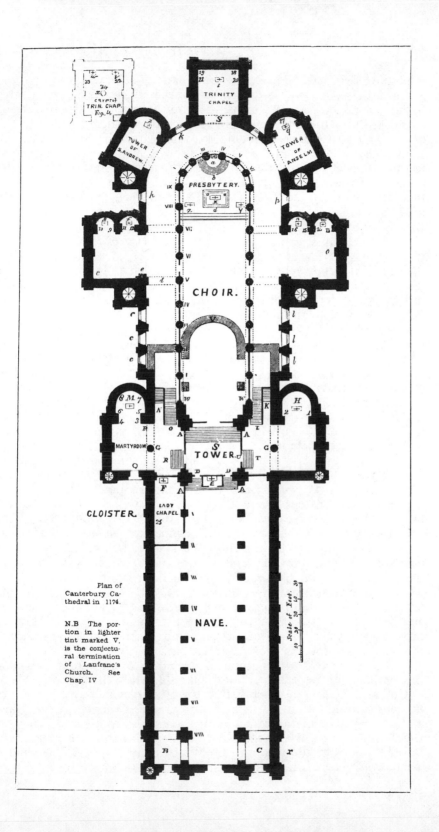

TRINITY CHAPEL.

CRYPT of
TRIN. CHAP.
Fig. 4.

TOWER
OF
S.ANDREW

TOWER
OF
ANSELM

PRESBYTERY.

CHOIR.

MARTYRDOM

TOWER.

CLOISTER.

LADY
CHAPEL

NAVE.

Plan of
Canterbury Ca-
thedral in 1174.

N.B The por-
tion in lighter
tint marked V.
is the conjectu-
ral termination
of Lanfranc's
Church. See
Chap. IV

Scale of Feet.

aforesaid great tower had a cross from each side, to wit, a south cross and a north cross, each of which had in the midst a strong pillar; this (pillar) sustained a vault which proceeded from the walls on three of its sides; the plan of the one cross is exactly the same as that of the other. The south cross was employed to carry the organ upon the vault. Above and beneath the vault was an apse (*H*), extended towards the east. In the lower part was the altar of St. Michael, in the upper part the altar of All Saints. Before the altar of St. Michael to the south was buried Archbishop Feologild (*I*). On the north the holy virgin Siburgis (*2*), who for her sanctity was buried in the church by St. Dunstan.

Between this apse and the choir the space is divided into two, that is, for the few steps (*K*) by which the crypt is gained, and for the many steps (*L*) by which the upper parts of the church are reached. The north cross similarly had two apses (*M*). In the upper one is the altar of St. Blasius, in the lower that of St. Benedict. In this lower one, to the right of the entrance, was buried Archbishop William (*3*), who with great glory dedicated the church of Christ which I am describing. He also founded the church of St. Martin for monks of Dover. To the left lies the predecessor of William, Archbishop Radulf (*4*), who, although discreet in wisdom and of renowned eloquence, yet did Pope Calixtus prefer before him Thurstan, archbishop of York, and Hugo, abbot of St. Augustine. In the same apse, before the altar on the right, lies Archbishop Egelnoth (*5*), and to the left Vulfelm (*6*). Behind the altar to the right Adelm (*7*), to the left Chelnoth (*8*). And thus is the aforesaid apse graced. Between this apse and the choir the space is divided into two, that is, for the steps (*N*) which descend to the crypt, and for the steps (*O*) which serve those who ascend to the eastern parts of the church.

Between this space and the aforesaid apse is a solid wall (*P*), before which that glorious companion of martyrs, and guest of the Apostles, the holy Thomas, fell in the body by the swords of raging men, but transmitted his unconquered soul to heaven to be straightway crowned with the glory and honour of the eternal kingdom. This place of martyrdom is opposite to the door of the cloister (*Q*) by which those four notaries of the devil entered that they might stamp the seal of the genuine preogative of the martyr between the anvil and hammer, that is, that they might adorn the head of St. Thomas, prostrate between the pavement and their swords, with the stamp of the Most High, the chaplet of martyrdom.

The pillar (*G*) which stood in the midst of this cross, as well as the vault which rested on it, were taken down in the process of time out of respect for the martyr, that the altar, elevated on the place of the martyrdom, might be seen from a greater distance. Around and at the height of the aforesaid vault a passage was constructed from which *pallia* and curtains might be suspended. From the cross to the tower, and from the tower to the choir many steps (*RS*) ascended. There was a descent (*T*) from the tower into the south cross by a new entrance (*U*). Also a descent from the tower to the nave through two doors (*DD*). Thus much for the church of Lanfranc. Now let us describe the choir, lest the memory thereof be utterly lost.

4. Of the Choir of Conrad.

I have described, as shortly as I might, the church constructed by Archbishop Lanfranc; that is, the nave, crosses, towers, and their appurtenances. Still the actual sight of them will explain them as much more rapidly as it will effectually.

You must know however, good reader, that I never saw the choir of Lanfranc, neither have I been able to meet with any description of it. Edmer, indeed, describes the old church, which before the time of Lanfranc was constructed after the Roman manner. Also he mentions, but does not describe, the work of Lanfranc which succeeded this old church, and the choir of Conrad constructed in the time of St. Anselm. Now, therefore, that this choir of Conrad, so gloriously completed, has been in our own days miserably comsumed by fire; my poor and simple pen shall attempt its description, lest the memory of so great a man and so noble a work be utterly lost. And although my purpose is not to describe the mere arrangement of stones, yet it is impossible clearly to shew the places of the Saints and of their repose, which are in various parts of the church, without first describing the building itself in which they were arranged, under the inspection and with the assistance of their historian Edmer. Let us begin therefore with the aforesaid great tower, which, as already explained, is placed in the midst of the whole church, and proceed eastward. The eastern pillars of the tower projected as a solid wall, and were formed each into a round semi-pillar (*W*). Hence in line and order were nine pillars on each side of the choir, nearly equidistant from each other; after these six in a circuit were arranged circularly, that is, from the ninth on the south side to the ninth on the north, of which the two extreme ones were united by the same one arch. Upon these pillars, as well those in the straight line as those in the circuit, arches were turned from pillar to pillar; above these the solid wall was set with small blank windows. This wall, (on either side), bounding the choir, met the corresponding one at the head of the church in that circuit of pillars. Above the wall was the passage which is called *triforium*, and the upper windows. This was the termination upwards of the interior wall. Upon it rested the roof and a ceiling decorated with excellent painting. At the bases of the pillars there was a wall built of marble slabs, which, surrounding the choir and presbytery, divided the body of the church from its sides, which are called aisles (*alæ*).

This wall inclosed the choir of the monks, the presbytery, the great Altar (*X*) dedicated in the name of Jesus Christ, the altar of St. Dunstan (*Y*), and the altar of St. Elfege (*Z*), with their holy bodies.

Above the wall, in the circuit behind and opposite to the altar, was the patriarchal seat (*a*) formed out of a single stone, in which, according to the custom of the Church on high festivals, the arch-bishops were wont to sit during the solemnities of the mass, until the consecration of the Sacrament; they then descended to the Altar of Christ by eight steps (*a b*).

From the choir to the presbytery there were three steps (*ZY*); from the pavement of the presbytery to the altar three steps (*d*); but to the partiarchal seat eight steps (*b a*). At the eastern horns of the altar were two wooden columns, gracefully ornamented with gold and silver, and sustaining a great beam, the extremities of which rested upon the capitals of two of the pillars (ix. ix.). This beam, carried across the church above the altar, and decorated with gold, sustained the representation of the Lord (*majestatem Domini*), the images of St. Dunstan and of St. Elfege, together with seven chests (*scrinia*), covered with gold and silver, and filled with the relics of divers saints. Between the columns there stood a gilded cross, of which the cross itself was surrounded by a row of sixty transparent crystals. In the crypt, under this altar of Christ, stood the altar of the holy Virgin Mary, to whose honor the entire crypt was dedicated. Which crypt occupied precisely the same space and compass in length and breadth as did the choir above it. In the midst of the choir hung a gilded corona carrying four and twenty wax lights. This was the fashion of the choir and presbytery. But the exterior wall of the aisles was as follows. Beginning from the martyrium of St. Thomas, that is to say from the cross of Lanfranc, and proceeding towards the east as far as the upper cross, the wall contained three windows (*ccc*) and no more. Opposite to the fifth pillar of the choir, the wall received an arch (*d*) from it, and turning towards the north (*e e*) it formed the north cross. The breadth of this cross extended from the fifth to the seventh pillar. For the wall proceeding northwards from the seventh pillar as from the fifth, and making two apses (*fg*), completed the cross of the eastern part. In its southern apse (*f*) was the altar of St. Stephen, under which, in the crypt, was the altar of St. Nicholas. In the northern apse (*g*) was the altar of St. Martin; and under it, in the crypt, the altar of St. Mary Magdalene. At the altar of St. Martin two archbishops were laid, to the right Vulfred (*9*), to the left Living (*10*); and similarly at the altar of St. Stephen, to the left Athelard (*11*), and to the right the venerable Cuthbert (*12*).

He it was who, being endowed with great wisdom, procured for Christ Church the right of free sepulture. For the bodies not only of the archbishops, but of all who died in the city, were wont, from the time of St. Augustine, to be carried to the church of the Apsotles Peter and Paul, without the city, and there buried. For in those days it was said that the city was for the living and not for the dead. But the blessed Cuthbert was grieved to think that after death he must be separated from his church and his children, that in life were the delights of his affection. Wherefore he sought and obtained from Rome the right of free burial for Christ Church. He was the first who, by the will of God, the authority of the high pontiff, and the permission of the king of England, was buried in Christ Church, and so also were all his successors, save one alone named Jambert.

From this apse of St. Stephen, the aforesaid wall proceeding eastward had a window (*h*) opposite to the side of the great Altar (*X*). Next after came a lofty tower, placed as it were outside the said wall, which was called the tower of St. Andrew because of the altar of St. Andrew (*i*) which was therein, below which, in the crypt, was the altar of the Innocents. From this tower the wall proceeding, slightly curved and opening into a window (*k*) reached a chapel, which was extended towards the east at the front of the church, and opposite to the high seat of the archbishop. But as there are many things to be said of the interior of this chapel, it will be better to pause before its entrance until the south wall with its appurtenances has been traced up to the same point. This south wall, beginning from the the the apse of St. Michael (*H*) in the cross of Lanfranc, reaches the upper cross after three windows (*l l l*). This cross at its eastern side, like the other, had two apses. In the southern apse (*m*) was the altar of St. Gregory, where two holy archbishops were deposited; to the south St. Bregwin (*13*), to the north St. Plegemund (*14*), underneath in the crypt was the altar of St. Audoen, archbishop of Rouen. In the other apse (*n*) was the altar of St. John the Evangelist, where two archbishops reposed; to the right Ethelgar (*15*); to the left Elfric (*16*); underneath in the crypt was the altar of St. Paulinus, where Archbishop Siric was buried. Before the altar of St. Audoen and nearly in the middle of the floor was the altar of St. Katherine (*o*). The wall proceeding from the above cross had a window (*p*) opposite to the great Altar, and next a lofty tower, in which was the altar of. the Apostles Peter and Paul (*q*).

But St, Anselm (*17*) having been translated there and placed behind the altar gave his name to the altar and to the tower. From this tower the wall proceeding for a short space and opening into a window (*r*) in its curve, arrived at the aforesaid chapel of the Holy Trinity, which was placed at the front of the church. An arch (*s*) springing from each wall, that is, from the south and from the north, completed the circuit.

The chapel placed outside the wall but joined to it and extended towards the east, had the altar of the Holy Trinity (*t*), where the blessed martyr Thomas celebrated his first mass on the day of his consecration. In this chapel, before and after his exile, he was wont to celebrate mass, to hear service, and frequently to pray. Behind the altar there lay two archbishops, to the right St. Odo (*18*), to the left St. Wilfrid (*19*), archbishop of York; to the south, close to the wall, the veneralbe Archbishop Lanfranc (*20*), and to the north Theodbald (*21*). In the crypt beneath, there were two altars, on the south (*v*) that of St. Augustine, the apostle of the English, and on the north (*w*) that of St. John Baptist. Close to the south wall Archbishop Ethelred (*22*) was deposited, and Eadsin (*23*) against the north wall. In the middle of this chapel there stood a column (*x*) which sustained arches and a vault, that came from all sides. At the base of this column, on the eastern side, . . . was the place (*24*) where the blessed martyr Thomas was buried on the day after his martyrdom. . . .

And now the description, as concise as I could make it, of the church which we are going to pull down, has brought us to the tomb of the martyr, which was at the end of the church; let therefore the church and the description come to an end together; for although this description has already extended itself to a greater length than was proposed, yet many things have been carefully omitted for the sake of brevity. Who could write all the turnings, and windings, and appendages of such and so great a church as this was? Leaving out, therefore, all that is not absolutely necessary, let us boldly prepare for the destruction of this old work and the marvellous building of the new, and let us see what our master William has been doing in the meanwhile.

5. Operations of the first five years.

The Master began, as I stated long ago, to prepare all things necessary for the new work, and to destroy the old. In this way the first year was taken up. In the following year, that is, after the feast of St. Bertin, (Sept. 5, 1175), before the winter, he erected four pillars, that is, two on each side, and after the winter two more were placed, so that on each side were three in order, upon which, and upon the exterior wall of the aisles he framed seemly arches and a vault, that is, three *claves* on each side. I put *clavis* for the whole *ciborium* because the *clavis* placed in the middle locks up and binds together the parts which converge to it from every side. With these words the second year was occupied.

In the third year he placed two pillars on each side, the two extreme ones of which he decorated with marble columns placed around them, and because at that place the choir and the crosses were to meet, he constituted these principal pillars. To which, having added the key-stones and vault, he intermingled the lower triforium from the great tower to the aforesaid pillars, that is, as far as the cross, with many marble columns. Over which he adjusted another triforium of other materials, and also the upper windows. And in the next place, three *claves* of the great vault, from the tower, namely, as far as the crosses. All which things appeared to us and to all who saw them, incomparable and most worthy of praise. And at so glorious a beginning we rejoiced and conceived good hopes of the end, and provided for the acceleration of the work with diligence and spirit. Thus was the third year occupied and the beginning of the fourth.

In the summer of which, commencing from the cross, he erected ten pillars, that is, on each side five. Of which the two first were ornamented with marble columns to correspond with the other two principal ones. Upon these ten he placed the arches and vaults. And having, in the next place, completed on both sides the triforia and upper windows, he was, at the beginning of the fifth year, in the act of preparing with machines for the turning of the great vault, when suddenly the beams broke under his feet, and he fell to the ground, stones and timbers accompanying his fall, from the height of the capitals of the upper vault, that is to say, of fifty feet. Thus sorely bruised by the blows from the beams and stones, he was rendered helpless alike to himself and for the work, but no other person than himself was in the least injured. Against the master only was this vengeance of God or spite of the devil directed.

The master, thus hurt, remained in his bed for some time under medical care in expectation of recovering, but was deceived in this hope, for his health amended not. Nevertheless, as the winter approached, and it was necessary to finish the upper vault, he gave charge of the work to a certain ingenious and industrious monk, who was the overseer of the masons; an appointment whence much envy and malice arose, because it made this young man appear more skilful than richer and more powerful ones. But the master reclining in bed commanded all things that should be done in order. And thus was completed the ciborium between the four principal pillars. In the key-stone of this ciborium the choir and crosses seem as it were to meet. Two ciboria on each side were formed before the winter; when heavy rains beginning stopped the work. In these operations the fourth year was occupied and the beginning of the fifth. But on the eighth day from the said fourth year, on the idus of September, there happened an eclipse of the sun at about the sixth hour, and before the master's accident.

And the master, perceiving that he derived no benefit from the physicians, gave up the work, and crossing the sea, returned to his home in France. And another succeeded him in the charge of the works; William by name, English by nation, small in body, but in workmanship of many kinds acute and honest. He in the summer of the fifth year finished the cross on each side, that is, the south and the north, and turned the ciborium which is above the great Altar, which the rains of the previous year had hindered, although all was prepared. Moreover, he laid the foundation for the enlargement of the church at the eastern part, because a chapel of St. Thomas was to be built there.

For this was the place assigned to him; namely, the chapel of the Holy Trinity, where he celebrated his first mass, where he was wont to prostrate himself with tears and prayers, under whose crypt for so many years he was buried, where God for his merits had performed so many miracles, where poor and rich, kings and princes, had worshipped him, and whence the sound of his praises had gone forth into all lands.

The master William began, on account of these foundations, to dig in the cemetery of the monks, from whence he was compelled to disturb the bones of many holy monks. These were carefully collected and deposited in a large trench, in that corner which is between the chapel and the south side of the infirmary house. Having, therefore, formed a most substantial foundation for the exterior wall with stone and cement, he erected the wall of the crypt as high as the bases of the windows.

Thus was the fifth year employed and the beginning of the sixth.

6. The entry into the new Choir.

In the beginning of the sixth year from the fire, and at the time when the works were resumed, the monks were seized with a violent longing to prepare the choir, so that they might enter it at the coming Easter. And the master, perceiving their desires, set himself manfully to work, to satisfy the wishes of the convent. He constructed, with all diligence, the wall which encloses the choir and presbytery. He erected the three altars of the presbytery. He carefully prepared a resting-place for St. Dunstan and St. Elfege. A wooden wall to keep out the weather was set up transversely between the penultimate pillars at the eastern part, and had three glass windows in it.

The choir, thus hardly completed even with the greatest labour and diligence, the monks were resolved to enter on Easter Eve with the new fire. As all that was required could not be fully performed on the Saturday because of the solemnities of that sacred day, it became necessary that our holy fathers and patrons, St. Dunstan and St. Elfege, the co-exiles of the monks, should be transferred to the new choir beforehand. Prior Alan, therefore, taking with him nine of the brethren of the church in whom he could trust, went by night to the tombs of the saints, that he might not be incommoded by a crowd, and having locked the doors of the church, he commanded the stone-work that enclosed them to be taken down.

The monks and servants of the church therefore, in obedience to the Prior's commands, took the structure to pieces, opened the stone coffins of the saints, and bore their relics to the *vestiarium*. Then, having removed the cloths in which they had been wrapped, and which were half consumed from age and rottenness, they covered them with other and more handsome palls, and bound them with linen bands. They bore the saints, thus prepared, to their altars, and deposited them in wooden chests, covered within and without with lead; which chests, thus lead-covered, and strongly bound with iron, were enclosed in stone-work that was consolidated with melted lead. Queen Ediva also, who had been placed under the altar of the holy cross after the fire, was similarly conveyed to the vestiarium. These things were done on the night preceding the fifth feria before the holy Easter; that is, on the sixteenth calend of May. On the morrow, however, when this translation of the saints became known to the whole convent, they were exceedingly astonished and indignant that it should have been done without their consent, for they had intended that the translation of the fathers should have been performed with great and devout solemnity.

They cited the prior and those who were with him, before the venerable Archbishop Richard, to answer for the slight thus presumptuously cast upon themselves and the holy patrons of the church, and endeavoured to compel the prior and his assistants to renounce their offices. But by the intervention of the archbishop and other men of authority, and after due apology and repentance, the convent was appeased; and harmony being thus restored, the service of Holy Saturday was performed in the chapter-house, because the station of the monks and the altar which had been in the nave of the church, were removed to prepare for the solemnities of the following Easter Sunday. About the sixth hour the archbishop in cope and mitre, and the convent in albs, according to the custom of the church, went in procession to the new fire, and having consecrated it, proceeded towards the new choir with the appointed hymn. At the door of the church which opens to the martyrium of St. Thomas, the archbishop reverently received from a monk the pix, with the Eucharist, which was usually suspended over the great Altar. This he carried to the great Altar of the new choir. Thus our Lord went before us into Galilee, that is, in our transmigration to the new church. The remainder of the offices that appertain to the day were devoutly celebrated. And then the pontiff, standing at the Altar and vested with the infula, began the Te Deum laudamus; and the bells ringing, the convent took up the song with great joy, and shedding sweet tears, they praised God with voice and heart for all His benefits.

The convent was ejected by the fire from the choir, even as Adam from paradise, in the year of the Word 1174, in the month of September, on the fifth day of the month, and about the ninth hour. They remained in the nave of the church five years, seven months, and thirteen days. And returned into the new choir in the year of grace 1180, in the month of April, on the nineteenth day of the month, at about the ninth hour of Easter Eve.

7. *The remaining operations of the sixth year.*

Our craftsman had erected outside the choir four altars, where the bodies of the holy archbishops were deposited, as they were of old, and as we have above described. At the altar of St. Martin; Living, and Wilfrid. At the altar of St, Stephen; Athelard, and Cuthbert. In the south cross at the altar of St. John; Elfric, and Ethelgar. At the altar of St. Gregory; Bregwin, and Plegemund. But Quenn Ediva, who before the fire reposed under a gilded *feretrum* in nearly the middle of the south cross, was now deposited at the altar of St. Martin, under the *feretrum* of Living.

Moreover, in the same summer, that is of the sixth year, the outer wall round the chapel of St. Thomas, begun before the winter, was elevated as far as the turning of the vault. But the master had begun a tower at the eastern part outside the circuit of the wall as it were, the lower vault of which was completed before the winter.

The chapel of the Holy Trinity above mentioned was then levelled to the ground; this had hitherto remained untouched out of reverence to St. Thomas, who was buried in the crypt. But the saints who reposed in the upper part of the chapel were translated elsewhere, and lest the memory of what was then done should be lost, I will record somewhat thereof. On the eighth idus of July the altar of the Holy Trinity was broken up, and from its materials the altar of St. John the Apostle was made; I mention this lest the history of the holy stone should be lost upon which St. Thomas celebrated his first mass, and many times after performed the divine offices. The stone structure which was behind this altar was taken to pieces. Here, as before said, St. Odo and St. Wilfrid reposed for a long period. These saints were raised in their leaden coffins (*capsis plumbeis*) and carried into the choir. St. Odo, in his coffin, was placed under the feretrum of St. Dunstan, and St. Wilfrid under the feretrum of St. Elphege.

Archbishop Lanfranc was found enclosed in a very heavy sheet of lead, in which, from the day of his first burial up to that day, he had rested untouched, in mitre and pall, for sixty-nine years and some months. He was carried to the vestiarium in his leaden covering, and there deposited until the community should decide what should be done with so great a Father. When they opened the tomb of Archbishop Theodbald, which was built of marble slabs, and came to his sarcophagus, the monks who were present expecting to find his body reduced to dust, brought wine and water to wash his bones. But when the lid of the sarcophagus was raised, he was found entire and rigid, and still subsisting in bones and nerves, skin and flesh, but somewhat attenuated. The bystanders marvelled at this sight, and placing him upon a bier (*tabulam gestatoriam*), they carried him as they had done Lanfranc, to the vestiarium, to await the decision of the convent. But the rumour began to spread among the people, and already, for this unwonted incorruption, many called him St. Theodbald. He was exhibited to some who desired to see him, and they helped to spread the tale among the rest.

He was thus raised from his sepulchre in the nineteenth year from his death, his body being incorrupted, and his silk vestments entire, And by the decision of the convent was buried in a leaden coffin (*in arca plumbea*) before the altar of St. Mary, in the nave of the church, which place he had wished for while living. The marble tomb was put together over him, as it was before. But Lanfranc having remainded, as before said, untouched for sixty-nine years, his very bones were consumed with rottenness, and nearly all reduced to powder. The length of time, the damp vestments, the natural frigidity of the lead, and above all, the frailty of the human structure, had conspired to produce this corruption. But the larger bones, with the remaining dust, were collected in a leaden coffer, (*in capsa plumbea*), and deposited at the altar of St. Martin. The two archbishops who lay to the right and left of St. Thomas in the crypt were taken up, and placed for the time in their leaden coffins (*capsis*) under the altar of St. Mary, in the crypt.

The translation of these Fathers having been thus effected, the chapel, together with its crypt, was destroyed to the very ground; only that the translation of St. Thomas was reserved until the completion of his chapel. For it was fitting and manifest that such a translation should be most solemn and public. In the mean time, therefore, a wooden chapel, sufficiently decent for the place and occasion, was prepared around and above his tomb. Outside of this a foundation was laid of stones and cement, upon which eight pillars of the new crypt, with their capitals, were completed. The master also carefully opened an entrance from the old to the new crypt. And thus the sixth year was employed, and part of the seventh. But before I follow the works of this seventh year, it may not be amiss to recapitulate some of the previous ones which have either been omitted from negligence or purposely for the sake of brevity.

8. Explanations.

It has been above stated, that after the fire nearly all the old portions of the choir were destroyed and changed into somewhat new and of a more noble fashion. The differences between the two works may now be enumerated. The pillars of the old and new work are alike in form and thickness but different in length. For the new pillars were elongated by almost twelve feet. In the old capitals the work was plain, in the new ones exquisite in sculpture. There the circuit of the choir had twenty-two pillars, here are twenty-eight. There the arches and every thing else was plain, or sculptured with an axe and not with a chisel. But here almost throughout is appropriate sculpture. No marble columns were there, but here are innumerable ones. There, in the circuit around the choir, the vaults were plain, but here they are arch-ribbed and have keystones. There a wall set upon pillars divided the crosses from the choir, but here the crosses are separated from the choir by no such partition, and converge together in one keystone, which is placed in the middle of the great vault which rests on the four principal pillars. There, there was a ceiling of wood decorated with excellent painting, but here is a vault beautifully constructed of stone and light tufa. There, was a single triforium, but here are two in the choir and a third in the aisle of the church. All which will be better understood from inspection than by any description.

This must be made known, however, that the new work is higher than the old by so much as the upper windows of the body of the choir, as well as of its aisles, are raised above the marble tabling.

And as in future ages it may be doubtful why the breadth which was given to the choir next the tower should be so much contracted at the head of the church, it may not be useless to explain the causes thereof. One reason is, that the two towers of St. Anselm and of St. Andrew, placed in the circuit on each side of the old church, would not allow the breadth of the choir to proceed in the direct line. Another reason is, that it was agreed upon and necessary that the chapel of St. Thomas should be erected at the head of the church, where the chapel of the Holy Trinity stood, and this was much narrower than the choir.

The master, therefore, not choosing to pull down the said towers, and being unable to move them entire, set out the breadth of the choir in a straight line, as far as the beginning of the towers (I. . .IX). Then, receding slightly on either side from the towers, and preserving as much as he could the breadth of the passage outside the choir on account of the processions which were there frequently passing, he gradually and obliquely drew in his work, so that from opposite the altar (IX), it might begin to contract, and from thence, at the third pillar (XI), might be so narrowed as to coincide with the breadth of the chapel, which was named of the Holy Trinity. Beyond these, four pillars (XII. XIII.) were set on the sides at the same distance as the last, but of a different form; and beyond these other four (XIV. XV.) were arranged in a circle, and upon these the super-posed work (of each side) was brought together and terminated. This is the arrangement of the pillars.

The outer wall, which extends from the aforesaid towers, first proceeds in a straight line, is then bent into a curve, and thus in the round tower the wall on each side comes together in one, and is there ended. All which may be more clearly and pleasantly seen by the eyes than taught in writing. But this much was said that the differences between the old and new work might be made manifest.

9. *Operations of the seventh, eighth, and tenth years.*

Now let us carefully examine what were the works of our mason in this seventh year from the fire, which, in short, included the completion of the new and handsome crypt, and above the crypt the exterior walls of the aisles up to their marble capitals. The windows, however, the master was neither willing nor able to turn, on account of the approaching rains. Neither did he erect the interior pillars. Thus was the seventh year finished, and the eighth begun.

In this eighth year the master erected eight interior pillars, (XII. . .XV), and turned the arches and the vault with the windows in the circuit. He also raised the tower up to the bases of the highest windows under the vault. In the ninth year no work was done for want of funds. In the tenth year the upper windows of the tower, together with the vault, were finished. Upon the pillars was placed a lower and upper triforium, with windows and the great vault. Also was made the upper roof where the cross stands aloft, and the roof of the aisles as far as the laying of the lead. The tower was covered in, and many other things done this year. In which year Baldwin bishop of Worcester was elected to the rule of the church of Canterbury on the eighteenth kalend of January, and was enthroned there on the feast of St. Dunstan next after. . . .

The Technique of Manuscript Illumination

The act of embellishing or illuminating manuscripts with designs and pictures represents a major art form of the high Middle Ages. The following anonymous work, *De arte illuminandi*, although probably written toward the end of the fourteenth century presents numerous techniques and formulas that were commonly used by illuminators throughout the Middle Ages.

1. Introduction.

IN THE NAME OF THE HOLY & INDIVISIBLE TRINITY. AMEN. To begin with, I intend to write quite straightforwardly and without any reference to authority, but liberally nevertheless, about various subjects which concern the practice of illuminating, with the pen as well as with the brush. And although many have gone back through the ages and expounded it on the basis of their writings, nevertheless, in order to cast more light on satisfactory and briefer methods, so that the experienced may be confirmed in their perhaps better views, and the inexperienced who desire to master this profession may be able to understand it distinctly and clearly, and even to practice it, I shall, in writing concisely here about the colors and their temperas, explain methods correct and tested.

So while, according to physics, the primary colors are three, namely, black, white, and red, and all other colors are intermediates of those, as is laid down in the books of all the physicists, nevertheless, the colors which are natural and necessary for illuminating are eight, namely, black, white, red, yellow, blue, violet, rose and green. And some of those are natural and some artificial. Ultramarine blue and azurite are natural. And the black color is a certain black earth or natural stone. The red color is likewise a certain red earth, commonly called "macra"; and the green, an earth, or malachite. And the yellow is yellow earth, or orpiment, or fine gold, or saffron. And all the other colors are artificial, namely: the black, which is made from the charcoal of vines or other kinds of wood, or from smoke of candles, wax, oil, or tallow, collected on a basin or a glazed porringer; the red color, such as vermilion, which is made from sulphur and quicksilver, or red lead, otherwise known as "stupium," which is made from lead; the white color which is made from lead, that is, white lead, or from the calcined bones of animals; the yellow, which is made from the turmeric root or fuller's weed with white lead, and in another way, by sublimation, and is called "purpurina" or mosaic gold, and it is made in another way out of glass and is called giallorino. Even an artificaial blue is made from the plant which is called turnsole, and a violet color is made from the same plant according to circumstances. The artificial green color is made out of copper; also out of the berries which are popularly called "prugnameroli" and gathered in the vintage season along the vineyard hedges; and it is also made in another way from the flowers of the blue lilies.

2. Binders for gilding.

The binders for gilding are as follows: stag's horn glue, parchment or fish glue, and things like these.

3. The solutions with which colors are tempered for use on parchment.

The solutions with which colors are laid are as follows: the glair of hens' eggs, and their yolks, gum arabic and gum tragacanth dissolved in pure spring water. And solutions of honey or sugar or sugar candy are required for sweetening them now and then, as I shall explain in detail, God willing, in connection with their preparation.

4. How the artificial colors are made: first of all, black.

The black color is made in several ways. First, and most generally, it is made very satisfactorily out of vine-twig charcoal, that is, by burning twigs of the vine from which wine comes; and before they turn to ashes, water is thrown on them, a little at a time, and they are allowed to go out, and the clean coals are separated from the ashes. It is also made in another way, as follows: get a clean basin of brass or glazed earthenware, and put under it a lighted candle of clean wax, and have the flame almost reach the hollow of the basin; and carefully collect that black which is produced by the smoke. And put (the candle back again) and make as much of it as you want.

5. White.

I have found that there is only one white color which is fit for the practice of illuminating, namely, white lead, known also as ceruse; for the white from calcined bones will not do, because it is too pasty. And it is not worth while to include a method for making white lead, because it is common enough knowledge to practically every one that it is made out of lead, and it is readily available everywhere.

6. The artificial red color.

The artificial red color is made from sulphur and quicksilver, and is called vermilion. And it is made in another way, namely, from lead, and is known as red lead or "stupium." And since these colors are readily available everywhere, I have not included the method of manufacture.

7. Yellow.

The artificial yellow color is made in many ways: first, as mentioned above, it is made from the root of the turmeric or from the rocket plant. It is made in this way: take one ounce of turmeric roots shaved good and thin with a knife, and put them into a half *petita* of plain water, and add an eighth of on ounce of rock alum, in a glazed earthenware dish. And let it soften for a day and a night; and when it is quite yellow, put an ounce of white lead into it, well worked up, and stir it with a stick. And let it stand on the fire for a while, constantly mixing it with the stick to keep it from boiling over. Then strain it through a linen cloth into an earthenware dish, fired but not glazed, and let it settle. And pour off the water carefully, and dry it, and put it aside for your use.

It is also made in a similar way out of that dyers' weed. Take this and cut it up fine with a knife, and put it into plain water or fairly strong lye, and have the water or lye stand over the weed in good measure. Boil it hard for a while; then, if there is one handful of the plant, put in an ounce and a half of white lead, well worked up. But, before you put in the white lead, work up one ounce of rock alum thoroughly, and put it into this dish with the decoction of the plant, and get it dissolved. And when it is dissolved, add the white lead gradually, constantly stirring it with a stick until all those things are thoroughly incorporated. And then strain it through a linen cloth into an earthenware porringer, fired but not glazed, and let it settle. And pour off the water, and again put in some clear plain water. And when the substance settles pour off the water; and let it dry, and put it away.

White lead can also be stained with saffron in the same way. And know that if it were not well stained, it could be given more color; and if there is too much color in it, put in more white lead.

8. An imitation gold color.

There is another artificial yellow color, which is known as mosaic gold or "purpurina," and it is made this way. Take one part of tin, and melt it, and throw upon it one part of pure quicksilver; and take it right off the fire, and work it up with vinegar and a little common salt. And wash it with clear water, hot or cold, until the water comes off clear and free from salt. And then melt the material again over the fire, and put it on the marble. And then take one part of sulphur, as clean and pure as amber, and one part of sal ammoniac, and work them up very thoroughly, and combine all together with the aforesaid mercury and tin, until it all turns black like coal, and is thoroughly combined. Then have a glass jar, like a bottle, with a wide, short neck and (have the jar) so big that when the material is put into it, at least half of it will be empty. This jar is to be thoroughly luted to the thickness of one finger with good clay, well thickened with asses' dung and shearings of cloths; and the jar should be luted as far up as the material reaches. And when this material has been put inside, place it in a furnace with an opening large enough to hold the luted part of the bottle, and seal up the joints and the opening in the furnace with ashes moistened with water. And at first, kindle underneath it a slow fire of willow wood or reeds or something of this kind, strengthening the fire for nine hours, more or less, up to the critical moment described below. And the jar should be covered with a loose tile in such a way that it can be taken off and replaced at will. And first a black smoke will appear, and then a white one; afterwards a mixed one. And a dry, clean stick is frequently inserted, that is, into the jar where the material is, in such a way as not to touch the material; and the heat is gradually but steadily increased until golden sparkles are noticed on the stick. And then the fire is withdrawn, because it is done. And after breaking the jar when it has cooled off, the material is taken out, and used. *Deo gratias.*

9. The natural color yellow.

Natural yellow color occurs: namely, fine gold, and yellow earth, and saffron, and also orpiment.

10. Blue, or sky color, natural and artificial.

Blue occurs in various forms, as, for example, the ultramarine, which is made from lapis lazuli (and I shall include the way to make it at the end of this book) and which still surpasses all the rest. There is another blue which is made from a stone found in Germany; and still another is made from silver plates as Albertus Magnus notes. Another, a coarse blue, is made artificially, namely, with the best indigo and white lead.

It is made also in another way from the plant called turnsole, and it stays blue in color for a year; afterwards it turns into a violet color. Now this is the way to make the color from this plant. Take the seeds of this plant, which are gathered from the middle of July up to the middle of Septimber. And it has yellow [   ] and its fruits, that is, those seeds, are triangular. That is because there are three seeds joined in one. And they should be gathered when the weather is fair. And the seeds are to be freed from the stems from which they hang, and put into an old, clean, linen or hempen cloth. And fold up the cloth, and draw it through your hands, until the cloth is saturated with the juice; and the kernels of the seeds do not get broken. And have a glazed porringer and squeeze the juice out of this cloth into this porringer; and again take some more fresh seeds of the plant and extract the juice in the same way, until you have enough of it. Then take some other good clean linen cloths which have been wet down first once or twice in a lye made with water and quicklime; and then wash them very thoroughly with clear water and dry them. (They can even be prepared plain, without the lime.) And when they are dry, put them into this porringer where the juice of the aforesaid plant is; and let the cloths soak up enough of this juice to saturate them thoroughly. And let them stand in this porringer for one day or a night.

Then have a dark, moist place, where you may put some garden loam in a winecup or other suitable dish, or upon screens, where neither wind, sun, rain nor water may get at it; and let there be voided upon this loam a quantity of the urine of a healthy man who has been drinking wine. And over it, furthermore, you put up a structure of light reeds or other little wooden rods, so that the cloths soaked in this liquid may be spread out above the vapor of the urine, (but) in such a way as not to touch the wine-soaked earth described above, because they would be spoiled. And then let them stay this way for three or four days, or until they dry there. Then put these cloths under books and keep them in a box; or put them into a glass jar, close it up, put it in quicklime, not slaked, in a quiet, dry spot, and keep it.

11. Green color.

Natural green color occurs as follows: namely, terre-verte, which painters regularly use, and malachite. Besides these, other kinds of green color are artificially extracted from compounds of natural materials in which that character is made effective. And in those it exists potentially and not yet developed in fact, but by appropriate treatment they are converted from potentiality to fact, as may be seen, for example, in the case of copper, which is red and under treatment becomes green. And it may be seen, likewise, in the case of the buckthorn berries, the *prugnameroli* which I mentioned above, so-called in the dialect of Rome, in the neighborhood of which city they abound. And it may be seen, in the third place, in blue lilies, which are called iris, and yet are changed into a very pure green color by treatment.

The color is made from these lilies as follows. Take these fresh flowers in the springtime when they are blooming, and pound them in a marble or bronze mortar; and squeeze the juice with a cloth into a glazed porringer. And in this juice soak other linen cloths, clean and soaked once or twice in a solution of rock alum and dried. And when the cloths are thoroughly saturated with the juice of the lilies in this way, let them dry in the shade, and keep them between the leaves of books; for a very lovely green, splendid for use on parchment, is made out of this juice preserved in this way by combining it with giallorino. And note that after the cloths are dry, if they are again soaked in this juice and dried, they will be better.

And you do the same thing with those buckthorn berries which are gathered in the vintage season, namely, in this fashion. Take the aforesaid seeds or berries, put them into a glazed porringer, and break or crush them well with your fingers. Then dissolve in clear lye, not too strong, as much rock alum as it will dissolve on the fire. And pour enough of this lye and alum over the berries in the porringer to cover these berries, crushed as directed. And let them stand so, out of the way, for three days; and then wring them out with your hands in a linen cloth, and strain the juice into another glazed porringer. And if you want, you can keep it in linen cloths; do throughout as directed above for the juice of the lilies. But otherwise put in into a glass bottle, and keep it by sealing the bottle. And you can grind verdigris with that juice; it is very good; and if you were to grind azurite (with it), it would change to a very lovely green. And it is mixed with giallorino or white lead for brush work; and leaves, etc., are laid in (with this), shaded with the lily juice, extracted from the cloths with glair of eggs. And it can be shaded likewise with the juice of the berries themselves, or with straight blue changed to green color, tempering it lightly with gum-water or glair. Another green is made with orpiment and good indigo; but it is not a good plan to use orpiment on parchment, because by its odor it reduces white lead, red lead, and green to a sort of metallic color; and therefore I have not undertaken to explain the way to make (greens) with it or with verdigris. . . .

20. The colors: how they should be ground and mixed together and laid on parchment.

You should know that the black color of charcoal or natural stone ought to be ground with plain water on a slab of porphyry (or of some other very hard sort of stone), until it becames impalpable, and then put into glazed earthenware dishes. And when it has settled, the water is carefully poured off and replaced with fresh; and so they are kept, in one (and the best) way, to await the convenience of the worker. And if the water gives out, or goes bad, it should always be replaced with fresh. And in the same way, for the most part, all colors which have body are worked up; except verdigris, which is worked up with vinegar, or with the juice of the leaves of the blue lilies, or with the juice of the berries mentioned above. And some people work it up with the juice of rue and a little saffron, and temper it with yolk of egg. The rest of the colors are worked up and kept in the same way, as I have described. And know that if the ultramarine blue is very fine and clean, it can be mixed with your fingers in the dish or in the horn with the tempera or solution. But if it is not very fine, then it must be ground on a slab which will not get scratched when it is ground; because blue and the other hard colors, such as giallorino, would be spoiled; because it would not be so important with the other, softer colors. I return to the ultramarine blue, the coarse and not very well washed (variety). This should be worked up with a fourth part, or less, of sal ammoniac; and then with plain water, or with lye, not too strong. And, when it has been ground to the desired degree of coarseness or fineness, put it into an earthenware dish, glazed and of a size proportionate to the amount of the blue; and put some clear plain water on it, to cover it. And mix it up with your hand or a stick, and let it settle; and pour off the water carefully; and put in some more fresh water, and mix it up; and after it has stood, pour it off again. And continue to do this until the water comes off clear and the blue remains pure and free from saltiness. And dry it in the shade, and keep it. And, if you want it to be of the utmost fineness, work it up into an impalpable condition, put it into a dish with plenty of plain water, mix it up well, and strain it through a fine muslin or linen cloth, until as much comes through as can. And let it settle, and pour off the water; and dry what remains in the bottom of the dish in the air, out of the sun; because it will be very good for any type of handling, as far as fineness goes, either with the pen or with the brush.

And then I must speak about azurite. You should know that, when the blue is coarse and ugly and you want to improve it, you do it in this way. Take the azurite, and work it up in the slab as above, as fine as you want to get it. And do this with a fairly thick solution of gum, and then put it into a good-sized glazed dish, and pour over it some clear plain water, and mix it up well. And when it has pretty much settled, pour off the water carefully into another glazed dish, so that, if any of the good were to go off with the water, it would not be lost. And again put in some plain water, and do as before. And go on repeating this process until the blue comes out pure and clean; and though it may be reduced in quantity, still it will be greatly improved. And if you want to, you can do it the same way as with ultramarine blue, by grinding it and passing it through cloth or silk; but that azurite would lose too much color in that way to be worth anything afterwards without some addition. And then dry it and keep it.

And when you want to apply blue with a brush, temper it with gum water; and some people put in two or three drops of the glair of eggs. Do whichever seems to you better after experimenting.

Also, when you want to make the bodies of letters with a pen: I will inform you that some people temper the blue with the solution of gum; and some with the glair of eggs, and they put in a little sugar, about as much as a grain of wheat; and some put in three parts of the solution of gum and one part of the glair. Do as you wish, because any of these is good.

To flourish with ultramarine blue. First you should know that it ought to be very fine, and tempered with glair of eggs, and some sugar or honey solution may be added, as above. Do whichever you please; because, if you become familiar with the character of these ingredients, it will come out all right for you. Know that, wherever the solution of honey or sugar is mentioned, candy sugar can be substituted; but it should be added in somewhat larger quantity, tempered with the solution or (glair). And know this: if the tempera of the blue ever gets dirty in the horn, put in clear water or grind it on the slab with a fresh tempera; and of it is too thick, put in some clear water or grind it on the slab with fresh tempera. And keep it well stirred in the horn with a little stick. And know that, when vermilion gets dirty, it is worked up in the same way. And if the glair gets dirty and thick, a drop or two of lye is put in, according to the amount of material; and it will flow more readily, because lye reduces the viscosity of the glair. . . .

23. To flourish with vermilion.

Take some of the best vermilion and work it up well on the slab with fairly strong lye. And when you have got it thoroughly ground, impalpable, put it into a glazed porringer, and pour plenty of plain water on it, and mix it up well with your fingers, and filter it, through a cloth of silk or fine close linen, into another glazed dish. And the coarse part, which stays behind, you grind and filter over again as before; and then let it settle, pour off the water, dry it in a breeze, and keep it. And some, when they are working up the vermilion put in a little *stupium,* that is, red lead, about an eighth part of it, and proceed as with the plain vermilion above. Do whichever you wish, and keep to the method which suits you, because either one is good. And when you want to make flowers with it, temper it with the glair of eggs on the slab, and put it into a glass horn or cow's horn. And if the glair makes a froth, human earwax will break that up at once, if you put in a little of it; and this is a secret.

And know that blue, and especially ultramarine, and vermilion are best used for flourishing, or for making flowers, in this way: namely, first work them up sufficiently on the porphyry with the gum or glair, or whatever, and a little sugar or candy, and let them dry on the slab, watching out for dust. When this is dry, soften the blue up with a fresh glair. And you temper the vermilion with glair and a few drops of good clear lye; and put it into the horn, and use it. And know that this method is superior to all others, and that, even, for making the bodies of letters. *Deo gratias.*

24. To make the bodies of letters with vermilion.

Take some of the best vermilion, and work it up very thoroughly, dry. Then temper it with the glair of eggs; and after you reduce it to an impalpable condition, let it dry on the same slab. Then temper it with some more fresh glair of eggs; and when it gets all soft, put it into the horn; and put in some earwax, and a little bit of honey so that when it is laid on the parchment the vermilion will be shiny and not brittle. And know that, if you put in much of the honey, it would be spoiled. And always keep a little realgar or something in the bottle with the glair of eggs to keep it from spoiling, as I have told you before.

25. Colors for illuminating with the brush.

Know, moreover, that when the colors have been worked up well with water, the water poured off, and the colors dried, you can then grind them with gum water; and let them stay in their dishes. And if they dry up, they can be softened afterward with clear plain water. And temper them over again on the slab or with your finger in the dish, and they work better. . . .

Note: How to paint the flesh of faces and other parts of the body.

If you want to make the flesh color of faces or other parts of the body, you should first lay in the whole area in which you are to do the flesh with terre-verte, and a great deal of white, so that the greenness is not very conspicuous. And then, with a wash, using *terretta* (which is made with yellow and black, indigo and red), lay in the features of the figures again with a wash, shading down the proper areas. Then with white and a little green you relieve or lighten the areas which are to brought up in relief, just as the painters do. And then take some red and a little white, and paint the areas which need to be colored, and gradually lay some of this same mixture on the shaded areas. And, finally, with lots of white and a little red, according to how you want to color the flesh, you coat the whole of the flesh with a very thin wash, but the areas of relief more than the shaded ones. And should the figures be too small, you would hardly touch anything except the areas of relief. And at the last you carry the modeling further with pure white, if you want to, and put the white and the black in the eyes; and make outlines in the proper places with red and black and a little yellow mixed together, or with indigo, if you wish, or black, which is better; and shape it up as you know how. And these remarks must do as a rough guide. . . .

32. An exceptional rule for making the very best gum for the illumination of letters with the brush and also with the pen.

And first, the glair of eggs is made with a sponge as described above; then the solution of gum, as before explained. And after that, the solution of honey; and in this solution is dissolved as much candy sugar as the solution will take up. And then take one part of the gum and another part of the glair of eggs, and mix them up in a bottle; and put into it one part, or less, of the solution of honey with the sugar; and let them stand together. And when they have become clear, the colors may be most beautifully laid with this tempera, if the master understands how to use it. And know that it is better for you to put in less of the solution of honey than of the other ingredients; and the reason is that, if too much were put in, it would soon soften up under the influence of moisture; and if too little, the colors would soon crack. And one has to take care to observe moderation in this.

Furthermore, you must know that gold and silver can be laid upon parchment wonderfully well with this mixture of solutions. And first do as follows; take three parts of the best painters' gesso, and one part of Armenian bole, and work them up very thoroughly on the porphyry slab. Then moisten them and work them up with this liquid, until it comes out like the vermilion for writing. And work it up very thoroughly on this slab, and let it dry in the sun on this slab. And when it is dry, scrape it off the slab with a knife, and put it away in a parchment in a dry place. And when you want to use it, take as much of it as you want, and put it into a glass horn, and put enough clear plain water on it to cover that material, and let it soften. Then pour off enough of the water to leave the material liquid. This you work up on the slab again, and put it back into the horn, and write with it like vermilion. And when it has dried, warm it a little with your breath and lay the gold or silver leaf on it, and press it down with the burnishing tooth, and burnish it over a panel. And do as you know how, for it will be excellent. *Deo gratias. Amen.*

Notes

9. THE TWELFTH CENTURY: CURRENTS OF DEBATE

A History of the Calamities of Abelard

Peter Abelard

The dynamic nature of twelfth-century culture, which sees the flowering and withering of older trends and the growth of new ones, is well mirrored by the dispute between two of the centuries greatest figures, Peter Abelard (d. 1142) and Bernard of Clairvaux (d. 1153). The former should be as well remembered for his activities as a teacher as he is for his fateful love affair with Heloise. His *Historia calamitatum,* excerpted below, privides, through an unusually candid autobiography for the period, insights into the nascent universities of the twelfth century and the debates that enlivened them as the older monastic culture of the early Middle Ages clashed with the trend toward rationalism and speculative thought that characterizes the scholasticism of the thirteenth century.

Often examples serve better than words to excite or to mitigate human passions. Wherefore, after certain comfort offered thee in speech in thy presence, I have decided in absence to write by way of comfort the experience of my own calamities, that in comparison with mine thou mayest see thy trials to be none at all, or but slight matters, and may be better able to endure them.

Chapter 1. Of the birthplace of Peter Abelard *and of his parentage.*

I then was born in a certain town which, situated at the entering into Brittany, distant from the city of Nantes about eight miles, I believe, in an easterly direction, is properly known as Palatium. As by the nature of the soil or of my blood I am light of heart, so also I grew up with an aptitude for the study of letters. A father, moreover, I had who was to no small extent imbued with letters before he girded on himself the soldier's belt. Whence, at a later time, he was seized with so great a love of letters that whatever sons he had he was disposed to instruct in letters rather than in arms. And so it befell us. I too, being the first-born, in so far as I was dearer to him than the rest, so much the more diligently did he care for my education. And I, when I advanced farther and had more facility in the study of letters, so much the more ardently did I adhere to it, and with such love of that study was I consumed that, abandoning the pomp of military glory with the inheritance and the privileges of a first-born son to my brother, I finally relinquished the court of Mars that I might be educated in the lap of Minerva. And inasmuch as I preferred the equipment of dialectic to all the teachings of philosophy; I exchanged those weapons for these and to the trophies of war preferred the conflicts of discussion. Thereafter, perambulating divers provinces in search of discussion, wherever I had heard the study of this art to flourish, I became an emulator of the Peripatetics.

Chapter 2. Of the persecution of him by his master William. *Of his mastership at Melun, at Corbeil and in Paris. Of his retirement from the city of Paris to Melun, his return to Mont Sainte-Genevieve and to his own country.*

I came at length to Paris, where this study had long been greatly flourishing, to *William* styled "of Champeau," my preceptor, a man at that time pre-eminent, rightly and by common repute, in this teaching: with whom I stayed for a while, welcomed by him at first but afterwards a grave burden to him, since I endeavoured to refute certain of his opinions and often ventured to reason with him, and at times shewed myself his superior in debate. Which things indeed those who among our fellow-scholars were esteemed the foremost suffered with all the more indignation in that I was junior to them in age and in length of study. Hence arose the beginnings of my calamities which have continued up to the present time, and the more widely my fame extended, the more the envy of others was kindled against me. At length it came to pass that, presuming upon my talents beyond the capacity of my years, I aspired, boy as I was, to the mastership of a school, and found myself a place in which to practise, namely Melun, at that time a town of note and a royal abode. My master afore-named suspected this plan and, seeking to remove my school as far as possible from his own, secretly employed all the means in his power to contrive that before I left his school he might take from me mine and the place that I had selected. But inasmuch as among the powerful in the land he numbered several there who were jealous of him, relying upon their help I succeeded in obtaining my desire and won the support of many for myself by the manifest display of his envy. And from this beginning of my school, so much did my name in the art of dialectic begin to be magnified that not only the repute of my fellow-scholars but that of the master himself began to decline and was gradually extinguished. Hence it came about that, presuming more largely upon myself, I made haste to transfer my school to the town of Corbeil, which is nearer to the city of Paris, so that there opportunity might furnish more frequent contests of disputation. Not long afterwards, however, being stricken with an infirmity by the immoderate burden of my studies, I was obliged to return home, and for some years, being banished, so to speak, from France, I was sought out more ardently by those to whom the teaching of dialectic appealed.

But a few years having gone by, when for some time I had recovered from my infirmity, that teacher of mine, *William,* Archdeacon of Paris, laying aside his former habit transferred himself to the order of the regular clergy, with the intention, as was said, that being thought to be more religious he might be promoted to a higher grade in the prelacy, as shortly happened, he being made Bishop of Chalons. Nor did this change of habit call him away either from the city of Paris or from his wonted study of philosophy; but in that same monastery to which for religion's sake he had repaired, he at once opened public classes in his accustomed manner. Then I returning to him that from his lips I might learn rhetoric, among the other efforts of our disputations, contrived, by the clearest chain of argument, to make him alter, nay shatter, his former opinion with regard to universals. For he had been of this opinion touching the community of universals, that he maintained a thing as a whole to be essentially the same in each of its individuals, among which, forsooth, there was no difference in essence but only variety in the multitude of their accidents. He now so corrected this opinion that thereafter he proclaimed the thing to be the same not essentially, but indiscriminately. And inasmuch as this has always been the main question among dialecticians concerning universals so much so that even *Porphyry* in his Isagoga, when he treats of universals, does not presume to define it, saying: "For this is a most weighty business," after he had corrected and then perforce abandoned his opinion, into such neglect did his instruction fall that he was scarcely admitted to be a teacher of dialectic at all; as if in this opinion about universals consisted the sum total of that art. Hence did my teaching acquire so great strength and authority that they who formerly adhered most vehemently to our said master and attacked my doctrine most strongly now flocked to my school, and he who had succeeded to our master's chair in the school of Paris offered me his own place, that there among the rest he might submit himself to my teaching where formerly his master and mine had flourished.

And so after a few days, I reigning there in the study of dialectic, with what envy our master began to consume away, with what rage to boil, is not easily expressed. Nor long sustaining the heat of the affliction that had seized him, he cunningly attempted to remove me once again. And because in my conduct there was nothing whereon he could openly act, he laboured to remove the school from him who had yielded up his chair to me (charging him with the vilest accusations), and to substitute a certain other, one of my jealous rivals, in his place. Then I, returning to Melun, established my school there as before; and the more openly his jealousy pursued me, the more widely it enlarged my authority, according to the words of the poet:

Envy seeketh the heights, the winds blow on the mountain-tops.

Not long after this, when it came to his knowledge that well-nigh all his disciples were in the utmost hesitation as to his religion, and were murmuring vehemently as to his conversion, in that evidently he had not retired from the city, he transferred himself and his conventicle of brethren, with his school, to a certain village at some distance from the city. And immediately I returned from Melun to Paris, hoping that thenceforth I should have peace from him. But seeing that, as I have said, he had caused my place there to be filled by one of my rivals, outside the city on the Mount of Saint Genevieve I pitched the camp of our school, as though to beleaguer him who had occupied my place. Hearing which, our master straightway returning unashamed to the city, brought back such pupils as he might still have, and the conventicle of brethren to their former monastery, as though to deliver his soldier, whom he had abandoned, from our siege. In truth, whereas he intended to advantage him, he greatly harmed him. He, forsooth, had until then retained sundry disciples, principally for the lectures on *Priscian* in which he was considered to excel. But after the master arrived he lost them one and all, and so was compelled to cease from the tenour of his school. And not long after this, as though despairing for the future of any worldly fame, he too was converted to the monastic life. Now after the return of our master to the city, the conflicts of discussion which our scholars waged as well with him as with his disciples, and the results which fortune in these wars gave to my people, nay to myself in them, thou thyself hast long known as matters of fact. But this saying of *Ajax* I may with more modesty than he repeat and more boldly utter:

> Shouldst thou demand the issue of this fight,
> I was not vanquished by mine enemy.

As to which, were I silent, the facts themselves speak and its outcome indicates the whole matter. But while these things were happening my dearest mother *Lucy* obliged me to return home. Who, to wit, after the conversion of *Berenger,* my father, to the monastic profession, was preparing to do likewise. Which being accomplished, I returned to France, principally that I might learn divinity, when our afore-mentioned master *William* attained to the Bishopric of Chalons. In the study, moreover, his own master, *Anselm* of Laon, was of great and long-established authority.

Chapter 3. How he came to Laon to the master Anselm.

I came therefore to this old man, who owed his name rather to long familiarity than to his intelligence or his memory. To whom if any came knocking upon his door in uncertainty as to some question, he departed more uncertain still. Indeed, he was admirable in the eyes of his hearers, but of no account in the sight of questioners. His fluency of words was admirable but in sense they were contemptible and devoid of reason. When he kindled a fire he filled his house with smoke, rather than lighted it with the blaze. His tree, in full life, was conspicuous from afar to all beholders, but by those who stood near and diligently examined the same it was found to be barren. To this tree therefore when I had come that I might gather fruit from it, I understood that it was the fig-tree which the Lord cursed, or that old oak to which *Lucan* compares *Pompey,* saying:

> There stands the shadow of a mighty name,
> Like to a tall oak in a fruitful field.

Having discovered this, not for many days did I lie idle in his shadow. But as I gradually began to come to his lectures more rarely, certain among the more forward of his disciples took it amiss, as though I were shewing contempt for so great a master. Thereafter him also secretly exciting against me with vile suggestions, they made me offensive in his sight. But it fell upon a day that after certain controversies of opinion we scholars were disporting ourselves. When, after a certain one had inquired of me with menacing intent what I thought as to the reading of the Holy Scriptures, I, who had as yet studied nothing save physics only, replied that it was indeed most salutary, the study of this lore in which the salvation of the soul is revealed, but that I marvelled greatly that, to them who were literate men, the Scriptures themselves or the glosses upon them should not be sufficient, so that they should require no other instruction. Many of those present, laughing at me, asked whether I was able and presumed to approach this task. I replied that I was ready to try it if they wished. Then, shouting together and laughing all the more: "Certainly," they said, "we agree. Let some one find, therefore, and bring to us here an expositor of some little read Scripture, and let us put what you promise to the proof."

And they all agreed upon the most obscure prophecy of *Ezekiel.* And so, taking up the expositor, I at once invited them to attend my lecture on the morrow, who, pouring counsels into my unwilling ears, said that in so weighty a matter there was nothing to be gained by haste, but that seeing my inexperience I must give longer thought to the examination and strengthening of my exposition. But I indignantly replied that it was not my custom to advance by practice but rather by intelligence; and added that either I abandoned the contest altogether or they, abiding by my judgment, must come to my lecture without delay. And my first lecture indeed few attended, since that to all it seemed ridiculous that I, who hitherto had been almost wholly unacquainted with Holy Writ, should so hastily approach it. To all, however, who did attend, that lecture was so pleasing that they extolled it with singular commendation, and compelled me to furnish further glosses in the style of my first lecture. Which becoming known, those who had not been present began to flock eagerly to my second lecture and my third, and all alike were solicitous at the start of each to take down in writing the glosses which I had begun on the first day.

Chapter 4. Of the persecution of him by his master Anselm.

Wherefore the old man aforesaid, being stirred by vehement envy, and having already been stimulated against me by the persuasion of divers persons, as I have before recounted, began no less to persecute me over the Holy Scriptures than our *William* had aforetime done over philosophy. Now there were at the time in this old man's school two who appeared to predominate over the rest, namely *Alberic* of Rheims and *Lotulph,* a Lombard: who, the more they presumed upon themselves, were the more kindled against me. And so, his mind greatly perturbed by their suggestions, as later it came to light, this old man boldly forbade me to continue further the work of interpretation which I had begun in his place of teaching. Advancing this pretext forsooth, that if perchance I were to write anything in error in my work, being still untrained in that study, it might be imputed to him. This coming to the ears of the scholars, they were moved with the utmost indignation against so manifest a calumny of envy, the like of which had never befallen any man yet. Which, the more manifest it was, the more honourable was it to me, and so by persecution my fame increased.

Chapter 5. How, having returned to Paris, he completed the interpretaions which he had begun to deliver at Laon.

So, after a few days, returning to Paris, the schools that had long before been intended for me and offered to me, from which I had at first been driven out, I held for some years in quiet, and there at the opening of my course I strove to complete those interpretations of *Ezekiel* which I had begun at Laon. Which indeed were so acceptable to their readers that they believed me to be no less adept in the Holy Scriptures than they had seen me to be in philosophy. Whence in both kinds of study our school vehemently multiplying, what pecuniary gain and what reputation it brought me cannot have failed to reach your ears. But inasmuch as prosperity ever puffs up fools, and worldly tranquillity enervates the vigour of the mind, and easily loosens it by carnal allurements, when now I esteemed myself as reigning alone in the world as a philosopher, nor was afraid of any further disturbance, I began to give rein to my lust, who hitherto had lived in the greatest continence. And the farther I advanced in philosophy or in the Holy Scriptures, the farther I receded by the impurity of my life from philosophers and divines. For it is well known that philosophers, not to say divines, that is to say men intent on the exhortations of Holy Scripture, have excelled principally by the grace of continence. When, therefore, I was labouring wholly in pride and lechery, the remedy for either malady was by divine grace conferred on me, albeit unwilling; and first for lechery, then for pride. For lechery, indeed, by depriving me of those parts with which I practised it; but for the pride which was born in me from my surpassing knowledge of letters, as is said by the Apostle: "Knowledge puffeth up"—by humiliating me by the burning of that book in which most I gloried. The story of both which things I wish you now to learn more accurately from a statement of the facts than by common hearsay, in the order in which they befell me. Since, therefore, I ever abhorred the uncleanness of harlots, and was withheld from the society of noble women by the assiduity of my studies, nor had ever held much conversation with those of the common sort, lewd fortune, as the saying is, caressing me, found a more convenient opportunity whereby she might the more easily dash me down from the pinnacle of this sublimity; so that in my overweening pride, and unmindful of the grace I had received, divine pity might recall me humbled to itself.

Chapter 6. How having fallen in love with Heloise *he was thereby wounded as well in body as in mind.*

Now there was in this city of Paris a certain young maiden by the name of *Heloise,* the niece of a certain Canon who was called *Fulbert,* who, so great was his love for her, was all the more diligent in his zeal to instruct her, so far as was in his power, in the knowledge of letters. Who, while in face she was not inferior to other women, in the abundance of her learning was supreme. For inasmuch as this advantage, namely literary knowledge, is rare in women, so much the more did it commend the girl and had won her the greatest renown throughout the realm. Seeing in her, therefore, all those things which are wont to attract lovers, I thought it suitable to join her with myself in love, and believed that I could effect this most easily. For such renown had I then, and so excelled in grace of youth and form, that I feared no refusal from whatever woman I might deem worthy of my love. All the more easily did I believe that this girl would consent to me in that I knew her both to possess and to delight in the knowledge of letters; even in absence it would be possible for us to reach one another's presence by written intermediaries, and to express many things more boldly in writing than in speech, and so ever to indulge in pleasing discussions.

So, being wholly inflamed with love for this girl, I sought an opportunity whereby I might make her familiar with me in intimate and daily conversation, and so the more easily lead her to consent. With which object in view, I came to terms with the aforesaid uncle of the girl, certain of his friends intervening, that he should take me into his house, which was hard by our school, at whatever price he might ask. Putting forward this pretext, that the management of our household gravely hindered my studies, and the expense of it was too great a burden on me. Now he was avaricious, and most solicitous with regard to his niece that she should ever progress in the study of letters. For which two reasons I easily secured his consent and obtained what I desired, he being all agape for my money, and

believing that his niece would gain something from my teaching.
Whereupon earnestly beseeching me, he acceded to my wishes farther
than I might presume to hope and served the purpose of my love:
committing her wholly to my mastership, that as often as I returned
from my school, whether by day or by night, I might devote my
leisure to her instruction, and, if I found her idle, vehemently
chastise her. In which matter, while marvelling greatly at his
simplicity, I was no less stupefied within myself than if he had
entrusted a tender lamb to a ravening wolf. For in giving her to me,
not only to be taught but to be vehemently chastised, what else was
he doing than giving every licence to my desires and providing an
opportunity whereby, even if I did not wish, if I could not move her
by blandishments I might the more easily bend her by threats and
blows. But there were two things which kept him most of all from
base suspicions, namely his love for his hiece and the fame of my
continence in the past.

What more need I say? First in one house we are united, then in
one mind. So, under the pretext of discipline, we abandoned ourselves utterly to love, and those secret retreats which love demands,
the study of our texts afforded us. And so, our books lying open
before us, more words of love rose to our lips than of literature,
kisses were more frequent than speech. Oftener went our hands to
each other's bosom than to the pages; love turned our eyes more
frequently to itself than it directed them to the study of the texts.
That we might be the less suspected, blows were given at times, by
love, not by anger, affection, not indignation, which surpassed all
ointments in their sweetness. What more shall I say? No stage of love
was omitted by us in our cupidity, and, if love could elaborate anything new, that we took in addition. The less experienced we were in
these joys, the more ardently we persisted in them and the less
satiety did they bring us. And the more this pleasure occupied me
the less leisure could I find for my philosophy and to attend to my
school. Most tedious was it for me to go to the school or to stay
there, laborious likewise when I was keeping nightly vigils of love
and daily of study. Which also so negligently and tepidly I now performed that I produced nothing from my mind but everything from
memory; nor was I anything now save a reciter of things learned in
the past, and if I found time to compose a few verses, they were
amorous, and not secret hymns of philosophy. Of which songs the
greater part are to this day, as thou knowest, repeated and sung in
many parts, principally by those to whom a like manner of life
appeals.

What was the sorrow, what the complaints, what the lamentations
of my scholars when they became aware of this preoccupation, nay,
perturbation of my mind, it is not easy even to imagine. For few
could fail to perceive a thing so manifest, and none, I believe, did fail
save he to whose shame it principally reflected, namely the girl's
uncle himself. Who indeed, when divers persons had at divers times

suggested this to him, had been unable to believe it, both, as I have said above, on account of his unbounded affection for his niece and on account also of the well known continence of my previous life. For not readily do we suspect baseness in those whom we most love. Nor into vehement love can the base taint of suspicion find a way. Whence cometh the saying of Saint *Jerome* in his Epistle to *Sabinian* (the eight-and-fortieth): "We are always the last to learn of the evils of our own house, and remain ignorant of the vices of our children and wives when they are a song among the neighbours. But what one is the last to know one does at any rate come to know in time, and what all have learned it is not easy to keep hidden from one." And thus, several months having elapsed, it befell us also. Oh, what was the uncle's grief at this discovery!

What was the grief of the lovers themselves at their parting! What blushing and confusion for me! With what contrition for the girl's affliction was I afflicted! What floods of sorrow had she to bear at my shame! Neither complained of what had befallen himself, but each the other's misfortune. But this separation of our bodies was the greatest possible coupling of our minds, the denial of its satisfaction inflamed our love still further, the shame we had undergone made us more shameless, and the less we felt our shame the more expedient our action appeared. And so there occurred in us what the poets relate of Mars and Venus when they were taken. Not long after this, the girl found that she had conceived, and with the greatest exultation wrote to me on the matter at once, consulting me as to what I should decide to do; and so on a certain night, her uncle being absent, as we had planned together I took her by stealth from her uncle's house and carried her to my own country without delay. Where, in my sister's house, she stayed until such time as she was delivered of a man child whom she named *Astrolabe*.

Her uncle, however, after her flight, being almost driven mad, with what grief he boiled, with what shame he was overwhelmed no one who had not beheld him could imagine. How he should act towards me, what snares he should lay for me he knew not. If he were to kill me, or to injure my body in any way, he feared greatly lest his beloved niece might be made to pay the penalty in my country. To seize my person and coerce me anywhere against my will was of no avail, seeing that I was constantly on my guard in this respect, because I had no doubt that he would speedily assault me if it were worth his while or if he dared. At length I, in some compassion for his exceeding anxiety and vehemently accusing myself of the fraud which my love had committed, as though of the basest treachery, went to supplicate the man, promising him also such further amends as he himself should prescribe. Nor, I asserted, did it appear remarkable to any who had experienced the force of love and retained a memory of the ruin to which even the greatest men, from the very beginning of the human race, had been brought down by women. And, that I might conciliate him beyond all that he could

hope, I offered him the satisfaction of joining her whom I had cor-
rupted to myself in marriage, provided that this were done in secret
lest I incurred any detriment to my reputation. He assented, and
with his own word and kiss, as well as with those of his household,
sealed the concord that I had required of him, the more easily to
betray me. . . .

*Chapter 9. Of the book of his Theology, and of the persecution which he
bore from his fellow-students. A Council is held against him.*

Now it so happened that I applied myself first to lecturing on
the fundamentals of our faith by the analogy of human reason, and
composed a certain tractate of theology, Of Unity and the Holy
Trinity, for our scholars, who were asking for human and philosophical reasons, and demanded rather what could be understood
than what could be stated, saying indeed that the utterance of words
was superfluous which the intelligence did not follow, nor could anything be believed unless first it had been understood, and that it was
ridiculous for anyone to preach to others what neither he himself nor
they whom he taught could comprehend with their intellect, Our
Lord Himself complaining that such were "blind leaders of the
blind." Which tractate indeed, when numbers had seen and read it,
began generally to please its readers, because it appeared to satisfy all
alike upon these questions. And inasmuch as these questions
appeared difficult beyond all others, the more their gravity was
admitted, the more subtle my solution of them was considered to be,
whereupon my rivals, vehemently incensed, assembled a Council
against me, principally those two old plotters, namely *Alberic* and
Lotulph, who now that their and my masters, to wit *William* and
Anselm, were defunct, sought as it were to reign alone in their room
and also to succeed them as if they had been their heirs. Since moreover both of them were conducting schools at Rheims, by repeated
suggestions they moved their Archbishop *Rodulph* against me, that
associating with himself *Cono* Bishop of Palestrina, who then held
the office of Legate in France, he should assemble a conventicle
under the name of Council in the city of Soissons, and should invite
me to appear there, bringing with me that famous work which I had
written about the Holy Trinity. And so it came to pass. But before I
came there, those two rivals of mine so diffamed me among the
clergy and the people, that almost the people stoned me and the few
of my disciples who had come with me on the first day of our arrival;
saying that I preached and had written that there were three Gods, as
they themselves had been assured.

I, however, as soon as I had reached the town sought out the
Legate; I gave him my book for his perusal and judgment, and
declared myself, if I had written anything that was dissentient from
the Catholic Faith, ready to receive correction or to give satisfaction.
But he at once enjoined me to take the book to the Archbishop and

to my two rivals, that they themselves might judge me who were my accusers on that count, that it might be fulfilled in me: "even our enemies themselves being judges." They, however, repeatedly perusing and searching the book, and finding nothing that they dared bring forward against me in the audience, adjourned to the end of the Council the condemnation of the book for which they were panting. But I, on each several day before the Council sat, publicly expounded the Catholic Faith to all according to what I had written and all who heard me with great admiration commended both my exposition of the words and my sense. Which when the people and the clergy saw they began in turn to say: "Lo, now he speaks in public and no one answers him anything. And the Council is coming rapidly to an end, that was convened principally, as we have heard, against him. Can it be that his judges have recognised that they, rather than he, are in error?" Wherefore my rivals were daily more and more inflamed.

And so one day *Alberic* coming to me with evil intent, and certain of his disciples, after divers bland words said that he marvelled at one thing which he had noticed in that book: namely that whereas God begat God, and there was but one God, I denied that God had begotten Himself. To which straightway I replied: "On this point, if you wish it, I will reason." "We pay no heed," said he, "to human reason, nor to our own sense in such matters, but only to the words of authority." To which I: "Turn the page of the book, and you will find the authority." And there was a copy of the book at hand, which he had brought with him. I turned to the place, which I knew, and which he had failed to observe, or else he sought there only what might harm me. And there was a sentence entitled: *Augustine* On the Trinity, Book I, Chapter 1: "Whoso supposes God to be so powerful as Himself to have begotten Himself, errs the more greatly in that not only God is not so; but no creature, either spiritual or corporeal. For there is nothing whatsoever that may beget itself." Which when his disciples, who were present, had heard, they were stupefied and blushed. But he, that he might cover himself as best he could, said: "It is well that it should be understood." To which I subjoined that this was nothing new, but for the present it was of little import, since he had required of me words only, and not sense. If, however, he wished me to give him sense and reason, I declared myself ready to shew him, according to his own opinion, that he had fallen into that heresy by which the Father is His own Son.

Which when he had heard, as though straightway made furious, he turned to threats, asserting that neither my reasons nor the authorities would avail me in this case. And so he withdrew. But on the last day of the Council, before they took their seats, the Legate and the Archbishop began to discuss at length with my rivals, and with divers persons, what should be decided about me and my book, the matter for which principally they had been called together. And as neither in my speech nor in the writings that were before them had they aught that they might charge against me, all being silent for a little space, or less open in their detraction of me, *Geoffrey*, Bishop of Chartres, who had precedence over the other Bishops by the fame of his piety and the dignity of his see, thus began: "All of you, Sirs, that are here present know that this man's teaching, whatsoever it be, and his intellect have had many supporters and followers in whatsoever he has studied, that he has greatly diminished the fame as well of his own masters as of ours, and that, so to speak, his vine has spread its branches from sea to sea. If, as I do not think, ye condemn him by prejudice, even rightly, ye must know that ye will offend many, and there will not be wanting those who will wish to defend him; especially as in the writing here present we see nothing which may deserve any open calumny; and as is said by *Jerome:* 'Strength that is manifest ever excites jealousy, and the lightnings strike the highest mountain peaks.' Take heed lest ye confer more renown on him by violent action, and lest we earn more reproach for ourselves by the envy than for him by the justice of the charge. For a false rumour, as the aforesaid Doctor, in his Tenth Epistle, reminds us, is quickly stifled, and a man's later life pronounces judgment on his past. But if ye are disposed to act canonically against him, let his dogma or his writing be brought into our midst, and let him be questioned and allowed freely to reply, that convicted or confessing his error he be henceforward silent. Following at least those words of Saint *Nicodemus,* when, desirous of setting Our Lord Himself at liberty, he said: 'Doth our law judge any man before it hear him and know what he doeth?' "

Hearing which straightway my rivals interrupting him cried out: "O wise counsel, that we should contend against his verbosity whose arguments or sophisms the entire world could not withstand!" But of a surety it was far more difficult to contend with Christ Himself, and yet *Nicodemus* invited that He should be heard according to the sanction of the law. When therefore the Bishop could not induce their minds to consent to what he had proposed, he tried by another way to restrain their envy; saying that for the discussion of so weighty a matter the few who were present could not suffice, and that this case needed a greater examination. His advice was, further, that to my Abbey, that is the monastery of Saint Denis, my Abbot, who was there present, should recall me; and that there, a greater number of more learned persons being called together, by a more diligent examination it should be decided what was to be done in the matter. The Legate assented to this last counsel, and so all the rest. Thereafter presently the Legate rose that he might celebrate Mass, before he entered the Council, and sent to me by the Bishop the licence that had been granted, namely to return to my monastery, and there to await what should be determined.

Then my rivals, considering that they had achieved nothing if this business should be carried on outside their diocese, where forsooth they would not be able to sit in judgment, little trusting evidently in justice, persuaded the Archbishop that it was assuredly ignominious to himself if this case were to be transferred to another audience, and that it would be most dangerous if in that way I escaped. And straightway hastening to the Legate, they succeeded in altering his opinion and brought him reluctantly to the position that he should condemn the book without any inquiry, and at once burn it in the sight of all, and condemn me to perpetual enclosure in a strange monastery. For they said that for the condemnation of the book this ought to be sufficient, that I had ventured publicly to read it, though commended by the authority neither of the Roman Pontiff nor of the Church, and had given it to be copied by many. And this would be of great benefit to the Christian faith, if by my example a similar presumption were prevented in others. And because the Legate was less a scholar than he should have been he relied principally on the Archbishop's advice, as the Archbishop on theirs. Which the Bishop of Chartres foreseeing straightway reported these machinations to me, and vehemently exhorted me that I should suffer them the more quietly, the more violently it was evident to all that they were acting. And that I must not doubt that this violence of so manifest an envy would go greatly against them and in my favour. Nor should I be at all perturbed over my confinement in a monastery, knowing that the Legate himself, who was doing this under compulsion, after a few days, when he had removed from the place, would set me wholly at liberty. And so he gave me what comfort he might, and to himself also, both of us in tears.

Chapter 10. Of the burning of his book. Of his persecution by the Abbot and his brethren.

And so being summoned I went straightway before the Council, and without any process of discussion they compelled me to cast my aforesaid book upon the fire. And thus it was burned, when, as they seemed to be saying nothing, one of my adversaries was heard to murmur that he understood it to be written in the book that God the Father alone was Almighty. Which when the Legate understood, greatly marvelling, he answered him that it was not to be believed of any little child that he would so err: "When our common Faith," he said, "holds and professes that there are Three Almighty." Hearing which a certain *Terric,* a master of a school, laughingly quoted the words of *Athanasius* (in the Creed): "yet there are not Three Almighties but One Almighty." And, when the Bishop began to chide and reprove him as one guilty of speaking against authority, boldly gainsaid him and, recalling the words of *Daniel,* said: "Thus, ye foolish children of Israel, neither judging nor knowing the truth, ye have condemned the daughter of Israel. Return to judgment," and judge the judge himself, ye who have set up such a judge for the instruction of the Faith and the correction of error: who when he ought to judge out of his own mouth hath condemned himself. This day, by divine mercy, deliver him who is plainly innocent, like Susanna of old, from his false accusers.

Then the Archbishop rising confirmed the sentence of the Legate, changing the words as was required. "Verily, Sir," he said, "the Father is Almighty, the Son is Almighty and the Holy Ghost is Almighty, and whoso dissenteth from this is evidently in error, nor is he to be heard. And yet, if it please thee, it is well that this our brother expound his faith before us all, that it be either approved or disapproved and corrected, as may be fitting." But when I rose to profess and expound my faith, that what I felt, I might express in my own words; my adversaries said that nothing else was necessary than that I should recite the Creed of *Athanasius,* which any boy could have done as well as I. And lest I should put forward the excuse of ignorance, as though I were not familiar with the words they had the written text brought for me to read.

I read it amid sighs, sobs and tears as best I could. Then like a criminal and a convict I was handed over to the Abbot of Saint Medard, who was present, and committed to his cloister as though to a gaol. And straightway the Council was dissolved. Now the Abbot and monks of that monastery, thinking that I was to remain longer with them, received me with the greatest exultation and using every diligence tried in vain to comfort me. God, Who judgest equity, with what gall then, with what bitterness of mind did I, wretch that I was, challenge Thee, did I finally accuse Thee, constantly repeating that plaint of Saint *Anthony:* "Good Jesus, where wert Thou?" But with what grief I boiled, with what blushing I was confounded, with what desperation perturbed, I then could feel, I cannot now express. I compared with what I had aforetime suffered in my body what I was now enduring, and of all men reckoned myself the most unhappy. That other I regarded as a small betrayal in comparison with this outrage, and lamented far more the detriment to my fame than that to my body: since to the former I had come through my own fault, but to this so open a violence, a sincere intent and love of our Faith had brought me which had compelled me to write. But when all those to whom the report of it came vehemently protested that this had been cruelly and inconsiderately done, the several persons who had taken part in it, repelling the blame from themselves, heaped it each on the others, so much so that my rivals themselves denied that it had been done by their counsel, and the Legate publicly deplored the jealousy of the French in this matter. Who being straightway moved to repentance, after some days, since at the time under compulsion he had given satisfaction to their jealousy, transferred me from the strange monastery to my own, where almost all the monks that had been there before were now, as I have already said, my enemies, for the vileness of their lives and their shameless conversation made suspect to them a man whose reproaches they could ill endure. And a few months having elapsed, fortune furnished them with an opportunity whereby they strove to undo me.

For it happened one day when I was lecturing that there came up a certain saying of *Bede,* when in expounding the Acts of the Apostles he asserts that *Denys* the Areopagite was Bishop of Corinth and not of Athens. Which seemed contrary to their taste, who boast that the famous Areopagite was their own *Denys,* whom his Acts profess to have been Bishop of Athens. Coming upon this I shewed it, as though jestingly, to certain of the brethren who were standing by. But they, greatly indignant, said that *Bede* was a most mendacious writer, and that they had a more truthful witness in *Hilduin,* their Abbot, who to investigate this matter had travelled long in Greece, and, having acquainted himself with the facts, had in the Acts of that Saint, which he compiled, veraciously removed all doubt. Whereupon one of them challenged me with an importunate question: what seemed to me the truth in this controversy, namely between *Bede* and *Hilduin?* I replied that the authority of *Bede,* whose writings the entire body of the Latin Churches consult, seemed to me the more acceptable. Whereat they, vehemently incensed, began to cry out, that now I had openly shewn that I had ever been the enemy of that our monastery, and that now I had greatly detracted from the whole realm, taking from it that honour wherein it singularly gloried when I denied that their Patron had been the Areopagite. I replied that neither had I denied this, nor was it any great matter whether he had been the Areopagite or had come from elsewhere, since he had won so bright a crown before God.

But they hastening straightway to the Abbot told him what they had made me say. Who readily gave ear to them, rejoicing to find any occasion whereby he might oppress me, fearing me the more as he himself lived so much more vilely than the rest. Then, his chapter summoned and the brethren congregated, he threatened me severely and said that he would send me immediately before the King. And I offered myself to the discipline of the rule, if I had in any way offended, but in vain. Then, horrified at their villainy and having borne for so long such adverse fortune, utterly despairing as though the whole world had conspired against me, with the help of a certain consensus of the brethren who took pity on me, and of certain of my disciples, I stole out secretly by night and made for the neighbouring lands of Count *Theobald,* where formerly I had sojourned in a cell. He moreover was both somewhat acquainted with me and was full of compassion for my oppressions, whereof he had heard. And so there I began to dwell in the town of Provins, to wit in a certain cell of monks of Troyes whose Prior had formerly been my bosom friend, and loved me dearly. Who, greatly rejoicing at my advent, cared for me with the utmost diligence.

Now it fell upon a day that our Abbot came to that town, to the aforesaid Count, upon certain business. Hearing of which, I went to the Count with this Prior, asking him to intercede for me with our Abbot, that he should pardon me and give me leave to live monastically wheresoever a suitable place might be found. And he and

they that were with him took the matter into consideration, promising to reply to the Count that same day before they departed.
But when they began their discussion, they decided that I wished to
transfer myself to another Abbey, and that this would be a great
disgrace to them. For they regarded it as the greatest glory to themselves that I had come to them on my conversion, as though
despising all other Abbeys; and now they said that it would be the
greatest reproach to them if, casting them off, I went elsewhere.
Hence they would listen to nothing from me or from the Count on
this matter. Nay, they straightway threatened me that if I did not
speedily return they would excommunicate me. And that Prior, with
whom I had taken refuge, they forbade in every way that he should
not harbour me any longer, else he must share my excommunication.
Hearing which, both the Prior and I were greatly troubled. But the
Abbot departing in this obstinacy, a few days later died. And when
another had succeeded him, I approached him with the Bishop of
Meaux, that he might grant me what I had sought from his predecessor. And as he too did not a first acquiesce in the matter, certain
of my friends thereafter intervening, I appealed to the King and his
Council, and so obtained what I desired.

A certain *Stephen* who was the King's Steward at that time,
summoning the Abbot and his friends, inquired of them why they
wished to retain me against my will, whereby they might easily incur
scandal and could gain nothing, since my life and theirs could in no
way be made to agree. And I knew the opinion of the King's Council
in the matter to be this, that the less regular that Abbey was the
more it should be subject to the King and profitable, that is to say in
temporal wealth. Wherefore I had believed that I should easily secure
the consent of the King and his servants. And so it came to pass. But
lest the monastery should lose the glorification which it had from
me, they conceded me the right to remove to what wilderness I
would, provided that I placed myself under the yoke of no Abbey.
And this, in the presence of the King and his servants, was agreed and
comfirmed on either side.

I therefore took myself to a certain wilderness in the Troyes
country which was known to me aforetime, and there, land having
been given to me by certain persons with the assent of the Bishop of
the place, built an oratory in the name of the Holy Trinity, making
it at first of reeds and thatch. Where lying hidden with one of my
clerks, I could truly declaim with the Lord: "Lo then did I wander
far off and remain in the wilderness." . . .

Against Certain Heads of Abelard's Heresies

Bernard of Clairvaux

The other side of the Abelard-Bernard controversy was presented by the famous Abbot of Clairvaux and leader of the Cistercians in a letter to Pope Innocent II dated 1140, one year before Abelard's teachings were condemned at the Council of Sens. In it, after refuting Abelard's teachings and beliefs as he understood them, Bernard presented his own Christ-centered theology, which gained him much popularity not only in his own lifetime but over the next few centuries as well. Such letters, most of which were written from the seclusion of Clairvaux, acted as vehicles through which the *"thaumaturgus"* of the West helped direct the course of events in his day.

Introduction.

To his most loving Father and Lord, *Innocent,* Supreme Pontiff, Brother *Bernard,* called Abbot of Clairvaux, sends humble greeting.

The dangers and scandals which are coming to the surface in the Kingdom of God, especially those which touch the faith, ought to be referred to your Apostolic authority. For I judge it fitting that there most of all, the losses suffered by the faith should be repaired, where faith cannot suffer defect. This, truly, is the prerogative of your see. For to what other person [than Peter] has it ever been said, *I have prayed for thee, Peter, that thy faith fail not?* (S. Luke xxii. 32). Therefore that which follows is required from the successor of Peter: *And when thou art converted strengthen thy brethren.* That, indeed, is necessary now. The time is come, most loving Father, for you to recognize your primacy, to prove your zeal, to do honour to your ministry. In this plainly you fulfil the office of Peter, whose seat you occupy, if by your admonition you strengthen the hearts that are wavering in the faith, if by your authority you crush the corrupters of the faith.

Chapter 1.

1. We have in France an old teacher turned into a new theologian, who in his early days amused himself with dialectics, and now gives utterance to wild imaginations upon the Holy Scriptures. He is endeavouring again to quicken false opinions, long ago condemned and put to rest, not only his own, but those of others; and is adding

fresh ones as well. I know not what there is in heaven above and in the earth beneath which he deigns to confess ignorance of: he raises his eyes to Heaven, and searches the deep things of God, and then returning to us, he brings back unspeakable words which it is not lawful for a man to utter, while he is presumptuously prepared to give a reason for everything, even of those things which are above reason; he presumes against reason and against faith. For what is more against reason than by reason to attempt to transcend reason? And what is more against faith than to be unwilling to believe what reason cannot attain? For instance, wishing to explain that saying of the wise man: *He who is hasty to believe is light in mind* (Ecclus. xix. 4). He says that a hasty faith is one that believes before reason; when Solomon says this not of faith towards God, but of mutual belief amongst ourselves. For the blessed Pope Gregory denies plainly that faith towards God has any merit whatever if human reason furnishes it with proof. But he praises the Apostles, because they followed their Saviour when called but once (Hom. in Evang. 26). He knows doubtless that this word was spoken as praise: *At the hearing of the ear he obeyed me* (Ps. xvii. 44), that the Apostles were directly rebuked because they had been slow in believing (S. Mark xvi. 14). Again, Mary is praised because she anticipated reason by faith, and Zacharias punished because he tempted faith by reason (S. Luke i. 20, 45), and Abraham is commended in that *against hope he believed in hope* (Rom. iv. 18).

2. But on the other hand our theologian says: "What is the use of speaking of doctrine unless what we wish to teach can be explained so as to be intelligible?" And so he promises understanding to his hearers, even on those most sublime and sacred truths which are hidden in the very bosom of our holy faith; and he places degrees in the Trinity, modes in the Majesty, numbers in the Eternity. He has laid down, for example, that God the Father is full power, the Son a certain kind of power, the Holy Spirit no power. And that the Son is related to the Father as force in particular to force in general, as species to genus, as a thing formed of material, to matter, as man to animal, as a brazen seal to brass. Did Arius ever go futher? Who can endure this? Who would not shut his ears to such sacrilegious words? Who does not shudder at such novel profanities of words and ideas? He says also that "the Holy Spirit proceeds indeed from the Father and the Son, but not from the substance of the Father or of the Son." Whence then? Perhaps from nothing, like everything created. But the Apostle does not deny that they are of God, nor is he afraid to say: *Of whom are all things* (Rom. xi. 36). Shall we say then that the Holy Spirit proceeds from the Father and the Son in no other way than all things do, that is, that He exists not essentially but by way of creation, and is therefore a creature like all other things. Or will this man, who is always seeking after new things, who invents what he does not find, affirms those things which are not, as though they are, will he find for himself some third way, in which he may produce Him from the Father and the Son? But, he says, "if He were

of the substance of the Father, He would surely have been begotten, and so the Father would have two Sons." As though everything which is from any substance has always as its father that from which is. For lice and phlegm and such things, are they sons of the flesh, and not rather of the substance of the flesh? Or worms produced by rotten wood, whence derive they their substance but from the wood? yet are they not sons of the wood. Again, moths have their substance from the substance of garments, but not their generation. And there are many instances of this kind.

3. Since he admits that the Holy Spirit is consubstantial with the Father and the Son, I wonder how an acute and learned man (as at least he thinks himself) can yet deny that He proceeds in substance from the Father and the Son, unless perchance he thinks that the two first persons proceed from the substance of the third. But this is an impious and unheard of opinion. But if neither He proceeds from their substance, nor They from His, where, I pray, is the consubstantiality? Let him then either confess with the Church that the Holy Spirit is of their substance, from whom He does not deny that He proceeds, or let him with Arius deny His consubstantiality, and openly preach His creation. Again he says, if the Son is of the substance of the Father, the Holy Spirit is not; they must differ from each other, not only because the Holy Spirit is not begotten, as the Son is, but also because the Son is of the substance of the Father, which the Holy Spirit is not. Of this last distinction the Catholic Church has hitherto known nothing. If we admit it, where is the Trinity? where is the Unity? If the Holy Spirit and the Son are really separated by this new enumeration of differences, and if the Unity is split up, then especially let it be made plain that that distinction which he is endeavouring to make is a difference of substance. Moreover, if the Holy Spirit does not proceed from the substance of the Father and the Son, no Trinity remains, but a duality. For no Person is worthy to be admitted into the Trinity whose substance is not the same as that of the others. Let him, therefore, cease to separate the procession of the Holy Spirit from the substance of the Father and the Son, lest by a double impiety he both take away number from the Trinity and attribute it to the Unity, each of which the Christian faith abhors. And, lest I seem in so great a matter to depend on human reasonings only, let him read the letter of Jerome to Avitus, and he will plainly see, that amongst the other blasphemies of Origen which he confutes, he also rejects this one, that, as he said, the Holy Spirit is not of the substance of the Father. The blessed Athanasius thus speaks in his book on the Undivided Trinity: "When I spoke of God alone I meant not the Person only of the Father, because I denied not that the Son and the Holy Spirit are of this same Substance of the Father."

Chapter 2.

4. Your holiness sees how in this man's scheme, which is not reasoning but raving, the Trinity does not hold together and the Unity is rendered doubtful, and that this cannot be without injury to the Majesty. For whatever That is which is God, it is without doubt That than which nothing greater can be conceived. If, then, in this One and Supreme Majesty we have found anything that is insufficient or imperfect in our consideration of the Persons, or if we have found that what is assigned to one is taken from another, the whole is surely less than That, than which nothing greater can be conceived. For indubitably the greatest which is whole is greater than that which consists of parts. That man thinks worthily, as far as man can, of the Divine Majesty who thinks of no inequality in It where the whole is supremely great; of no separation where the whole is one; of no chasm where the whole is undivided; in short, of no imperfection or deficiency where the whole is a whole. For the Father is a whole, as are the Father, the Son and the Holy Spirit; the Son is a whole, as are He Himself and the Father and the Holy Spirit; the Holy Spirit is a whole, as are He Himself and the Father and the Son. And the whole Unity is a whole neither superabounding in the Three, nor diminished in Each Person. For they do not individually divide between Them that real and highest Good which they are, since they do not possess It in the way of participation, but are essentially the very Good. For those phrases which we most rightly use, as One from Another, or One to Another, are designations of the Persons, not division of the Unity. For although in this ineffable and incomprehensible essence of the Deity we can, by the requirements of the properties of the Persons, say One and Another in a sober and Catholic sense, yet there is not in the essence One and Another, but simple Unity; nor in the confession of the Trinity any derogation to the Unity, nor is the true assertion of the Unity any exclusion of the *propria* of the Persons. May that execrable similitude of genus and species be accordingly as far from our minds as it is from the rule of truth. It is not a similitude, but a dissimilitude, as is also that of brass and the brazen seal; for since genus and species are to each other as higher and lower, while God is One, there can never be any resemblance between equality so perfect and disparity so great. And again, with regard to his illustration of brass, and the brass which is made into a seal, since it is used for the same kind of similitude, it is to be similarly condemned. For since, as I have said, species is less than and inferior to genus, far be it from us to think of such diversity between the Father and the Son. Far be it from us to agree with him who says that the Son is related to the Father as species to genus, as man to animal, as a brazen seal to brass, as force to force absolutely. For all these several things by the bond of their common nature are to each other as superiors and inferiors, and therefore no comparison is to be drawn from these things with That in which there is no

inequality, no dissimilarity. You see from what unskillfulness or impiety the use of these similitudes descends. . . .

Chapter 4.

9. It is no wonder if a man who is careless of what he says should, when rushing into the mysteries of the Faith, so irreverently assail and tear asunder the hidden treasures of godliness, since he has neither piety nor faith in his notions about the piety of faith. For instance, on the very threshold of his theology (I should rather say his stultology) he defines faith as private judgment; as though in these mysteries it is to be allowed to each person to think and speak as he pleases, or as though the mysteries of our faith are to hang in uncertainty amongst shifting and varying opinions, when on the contrary they rest on the solid and unshakable foundation of truth. Is not our hope baseless if our faith is subject to change? Fools then were our martyrs for bearing so cruel tortures for an uncertainty, and for entering, without hesitation, on an everlasting exile, through a bitter death, when there was a doubt as to the recompense of their reward. But far be it from us to think that in our faith or hope anything, as he supposes, depends on the fluctuating judgment of the individual, and that the whole of it does not rest on sure and solid truth, having been commended by miracles and revelations from above, founded and consecrated by the Son of the Virgin, by the Blood of the Redeemer, by the glory of the risen Christ. These infallible proofs have been given us in superabundance. But if not, the Spirit itself, lastly, bears witness with our spirit that we are the sons of God. How, then, can any one dare to call faith opinion, unless it be that he has not yet received that Spirit, or unless he either knows not the Gospel or thinks it to be a fable? *I know in whom I have believed, and I am confident* (2 Tim. i. 12), cries the Apostle, and you mutter in my ears that faith is only an opinion. Do you prate to me that that is ambiguous than which there is nothing more certain? But Augustine says otherwise: "Faith is not held by any one in whose heart it is, by conjectures or opinions, but it is sure knowledge and has the assent of the conscience." Far be it from us, then, to suppose that the Christian faith has as its boundaries those opinions of the Academicians, whose boast it is that they doubt of everything, and know nothing. But I for my part walk securely, according to the saying of the teacher of the Gentiles, and I know that I shall not be confounded. I am satisfied, I confess, with his definition of faith, even though this man stealthily accuses it. *Faith,* he says, *is the substance hoped for, the evidence of things not seen* (Heb. xi. 1). The substance, he says, of things hoped for, not a phantasy of empty conjectures. You hear, that it is a substance; and therefore it is not allowed you in our faith, to suppose or oppose at your pleasure, not to wander hither and thither amongst empty opinions, through devious errors. Under the name of substance something certain and

fixed is put before you. You are enclosed known bounds, shut in
within fixed limits. For faith is not an opinion, but a certitude.

10. But now notice other points. I pass over his saying that the
spirit of the fear of the Lord was not in the Lord; that there will be
no holy fear of the Lord in the world to come; that after the consecration of the bread and of the cup, the former accidents which
remain are suspended in the air; that the suggestions of devils come
to us, as their sagacious wickedness knows how, by the contact of
stones and herbs; and that they are able to discern in such natural
objects strength suited to excite various passions; that the Holy Spirit
is the *anima mundi;* that the world, as Plato says, is so much a more
excellent animal, as it has a better soul in the Holy Spirit. Here while
he exhausts his strength to make Plato a Christian, he proves himself
a heathen. All these things and his other numerous silly stories of the
same kind I pass by, I come to graver matters. To answer them all
would require volumes. I speak only of those on which I cannot
keep silence.

Chapter 5.

11. I find in a book of his sentences, and also in an exposition
of his of the Epistle to the Romans, that this rash inquirer into the
Divine Majesty attacks the mystery of our Redemption. He admits in
the very beginning of his disputation that there has never been but
one conclusion in our ecclesiastical doctors on this point, and this he
states only to spurn it, and boasts that he has a better; not fearing,
against the precept of the Wise Man, *To cross the ancient boundaries
which our fathers have marked out* (Prov. xxii. 28). It is needful to
know, he says, that all our doctors since the Apostles agree in this,
that the devil had power and dominion over man, and that he rightly
possessed it, because man, by an act of the free will which he had,
voluntarily consented to the devil. For they say that if any one conquers another, the conquered rightly becomes the slave of his
conqueror. Therefore, he says, as the doctors teach, the Son of God
became incarnate under this necessity, that since man could not
otherwise be freed, he might, by the death of an innocent man, be
set free from the yoke of the devil. But as it seems to us, he says,
neither had the devil ever any power over man, except by the permission of God, as a jailer might, nor was it to free man that the Son
of God assumed flesh. Which am I to think the more intolerable in
these words, the blasphemy or the arrogance? Which is the more to
be condemned, his rashness or his impiety? Would not the mouth of
him who speaks such things be more justly beaten with rods than
confuted with reasons? Does not he whose hand is against every man,
rightly provoke every man's hand to be raised against him? All, he
says, says so, but so do not I. What, then do you say? What better
statement have you? What more subtle reason have you discovered?
What more secret revelation do you boast of which has passed by the

Saints and escaped from the wise? He, I suppose, will give us secret waters and hidden bread.

12. Tell us, nevertheless, that truth which has shown itself to you and to none else. Is it that it was not to free man that the Son of God became man? No one, you excepted, thinks this; you stand alone. For not from a wise man, nor prophet, nor apostle, nor even from the Lord Himself have you received this. The teacher of the Gentiles *received from the Lord what he has handed down to us* (1 Cor. xi. 23). The Teacher of all confesses that His doctrine is not His own, for *I do not,* He says, *speak of Myself* (S. John vii. 16 and xiv. 10), while you give us of your own, and what you have received from no one. *He who speaketh a lie speaketh of his own* (*ibid.* viii. 44). Keep for yourself what is your own. I listen to Prophets and Apostles, I obey the Gospel, but not the Gospel according to Peter. Do you found for us a new Gospel? The Church does not receive a fifth Evangelist. What other Gospel do the Law, the Prophets, apostles, and apostolic men preach to us than that which you alone deny, viz., that God became man to free man? And if an angel from heaven should preach to us any other Gospel, let him be anathema.

13. But you do not accept the Doctors since the Apostles, because you perceive yourself to be a man above all teachers. For example, you do not blush to say that all are against you, when they all agree together. To no purpose, therefore, should I place before you the faith and doctrine of those teachers whom you have just proscribed. I will take you to the Prophets. Under the type of Jerusalem the prophet speaks, or rather the Lord in the prophet speaks to His chosen people: *I will save you and deliver you, fear not* (Wisd. iii. 16). You ask, from what power? For you do not admit that the devil has or ever has had power over man. Neither, I confess, do I. It is not, however, that he has it not because you and I wish it not. If you do not confess it, you know it not; they whom *the Lord has redeemed out of the hand of the enemy,* they know it and confess it. And you would by no means deny it, if you were not under the hand of the enemy. You cannot give thanks with the redeemed, because you have not been redeemed. For if you had been redeemed you would recognize your Redeemer, and would not deny your redemption. Nor does the man, who knows not himself to be a captive, seek to be redeemed. Those who knew it called unto the Lord, and the Lord heard them, and redeemed them from the hand of the enemy. And that you may understand who this enemy is, He says; *Those whom He redeemed from the hand of the enemy He gathered out of all lands* (Ps. cvii. 2, 3). But first, indeed, recognize Him Who gathered them, of Whom Caiaphas in the Gospel prophesied, saying that Jesus should die for the people, and the Evangelist proceeds thus: *And not for that nation only, but that He might gather together into one all the children of God which were scattered abroad* (S. John xi. 51, 52). Whither had they been scattered? Into all lands. Therefore those whom He redeemed He gathered together

from all lands. He first redeemed, then gathered them. For they were not only scattered, but also taken captive. He redeemed and gathered them; but redeemed them from the hand of the enemy. He does not say of the enemies, but of the enemy. The enemy was one, the lands many. Indeed, he gathered them not from one land, but from the lands, from the east and from the west, from the north and from the south. What Lord was there so powerful, who governed not one land but all lands? No other, I suppose, than He who by another prophet is said to drink up a river, that is, the human race, and not to wonder; and to trust that he can also draw up into his mouth Jordan, *i.e.,* the elect (Job xl. 18). Blessed are they who so flow in that they can flow out, who so enter that they can go out.

14. But now perhaps you do not believe the Prophets, thus speaking with one accord of the power of the devil over man. Come with me then to the Apostles. You said, did you not? that you do not agree with those who have come since the Apostles; may you agree then with the Apostles; and perhaps that may happen to you which one of them describes, speaking of certain persons: *If God, peradventure, will give them repentance to the acknowledging of the truth, and that they may recover themselves out of the snare of the devil, who are taken captive by him at his will* (2 Tim. ii. 25, 26). It is Paul who thus asserts that men are taken captive by the devil at his will. Do you hear? "at his will;" and do you deny his power? But if you do not believe Paul, come now to the Lord Himself, if perchance you may listen to Him and be put to silence. By Him the devil is called *the prince of this world* (S. John xiv. 30), and the *strong man armed* (S. Luke xi. 21), and the *possessor of goods* (S. Matt. xii. 29), and yet you say that he has no power over men. Perhaps you think the house in this place is not to be understood of the world, nor the goods of men. But if the world is the house of the devil and men his goods, how can it be said he has no power over men? Moreover, the Lord said to those who took Him: *This is your hour and the power of darkness* (S. Luke xxii. 53). That power did not escape him who said: *Who hath delivered us from the power of darkness, and hath translated us into the kingdom of His dear Son* (Col. i. 13). The Lord then neither denied the power of the devil even over Him, nor that of Pilate, who was a member of the devil. He said: *Thou couldst have no power against me at all except it were given thee from above* (S. John xix. 11). But if that power given from above so violently raged against the green tree, how is it that it did not dare to touch the dry? Nor I suppose will he say, that it was an unjust power which was given from above. Let him, therefore, learn that not only had the devil power over man, but also a just power, and in consequence let him see this, that the Son of God came in the flesh to set man free. But though we say that the power of the devil was a just one we do not say that his will was. Whence it is not the devil who usurped the power, who is just, nor man who deservedly was subjected to it; but the Lord is just, who permitted the subjection. For any one is called

just and unjust, not from his power but from his will. This power of the devil over man though not rightly acquired, but wickedly usurped, was yet justly permitted. And in this way man was justly taken captive, viz., that the justice was neither in the devil, nor in man, but in God.

Chapter 6.

15. Man therefore was lawfully delivered up, but mercifully set free. Yet mercy was shown in such a way that a kind of justice was not lacking even in his liberation, since, as was most fitting for man's recovery, it was part of the mercy of the liberator to employ justice rather than power against man's enemy. For what could man, the slave of sin, fast bound by the devil, do of himself to recover that righteousness which he had formerly lost? Therefore he who lacked righteousness had another's imputed to him, and in this way: The prince of this world came and found nothing in the Saviour, and because he notwithstanding laid hands on the Innocent he lost most justly those whom he held captive; since He who owed nothing to death, lawfully freed him who was subject to it, both from the debt of death, and the dominion of the devil, by accepting the injustice of death; for with what justice could that be exacted from man a second time? It was man who owed the debt, it was man who paid it. *For if one,* says S. Paul, *died for all, then were all dead* (2 Cor. v. 14), so that, as One bore the sins of all, the satisfaction of One is imputed to all. It is not that one forfeited, another satisfied; the Head and body is one, viz., Christ. The Head, therefore, satisfied for the members, Christ for His children, since, according to the Gospel of Paul, by which Peter's falsehood is refuted, He who died for us, *quickened us together with Himself, forgiving us all our trespasses, blotting out the handwriting of ordinances that was against us, and took it out of the way, nailing it to His cross, having spoiled principalities and powers* (Col. ii. 13, 14).

16. May I be found amongst those spoils of which the opposing powers were deprived, and be handed over into the possession of my Lord. If Laban pursue me and reproach me for having left him by stealth, he shall be told that I came to him by stealth, and therefore so left him. The secret power of sin subjected me, the hidden plan of righteousness freed me from him; or I will reply, that if I was sold for nothing shall I not be freely redeemed? If Asshur has reproached me without cause, he has no right to demand the cause of my escape. But if he says, "Your father sold you into captivity," I will reply, "But my Brother redeemed me." Why should not righteousness come to me from another when guilt came upon me from another? One made me a sinner, the other justifies me from sin; the one by genera-ation, the other by His blood. Shall there be sin in the seed of the sinner and not righteousness in the blood of Christ? But he will say, "Let righteousness be whose it may, it is none of yours." Be it so.

But let guilt also be whose it may, it is none of mine. *Shall the right-eousness of the righteous be upon him, and the wickedness of the wicked not be upon him?* It is not fitting for the son to bear the iniquity of the father, and yet to have no share in the righteousness of his brother. But now by man came death, by Man also came life. *For as in Adam all die, even so in Christ shall all be made alive* (1 Cor. xv. 21, 22). I attain to one and to the other in the same way: to the one by the flesh, to the other by faith. And if from the one I was infected with concupiscence from my birth, by Christ spiritual grace was infused into me. What more does this hired advocate bring against me? If he urges generation, I oppose regeneration; and add that the former is but carnal, while the latter is spiritual. Nor does equity suffer that they fight as equals, but the higher nature is the more efficacious cause, and therefore the spirit must necessarily over-come the flesh. In other words, the second birth is so much the more beneficial as the first was baneful. The offence, indeed, came to me, but so did grace; and *not as the offence so also is the free gift; for the judgment was by one to condemnation, but the free gift is of many offences unto justification* (Rom. v. 16). From the first man flowed down the offence, from the highest heaven came down the free gift: both from our father, one from our first father, the other from the Supreme Father. My earthly birth destroys me, and does not my heavenly much more save me? And I am not afraid of being rejected by the Father of lights when I have been rescued in this way from the power of darkness, and justified through His grace by the blood of His Son: *It is God that justifieth, who is he that condemneth?* He who had mercy on the sinner will not condemn the righteous; I mean that I am righteous, but it is in His righteousness, for *Christ is the end of the law for righteousness to every one that believeth* (Rom. x. 4). In short, *He was made our righteousness by God the Father* (1 Cor. i. 30). Is not that righteousness mine which was made for me? If my guilt was inherited, why should not my righteousness be accorded to me? And, truly, what is given me is safer than what was born in me. For this, indeed, has whereof to glory, but not before God; but that, since it is effectual to my salvation, has nothing whereof to glory save in the Lord. *For if I be righteous,* says Job, *yet will I not lift up my head* (Job x. 15), lest I receive the answer: *What hast thou that thou didst not receive? now if thou didst receive it, why dost thou glory as if thou hadst not received it?* (1 Cor. iv. 7). . . .

Chapter 8.

19. Then he labours to teach and persuade us that the devil could not and ought not to have claimed for himself any right over man, except by the permission of God, and that, without doing any injustice to the devil, God could have called back His deserter, if He wished to show him mercy, and have rescued him by a word only, as

though any one denies this; then after much more he proceeds: "And
so what necessity, or what reason, or what need was there, when the
Divine compassion by a simple command could have freed man from
sin, for the Son of God to take flesh for our redemption, to suffer so
many and such great privations, scorn, scourgings, and spittings on,
in short, the pain and ignominy of the cross itself, and that with evil
doers?" I reply: The necessity was ours, the hard necessity of those
sitting in darkness and the shadow of death. The need, equally ours,
and God's, and the Holy Angels! Ours, that He might remove the
yoke of our captivity; His own, that He might fulfil the purpose of
His will; the Angels', that their number might be filled up. Further,
the reason of this deed was the good pleasure of the Doer. Who
denies that there were ready for the Almighty other and yet other
ways to redeem us, to justify us, to set us free? But this takes
nothing from the efficacy of the one which He chose out of many.
And, perhaps, the greatest excellence of the way chosen is that in a
land of forgetfulness, of slowness of spirit, and of constant
offending, we are more forcibly and more vividly warned by so many
and such great sufferings of our Restorer. Beyond that no man
knows, nor can know to the full, what treasures of grace, what
harmony with wisdom, what increase of glory, what advantages for
salvation the inscrutable depth of this holy mystery contains within
itself, that mystery which the Prophet when considering *trembled at,
but did not penetrate* (Habak. iii. 2 in LXX.), and which the
forerunner of the Lord thought himself *unworthy to unloose*
(S. John i. 27).

20. But though it is not allowed us to scrutinize the mystery of
the Divine Will, yet we may feel the effect of its work and perceive
the fruit of its usefulness. And what we may know we may not keep
to ourselves, for to conceal their word is to give glory to kings, but
God is glorified by our investigating His sayings. [Prov. xxv. 2. But
the sense of the text is the reverse of this.] Faithful is the saying and
worthy of all acceptation, that *while we were yet sinners we were
reconciled to God by the death of His Son* (Rom. v. 10). "Where
there is reconciliation there is also remission of sins. For if, as the
Scripture says, *our sins separate between us and God"* (Is. lix. 2),
there is no reconciliation while sin remains. In what, then, is
remission of sins? *This cup,* He says, *is the new testament in My
Blood which shall be shed for you for the remission of sins* (S. Matt.
ccvi. 28). Therefore where there is reconciliation there is remission of
sins. And what is that but justification? Whether, therefore, we call it
reconciliation, or remission of sins, or justification, or, again,
redemption, or liberation from the chains of the devil, by whom we
were taken captive at his will, at all events by the death of the Only
Begotten, we obtain that we have been justified freely by His blood,
in whom, as S. Paul says again, *we have redemption through His
blood, the forgiveness of sins, according to the riches of His grace*
(Eph. i. 7). You say, Why by His blood when He could have wrought

it by His Word? Ask Himself. It is only allowed me to know that it is so, not why it is so. *Shall the thing formed say to Him that formed it, "Why hast Thou made me thus?"*

21. But these things seem to him foolishness, he cannot restrain his laughter; listen to his jeering. "Why does the Apostle say," he asks, "that we are justified, or reconciled to God by the death of His Son, when He ought to have been the more angry with man, as he sinned more deeply in crucifying His Son, than in transgressing His first command by tasting of the apple?" As if the iniquity of the malignant were not able to displease, and the godliness of the sufferer to please God, and that in one and the same act. "But," he replies, "if that sin of Adam was so heinous that it could not be expiated but by the death of Christ, what expiation shall suffice for that homicide which was perpetrated upon Christ?" I answer in two words, That very Blood which they shed, and the prayer of Him whom they slew. He asks again: "Did the death of His innocent Son so please God the Father that by it He was reconciled to us, who had committed such a sin in Adam, that because of it our innocent Lord was slain? Would He not have been able to forgive us much more easily if so heinous a sin had not been committed?" It was not His death alone that pleased the Father, but His voluntary surrender to death; and by that death destroying death, working salvation, restoring innocence, triumphing over principalities and powers, spoiling hell, enriching heaven, making peace between things in heaven and things on earth, and renewing all things. And since this so precious death to be voluntarily submitted to against sin could not take place except through sin, He did not indeed delight in, but He made good use of, the malice of the wrong-doers, and found the means to condemn death and sin by the death of His Son, and the sin [of those who condemned Him]. And the greater their iniquity, the more holy His will, and the more powerful to salvation; because, by the interposition of so great a power, that ancient sin, however great, would necessarily give way to that committed against Christ, as the less to the greater. Nor is this victory to be ascribed to the sin or to the sinners, but to Him who extracted good from their sin, and who bore bravely with the sinners, and turned to a godly purpose whatever the cruelty of the impious ventured on against Himself.

22. Thus the Blood which was shed was so powerful for pardoning that it blotted out that greatest sin of all, by which it came to pass that it was shed; and, therefore, left no doubt whatever about the blotting out of that ancient and lighter sin. Thus he rejoins: "Is there any one to whom it does not seem cruel and unjust, that any one should require the blood of an innocent man as the price of some thing, or that the death of an innocent man should in any way give him pleasure, not to say that God should hold so acceptable the death of His Son as by it to be reconciled to the whole world?" God the Father did not require the Blood of His Son, but, nevertheless, He accepted it when offered; it was not blood He

thirsted for, but salvation, for salvation was in the blood. He died, in short, for our salvation, and not for the mere exhibition of charity, as this man thinks and writes. For he so concludes the numerous calumnies and reproaches, which he as impiously as ignorantly belches out against God, as to say that "the whole reason why God appeared in the flesh was for our education by His word and example," or, as he afterwards says, for our instruction; that the whole reason why He suffered and died was to exhibit or commend to us charity.

Chapter 10.

23. But what profits it that He should instruct us if He did not first restore us by His grace? Or are we not in vain instructed if the body of sin is not first destroyed in us, that we should no more serve sin? If all the benefit that we derive from Christ consists in the exhibition of His virtues, it follows that Adam must be said to harm us only by the exhibition of sin. But in truth the medicine given was proportioned to the disease. *For as in Adam all die, even so in Christ shall all be made alive* (1 Cor. xv. 22). As is the one, so is the other. If the life which Christ gives is nothing else but His instruction, the death which Adam gave is in like manner only his instruction; so that the one by his example leads men to sin, the other by His example and His Word leads them to a holy life and to love Him. But if we rest in the Christian faith, and not in the heresy of Pelagius, and confess that by generation and not by example was the sin of Adam imparted to us, and by sin death, let us also confess that it is necessary for righteousness to be restored to us by Christ, not by instruction, but by regeneration, and by righteousness life (Rom. v. 18). And if this be so, how can Peter say that the only purpose and cause of the Incarnation was that He might enlighten the world by the light of His wisdom and inflame it with love of Him? Where, then, is redemption? There come from Christ, as he deigns to confess, merely illumination and enkindling to love. Whence come redemption and liberation?

24. Grant that the coming of Christ profits only those who are able to comform their lives to His, and to repay to Him the debt of love, what about babes? What light of wisdom will he give to those who have barely seen the light of life? Whence will they gain power to ascend to God who have not even learned to love their mothers? Will the coming of Christ profit them nothing? Is it of no avail to them that they have been planted together with Him by baptism in in the likeness of His death, since through the weakness of their age they are not able to know of, or to love, Christ? Our redemption, he says, consists in that supreme love which is inspired in us by the passion of Christ. Therefore, infants have no redemption because they have not that supreme love. Perhaps he holds that as they have no power to love, so neither have they necessity to perish, that they

have no need to be regenerated in Christ because they have received no damage from their generation from Adam. If he thinks this, he thinks foolishness with Pelagius. Whichever of these two opinions he holds, his ill-will to the sacrament of our salvation is evident; and in attributing the whole of our salvation to devotion, and nothing of it to regeneration, it is evident too that, as far as he can, he would empty of meaning the dispensation of this deep mystery; for he places the glory of our redemption and the great work of salvation, not in the virtue of the Cross, not in the blood paid as its price, but in our advances in a holy life. But *God forbid that I should glory save in the Cross of our Lord Jesus Christ* (Gal. vi. 14), in which are our salvation, life, and resurrection.

25. And, indeed, I see three chief virtues in this work of our salvation: the form of humility in which God emptied Himself; the measure of charity which He stretched out even to death, and that the death of the Cross; the mystery of redemption, by which He bore that death which He underwent. The former two of these without the last are as if you were to paint on the air. A very great and most necessary example of humility, a great example of charity, and one worthy of all acceptation, has He set us; but they have no foundation, and, therefore, no stability, if redemption be wanting. I wish to follow with all my strength the lowly Jesus; I wish Him, who loved me and gave Himself for me, to embrace me with the arms of His love, which suffered in my stead; but I must also feed on the Paschal Lamb, for unless I eat His Flesh and drink His Blood I have no life in me. It is one thing to follow Jesus, another to hold Him, another to feed on Him. To follow Him is a life-giving purpose; to hold and embrace Him a solemn joy; to feed on Him a blissful life. *For His flesh is meat indeed, and His blood is drink indeed. The bread of God is He who cometh down from Heaven and giveth life to the world* (S. John vi. 56, 33). What stability is there for joy, what constancy of purpose, without life? Surely no more than for a picture without a solid basis. Similarly neither the examples of humility nor the proofs of charity are anything without the sacrament of our redemption.

26. These results of the labour of the hands of your son, my lord and father, you now hold, such as they are, against a few heads of this new heresy; in which if you see nothing besides my zeal, yet I have meanwhile satisfied my own conscience. For since there was nothing that I could do against the injury to the faith, which I deplored, I thought it worth while to warn him, whose arms are the power of God, for the destruction of contrary imaginations, to destroy every high thing that exalteth itself against the knowledge of God, and to bring every thought into captivity to the obedience of Christ. There are other points in his other writings, not few nor less evil; but the limits of my time and of a letter do not allow me to reply to them. Moreover, I do not think it necessary, since they are so manifest, that they may be easily refuted even by ordinary faith. Still, I have collected some and sent them to you.

Notes

10. SCHOLASTIC PHILOSOPHY AND THEOLOGY

Opus majus

Roger Bacon

Intellectual activity in the thirteenth century was animated by one overriding issue: the role philosophy should play in the study of theology. One opinion regarding this matter is sketched out below as written by the master who may have been the first to lecture on the works of Aristotle at the University of Paris after their ban there in 1210 and 1231, Roger Bacon (ca. 1219-1292). Bacon's *Opus majus* (written 1266-1268) provides as well an insight into the historical perspective scholars of the thirteenth century assumed in their writing.

PART TWO

Chapter 1.

Accordingly after the four general causes of all human error have been banished to the lower regions and have been completely removed from this plea, I wish to show in this second part that there is one wisdom that is perfect and that this is contained in the Scriptures. From the roots of this wisdom all truth has sprung. I say, therefore, that one science is the mistress of the others, namely, theology, to which the remaining sciences are vitally necessary, and without which it cannot reach its end. The excellence of these sciences theology claims for her own law, whose nod and authority the rest of the sciences obey. Or better, there is only one perfect wisdom, which is contained wholly in the Scriptures, and is to be unfolded by canon law and philosophy. . . .

Chapter 2.

This moreover becomes clearer as we estimate and consider the division of the sciences. For if we should try to separate the sciences one from another, we cannot say that theology is not both the science of canon law and philosophy; for under one division of philosophy, namely, moral science, which Aristotle named civil, is contained the civil law, as will be shown below. But canon law is named from the canonical Scriptures, not from others, just as the name shows. The books of the Old Testament are called the canonical Scriptures, as is the practice in the first part of the Decreta in the ninth section, and elsewhere; or the Scriptures are called canonical from this same word canon, for *canon* in Greek is called *regula* in Latin; and the law, canonical as well as divine, is acknowledged to give us the way of living according to rule. But canon law is wholly founded on the authority of Scripture and its expositors, as is clearly shown throughout the whole body of the Decretum and of the Decretals. For either in support of the ordinances of the canons there are brought forward the authorities of the expositors of Scripture, as Augustine, Jerome, Gregory, Ambrose, Isidore, Cyprian, Hilary, and others; or the holy and exalted pontiffs in support of their own decrees cite the authorities and examples of the New and Old Testaments; and hence this law is nothing else but an explanation of the will of God in the Scriptures. Canon law is likewise called ecclesiastical law, by which the Church of God is ruled in spiritual matters both in its head and in its members. But the Scripture, has no other interest outside this direction of the Church. Moreover, the natural law is contained in the Scripture, as is taught in the beginning of the Decretum, but whatever has been accepted in customs or included in writings, if it should be opposed to natural law, must be considered vain and without reason, as is set forth in the first part, eighth section. Therefore canon laws cannot be different from divine law, nay, they must be derived from its sources. The common law, moreover, is either divine or human. It is divine, since it was proclaimed to the world by the mind and spirit of God in his Scriptures; it is human, since it was discovered by the mind of man. But we agree that the Church is ruled by the divine mind and spirit, and therefore by the divine law which is included in the Scriptures, and it is certain that the Church is ruled by canon law. Therefore this divine law must be drawn out of the treasure-house of the Scriptures. This, moreover, is clear if we consider the divisions of canon law. For it orders the gradations of ecclesiastical offices, determines the sacraments of God, discusses the forum of the conscience, and settles ecclesiastical cases. But the roots of all these matters and the erect stalk itself are found in the Scriptures; the branches belong to the expositors of the same, so that in the body of the canons are to be had the leaves, flowers, and fruit bringing salvation. For the pleasing embellishment of the language of the canon is compared to leaves according to the Scriptures, but the utility of the flowers and fruits is comprised in the four divisions already mentioned under their appropriate metaphors. And for this reason the canons are merely the golden heads of grain, and the branches, the ripeness of the grapes, are to be offered through the virtue in their own Scriptures. Since therefore canon law is thus subject to Scripture, it is contained in one body, just as the body of a single tree is composed of roots and stalk, branches, flowers, and fruits.

Chapter 3.

We must show, moreover, both in general and in particular, that the power of philosophy is not foreign to the wisdom of God, but is included in it. After this has been made clear by authorities, examples, and arguments of a general nature, a fuller exposition will then be made covering the four or five divisions of philosophy in regard to the power of the separate sciences and arts. For if Christians ought to snatch from the philosophers as from unlawful possessors the useful facts contained in their books, even as in the beginning I quoted from Augustine, it is evident that philosophy is wholly worthy and belongs to sacred truth. In the same book he says that the gold and silver of the philosophers did not originate with them but are dug out of certain mines as it were of divine providence, which is present everywhere, and he shows that this had been prefigured saying, "Just as the Egyptians possessed vessels and ornaments of gold and silver and raiment, which that people on its departure from Egypt claimed for itself on the ground that it would make a better use of these things; so the systems of the Gentiles contain liberal instruction better adapted to the service of truth and moral precepts of the most useful kind, and some facts are discovered in these philosophers concerning the worship of God himself, and this gold as it were and silver of theirs the Christian should take from them and apply to good use in preaching the Gospel."

And he explains this statement in all matters subject to human management which relate to either morals, or history, or arts, or nature, or logic and grammar. For as regards morals, he says, "The raiment also of those men, that is certain human institutions, but yet adapted to human society, which we cannot do without in this life, must be converted to Christian use." Of matters pertaining to history, he says, "The history of the Gentiles aids us greatly in understanding the Scriptures. For both by means of the Olympiads and the names of the consuls we frequently seek an answer to our question, and ignorance of the consulship in which our Lord suffered has caused some to err in thinking that our Lord suffered in the forty-sixth year of his age, because it was said by the Jews that their temple had been so many years in building, which was a figure of our Lord's body." This fact is made clear in almost innumerable places in the New and Old Testament. Concerning other human considerations relating to the arts as well as nature he says, "Of all the other arts, by which something is made or remains after the action, as a house, bench, vessel or any object of this kind, or medicine and agriculture and the art of navigation, or of those activities whose whole effect is the action itself, as dancing, running, wrestling"—a knowledge of these, I say, must be employed in froming a judgment, lest we should

be wholly ignorant of that which the Scriptures wish to inculcate
when they employ certain forms of expression derived from these
arts, and we may take the term *naturalia* in a wider sense so as to
include medicine and agriculture. For those sciences are based on
nature, and are two of the eight sciences dealing especially with
nature, as will be explained below. Yet in general he says in regard
to all the natual sciences, "That man would indeed do the Scriptures
a kind service who should collect the characteristics of times and
places, of stones and the rest of inanimate things, of plants and
animals." Moreover, in behalf of logic he says, in the first place,
that a training in disputation is valuable in regard to all kinds of
questions that must be examined and solved in sacred writings. Elsewhere in the same book he says there is a difference in the case of
logic from the other sciences. For certain necessary and important
things can be inferred from these sciences on behalf of theology, but
I do not see, as he says, whether this can be the case with logic, since
it, like nerves, is inferred throughout the whole text of the
Scriptures. Also in the third book concerning the order of discipline
he says that no one should approach the sacred science without a
knowledge of the power of logic. His second, third, and fourth books
almost throughout exhort us in regard to the application of grammar
to sacred things. Jerome, moreover, in his commentary on the
Epistle to Titus, speaking of the usefulness of grammar in regard to
theology in comparison with many other sciences, says, "The
teaching of the grammarians can benefit life provided it be applied to
better uses," a subject concerning which many important statements
must be made in what follows. But concerning mathematics,
Cassiodorus says in his book on this science, "These four sciences,
geometry, arithmetic, astronomy, music, we ponder over with an
attentive mind, they sharpen our perception, they wipe away the
mire of ignorance, and produce that speculative contemplation by
the gift of the Lord. Rightly do the holy fathers persuade us to read
these four, since in a great measure through them our appetite is
drawn away from carnal things, and we are caused to desire those
things which we can view in spirit only with the help of the
understanding." But these matters will be shown fully in their proper
place. If such is the case in regard to these sciences, much more is
metaphysics in accord with divine utterances. For with the philosophers metaphysics occupies the place of one part of theology,
being named by them together with moral philosophy the divine
science and the theology of physics, as is clear from the first and
eleventh books of the Metaphysics of Aristotle and from the ninth
and tenth of the Metaphysics of Avicenna. For it considers many
things concerning God and the angels and divine topics of this kind,
and thus it is clear that Scripture lays claim to the power of the
whole science. But not only Augustine gives us the above instruction,
but he states that many sacred writers have done so when he asks,
"Do we not see with how great a load of gold Cyprian came out of

Egypt, that very sweet teacher and most blessed martyr; likewise Lactanius, Victorinus, Optatus, and Hilary, to be silent about the living; likewise innumerable Greeks, as in former days Moses himself a most faithful servant of God had done, concerning whom it was written that he was learned in all the wisdom of the Egyptians?". . . .

Chapter 5,

The reasons can be given why the sacred writers so affirm the point in question and declare that it was set forth in a figure and seized upon in effect by the saints. In the first place the truth where-ever found is thought to belong to Christ, as evidenced by the opinion and authorities of Augustine quoted above; in the second place, although in some measure the truth may be said to belong to the philosophers, yet for possessing it the divine light first flowed into their minds, and illumined them from above. For it lighteth every man that cometh into this world, as the Scripture says, with which sentiment the philosophers themselves agree. For they main-tain that there is an active intellect and a possible intellect. The human soul is called possible by them, because it has of itself capacity for sciences and virtues and receives these from another source. The active intellect is the one which flows into our minds, illuminating them in regard to knowledge and virtue, because although the possible intellect may be called active from the act of understanding, yet in assuming an active intelligence, as they do, it is so called as influencing and illuminating the possible intellect for the recognition of truth. And thus the active intellect, according to the greater philosophers, is not a part of the soul, but is an intel-lectual substance different and separated essentially from the possible intellect. . . .

Chapter 6.

The third reason why the wisdom of philosophy is reduced to the divine wisdom is that God not only has enlightened their minds for the acquisition of a knowledge of wisdom, but they have secured it from him, and he has revealed, presented, and given it to them. For all wisdom is from the Lord God, just as the authority of Scripture states, because, as the Apostle says, "What is known of God is mani-fest in them, for God has revealed it to them." Augustine says on John that he gave it to them, and the greatest philosopher Aristotle in the book of the Secrets asserts that the whole of philosophy was evidently given and revealed by God. Also one of the greatest of philosophers, Marcus Tullius, in the first book of the Tusculan Disputations asks, "What is philosophy, as Plato says, but the gift, as I say, the invention of God?" Whence he also says that not even a poet has poured forth a theme filled with weighty meaning without some divine instigation of his mind. Moreover, Augustine in the eighth book of the City of God teaches and approves of what Socrates, the father of the great philosophers, maintained, that a man cannot know the causes of things except in the divine light and by its gift, and any one can prove for himself that nothing in the first instance is discovered by man which is within the range of philosophy. I offer an example in a very small matter; for although the Universals of Porphyry have been pretty adequately explained by him, and elsewhere have been stated sufficiently in logic, metaphysics, and natural and speculative philosophy, yet there is no man so well grounded as not to need in many ways to have teachers and to listen to them for a long time and to study before he knows the whole truth of the Universals. And no one with difficulty learns enough about these before death, no matter how many teachers he may have, as is clear owing to the disagreement of all in this matter: since some maintain that these exist only in the mind, others that they exist only outside of it, while still others maintain that in respect to being they are in things, but in their universal aspect they are in the mind. Avicenna shows in his commentary on Porphyry that he lacked the sixth Universal and that he made several false statements. If, therefore, ignorance of these exists in any man you please, although he may study throughout his whole life the books of the philosophers, and though he may have honored teachers, much more will he be ignorant of these weightier matters and never discover them for himself without books and teachers. Wherefore of necessity the truth of these matters was revealed to man in the beginning. If also any one, however well versed in the Universals, had handed over the book of Porphyry to oblivion and all things necessary for a knowledge of Universals, and could not have books or teachers, it would be impossible that he should ever unfold the truth of the Universals. I am speaking of the Universals in respect to their true being, as a metaphysician must consider them, and not merely in respect to the puerile teaching of Porphyry and the method of logic. Wherefore any one can consider for himself that revelation is necessary in this direction; and since these are puerile and very small matters, my position will be much stronger as applied to the whole knowledge of philosophy. But what is from God and what he himself has revealed, presented, and given, should be in absolute conformity with his own wisdom.

Chapter 7.

But the whole aim of philosophy is that the Creator may be known through the knowledge of the creature, to whom service may be rendered in a worship that gives him honor, in the beauty of morals, and in the integrity of useful laws, because of the reverence due his majesty and the benefits of creation and preservation and of future happiness, so that men may live in peace and justice in this life. For the end of speculative philosophy is the knowledge of the

Creator through the creatures, and moral philosophy establishes the dignity of morals, just laws, and the worship of God, and persuades us of our future felicity in a profitable and glorious manner so far as lies in the power of philosophy. These things are known as facts by those who peruse all the principal parts of philosophy, as what follows will show. Since, therefore, these things are altogether necessary for Christians and are in complete accord with the wisdom of God, it is clear that philosophy is necessary to the divine law and to the faithful who glory in it. . . .

Chapter 9.

This general proposition can be proved finally by the fact that the full measure of philosophy was given to the same men to whom also the law of God was given, namely, the holy patriarchs and prophets from the beginning of the world. And not only is this necessary for establishing the point under consideration, but also for certifying the whole range of knowledge. For one could not unaided acquire the principles of the sciences and arts, but needed a revelation. If we prove a revelation, we should have no doubt in regard to the secrets of wisdom discovered by the investigators, although we have had not experience in them. But there is no single point within the realm of knowledge so difficult of proof as this, because it is the main foundation of all human comprehension, and objections and doubts frequently present themselves, and authorities and books must be explained more fully than for any other proposition discoverable in the whole range of knowledge. I say, therefore, that the power of philosophy was given by God to the same persons as the sacred Scripture, namely, the saints at the beginning, so that there thus appears to be one wisdom in its entirety necessary for mankind. For the partiarchs and prophets alone were true philosophers, knowing all things, to wit, not only the law of God, but all the parts of philosophy. For sacred Scripture proves this to us with sufficient clearness, stating that Joseph instructed the princes of Pharaoh and taught the old men of Egypt prudence, and Moses was skilled in all the wisdom of the Egyptians. Bezaleel and Aholiab also proved this point, who had a full grasp and knowledge of the things of nature; for with one breath the Holy Spirit illumined them and taught them the whole of nature's power in metals and other minerals. But Solomon, wiser than all preceding or following him, according to the testimony of Scripture, possessed the full power of philosophy. Josephus in the first book of his Antiquities says that since the sons of Adam through Seth were religious men and made by God himself, God granted them a life of six hundred years on account of the glorious parts of philosophy in which they studied, in order that they might know by experience through the length of their life what God revealed to them. He adds that Noah and his sons taught the Chaldeans the parts of philosophy, and that Abraham entered Egypt and taught the Egyptians. And he adds that Solomon left no part of nature unexamined, but philosophized about all things and clearly set forth his teaching in regard to their properties, and he mentions how Solomon in treating of things singly composed four thousand and five books; and he adds many things which we know nature as she generally functions does not in any way do. . . .

Chapter 10.

After this in the time of Othniel, judge of Israel, Cadumus the Theban reigned, who first gave letters to the Greeks, as is shown in the Cluniac chronicles. Bede also in his smaller chronological work and other writers agree that under Aoth the judge, Amphion the musician flourished. This Aoth was first after Othniel under Deborah and Barak. There was another Apollo, a philosopher, according to the Cluniac chronicle, the founder of medicine, a contemporary of the second Hercules, whose deeds are famous, as Augustine says in the eighteenth book of the City of God. This Hercules in the time of Abimelech the judge laid waste Troy, set up his pillars in India, erected his columns at Gades, and refusing to bear the pain of his disease cremated himself in the time of Jephthah the judge, as is confirmed by Augustine and the chronicle mentioned. I have spoken of this second Hercules, because there was another Hercules near the time of the greater Mercury who was a little after him, as Augustine states. After him there was a third, who established the Olympian contest, which after an intermission his son Picus restored in the four hundred and eighth year after the destruction of Troy, as Solinus writes. Whence many have been deceived thinking that there was but one Hercules, who did all the things that were written concerning several, as Augustine says. There was a similar mistake in regard to this philosopher Apollo. For all, as Augustine says, reckon him to have been the one who was worshiped as a god in the island of Delos, under the impression that he was one and the same person, whereas the contrary is shown to be the fact by much evidence. For that Apollo who gave responses in temples is found at least to have given a response when the city of Athens was founded, that Athena, who is Minerva, might be worshiped as a goddess, and for this reason this philosopher cannot be he who was worshiped as the Dephic god. But according to Augustine he was the son of Latona, whose sister was Diana. Isidore also mades the same statement in the eighth book. Similarly he does not seem to be the one of whom Jerome writes in the Epistle to Paul which is placed before the Bibles of the Latins. For that one discovers Hiarchus seated on a golden throne and teaching, and this Hiarchus is said to be Abrachis, the astronomer, who lived after the death of Alexander the Great, as Ptolemy shows in the Almagest. And therefore according to this there were three Apollos as well as three Hercules. Then under Gideon Orpheus and Linus won fame, as Bede states. And these men, namely, Amphion,

Orpheus, Linus, and such men of their day, were called theological
poets, as Augustine says, because they composed hymns to the gods.
According to Solinus, Nicostrate, mother of the Roman king
Evander, was called Carmentis from her gift of prophecy, who dwelt
on the Capitoline hill in Rome, and was first to give the Latins
letters. And this, as Bede states, was the time of Jair, judge of Israel,
but according to the Cluniac chronicle it was in the time of the judge
who filled that office seventeen years after Jair. But this question is
not within the scope of the present discussion.

On account of the Sibyls and especially the Erythraean Sibyl,
who far surpassed all the unbelieving philosophers previously
mentioned, the date of the fall of Troy must be settled definitely.
For Augustine states in the eighth book of the City of God that
many authorities have written that this Sibyl lived in the time of the
Trojan war, although others held that she lived in the time of
Romulus and Ahaz, or of Hezekiah, king of Judah, as Augustine says.
Now the fall of Troy was four hundred years before Romulus. For
Solinus proves that Rome was founded in the seventh Olympiad,
four hundred and thirty-three years after the Trojan war. as he
clearly shows by Hercules and Picus his son mentioned above and by
others. And Augustine in the eighth book mentioned above main-
tains that Troy was captured when Labdon spoken of above judged
the Hebrews, whence in the Cluniac chronicles it is stated that Troy
was captured in the third year of Labdon. Then in the time of
Samuel according to the Cluniac chronicle, but more explicitly in the
Deeds of the Greater Britons, lived Homer the famous poet. Then
Hesiod the philosopher succeeded Homer before the founding of
Rome, as Tullius says in his book of Tusculan Questions. And later
came Archilochus in the reign of Romulus, as is stated in the same
book, and therefore in the time of Ahaz or Hezekiah, kings of Judah.
For in the first year of Numitor, grandfather of Romulus, who was
the last king of the Albans in Italy, as Augustine states, Rome was
founded. And therefore Numitor and his grandson Romulus ruled at
the same time, and then the kingdom and the name of the Albans
ceased, and they were called Roman kings. The king at that time in
Judah was Ahaz; or, as some think, Hezekiah his successor, a most
excellent and pious king, ruled in the time of Romulus.

Chapter 11.

Augustine makes these statements; but in the time of this same
Romulus, according to Augustine, Thales is reported to have lived
who was the first of the seven wise men. For after the theological
poets wisdom increased and men devoted to it were called Sophists,
that is wise men. But according to Bede in his book of Chronologies
and according to Isidore in the fifth book of the Etymologies and
according to others also, Thales lived in the time of Josiah, who as a
natural philosopher examined nature and was an astrologer at the
time when the Hebrew people, as Augustine states, were led into

captivity. Another of the seven wise men appeared, Pittacus by name and a Mytilenean by nationality and race; and five others were in the time of the captivity, whose names are Solon the Athenian, Chilon the Lacedaemonian, Periander the Corinthian, Cleobulus the Lidian, Bias the Prienean. Of these Solon gave the Athenians laws, for the transfer of which the Roman people sent ten men, and they are called the laws of the twelve tables, as Isidore writes in his fifth book and Gratianus accepts the statement from him. But the four others left nothing in writing, as Augustine says. All these men, however, were called wise according to Augustine in the eighth book of the City of God, who were distinguished from other men in the nature of their life by certain precepts pertaining to right living, and according to Augustine in the eighth book these were the Ionic wise men, that is Greek. But another class of men devoted to wisdom arose after these in the Greek language, which, however, is called Italic, but they came from that part of Italy which in ancient times was called Great Greece. They were called the Italic school because they studied in Italy although they were Greeks and used the Greek language. Those men did not wish to be called wise, but lovers of wisdom, of whom the first was Pythagoras from the island of Samos. When he was asked who he was, he replied that he was a philosopher, that is a lover of wisdom, as Augustine says in the eighth book of the City of God; but in the eighteenth book of the City of God Augustine says that he appeared at the time of the Jewish restoration. According to Tullius in the first book of the Tusculan Questions in the time of the Roman king Tarquin the Proud, the seventh from Romulus and last of the Roman kings, after whom the cousuls arose, Pythagoras came into Italy and swayed Great Greece with his reputation, discipline, and authority. For many ages afterwards the name of Pythagoras had such weight that no others were considered learned. This Tarquin, as Bede writes, began to reign in the time of Cyrus, king of the Persians, who released the Jews from captivity, and reigned in the time of Cambyses, the son of Cyrus, and of his two brothers the Magians, and of Darius, in whose second year the temple was built, and at that time Pythagoras was considered famous, as Bede says, and Zorobabel, Aggaeus, Zachariah, and Malachi were renowned as prophets. Pythagoras was taught by Pherecydes the Syrian, as Tullius says in the book mentioned above, who was the first to maintain that the souls of men are immortal. His date is established only by the date of Pythagoras his pupil, although Isidore also says in the first book that Pherecydes wrote histories in the time of Esdras, which might have been toward the end of Pherecydes' own life and in the youth of Esdras. For from the time when Pythagoras was said to have flourished there passed the thirty-six years of the reign of Darius, the twenty-six of Xerxes, the seven months of Artabanus, and the six years of Artaxerxes Longimanus, before Esdras went up from Babylon to Jerusalem. For in the seventh year of his reign on the first day of the first month, according to the Scripture and the chronicle, Esdras set out.

Chapter 12.

These two classes of philosphers, the Ionic and the Italic, branched out through many schools and various successors up to the teaching of Aristotle, who corrected and changed the positions of all his predecessors, and attempted to complete philosophy. Archytas of Tarentum and Timaeus named especially among others succeeded Pythagoras. But the leading philosophers, Socrates, Plato, and Aristotle, did not descend from this line, but were Ionians and true Greeks, of whom the first was Thales of Miletus. How the rest succeeded him, Augustine shows in the eighth book of the City of God. For after Thales first came Anaximander his pupil, whose successor was Anaximenes, and these two were in the time of the Jewish captivity, as Augustine states in the eighteenth book of the City of God, and others likewise agree in this. Now Anaxagoras and Diogenes, auditors of Anaximenes, succeeded him under Darius Hydaspes, in whose second year the building of the temple began. Anaxagoras, as Augustine states, had as his successor Archelaus his pupil, whose auditor Democritus, according to Isidore in the eighth book, is said to have been the pupil of Archelaus. Socrates was born, according to Bede, under Artabanus, who reigned over the Persians for seven years, whom Artaxerxes Longimanus succeeded, in whose seventh year Esdras descended from Babylon. Esdras and Socrates were therefore contemporaries, but Esdras was the older, as is clear from what has now been said. For this reason Augustine says in his eighteenth book that Socrates was after Esdras, that is, later in respect to birth. For when Esdras was influential at the court of the Persian king and among the Jews, Socrates appeared. This is the Socrates who is called the father of the great philosophers, since he was the teacher of Plato and Aristotle, from whom all the schools of philsophers have descended. Now Plato, according to Bede in his larger work on Chronologies, was born under Sogdianus, who reigned for seven months, whom Darius surnamed Nothus, although Bede writes in his larger work on the Chronologies that Plato was born under the same Darius. But in that work he reckons the time of Sogdianus, since it was short, under the reign of Darius. For he joins him in succession with Artaxerxes Longimanus. Now at Plato's birth Hippocrates was famed as a physician, as Bede states, and at this time we find Empedocles and Parmenides. But Plato, first learning what Socrates and Greece had to teach, as a teacher of Athens sought Egypt and Archytas of Tarentum and Timaeus, and traversed most laboriously that same Italian coast which was called Great Greece, as Jerome states to Paulinus. And against Rufus Jerome writes that Plato, after founding the Academy and teaching innumerable pupils, when he perceived that much was lacking in his system of instruction, came to Great Greece, and there instructed by Archytas of Tarentum and Timaeus of Locri in the doctrine of Pythagoras united his own elegance and grace with teachings of this kind. Plato is placed before all other philosophers according to the sacred writers, because his books reached their hands, and because he wrote beautiful sentiments about God and much about morals and a future life, which accord closely with the sacred wisdom of God, as I shall explain in the part on moral philosophy. For this reason many Catholic writers have thought that he heard Jeremiah the prophet in Egypt. For he visited Egypt in his search for wisdom and was taught by the barbarian priests, as Tullius writes concerning him in the fifth book of the Academica. But Augustine says that he did not live in the time of Jeremiah. For Jeremiah, as he says in the eighteenth book of the City of God, first prophesied in the time of the fourth king from Romulus, who was called Ancus Martius, and in the time of the fifth king, namely Tarquinius Priscus. Plato, however, did not live at that time, but was born almost one hundred years after the time of Jeremiah, as Augustine states in the eighth book, and he did not, as some thought, find the Seventy Translators in order to receive their instruction. For as Augusine states in the eighth book and Tully in his book on Old Age, Plato died in the eighty-first year of his life, and this was at the end of the reign of Artaxerxes, who was called Ochus, as Bede states; and from the year of his death, as Augustine states, there were almost thirty years to the time of the Seventy Translators. Hence Plato was not instructed in divine matters by them. But Augustine thinks that owing to his desire for knowledge he learned Hebrew and read through the books of the Old Testament, as he shows in his account of the creation of the world which he has represented in conformity with Scripture, and by the name of God which God himself gave in Exodus, "I am that I am," when Moses asked him what his name was. This is the name used by Plato, who states that it is God's name.

Chapter 13.

Before the death of Socrates Aristotle was born, since he was his auditor for three years, as we read in the life of Aristotle. According to Bede he was born under Artaxerxes surnamed Memnon, the successor of Darius Nothus. In his seventeenth year he was an auditor of Socrates and listened to him for three years. After the death of Socrates he became an auditor of Plato, according to Bede, and remained so for twenty years, as we read in his life. After Plato's death he lived twenty-three years. As is clear from the statements made, the extent of his life was sixty-three years. This statement is likewise made in Censorinus' book on the natal day. Censorinus' book states that Aristotle maintained a struggle against a mortal disease for three years by the greatness of his soul rather than by the virtue of medicine. Aristotle became the teacher of Alexander the Great and on the authority of his pupil sent two thousand men throughout the world to inquire into the secrets of nature, as Pliny tells us in the eighth book of his Natural History, and Aristotle composed a thousand books, as we read in his life. He purged away the errors of preceding philosophers, and enlarged philosophy, aspiring to that full measure of this subject possessed by the ancient patriarchs, although he was not able to perfect each of its parts. For his successors have corrected him in some particulars, and have added many things to his works, and additions will continue to be made until the end of the world, because there is no perfection in human discoveries, as has been shown in what precedes. Nature made this man strong, as Averroës says in the third book on the Soul, that she might discover the ultimate perfection of man. Aristotle, on the testimony of all great philosophers, is the greatest of them all, and that alone must be ascribed to philosophy which he himself has affirmed; whence at the present time he is called by the title Philosopher in the realm of philosophy, just as Paul is understood by the title of Apostle in the doctrine of the sacred wisdom. But the larger portion of the philosophy of Aristotle received little attention either on account of the concealment of the copies of his work and their rarity, or on account of their difficulty, or unpopularity, or on account of the wars in the East, till after the time of Mahomet, when Avicenna and Averroës and others recalled to the light of full exposition the philosophy of Aristotle. Although only some of his works on logic and certain others have been translated from Greek by Boetius, yet from the time of Michael Scotus, whose translations with authentic expositions of certain parts of Aristotle's works on nature and metaphysics appeared in the year of our Lord 1230, the philosophy of Aristotle has grown in importance among the Latins. But in comparison with the vastness of his wisdom contained in a thousand books, only a very small portion up to the present time has been translated into Latin, and still less is in common use among students. Avicenna in particular, the imitator and expositor of Aristotle, and the man who completed philosophy as far as it was possible for him to do so, composed a threefold volume of philosophy, as he states in the prologue of his book Sufficiency: one part popular in character like the philosophical dicta of the Peripatetics who are of the school of Aristotle; the second part in conformity with the pure truth of philosophy, which does not fear the thrusts of the spears of contradicters, as he himself asserts; and the third part conterminous with his own life, in which he gave an exposition of the earlier parts and collected together the more hidden facts of nature and art. But of these volumes two have not been translated; the Latins have the first in certain parts; which is called the book of Assipha, that is the book of Sufficiency. After him came Averroës, a man of sound wisdom, correcting many statements of his predessors and adding much to them, although he must be corrected in some particulars and completed in many others. For of making many books there is no end, as Solomon writes in Ecclesiastes.

Chapter 14.

From these considerations the main conclusion is clear, and it is manifest that all unbelieving philosophers and poets and Sibyls and whosoever were devoted to wisdom, appeared after the true, believing, and perfect philosophers, who were the sons of Seth and Noah with their sons, to whom God granted a life of six hundred years to complete the study of wisdom, as Josephus says in the first book of Antiquities, saying that in less time they could not complete philosophy, especially on account of astronomy, in which there is the greater difficulty because mortal men are far distant from the heavenly bodies. But God revealed all things to them, and gave them length of life to complete philosophy through experience. But because of the evil of men, who have abused the paths of wisdom, as in the first instance did Nemroth and Zoroastes, Atlas, Prometheus, Mercurius Trismegistus, Aesculapius, Apollo, Minerva, and the like, who were worshiped as gods because of their wisdom, God darkened the foolish heart of the multitude: and gradually the knowledge of philosophy disappeared until Solomon again recalled and perfected it in its entirety, as Josephus shows in the eighth book of the Antiquities. And again on account of men's sins the study of philosophy vanished by degrees, until Thales of Miletus took it up again, and his successors broadened it, until Aristotle completed it, as far as was possible for that time. But those men learned all things from the Hebrews, as Aristotle says in the book of Secrets, as was shown above. Since, therefore, the first unbelieving philosophers, as Nemroth, Prometheus, Atlas, Apollo, and others were after Seth and Noah and Shem and Abraham and after their sons who completed philosophy; and since following Solomon, who a second time perfected it, were the rest of the unbelieving philosophers, Thales, Pythagoras, Socrates, Plato, and Aristotle, it is clear that philosophy in its perfection was first given to the holy patriarchs and prophets, to whom likewise was revealed the divine law by one and the same God. This would not have happened unless philosophy were wholly conformable with God's saints and holy law, and useful and necessary for the understanding, execution, and defense of that law. Moreover, a belief in philosophy must be secured, philosophy must be demonstrated, diffused, and enlarged, for it is necessary in all these ways, as will appear on going through the separate parts of philosophy. Therefore philosophy is merely the unfolding of the divine wisdom by learning and art. Hence there is one perfect wisdom which is contained in the Scriptures, and was given to the saints by God; to be unfolded, however, by philosophy as well as by canon law.

Chapter 15.

Hence it follows of necessity that we Christians ought to employ philosophy in divine things, and in matters pertaining to philosophy to assume many things belonging to theology, so that it is apparent that there is one wisdom shining in both. . . .

Summa contra gentiles

Thomas Aquinas

Scholasticism, the method of resolving doubts by presenting both sides of and issue (*sic et non*) and then reaching a conclusion that sides with one opinion and systematically rejects all others, is usually thought to find its greatest representive in the person of Thomas Aquinas (1225-1274). In the opening chapters of his summa aimed at setting aside the doubts of nonbelievers (*contra gentiles*), Aquinas, like Bacon, discusses the role philosophy should play in theology and brings in as well his famous "arguments in proof of God's existence."

Chapter 1. In what consists the office of a wise man.

My mouth shall mediate truth, and my lips shall hate wickedness.—Prov. viii. 7.

The general use which, in the Philosopher's opinion, should be followed in naming things, has resulted in those men being called *wise* who direct things themselves and govern them well. Wherefore among other things which men conceive of the wise man, the Philosopher reckons that *it belongs to the wise man to direct things.* Now the rule of all things directed to the end of government and order must needs be taken from their end: for then is a thing best disposed when it is fittingly directed to its end, since the end of everything is its good. Wherefore in the arts we observe that the art which governs and rules another is the one to which the latter's end belongs: thus the medical art rules and directs the art of the druggist, because health which is the object of medicine is the end of all drugs which are made up by the druggist's art. The same may be observed in the art of sailing in relation to the art of ship-building, and in the military art in relation to the equestrian art and all warlike appliances. These arts which govern others are called *master-arts (architectonicæ)*, that is *principal arts,* for which reason their craftsmen, who are called *master-craftsmen (architectores)*, are awarded the name of wise men. Since, however, these same craftsmen, through being occupied with the ends of certain singular things, do not attain to the universal end of all things, they are called wise about this or that, in which sense it is said (I Cor. iii. 10): *As a wise architect, I have laid the foundation:* whereas the name of being wise is reserved to him alone whose consideration is about the end of the universe, which end is also the beginning of the universe: wherefore according to the Philosopher, it belongs to the wise man to consider the *highest causes.*

Now the last end of each thing is that which is intended by the first author or mover of that thing: and the first author and mover of the universe is an intellect, as we shall prove further on. Consequently the last end of the universe must be the good of the intellect: and this is truth. Therefore truth must be the last end of the whole universe; and the consideration thereof must be the chief occupation of wisdom. And for this reason divine Wisdom, clothed in flesh, declares that He came into the world to make known the truth, saying (Jo. xviii. 37): *For this was I born, and for this cause came I into the world, that I should give testimony to the truth.* Moreover the Philosopher defines the First Philosophy as being the *knowledge of truth,* not of any truth, but of that truth which is the source of all truth, of that, namely, which relates to the first principle of being of all things; wherefore its truth is the principle of all truth, since the disposition of things is the same in truth as in being.

Now it belongs to the same thing to pursue one contrary and to remove the other: thus medicine which effects health, removes sicknesss. Hence, just as it belongs to a wise man to meditate and disseminate truth, especially about the first principle, so does it belong to him to refute contrary falsehood.

Wherefore the twofold office of the wise man is fittingly declared from the mouth of Wisdom, in the words above quoted; namely, to meditate and publish the divine truth, which antonomastically is *the* truth, as signified by the words, *My mouth shall meditate truth;* and to refute the error contrary to truth, as signified by the words, *and my lips shall hate wickedness,* by which is denoted falsehood opposed to divine truth, which falsehood is contrary to religion that is also called *godliness,* wherefore the falsehood that is contrary thereto receives the name of *ungodliness. . . .*

Chapter 3. In what way it is possible to make known the divine truth.

Since, however, not every truth is to be made known in the same way, *and it is the part of an educated man to seek for conviction in each subject, only so far as the nature of the subject allows,* as the Philosopher most rightly observes as quoted by Boethius, it is necessary to show first of all in what way it is possible to make known the aforesaid truth.

Now in those things which we hold about God there is truth in two ways. For certain things that are true about God wholly surpass the capability of human reason, for instance that God is three and one: while there are certain things to which even natural reason can attain, for instance that God is, that God is one, and others like these, which even the philosophers proved demonstratively of God, being guided by the light of natural reason.

That certain divine truths wholly surpass the capability of

human reason, is most clearly evident. For since the principle of all the knowledge which the reason acquires about a thing, is the understanding of that thing's essence, because according to the Philosopher's teaching the principle of a demonstration is *what a thing is,* it follows that our knowledge about a thing will be in proportion to our understanding of its essence. Wherefore, if the human intellect comprehends the essence of a particular thing, for instance a stone or a triangle, no truth about that thing will surpass the capability of human reason. But this does not happen to us in relation to God, because the human intellect is incapable by its natural power of attaining to the comprehension of His essence: since our intellect's knowledge, according to the mode of the present life, originates from the senses: so that things which are not objects of sense cannot be comprehended by the human intellect, except in so far as knowledge of them is gathered from sensibles. Now sensibles cannot lead our intellect to see in them what God is, because they are effects unequal to the power of their cause. And yet our intellect is led by sensibles to the divine knowledge so as to know about God that He is, and other such truths, which need to be ascribed to the first principle. Accordingly some divine truths are attainable by human reason, while others altogether surpass the power of human reason.

Again. The same is easy to see from the degrees of intellects. For if one of two men perceives a thing with his intellect with greater subtlety, the one whose intellect is of a higher degree understands many things which the other is altogether unable to grasp; as instanced in a yokel who is utterly incapable of grasping the subtleties of philosophy. Now the angelic intellect surpasses the human intellect more than the intellect of the cleverest philosopher surpasses that of the most uncultured. For an angel knows God through a more excellent effect than does man, for as much as the angel's essence, through which he is led to know God by natural knowledge, is more excellent than sensible things, even than the soul itself, by which the human intellect mounts to the knowledge of God. And the divine intellect surpasses the angelic intellect much more than the angelic surpasses the human. For the divine intellect by its capacity equals the divine essence, wherefore God perfectly understands of Himself what He is, and He knows all things that can be understood about Him: whereas the angel knows not what God is by his natural knowledge, because the angel's essence, by which he is led to the knowledge of God, is an effect unequal to the power of its cause. Consequently an angel is unable by his natural knowledge to grasp all that God understands about Himself: nor again is human reason capable of grasping all that an angel understands by his natural power. Accordingly just as a man would show himself to be a most insane fool if he declared the assertions of a philosopher to be false because he was unable to understand them, so, and much more, a man would be exceedingly foolish, were he to suspect of falsehood the things revealed by God through the ministry of His angels, because they cannot be the object of reason's investigations.

Furthermore. The same is made abundantly clear by the deficiency which every day we experience in our knowledge of things. For we are ignorant of many of the properties of sensible things, and in many cases we are unable to discover the nature of those properties which we perceive by our senses. Much less therefore is human reason capable of investigating all the truths about that most sublime essence.

With this the saying of the Philosopher is in accord (2 *Metaph.*) where he says that *our intellect in relation to those primary things which are most evident in nature is like the eye of a bat in relation to the sun.*

To this truth Holy Writ also bears witness. For it is written (Job xi. 7): *Peradventure thou wilt comprehend the steps of God and wilt find out the Almighty perfectly?* and (xxxvi. 26): *Behold God is great, exceeding our knowledge,* and (I Cor. xiii. 9): *We know in part.*

Therefore all that is said about God, though it cannot be investigated by reason, must not be forthwith rejected as false, as the Manicheans and many unbelievers have thought.

Chapter 4. That the truth about divine things which is attainable by reason is fittingly proposed to man as an object of belief.

While then the truth of the intelligible things of God is twofold, one to which the inquiry of reason can attain, the other which surpasses the whole range of human reason, both are fittingly proposed by God to man as an object of belief. We must first show this with regard to that truth which is attainable by the inquiry of reason, lest it appears to some, that since it can be attained by reason, it was useless to make it an object of faith by supernatural inspiration. Now three disadvantages would result if this truth were left solely to the inquiry of reason. One is that few men would have knowledge of God: because very many are hindered from gathering the fruit of diligent inquiry, which is the discovery of truth, for three reasons. Some indeed on account of an indisposition of temperament, by reason of which many are naturally indisposed to knowledge: so that no efforts of theirs would enable them to reach to the attainment of the highest degree of human knowledge, which consists in knowing God. Some are hindered by the needs of household affairs. For there must needs be among men some that devote themselves to the conduct of temporal affairs, who would be unable to devote so much time to the leisure of contemplative research as to reach the summit of human inquiry, namely the knowledge of God. And some are hindered by lazinesss. For in order to acquire the knowledge of God in those things which reason is able to investigate, it is necessary to have a knowledge of many things: since almost the entire consideration of philosophy is directed to the knowledge of God: for which reason metaphysics, which is about divine things, is the last of the parts of philosophy to be studied. Wherefore it is not possible to arrive at the inquiry about the aforesaid truth except after a most laborious study: and few are willing to take upon themselves this labour for the love of a knowledge, the natural desire for which has nevertheless been instilled into the mind of man by God.

The second disadvantage is that those who would arrive at the discovery of the aforesaid truth would scarcely succeed in doing so after a long time. First, because this truth is so profound, that it is only after long practice that the human intellect is enabled to grasp it by means of reason. Secondly, because many things are required beforehand, as stated above. Thirdly, because at the time of youth, the mind, when tossed about by the various movements of the passions, is not fit for the knowledge of so sublime a truth, whereas *calm gives prudence and knowledge,* as stated in 7 Phys. . Hence mankind would remain in the deepest darkness of ignorance, if the path of reason were the only available way to the knowledge of God: because the knowledge of God which especially makes men perfect and good, would be acquired only by the few, and by these only after a long time.

The third disadvantage is that much falsehood is mingled with the investigations of human reason, on account of the weakness of our intellect in forming its judgments, and by reason of the admixture of phantasms. Consequently many would remain in doubt about those things even which are most truly demonstrated, through ignoring the force of the demonstration: especially when they perceive that different things are taught by the various men who are called wise. Moreover among the many demonstrated truths, there is sometimes a mixture of falsehood that is not demonstrated, but assumed for some probable or sophistical reason which at times is mistaken for a demonstration. Therefore it was necessary that definite certainty and pure truth about divine things should be offered to man by the way of faith.

Accordingly the divine clemency has made this salutary commandment, that even some things which reason is able to investigate must be held by faith: so that all may share in the knowledge of God easily, and without doubt or error.

Hence it is written (Eph. iv. 17, 18): That *henceforward you walk not as also the Gentiles walk in the vanity of their mind, having their understanding darkened:* and (Isa. liv. 13): *All thy children shall be taught of the Lord.*

Chapter 5. That those things which cannot be investigated by reason are fittingly proposed to man as an object of faith.

It may appear to some that those things which cannot be investigated by reason ought not to be proposed to man as an object of faith: because divine wisdom provides for each thing according to the mode of its nature. We must therefore prove that it is necessary also for those things which surpass reason to be proposed by God to man as an object of faith.

For no man tends to do a thing by his desire and endeavour unless it be previously known to him. Wherefore since man is directed by divine providence to a higher good than human frailty can attain in the present life, as we shall show in the sequel, it was necessary for his mind to be bidden to something higher than those things to which our reason can reach in the present life, so that he might learn to aspire, and by his endeavours to tend to something surpassing the whole state of the present life. And this is especially competent to the Christian religion, which alone promises goods spiritual and eternal: for which reason it proposes many things surpassing the thought of man: whereas the old law which contained promises of temporal things, proposed few things that are above human inquiry. It was with this motive that the philosophers, in order to wean men from sensible pleasures to virtue, took care to show that there are other goods of greater account than those which appeal to the senses, the taste of which things affords much greater delight to those who devote themselves to active or contemplative virtues.

Again it is necessary for this truth to be proposed to man as an object of faith in order that he may have truer knowledge of God. For then alone do we know God truly, when we believe that He is far above all that man can possibly think of God, because the divine essence surpasses man's natural knowledge, as stated above. Hence by the fact that certain things about God are proposed to man, which surpass his reason, he is strengthened in his opinion that God is far above what he is able to think.

There results also another advantage from this, namely, the checking of presumption which is the mother of error. For some there are who presume so far on their wits that they think themselves capable of measuring the whole nature of things by their intellect, in that they esteem all things true which they see, and false which they see not. Accordingly, in order that man's mind might be freed from this presumption, and seek the truth humbly, it was necessary that certain things far surpassing his intellect should be proposed to man by God.

Yet another advantage is made apparent by the words of the philosopher (10 *Ethic.*). For when a certain Simonides maintained that man should neglect the knowledge of God, and apply his mind to human affairs, and declared that *a man ought to relish human things, and a mortal, mortal things:* the Philosopher contradicted him, saying that *a man ought to devote himself to immortal and divine things as much as he can.* Hence he says (11 *De Animal.*) that though it is but little that we perceive of higher substances, yet that little is more loved and desired than all the knowledge we have of lower substances. He says also (2 *De Cœlo et Mundo*) that when questions about the heavenly bodies can be answered by a short and probable solution, it happens that the hearer is very much rejoiced. All this shows that however imperfect the knowledge of the highest things may be, it bestows very great perfection on the soul: and consequently, although human reason is unable to grasp fully things that are above reason, it nevertheless acquires much perfection, if at least it hold things, in any way whatever, by faith.

Wherefore it is written (Ecclus. iii. 25): *Many things are shown to thee above the understanding of men,* and (I Cor. ii. 10, 11): *The things . . . that are of God no man knoweth, but the Spirit of God: but to us God hath revealed them by His Spirit.*

Chapter 6. That it is not a mark of levity to assent to the things that are of faith, although they are above reason.

Now those who believe this truth, of *which reason affords a proof,* believe not lightly, as though *following foolish fables* (2 Pet. i. 16). For divine Wisdom Himself, Who knows all things most fully, deigned to reveal to man *the secrets of God's wisdom:* and by suitable arguments proves His presence, and the truth of His doctrine and inspiration, by performing works surpassing the capability of the whole of nature, namely, the wondrous healing of the sick, the raising of the dead to life, a marvellous control over the heavenly bodies, and what excites yet more wonder, the inspiration of human minds, so that unlettered and simple persons are filled with the Holy Ghost, and in one instant are endowed with the most sublime wisdom and eloquence. And after considering these arguments, convinced by the strength of the proof, and not by the force of arms, not by the promise of delights, but—and this is the greatest marvel of all—amidst the tyranny of persecutions, a countless crowd of not only simple but also of the wisest men, embraced the Christian faith, which inculcates things surpassing all human understanding, curbs the pleasures of the flesh, and teaches contempt of all worldly things. That the minds of mortal beings should assent to such things, is both the greatest of miracles, and the evident work of divine inspiration, seeing that they despise visible things and desire only those that are invisible. And that this happened not suddenly nor by chance, but by the disposition of God, is shown by the fact that God foretold that He would do so by the manifold oracles of the prophets, whose books we hold in veneration as bearing witness to our faith. This particular kind of proof is alluded to in the words of Heb. ii. 3,4: *Which,* namely the salvation of mankind, *having begun to be declared by the Lord, was confirmed with us by them that heard Him, God also bearing witness by signs and wonders, and divers . . . distributions of the Holy Ghost.*

Now such a wondrous conversion of the world to the Christian faith is a most indubitable proof that such signs did take place, so that there is no need to repeat them, seeing that there is evidence of them in their result. For it would be the most wondrous sign of all if

without any wondrous signs the world were persuaded by simple and
lowly men to believe things so arduous, to accomplish things so
difficult, and to hope for things so sublime. Although God ceases not
even in our time to work miracles through His saints in confirmation
of the faith.

On the other hand those who introduced the errors of the sects
proceeded in contrary fashion, as instanced by Mohammed, who
enticed peoples with the promise of carnal pleasures, to the desire of
which the concupiscence of the flesh instigates. He also delivered
commandments in keeping with his promises, by giving the reins to
carnal pleasure, wherein it is easy for carnal men to obey: and the
lessons of truth which he inculcated were only such as can be easily
known to any man of average wisdom by his natural powers: yea
rather the truths which he taught were mingled by him with many
fables and most false doctrines. Nor did he add any signs of supernatural agency, which alone are a fitting witness to divine inspiration,
since a visible work that can be from God alone, proves the teacher
of truth to be invisibly inspired: but he asserted that he was sent in
the power of arms, a sign that is not lacking even to robbers and
tyrants. Again, those who believed in him from the outset were not
wise men practised in things divine and human, but beastlike men
who dwelt in the wilds, utterly ignorant of all divine teaching; and it
was by a multitude of such men and the force of arms that he compelled others to submit to his law.

Lastly, no divine oracles of prophets in a previous age bore
witness to him; rather did he corrupt almost all the teaching of the
Old and New Testaments by a narrative replete with fables, as one
may see by a perusal of his law. Hence by a cunning device, he did
not commit the reading of the Old and New Testament Books to his
followers, lest he should thereby be convicted of falsehood. Thus it is
evident that those who believe his words believe lightly.

*Chapter 7. That the truth of reason is not in opposition to the truth of the
Christian faith.*

Now though the aforesaid truth of the Christian faith surpasses
the ability of human reason, nevertheless those things which are
naturally instilled in human reason cannot be opposed to this truth.
For it is clear that those things which are implanted in reason by
nature, are most true, so much so that it is impossible to think them
to be false. Nor is it lawful to deem false that which is held by faith,
since it is so evidently confirmed by God. Seeing then that the false
alone is opposed to the true, as evidently appears if we examine
their definitions, it is impossible for the aforesaid truth of faith to be
contrary to those principles which reason knows naturally.

Again. The same thing which the disciple's mind receives from
its teacher is contained in the knowledge of the teacher, unless he
teach insincerely, which it were wicked to say of God. Now the

knowledge of naturally known principles is instilled into us by God, since God Himself is the author of our nature. Therefore the divine Wisdom also contains these principles. Consequently whatever is contrary to these principles, is contrary to the divine Wisdom; wherefore it cannot be from God. Therefore those things which are received by faith from divine revelation cannot be contrary to our natural knowledge.

Moreover. Our intellect is stayed by contrary arguments, so that it cannot advance to the knowledge of truth. Wherefore if conflicting knowledges were instilled into us by God, our intellect would thereby be hindered from knowing the truth. And this cannot be ascribed to God.

Furthermore. Things that are natural are unchangeable so long as nature remains. Now contrary opinions cannot be together in the same subject. Therefore God does not instill into man any opinion or belief contrary to natural knowledge.

Hence the Apostle says (Rom. x. 8): *The word is nigh thee even in thy heart and in thy mouth. This is the word of faith which we preach.* Yet because it surpasses reason some look upon it as though it were contrary thereto; which is impossible.

This is confirmed also by the authority of Augustine who says (*Gen. ad lit.* ii): *That which truth shall make known can nowise be in opposition to the holy books whether of the Old or of the New Testament.*

From this we may evidently conclude that whatever arguments are alleged against the teachings of faith, they do not rightly proceed from the first self-evident principles instilled by nature. Wherefore they lack the force of demonstration, and are either probable or sophistical arguments, and consequently it is possible to solve them. . . .

Chapter 12. Of the opinion of those who say that the existence of God cannot be proved, and that it is held by faith alone.

The position that we have taken is also assailed by the opinion of certain others, whereby the efforts of those who endeavour to prove that there is a God would again be rendered futile. For they say that it is impossible by means of the reason to discover that God exists, and that this knowledge is acquired solely by means of faith and revelation.

In making this assertion some were moved by the weakness of the arguments which certain people employed to prove the existence of God.

Possibly, however, this error might falsely seek support from the statements of certain philosophers, who show that in God essence and existence are the same, namely that which answers to the question, *What is He?* and that which answers to the question, *Is He?* Now it is impossible by the process of reason to acquire the knowledge of what God is. Wherefore seemingly neither is it possible to prove by reason whether God is.

Again. If, as required by the system of the Philosopher, in order to prove whether a thing is we must take as principle the signification of its name, and since according to the Philosopher (4 *Metaph.*) *the signification of a name is its definition:* there will remain no means of proving the existence of God, seeing that we lack knowledge of the divine essence or quiddity.

Again. If the principles of demonstration become known to us originally through the senses, as is proved in the *Posterior Analytics,* those things which transcend all sense and sensible objects are seemingly indemonstrable. Now such is the existence of God. Therefore it cannot be demonstrated.

The falseness of this opinion is shown to us first by the art of demonstration, which teaches us to conclude causes from effects. Secondly, by the order itself of sciences: for if no substance above sensible substance can be an object of science, there will be no science above Physics, as stated in 4 *Metaph.* Thirdly, by the efforts of the philosophers who have endeavoured to prove the existence of God. Fourthly, by the apostolic truth which asserts (Rom. i. 20) that the *invisible things of God are clearly seen, being understood by the things that are made.*

Nor should we be moved by the consideration that in God essence and existence are the same, as the first argument contended. For this is to be understood of the existence by which God subsists in Himself, of which we are ignorant as to what kind of a thing it is, even as we are ignorant of His essence. But it is not to be understood of that existence which is signified by the composition of the mind. For in this way it is possible to prove the existence of God, when our mind is led by demonstrative arguments to form a proposition stating that God is.

Moreover. In those arguments whereby we prove the existence of God, it is not necessary that the divine essence or quiddity be employed as the middle term, as the second argument supposed: but instead of the quiddity we take His effects as middle term, as is the case in *a posteriori* reasoning: and from these effects we take the signification of this word *God.* For all the divine names are taken either form the remoteness of God's effects from Himself, or from some relationship between God and His effects.

It is also evident from the fact that, although God transcends all sensibles and senses, His effects from which we take the proof that God exists, are sensible objects. Hence our knowledge, even of things which transcend the senses, originates from the senses.

Chapter 13. Arguments in proof of God's existence.

Having shown then that it is not futile to endeavour to prove the existence of God, we may proceed to set forth the reasons whereby both philosophers and Catholic doctors have proved that there is a God. In the first place we shall give the arguments by which Aristotle sets out to prove God's existence: and he aims at proving this from the point of view of movement, in two ways.

The *first way* is as follows. Whatever is in motion is moved by another: and it is clear to the sense that something, the sun for instance, is in motion. Therefore it is set in motion by something else moving it. Now that which moves it is itself either moved or not. If it be not moved, then the point is proved that we must needs postulate an immovable mover: and this we call God. If, however, it be moved, it is moved by another mover. Either, therefore, we must proceed to infinity, or we must come to an immovable mover. But it is not possible to proceed to infinity. Therefore it is necessary to postulate an immovable mover.

This argument contains two propositions that need to be proved: namely that *whatever is in motion is moved by another,* and that *it is not possible to proceed to infinity in movers and things moved.*

The first of these is proved by the Philosopher in *three ways. First,* thus. If a thing moves itself, it must needs have the principle of its movement in itself, else it would clearly be moved by another. Again it must be *moved primarily,* that is, it must be moved by reason of itself and not by reason of its part, as an animal is moved by the movement of its foot, for in the latter way not the whole but the part would be moved by itself, and one part by another. Again it must be divisible and have parts, since whatever is moved is divisible, as is proved in 6 *Phys.*

These things being supposed, he argues as follows. That which is stated to be moved by itself is moved primarily. Therefore if one of its parts is at rest, it follows that the whole is at rest. For if, while one part is at rest, another of its parts were in motion, the whole itself would not be moved primarily, but its part which is in motion while another is at rest. Now nothing that is at rest while another is at rest, is moved by itself: for that which is at rest as a result of another thing being at rest must needs be in motion as a result of the other's motion, and hence it is not moved by itself. Hence that which was stated to be moved by itself, is not moved by itself. Therefore whatever is in motion must needs be moved by another.

Nor is this argument traversed by the statement that might be made, that supposing a thing moves itself, it is impossible for a part thereof to be at rest, or again by the statement that to be at rest or in motion does not belong to a part except accidentally, as Avicenna quibbles. Because the force of the argument lies in this, that if a thing moves itself primarily and of itself, not by reason of its parts, it follows that its being moved does not depend on some thing; whereas with a divisible thing, being moved, like being, depends on its parts, so that it cannot move itself primarily and of itself. Therefore the truth of the conclusion drawn does not require that we suppose as an absolute truth that a part of that which moves itself is at rest, but that this conditional statement be true that *if a part were at rest,* the whole would be at rest. Which statement can be true even if the antecedent be false, even as this conditional proposition is true: *If a man is an ass he is irrational.*

Secondly, he proves it by induction, thus. A thing is not moved by itself if it is moved accidentally, since its motion is occasioned by the motion of something else. Nor again if it is moved by force, as is manifest. Nor if it is moved by its nature like those things whose movement proceeds from themselves, such as animals, which clearly are moved by their souls. Nor if it is moved by nature, as heavy and light things are, since these are moved by their generating cause and by that which removes the obstacle to their movement. Now whatsoever things are in motion are moved either *per se* or accidentally; and if *per se,* either by force or by nature: and if the latter, either by something in them, as in the case of animals, or not by something in them, as in the case of heavy and light bodies. Therefore whatever is in motion is moved by another.

Thirdly, he proves his point thus. Nothing is at the same time in act and in potentiality in respect of the same thing. Now whatever is in motion, as such, is in potentiality, because motion is *the act of that which is in potentiality, as such.* Whereas whatever moves, as such, is in act, for nothing acts except in so far as it is in act. Therefore nothing is both mover and moved in respect of the same movement. Hence nothing moves itself.

We must observe, however, that Plato, who asserted that every mover is moved, employed the term *movement* in a more general sense than Aristotle. For Aristotle took movement in its strict sense, for the act of a thing that is in potentiality as such, in which sense it applies only to divisible things and bodies, as is proved in 6 *Phys.* Whereas according to Plato that which moves itself is not a body; for he took movement for any operation, so that to understand or to think is a kind of movement, to which manner of speaking Aristotle alludes in 3 *De Anima.* In this sense, then, he said that the first mover moves itself, in as much as it understands, desires and loves itself. This, in a certain respect, is not in contradiction with the arguments of Aristotle; for it makes no difference whether with Plato we come to a first mover that moves itself, or with Aristotle to something first which is altogether immovable.

He proves the other proposition, namely that *it is impossible to proceed to infinity in movers and things moved,* by three arguments.

The *first* of these is as follows. If one were to proceed to infinity in movers and things moved, all this infinite number of things would necessarily be bodies, since whatever is moved is divisible and corporeal, as is proved in 6 *Phys.* Now every body that moves through being moved is moved at the same time as it moves. Therefore all this infinite number of things are moved at the same time as one of them is moved. But one of them, since it is finite, is moved in a finite time. Therefore all this infinite number of things are moved in a finite time. But this is impossible. Therefore it is impossible to proceed to infinity in movers and things moved.

That it is impossible for the aforesaid infinite number of things to be moved in a finite time, he proves thus. Mover and moved must needs be simultaneous; and he proves this by induction from each species of movement. But bodies cannot be simultaneous except by continuity or contact. Wherefore since all the aforesaid movers and things moved are bodies, as proved, they must needs be as one movable thing through their continuity or contact. And thus one infinite thing would be moved in a finite time, which is shown to be impossible in 6 *Phys*.

The *second argument* in proof of the same statement is as follows. In an ordinate series of movers and things moved, where namely throughout the series one is moved by the other, we must needs find that if the first mover be taken away or cease to move, none of the others will move or be moved: because the first is the cause of movement in all the others. Now if an ordinate series of movers and things moved proceed to infinity, there will be no first mover, but all will be intermediate movers as it were. Therefore it will be impossible for any of them to be moved: and thus nothing in the world will be moved.

The *third argument* amounts to the same, except that it proceeds in the reverse order, namely by beginning from above: and it is as follows. That which moves instrumentally, cannot move unless there be something that moves principally. But if we proceed to infinity in movers and things moved, they will all be like instrumental movers, because they will be alleged to be moved movers, and there will be nothing by way of principal mover. Therefore nothing will be moved.

We have thus clearly proved both statements which were supposed in the first process of demonstration whereby Aristotle proved the existence of a *first immovable mover*.

The *second way* is as follows. If every mover is moved, this statement is true either in itself or accidentally. If accidentally, it follows that it is not necessary: for that which is accidentally true is not necessary. Therefore it is a contingent proposition that no mover is moved. But if a mover be not moved, it does not move, as the opponent asserts. Therefore it is contingent that nothing is moved, since, if nothing moves, nothing is moved. Now Aristotle holds this to be impossible, namely, that at any time there be no movement. Therefore the first proposition was not contingent, because a false impossibility does not follow from a false contingency. And therefore this proposition, *Every mover is moved by another,* was not accidentally true.

Again, if any two things are found accidentally united in a certain subject, and one of them is to be found without the other, it is probable that the latter can be found without the former: thus if *white* and *musical* are found in Socrates, and *musical* without *white*

is found in Plato, it is probable that it is possible to find *white* without *musical* in some subject. Accordingly if mover and moved be
united together in some subject accidentally, and it be found that a
certain thing is moved without its being a mover, it is probable that
a mover is to be found that is not moved. Nor can one urge against
this the case of two things one of which depends on the other;
because those in question are united not *per se* but accidentally. If,
however, the aforesaid proposition is true in itself, again there follows
something impossible or unfitting. For the mover must needs be
moved either by the same kind of movement or by another kind. If
by the same kind, it follows that whatever causes alteration must
itself be altered, and furthermore that the healer must be healed, that
the teacher must be taught, and in respect of the same science. But
this is impossible: for the teacher must needs have science, while the
learner must needs not have it, and thus the same will be both
posessed and not possessed by the same, which is impossible. And if
it be moved by another kind of movement, so that, to wit, that
which causes alteration be moved in respect of place, and that which
moves in respect of place be increased, and so on, it will follow that
we cannot go on indefinitely, since the genera and species of movement are finite in number. And thus there will be some first mover
that is not moved by another. Unless, perchance, someone say that
a recurrence takes place, in this way, that when all the genera and
species of movement have been exhausted, a return must be made to
the first; for instance, if that which moves in respect of place be
altered, and that which causes alteration be increased, then again that
which is increased be moved in respect of place. But the consequence
of this will be the same as before; namely, that which moves by one
kind of movement is itself moved by the same kind, not immediately
indeed but mediately. It remains therefore that *we must needs
postulate some first mover that is not moved by anything outside
itself*.

   Since however, given that there is a first mover that is not moved
by anything outside itself, it does not follow that it is absolutely
immovable, Aristotle proceeds further, saying that this may happen
in two ways. First, so that this first mover is absolutely immovable.
And if this be granted, our point is established, namely that there is a
first immovable mover. Secondly, that this first mover is moved by
itself. And this seems probable: because what is of itself is always
prior to what is of another: wherefore also in things moved, it is
logical that what is moved first is moved by itself and not by another.

   But, if this be granted, the same consequence follows. For it
cannot be said that the whole of that which moves itself is moved by
its whole self, because then the absurd consequences mentioned
above would follow, namely that a person might teach and be taught
at the same time, and in like manner as to other kinds of movement;
and again that a thing would be at the same time in act and in
potentiality, since a mover, as such, is in act, while that which is

moved is in potentiality. It remains, therefore, that one part thereof is mover only, and the other part moved. And thus we have the same conclusion as before, namely that there is something that moves and is itself immovable.

And it cannot be said that both parts are moved, so that one is moved by the other; nor that one part moves both itself and the other; nor that the whole moves a part; nor that part moves the whole, since the above absurdities would follow, namely that something would both move and be moved by the same kind of movement, and that it would be at the same time in potentiality and in act, and moreover that the whole would move itself not primarily but by reason of its part. It remains, therefore, that in that which moves itself, one part must be immovable, and must move the other part.

Since, however, in those things among us which move themselves, namely animals, the part which moves, namely the soul, though immovable of itself, is nevertheless moved accidentally, he goes on to show that in the first mover, the part which moves is not moved neither of itself nor accidentally.

For in those things which among us move themselves, namely animals, since they are corruptible, the part which moves is moved accidentally. Now those corruptible things which move themselves must needs be reducible to some first self-mover that is everlasting. Therefore that which moves itself must have a mover, which is moved neither of itself nor accidentally.

It is clear that, in accordance with his hypothesis, some self-mover must be everlasting. For if, as he supposes, movement is everlasting, the production of these self-movers that are subject to generation and corruption must be everlasting. But no one of these self-movers, since it does not always exist, can be the cause of this everlastingness. Nor can all of them together, both because they would be infinite, and because they do not exist all together. It follows therefore that there must be an everlasting self-mover, that causes the everlastingness of generation in these lower self-movers. And thus its mover is not moved, neither of itself nor accidentally. Again, we observe that in self-movers some begin to be moved anew on account of some movement whereby the animal is not moved by itself, for instance by the digestion of food or a change in the atmosphere: by which movement the mover that moves itself is moved accidentally. Whence we may gather that no self-mover, whose mover is moved *per se* or accidentally, is always moved. But the first self-mover is always in motion, else movement could not be everlasting, since every other movement is caused by the movement of the first self-mover. It follows therefore that the first self-mover is moved by a mover who is not moved, neither *per se* nor accidentally.

Nor is this argument rebutted by the fact that the movers of the lower spheres cause an everlasting movement, and yet are said to be moved accidentally. For they are said to be moved accidentally not by reason of themselves, but by reason of the things subject to their motion, which follow the motion of the higher sphere.

Since, however, God is not part of a self-mover, Aristotle goes on in his *Metaphysics* to trace from this motor that is part of a self-mover, another mover altogether separate, which is God. For since every self-mover is moved through its appetite, it follows that the motor that is part of a self-mover, moves on account of the appetite for some appetible object. And this object is above the motor in moving, because the appetent is a moved mover, whereas the appetible is a mover altogether unmoved. Therefore *there must needs be a first mover separate and altogether immovable,* and this is God.

Now two things would seem to weaken the above arguments. The *first* of these is that they proceed from the supposition of the eternity of movement, and among Catholics this is supposed to be false. To this we reply that the most effective way to prove God's existence is from the supposition of the eternity of the world, which being supposed, it seems less manifest that God exists. For if the world and movement had a beginning, it is clear that we must suppose some cause to have produced the world and movement, because whatever becomes anew must take its origin from some cause of its becoming, since nothing evolves itself from potentiality to act, or from non-being to being.

The *second* is that the aforesaid arguments suppose that the first moved thing, namely the heavenly body, has its motive principle in itself, whence it follows that it is animated: and by many this is not granted.

To this we reply that if the first mover is not supposed to have its motive principle in itself, it follows that it is immediately moved by something altogether immovable. Hence also Aristotle draws this conclusion with an alternative, namely that either we must come at once to a first mover immovable and separate, or to a self-mover from which again we come to a first mover immovable and separate.

The Philosopher proceeds in a *different way* in 2 *Metaph.* to show that it is impossible to proceed to infinity in efficient causes, and that we must come to one first cause, and this we call God. This is how he proceeds. In all efficient causes following in order, the first is the cause of the intermediate cause, and the intermediate is the cause of the ultimate, whether the intermediate be one or several. Now if the cause be removed, that which it causes is removed. Therefore if we remove the first the intermediate cannot be a cause. But if we go on to infinity in efficient causes, no cause will be first. Therefore all the others which are intermediate will be removed. Now this is clearly false. Therefore we must suppose *the existence of a first efficient cause:* and this is God.

Another reason can be drawn from the words of Aristotle. For in 2 *Metaph.* he shows that those things which excel as true excel as beings: and in 4 *Metaph.* he shows that there is something supremely true, from the fact that we see that of two false things one is falser than the other, wherefore it follows that one also is truer than the other. Now this is by reason of approximation to that which is simply and supremely true. Wherefore we may further conclude that *there is something that is supremely being.* And this we call God.

Another argument in support of this conclusion is adduced by Damascene from the government of things: and the same reasoning is indicated by the Commentator in 2 *Phys.* It runs as follows. It is impossible for contrary and discordant things to accord in one order always or frequently except by someone's governance, whereby each and all are made to tend to a definite end. Now we see that in the world things of different natures accord in one order, not seldom and fortuitously, but always or for the most part. Therefore it follows that there is *someone by whose providence the world is governed.* And this we call God.

Notes

or dangerous
herefore with
at his doings
s lyfe. Truelye
to payne. Hee
which bee not
ent: and vayne
dness hee shall
of putrifaction
Man is made of
desire of fleshly
foule delight of
e. Hee is borne a
more myserable)
part daungerous,
s neighbours, or
l unhonest things,
science, and dis-
n vayne thynges,
nce: Hee doeth
nothing regardeth
chaffe to the fyre
shall be meate for
ur: and in fyne, he
d full of horror and

The First Booke.

I

al outlines of Christian theology,
, from the potential of our God-
d tendencies toward sin. Both
n during the high Middle Ages.
cities and how these could aid
en tended to emphasize the
rning sinners from their evil
e *De contempu mundi* of
d very wide circulation not
as well, as is attested to by
ely distributed during the

de. Chapter 2.

earth, which is more
ppeare by the second
es and starres, of the
e ayre: the fishes and
id forme of the earth.
s which bee made of
base: if hee have respec
of the ayre, hee shall
and if hee looke uppon
e shall iustly take him
compare him selfe with
preferre himselfe before
wne substance not farre
d shall acknowledge him
ee the death of men and
oth is equal, and man can
te: they be made of earth,
th. These be the wordes of
clude, what other thing is

yrst.

or sanctifyed in his
of him selfe these
behold with mine
my dayes should
ophet did speake
ny mother hath
woe is mee: and
why hast thou
? why did I not
I not perishe
ceyved in my
being bor
God the pl
y everla
not bin
found
e
p

of man in this his conversation? and the damnable
departure of the soule of man from the bodye? I will t
teares consider and declare whereof man is made, wl
are, and what perhappes shall become of him after thi
man is made of earthe, conceyved in sinne, and borne
doeth commit in this lyfe, wicked and shrewde turnes
lawfull: foule and uncleane actes which bee not dec
things which are not expedient. Through his wicke
become food to the fire, meat for worms, and a lumpe
lothesome to behold. I will expound it more plainly.
dust, of clay, of ashes: he is conceived in the wanton
luste, in the heate of carnall appetyte, in the
leacherye, and which is worse, in the spotte of sinn
servant to labour, feare, and sorowe: and (which is
a subiecte to deathe. His doyngs are for the most
whereby he eyther offendeth God, hurteth hi
impayreth him selfe. Hee practiseth unseemely an
whereby hee procureth infamye, defileth his co
honesteth him selfe. Hee occupyeth him selfe
whereby hee doth neglecte matters of import
despyse things which bee for his profitte, and
things which bee necessarye. Hee shall become
which alwayes doeth burne unquenchably: Hee
the worme which alwayes doeth gnawe and dev
shall be an immortall masse of putrifaction, heap
lothsomenesse.

Of the vile and base matter whereof man is ma

God hath made man of the slyme of the
base than bee the other Elements, as it doth a
Chapter of Genesis. For he made the Planett
fire: the blastes and wyndes he created of th
birdes of the water: but man and beasts he d
Therefore if man doe consider those thinge
water, hee shall finde his substance vyle and
to those living thinges which are created
acknowledge him selfe to be much inferior:
those creatures which bee made of fyre, he
selfe moste abjecte of all. Hee shall not
heavenly things, neyther shall he presume to
rthly creatures, for that hee findeth his
ering from the savage or brute beastes a
lyke unto them. For wee evidently s
s is all one, the condition of them b
more than the beaste in this respec
doe both returne agayne into ear
King Salomon. Wherefore to co

man, but clay and ashes? Hereuppon doth man saye unto God, Remember I beseech thee O Lord, that thou hast made mee lyke claye, and wilt reduce mee into dust. And heereuppon doth God say again unto man, thou arte dust, and shalt returne again into dust. I am compared (saieth holy Iob) to clay, and likened to embers and ashes. Clay is made of water and dust, both of them remayining, but ashes are made of wood and fire, both of them consuming or decaying. The mystery is manifest, but to be declared more playner in another place. Wherefore then doest thou were proude of insolent O thou claye? or why doest thou extoll and magnifie thy selfe O thou dust? and wherupon mayest thou boast, being nothing but ashes?

The corruption of mans Conception. Chapter 3.

Thou mayest perhappes refute these former reasons after this superficiall sort saying, that Adam was made of the slime of the earth and that thy being is from the seede of man. True it is thou sayest: but yet was Adam made of a pure and maydenlye earth, and thou art created of an uncleane and corrtupte seede. And who can make him cleane which is conceyved of an adultred and defiled seede? or what is man that hee should seeme pure and undefiled, and that beyng borne of a woman he shuld appeare iuste? For beholde (sayeht the Prophet David) I am conceyved in wickednesse, and my mother hath brought me forth in sinne: Not in one sinne onely, nor in one kynde of offence, but in a multitude of iniquities: That is to saye, in the iniquityes and sinnes of others. For Conception is of two sortes. The one is of seedes: and the other of natures. The former conception is to bee understanded, in offences personally committed: the seconde is, in offences contracted or taken by others. The parentes doe commit offence in the former conception: and the children doe incurre offence in the seconde. For who knoweth not that carnal knowledge (although it be in mariage) can not be had without the motion of the flesh, without the heat of carnall desire, and without the foule delight of wanton lust. Whereby the seedes conceived are adulterate, defiled, and corrupte: Of the which the soule or life at the length poured into the body doth gather the spot of sin, the blemish of offence, and the corruption of iniquitie, lyke as an evill seasoned vessell poysoneth good liquor, or as that which is uncleane defileth the contrary. For the soule of man hath three naturall operations or vertues. The first is, the use of reason, to the ende it may disceyrne good from evill. The seconde is an aptenesse or inclynation to dislyke, that thereby it may shunne or delyne from that which is evill. The thyrde is a disposition or pronenesse to affecte, that thereby it may desire and lyke that which is good. These three effectes or vertues are in man from his byrthe, greatly altered and obsured, by three contrary vices. For the use of reason is miscaried by ignorance, so that it cannot discerne the good from the evill. The inclination to dislike or to be offended with that which is evil, is headlong hurled downe by the fury of anger, which causeth the refusal oftentymes of that which is good: And the affection— to covet or desire that which is good, is wholy overthrowne through the desire of evil. The first of these vertues or operations bringeth fourth offence, which consisteth in omittyng, and in Latyne is called Delictum. The last bringeth foorth sinne or trespasse, which doth consist in committing, and in Latine is called Peccatum. The third (meane betwixte them both) bringeth forth bothe Delictum and Peccatum. For this worde Delictum signifieth nothing els but to omit that which ought to be done: and this word Peccatum doeth importe the doing of that which ought not to be done. These three vices doe spring through the corruption of our fleshe. For in the carnall acquaintance betwixt man and woman, the deepe consideration and force of reason is covered and supprest, and insteed therof ignorance taketh place: the flame of fleshly delight is kindled, whereby hir furie more increaseth: the great desire of pleasure is satiate, by the which concupiscence is ingendered. This is the Tyran of the fleshe, the lawe of the members, the nourishment and inflamation of sinne, the languishing and feblenesse of nature, and the foode of deathe. No man is borne without it: which if at any tyme wee happilye passe over, not yelding thereunto, yet doeth hir force alwayes remayne actually grafted in our flesh: for if we shall say we have no sinne, wee deceive our selves, and the trueth is not in us. O greevous necessitie, and unfortunate estate of man, before we can sinne we are fastened and straight linked to sinne. And before wee can offend, we are bounde with offence. By one man sinne entered into the world (saith saint Paul) and through sinne death hath gone over all men. Dyd not our fathers eate the bitter grape (saye the Prophets) and are not the teeth of their children set on edge therewith?

Of the feebleness and weaknesse of the yong infant. Chapter 4.

Why then is lighte given to this poore wretche, and lyfe to them which lyve in bitternesse of the soule? happye are they which dyed before they were borne, feelying death before they knewe what lyfe is. For some come into this world so deformed and monstrous, that they seeme rather to be abominations than men: for whom peradventure it had bin better provyded, if they had never come in sight, bicause they are set forth to be beholden as monsters. For manye of them are borne dismembred, and corrupt in their senses, to the heavinesse and sorowe of their frendes, to the ignominie of their parentes, and to the rebuke of their kinsfoks. To what end should I speake this particularly of some, seeing that generally wee bee all borne impotent, without knowledge, without speech, and without strength? Wee come into this worlde lamenting, feebly, faint, differing very little from brute beasts, yea in worse case than they bee in many respectes. For they as soone as they come forth, doe by and by march and go forwardes, and we can not only not go upright upon our feete, but being croked are not able to creepe with our handes.

Of the payne of the childes byrth, and of his pitifull crying out. Chapter 5.

Wee be all borne yelling and crying, to the end we may expresse our miserie. For the man childe newly borne cryeth, A: the female E: so that all crye, A: or E: which commeth from Eva. And what is Eva, but as much to say as Hev, Ha: which importeth alas, or fye uppon me. For these wordes bee both Interiections of him that soroweth or lamenteth, expressing the greatnesse of his grief, Hereuppon our first mother before hir sin committed in Paradise, was called Virago, but after she had sinned, she well deserved to bee named Eva: at the which tyme shee hearde God say unto hir: Thou shalte bring forth thy chylde in payne and sorow. For there is no payne like to the grief of a woman labouring with childe. Wherefore Rachel through the exceeding great payne of travail with hir childe departing out of this life, on hir death bed named hir son Benoni, which is as much to say, as the child of sorow and pain. The wife of Phinces through sodayn pangs coming uppon hir, was delivered of a childe and both of them died as it were at an instant, yet in the very point of hir death she called hir chyld Icabod: which is to say the child of no glory. But as he which escaped after shipwrack is glad, so the woman when she is in tavel is sad, but after shee is delivered, remembreth none or hir pain for ioy that there is brought forth a reasonable creature into the world. Then to conclude, she conceiveth hir childe in uncleannesse, shee bringeth it forth with heavinesse and sorrowe, shee nourisheth it with anguishe and payne, shee keepeth it with continuall care and feare.

Of the nakednesse of man. Chapter 6.

Naked commeth hee out of his mothers wombe into this worlde, and naked shall he returne againe from hence: he commeth poore and shall returne agayne poore: For I came naked out of my mothers wombe (sayth Iob) and out of this world I shall returne naked agayne: we brought nothing (doubtlesse) into this worlde, bycause wee can take nothing with us out of it. If anye man goe out of the worlde clothed, let him consider what kynde of apparell hee brought into it, which willingly I will passe over, as a thing undecent to bee spoken, and unseemely to bee heard.

What fruite man bringeth forth. Chapter 7.

O Most vile, unworthye, and miserable condition of man: O unseemelye and wretched estate. Search out diligently and make serious inquisition of the hearbes and trees: they doe of themselves

bring forth flowers, boughes, and fruites, and thou miserable wretche
bringest forth nittes, lyse, and wormes: They doe of their owne
nature yelde oyle, wyne, and balme, but thou utterest things
displeasant and odious: they doe send forth from them sweete and
pleasant odours, thou lothsome and unsavery smels: such as the tree
is such is the fruite, for an evill tree can not bring forth good fruit.
And what is man according to his forme, but a certayne tree turned
upside downe? whose rootes be the heares, whose trunke is the head
with the necke, whose stock is the brest with the belly, the
braunches bee the armes with the legges, the leaves be the fingers
with the ioyntes. This is the leafe which is toste with every wynde,
this is the tree that is overthrowne with every blast, and this is the
stubble which is dryed up with the sunne.

Of the incommodities of olde age and shortnesse of lyfe. Chapter 8.

In the beginning of mans estate, we reade that men lived nine
hundreth yeares and more: but the lyfe of man decling by little and
little, God sayde unto Noe, my spirit or breath shal not remain
alwayes in man, for that he is fleshe, and his dayes shal be an
hundreth and twentie yeares: which may be understoode as well of
the terme of mans life, as of the space of his repentance. For since
that time forwards, we seldom reade that man lived longer: but when
mans life was cut shorter, the Psalmist sayd. The dayes and tyme of
our lyfe and yeeres, doe consist in the very number of seventie
years, but if through the powers and forces of nature, they be
continued to the number of foure score yeres, yet that tyme is but
of more labour and sorow. Shal not the final number of my dayes
(saith Iob) be ended in a short time: our dayes passe over more swift
than the webbe which is cut off by the weaver. A man borne of a
woman liveth but a shorte tyme, and is replenished with many
myseries, which florisheth for a tyme, and vanisheth away agayne,
even as a flower: hee also flyeth away lyke a shadowe, and doeth
never continew in one estate. Fewe men now adayes doe come to the
terme of fortye yeeres, but more fewer doe attaine unto the age of
three score yeeres. If one proceed forward and come to old age, his
hart is by and by afflicted and tormented, his head is shaken and
tost, his spirites war fainte and weake, his breathe yeldeth a lothsome
ayre, his face becommeth wrinkled, his stature beginneth to be
crooked, his sight fayleth him, his ioyntes weaken, his nose runneth,
his heares fall of, his handes tremble and shake, his teeth ware rotten,
his eares become deafe, his vertue and strength doth vanishe and
decaye. The olde man is soone provoked and styrred to wrath, and
hardly and with much a doe hee is reconciled agayne to reason. Hee
is quicke of beleife, and slowly brought from it: he is ful of suspition
and complaints: he is for the most part sad, and seldom mery: he is
neare and covetous: he is swift to speake, but slow to heare: he
praiseth his old acquaintance, and despiseth his newe friends. He

doth reprehend that which is present, and commendeth that which is past: he sigheth and is carefull: hee is dull and impotent. Heare what the Poete sayeth: Manye incommodities beesette an olde man on every syde. But let neither old men boaste of them selves agaynst young men, nor yet let not young men become insolent agaynst olde men: for what wee bee, the olde man in times paste was, and what he now is, the very same in tyme to come if lyfe long last shall we bee.

Of the labour of mortall men. Chapter 9.

The byrd is created to flye, and man is borne to labour: all his dayes bee full of paynes, care and myserie, neyther doeth his mynde rest in the night. And what is this els, but vanitie? there is no man under the sun without labour or trouble, no man under the moone without some want or defecte, no none at any tyme without vanitie. Time through delay is the worker of all changeable things. Vanitie of vanities, and all is but vanitie sayeth the wyse man. O how dyvers be the studies and affections of men? how disagreeing or unlike be their exercises? And yet one ende is dew unto them all, and the selfe same effecte, labour, and affliction of the spirite is incident unto them all. There is great labour and exercise (saith the wyse man) ordayned for all men, and a heavy yoke is layde uppon the children of Adam, from the day that they come forth of their mothers wombe, until the day of their burriall in the mother of all men. . . .

Of divers griefes and sorowes of mankinde. Chapter 12.

O What sorowe and anguishe of minde doeth vexe mortall men. Thought consumeth them, pensivenesse doth possesse them, heavinesse harmeth them, feare putteth them out of comforte, tremblyng moveth all the partes of them, horror depryveth them of their perfite senses, terror doeth afflict them, sadnesse doeth trouble them, and trouble doeth make them sadde and heavye. The poore, and the riche: the sevante, and the master: the maried and the single man: to conclude, the good and bad, be all tormented with worldly vexations, and are all toste with worldly tempestes. Beleve in this a master that hath tryed it: If I shall bee wicked (sayth Iob) then woe unto mee: if I shall be iuste and upright, I shall not lifte up my heade beyng burdened and overcharged with affliction and misery.

The miserie of the poore and riche. Chapter 13.

The poore are prest with famine, supprest with sorow, opprest with thirst, colde, and needinesse. They be nothing esteemed, they consume and pine away, they be despised and discomforted. O how miserable is the condytion of him that beggeth. For to aske for Gods sake, hee is abashed through shame: and if he doeth not aske, he is pained and pyneth away through neede. And therefore is he

constrayned by meere necessitie to begge. He doth accuse and fynde
fault with God, as that he were unrightuous, and partiall: for so
much as he did not devyde these worldly thinges equally. Hee
blameth hys neighbour as wicked and unmercyfull, for that hee doth
not fully and sufficiently succour his neede. He doth fret and fume,
murmureth, and curseth. Marke what the wyse man sayth uppon
this. It is better (saith he) for a man to dye, than to stand in need.
The poore man shall be odious even to his neighbour. All the dayes
of the poore be evill and miserable, yea verilye his owne bretherne
oftentymes doe shunne him, hys friendes loathe hym, hys ennimyes
laughe at hym. And therefore uppon greate cause the Poet sayeth:
Whylest fortune doeth favour thee thou shalte fynde manye friendes,
but if woe doe bewytche thee, thou shalte be lefte alone. Out upon
this shamefull worldly consideration: that the person of a man
shoulde bee esteemed according to his fortune, whereas in deede,
the giftes of fortune ought rather to be esteemed according to the
goodnesse of the person that doethe possesse them. But suche is the
iniquitie of tyme, that a man is taken to be so good as hee is riche,
and so evill as hee is poore, whereas indeede eache, man oughte
rather to bee thought so riche as he is good, and so poore as he is
evill. The riche man is overthrowen through his abundance, hee is
caried away by vayne glory, and through the confidence that he hath
in his welthe, he braggeth and boasteth: being puft up with pride,
hee runneth at his pleasure, and falleth into that whiche is unlawful.
But those thyngs truely which were his delightes and causes of
offences, shall beest soones made the instrumentes of his tormentes.
The laboure in getting, the feare in possessing, and the sorow in
losing, doth alwayes trouble and disquiet his mind. For where thy
treasure is (sayth Christ) there is thy hart.

The miseries of Servantes and Masters. Chapter 14.

The sevante or bond man is vexed and weried about the
provision of his maisters necessaries, with watching and carying of
things from place to place: he is beaten with stripes, and spoyled of
his wealth. If he have no riches, his labour must make a painful
purchase: if he have ought he is compelled to spende it at his masters
pleasure. The offence of the master, is the peyne of the servant: the
offence of the sevant, turneth to the pray of hys master. For as the
Poete saith, Wherein soever the rulers do amisse, the poore subiects
feele the smart. The wilde asse in the wildernesse is the game or pray
for the Lion: even so is the poore man the pray for the riche. O
extreame condition of bondage. Nature hathe brought foorth all men
free, but fortune hath made slaves and bond men. The bondman is
forced to suffer, and no man is permitted to take compassion uppon
hym: hee is compelled to weepe, wayle, and to be sorowfull, and no
man is suffered to be sory with him: so is he not his owne man, and
in his miseries soroweth comfortlesse. The martiall mindes live in

miserable moodes: for besydes the great paynes they endure, and the continual daungers they stande in, they make theyr onely felicities of other mens miserie: and it is an odious thing to live uppon the spoyle of an othor. The cruell master lyveth alwayes in feare, least the treason of hys servantes shorten hys dayes. If he be gentle, then hys familiaritie breedeth contempte: feare then dothe vexe him if hee be severe: and contempte setteth him at nought if hee be curteous: For crueltie getteth hatred, and contempt foloweth familiaritie. Furthermore, familiar care causeth weerinesse, and private regarde bringeth griefe. Wherefore it behoveth a man to be readie and well senced on every syde, that hee may beware and take heede before hand, of the ambushes and the craftie fetches or deceytes of the malitious and envious men, whereby hee may repell and put away the iniuries of those whyche assaulte hym, to the overthrowe of hys enimies, and to be able to defende hys neyghbors, and protect hys countrey men: for one daye is not satisfyed in hir malice towards man in thys lyfe, but she bringeth foorth laboures and sorowes for an other: and one nyghte doeth shewe and declare knowledge to another. Wee therefore so leade our dayes in travell, and passe over many nightes without sleepe.

The miserie of the maried and unmaried man. Chapter 15.

So deepely rooted is lecherous lust in the fleshe of man, that if it be possible for fire not to burne, it is possible for man not to lust. For howsoever the fleshe shall bee kepte under, yet shall not that unquiet Iebusite bee dryven out or conquered. For although thou rebuke nature never so much, yet will she returne agayne. All men doe not understande this saying, or obtayne this grace, but hee which can conceyve or comprehende it, (sayth oure Lorde) lette hym. Whereuppon when GOD gave commandement unto Moses and Aaron for the ordering of the holy garmentes, and of the apparelling of theyr children, hee did not onely gyve commanndement for the covering of the thighes, but willed them to use linnen sloppes to cover their privities, when they shoulde enter into the Tabernacle of witnesse. The Apostle also sayth to those which be maried, Do not defraud one another, unlesse it be perhappes by consent for a time, that you may be more fervent in prayer, and afterwardes returne agayne unto the same, least the Sathan tempt you through incontinency: For it is better for a man to marrie, that to burne. For the Angell of Sathan, with suttle devises continually provoking lewde liking, doth alwayes warre and fighte with maidenly chastity and manly constancie: He kindleth the fire of nature with the blast of fraile suggestion: He also layeth matter before us, to worke our lewde lusts: He fighteth a combate with us, casting before our eyes the glorious shape of some gallant dame, whereby the feeble minde is secretly sauced with amorous desires. And the body made prone to perdition: He changeth our affections dayly with the sighte of sundry pleasant shapes. Let King David suffise for example, who in the after noone walking in his Princely palace, beholding Bersabe washing hir selfe on the other side, sent for hir, tooke hir and slepte with hir, for she was exceeding faire and beautifull. But the maried man is carefull for those thyngs which belong to his wiff and family, and is devided in himselfe. For divers cares draweth him sundry wayes, and sundry thoughts disquiete his troubled minde. The feare of evil fortune doth vexe him, the losse of welth doth torment him, and the charge of household doth devide him diversly. For all hys studie is howe to mayntayne his wife, to procure things necessary for his children, and to discharge the hire of his servants. And therefore most truly is it sayde, that such men have the troubles and cares of the flesh. Hys wife desireth to have pretious ornamentes and rich iewelles, shee craveth divers sutes of gorgious and sumptuous apparell, and sundry parcels of householde stuffe: yea and oftentimes the wives furniture, doth exceede the revenewe of hir husbands lands. But if she be denyed what she demandeth, then doth she mourne and sighe day and nighte, she frowneth and murmureth, she chatteth and checketh, with greevous complaintes of hir husbandes ingratitude, withoute ceasing. There be three things (saith Salamon) whiche doe not permitte a man to tarrie in his house, that is, a smokie chimney, a dropping roufe, and a shrewde wife. Often time she sayeth unto hir husbande, suche a mans wife goeth gorgeously and finely apparelled, and is esteemed and much made of by every one: but I poore wretche, all alone, am nothyng regarded amongst my neighbours: I am contemned and despised of every one. Shee only will bee loved and praysed: she thynketh the good countenance shewed unto an other, to procure hatred unto hir: and shee surmiseth the commendation of an other, to be for hir disgraces. All that she loveth, must be lyked of, and all that she hateth must bee disliked: she will be mistresse and cannot be maistred: she may not abide to serve as a subiect, but she must rule as a governour: shee will seeme experte in all things, and will shewe hir selfe ignorant in nothing. If shee be fayre, she is soone beloved of others: if she be foule, she is not hastily desired. But it is a hard matter to keepe that whiche is beloved of many, and it is a greefe to posssesse that which no man esteemeth. Some men assure hir by the comelynesse of theyr personage: some gayne victory by policie: some do move affection by merrie conceytes, or pleasant devises: other some doe winne good will through liberalitie: and needes muste there be some breach, where the batterie is layde on every side. The goodnesse of the horse, the Asse, the garmente, the bedde, the potte, and also the pitcher, are firste tryed, and after bought: but the manners or conditions of a woman are hardly knowen, least misliking growe before mariage. But after mariage whatsoever befall hir, bee shee foule or faire, wise or folish, patient or proud, lothsome or handsome, shee cannot bee separate, but onely for adultrie. Yea neyther can the man which putteth away hys wife for this cause marrie an other, neyther yet can the wife put so away, take another husbande. For whosoever shall forsake hys wife unlesse it bee for adultrie, gyveth hir occasion to committe adulterie: and hee whiche doethe marrie hir that is dismissed for adulterie, doeth also committe adulterie. If the wife shall goe from hir husbande for thys cause (sayeth the Apostle) she oughte eyther to remayne unmarryed, or else bee reconciled to hir husbande agayne.

Therefore the burthen of wedlocke is greevous. For as (Salomon sayth) he is foolish and unwise which keepeth his wife being an adultresse: and he is the patrone of his wives dishonestie, which doth cloke hir crime. If then a man put away his wife being an adultresse, he is punished without his faulte, for that he must so long as shee liveth remaine chast. And therefore Christes disciples said, If a mans condition and case be suche with his wife, it is better for man not to marrie. For no man can well brooke a mate in love: and who so ever is the subiect of ielousie, is the slave of suspition. Yea and although the Scripture dothe affirme, that man and wife shall be two in one fleshe, yet besydes that, the very love of the husbande it selfe, doethe cause him to be impatient of partners. . . .

Of the enimyes of man. Chapter 17.

The life of man is nothing else but warfare uppon the earth. Is it not a warfare in deede, whereas many kynde of enimyes lye in wayte on every syde, that they may take, persecute, and kill us? as the divil, the world, mankynde it selfe, and the fleshe. The devil with vyces and fleshly desires: man togither with beastes, and other creatures: the world with the elements: the flesh with sensualities. For the fleshe lusteth contrary to the spirite, and the spirite contrary to the fleshe. Yea we have not only a combat against flesh and bloud, but also against the spirituall authors of wickednesse, which be in the ayre, and agaynst the Lordes and rulers of darkenesse. For your adversary the devil (sayth saynt Peter) goeth about like a roring Lyon seeking whome hee may devour. The firy darts of our wicked enimies are alwayes kindled against us. Death entreth in by the windowes, the eye doth rob and spoyle the soule, the whole world doeth fight against us unwise men, for one nation warreth against an other, and great earthquakes are in divers places, pestilence and hungers, terrors and tempestes commeth downe amongest us from the heavens. The earth bringeth forth thornes and thistles: the water bringeth forth innundations and fluds: the ayre sendeth uppon us stormes, thunders, lightnings, and terrible fierye sightes. The earth (sayeht God to Adam) shall bee cursed in thy labour, it shall yelde unto thee thornes and thistles, and in the sweate of thy browes thou shalt eate thy bread, until thou doest returne againe into the earth. The wylde bore of the wooddes doth lye in waite for to devour us, and every wylde beast seeketh our destruction. The Woulf, the Bear, the Lybard, the Lyon, the Tygar, and the wylde Asse: the Crocodile,

the Grife, the Serpent, the Snake, the Basiliske, the venimous worme
called Aspis, the Dragon, the Cereastes, the Scorpion, and the Vyper:
also Nittes, Lyce, Emattes, Fleas, Gnattes, and Flyes, Hornettes, and
Waspes, Fishes and Foules, all these I say doe lye in waite to make a
praye of our persons. For wee which in the beginning were created to
beare rule over the fishes of the Sea, and foules of the ayre, and over
all living things whiche move uppon the earth, are nowe become a
praye for them to feed uppon. For it is written, I will set the teeth
of beasts uppon them. . . .

Of the innumerable kindes of sicknesses that man is subiect unto. Chapter 25.

The knowledge that man hath hadde to search oute the causes
and natures of things these many hundreth yeeres, could as yet never
finde out so many kindes of diseases, or such divers sortes of passions,
as the frailtie or weakenesse of man could endure and suffer. Shoulde
I call it tollerable impatience to sustayne suche infirmities or intollerable sufferance? It is better I ioyne them both togither: For it is
intollerable for the bitternesse of the passion, and tollerable for the
necessitie of suffering. Mans nature from day to day is more and
more corrupt: Inso much that many holsome experiments which in
tymes past were of great force, are nowe through the defect or
weakenesse of mans nature, become hurtfull and dangerous. For now
both the worlds, that is to say, the great world that contyneth all,
and man whyche is the little world contayned therein, waxe both
olde, and drawe towardes an ende. And howe muche the more the
age of them both is prolonged or encreased, so much the worse the
nature of them both is vexed and troubled.

Of divers kindes of torments which men sustayne. Chapter 26.

What shoulde I speake of the poore and miserable wretches of
thys worlde, which by innumerable kynds of tormentes sustayne
punishmente? Some of them are beaten to deathe with cudgels, some
cut off by the sword, some burnt with fire, some are stoned to
deathe, some are torne in pieces with horses and with the talents of
beasts, some are hanged on gibbets, some are rackte and strangled
to deathe, some are tormented with engins made of mettalles, and
they are crucifyed with a million more of miseries. Some are straitely
prest with fetters and bonds, and yoked with sundry engins. Some
are cast into prison, and there pine away for neede. Some are throwen
downe headlong from high places, some are drowned, flayed quicke,
dismembred, cut in peeces and perced through theyr bodyes. Upon
them falleth those punishments of the which the Prophete speaketh,
saying, some perishe under the sworde, some by famine, and some in
durance or captivitye. It is a heavie and pitifull syghte, that some
are given to feede the foules of the ayre, some the fishes of the Sea,
and some the beastes of the earth. Alas, and woe unto you most

wretched and miserable mothers, which bring forth such unfortunate children.

Of a certayn horrible fact committed by a woman compelled thereunto by extreame misery. Chapter 27.

To leave out nothing wherby the miseries of this worlde may bee manifest, I wil make rehersall of an horrible and dreadfull fact committed in the Jewes warres. A certayne woman of noble parentage and great wealth, did endure the common fortune in the siedge of Ierusalem, amongst the rest of the multitude which came thither from divers places: The goods which shee brought into the citie, were for the most part taken and spoyled by the Tyrantes: And that little which was lefte to sustayne hir weary life, the robbers and spoylers of the Citie (dayly entring into hir house) bereeved hir thereof. Whereby great trouble and griefe dyd so much move hir, that often times with opprobrious wordes she did attempte to stir up their choler, by their bloudy hands to end hir wretched life. But when by no meanes shee could provoke their anger to fulfill hir evil intent, nor yet could move them to take compassion uppon hir miserable estate, all hope of foode forsaking hir, and payne of penury pinching hir, using the worst counsail, did arme hir selfe against the lawes of nature. For having a yong babe sucking at hir breast, she cryed out and sayde, O unhappye chylde of an unfortunate mother, heavye is thy chaunce, but heavier is my choise: for I am forced to make foode of my owne fleshe: I will make my myserie knowne to all posteritie, and the crueltie of the Romaynes the cause of my calamitie. Come now therfore my little babe, whom I have borne full often in myne armes, whom I have nourished with my tender pappes, whom I have kissed full sweetly with my lippes, let thy flesh bee foode unto thy wofull mother, and let the womb which brought thee into light, be thy rufull grave. And when she had thus spoken, she murdered hir child, part of whom through famyne she presentlye devoured, the rest shee did reserve to feede hir furious appetite. And beholde, the hungry souldyers passing by, receyved the broyling savour of hir unnaturall dyet. Wherefore with force they came into the house to spoile hir of hir foode: whose desire to satisfie, shee playd hir parte most kyndly, saying, behold I have reserved the best portion for you: and by and by uncovered the remnant of hir child: which unkynde and cruell spectacle dyd so dismay them and move their senses, that trembling feare betooke them all, and the horror of the sight did bereave them of their speeche. But shee with a Tygres countenaunce, and most cruell harte, sayde unto them, eate friendes, it is parte of my chylde, of my deare sonne, whome I have brought into this worlde, and through penurie it is my deed: what wil you be more scrupulous than the mother? shall bloudy Souldiers have more tender harts than a silly woman? if pittie or naturall affection doe overcome you and cause you to abhor my dyet, I my selfe will feed thereon agayne. And after she had thus sayd, the souldiers departed as men all astonied at the sight, the which spoyling hir of all hir wealth and riches, left hir none other foode to feede uppon.

Of the punishing of the Innocent, and dismissyng of the guiltie. Chapter 28.

Let no man assure him selfe to bee free or exempt from payne, although he knowe him selfe to bee without offence. Hee that standeth, let him take heede that hee doe not fall. For the innocent is often tymes condemned, and the offendour delivered: the godly is punished, and the wicked is honored: Iesus is crucified, and Barrabas is dismist. In these our dayes a quyet man is esteemed unprofitable: and he that is addicted unto devotion, or to the service of god, is reputed for an hypocrite: and the simple man that is without deceite, is accompted for a foole. For the simplicitie of the rightuous man is laughed at, and hee whose vertue shineth before men as a lampe, in the imaginations of the riche is contemned.

An Account of the Mind's Journey to God

Bonaventura

Scholasticism, as epitomized by the Dominican, Thomas Aquinas, is synonymous with rational theology and the derivation of knowledge about God through the study of philosophy. Scholasticism, as epitomized by a second great thinker of the thirteenth century, the Franciscan, Bonaventura (1221-1274), admits room for another path to God, the mystic way. Bonaventura's *Itinerarium mentis in Deum,* proved popular not only in his own day but throughout the later Middle Ages as well when mysticism flourished far more than during the high Middle Ages.

Prologue.

In the beginning I invoke the First Principle, from whom, as from the Father of Lights, descend all illuminations, from whom is every best and every perfect gift—that is, I invoke the Eternal Father, through his Son, our Lord Jesus Christ, that, by the intercession of the Most Holy Virgin Mary, Mother of the same God and our Lord Jesus Christ, and by that of the Blessed Francis, our guide and father, He would illuminate the eyes of our soul, to guide our feet into the way of that peace which passeth all sense, the peace which our Lord Jesus Christ preached and gave, of which preaching our father, Saint Francis, was the repeater, in every sermon proclaiming peace at the beginning and end; in every salutation wishing peace; in every contemplation sighing for ecstatic peace, as a citizen of that Jerusalem, whereof it is said by that Man of Peace, who was peaceful with them who hated peace: "Seek ye those things which are for the peace of Jerusalem" (Psalms, 122:6). For He knew that the throne of Solomon was only in peace, as it is written: "In Salem (peace) also is his Tabernacle and his dwelling-place in Zion" (Psalms, 76:3). When, therefore according to the example of our most blessed father Francis, I panted after this peace—I, a sinner, who, though in all respects unworthy, have succeeded, the seventh in order since his transition, in the room of that most blessed Father, to the general ministry of the brethren—it happened that by the Divine will, in the thirty-third year after the transition of this blessed father, I, desiring to find peace of spirit, withdrew to Mount Alvernia as to a quiet place; and while I abode there and was considering in my mind certain mental ascensions to God, there occurred to me, among other things, that miracle which in the above-mentioned spot happened to the blessed Francis, namely, the vision of a winged seraph in the form of a crucifix. And, as I reflected thereupon, it immediately appeared to me that this vision typified the uplifting of our father in contemplation and the way that leads thereto; for by the six wings we may rightly understand the six upliftings of illumination, whereby, as by a kind of steps or paths, the soul is disposed to pass upward to peace through the ecstatic transports of Christian Wisdom. . . .

I purpose to divide my treatise into seven chapters, prefixing to each a title for the easier understanding of the things treated therein. I beg my readers, therefore, that they will regard the intention of the writer more than his work, the meaning of his words more than his uncouth speech, truth more than elegance of style, exercise of affection more than erudition of intellect. Those who will do this must not run lightly over the course of these speculations, but must with all care ruminate upon them.

THE SPECULATION OF THE POOR MAN IN THE WILDERNESS.

Chapter 1. On the degrees of ascension to God, and the beholding of Him through His footsteps in the universe.

"Blessed is the man whose strength is in thee; in whose heart are the highways to Zion. Passing through the valley of weeping, they make it a place of springs" (Psalms, 84:4-6). Since bliss is naught but the enjoyment of the Supreme Good, and the Supreme Good is above us, no one can become blest unless he ascend above himself, with ascension not of the body, but of the heart. But we cannot be lifted above ourselves, save through a higher power lifting us up. For, however much our inward steps may be ordered, nothing is done unless divine aid accompany. But divine aid accompanies those who ask it from the heart, humbly and devoutly, and this is to sigh for it in this vale of tears—which is done by fervent prayer. Prayer, therefore, is the mother and source of uprising to God. Wherefore Dionysius, in his "Mystic Theology," wishing to instruct us in the way to attain mental transports, sets down prayer as the first step. Let us each, therefore, pray and say to our Lord, God: "Lead me, O Lord, in thy way, and I will walk in thy truth. Let my heart rejoice to fear thee" (Psalms, 86:11). In praying this prayer, we are illuminated to know the steps of ascension to God. For, inasmuch as, in our present condition, this Universe of things is a stair whereby we may ascend to God; and, since among these things some are his footprints, some his image, some corpreal, some spiritual, some temporal, some eternal; and, hence, some outside of us, and some inside; in order that we may attain to the consideration of the First Principle, which is altogether spiritual, eternal, and above us, we must pass through the footsteps, which are corporeal, temporal, and outside of us; and this is to be led in the *way* of God. We must also enter into our own minds, which are the image of God, eternal, spiritual, and within us; and this is to enter into the *truth* of God. We most also rise aloft to the eternal, which is purely spiritual and above us, by looking at the First Principle; and this is to rejoice in the *knowledge* of God and in *reverence* for his majesty. This, then, is the three-days' journey in the wilderness. This is the threefold illumination of one day; the first is as the evening, the second as the morning, and the third as noon-day. This has regard to the threefold existence of things; that is, in matter, in intelligence, and in the divine art, as it is written: "Let there be made; He made, and it was made" (Gen. 1:2,3). This also has regard to the triple substance in Christ, who is our stair—that is, the corporeal, the spiritual, and the divine.

According to this triple progress, our minds have three principal outlooks. The first is toward corporeal things without, and with reference to this it is called animality or sensuality. The second is directed inward upon and into itself, and with reference to this it is called spirit. The third is directed upward above itself, and in reference to this it is called mind. With all these it must dispose itself to ascend to God, that it may love him with the whole mind, the whole heart, and the whole soul, in which consist at once perfect observance of the law and Christian Wisdom.

But, since every one of the aforesaid modes is doubled, according as we come to consider God as *Alpha* and as *Omega,* or according as we come to see God in each of the above modes through a glass and in a glass, or because each of these considerations has to be commingled with the other that is joined to it, and also to be considered in its purity, so it is necessary that these three grades should rise to the number of six; whence, as God finished the universal world in six days and rested on the seventh, so the smaller world is led in the most orderly way, by six successive grades of illumination, to the rest of contemplation. Typical of this are the six steps leading to the throne of Solomon: the six-winged Seraphim which Isaiah saw; the six days after which God called Moses from the midst of the darkness; the six days after which—as we read in Matthew, Christ led his disciples up into a mountain, and was transfigured before them.

Corresponding, therefore, to the six grades of ascension into God are the six grades of the powers of the soul, whereby we ascend from the lowest to the highest; from the external to the most internal; from the temporal to the eternal; namely: sense, imagination, reason, intellect, intelligence, and the apex of the mind, or the spark of synteresis. These grades are implanted in us by nature, deformed by sin, reformed by grace, to be purged by justice, exercised by knowledge, perfected by wisdom. . . .

And, since we must ascend Jacob's ladder, before we descend, let us place the first step in the ascent at the bottom, holding up this whole sensible world before us, as a mirror, through which we may rise to God, the supreme artificer, that we may be true Hebrews, passing forth from Egypt to the land promised to our fathers; also that we may be Christians, passing forth with Christ from this world to the Father; and that we may be lovers of Wisdom, that calleth and saith: "Come unto me all ye that desire me, and be ye filled with mine offspring" (Sirach, 24:20). "For, from the greatness and beauty of created things, their Creator may be seen and known" (Wisdom, 13:5). The supreme power, wisdom, and benevolence of the Creator is reflected in all created things, as is reported in threefold fashion by the sense of the flesh to the interior sense. For the sense of the flesh lends itself to the intellect when it investigates with reason, believes with faith, or contemplates with intellect. In contemplating, it considers the actual existence of things; in believing, their habitual course; in reasoning, their potential pre-excellence.

The first point of view, which is that of contemplation, considering things in themselves, sees in them weight, number, and measure; weight, which marks the point to which they tend; number, whereby they are distinguished; measure, whereby they are limited; and hereby it sees in them mode, species, order, as will as substance, virtue, and action, from which it may arise, as from footsteps, to understand the power, wisdom, and boundless goodness of the Creator.

The second point of view, which is that of faith, considering this world, attends to its origin, course, and termination. For by faith we believe that the ages were arranged by the Word of Life; by faith we believe that the epochs of the three laws—the law of nature, the law of scripture, and the law of grace—succeed each other and have elapsed in the most perfect order; by faith we believe that the world will be terminated by a final judgment. In the first we observe the power; in the second, the providence; in the third, the justice of the Supreme Principle.

The third point of view—that of reason—investigating, sees that some things are only, and some are and live only, wheras some are, live, and discern; and that the first are inferior; the second, middle; the third, superior. It sees, likewise, that some are only corporeal, and some partly corporeal, partly spiritual; whence it concludes that there are some purely spiritual, as better and worthier than either. It sees, moreover, that some are mutable and corruptible, as terrestrial things; others mutable and incorruptible, as celestial things; whence it concludes that some are immutable and incorruptible, as supercelestial things. From these visible things, therefore, it rises to consider God's power, wisdom, and goodness, as being, living, and intelligent, as purely spiritual, incorruptible, and intransmutable. . . .

Open, therefore, thine eyes; draw near thy spiritual ears; unseal thy lips, and apply thy heart, that in all created things thou mayest see, hear, praise, love, magnify, and honor God, lest, peradventure, the universal frame of things should rise up against thee. Yea, for this the universe will fight against them that are without senses, whereas to them that have senses it will be a matter of glory, who can say with the Prophet: "Thou, Lord, hast made me glad through thy work; I will triumph in the works of thy hands" (Psalms, 92:4). "O Lord, how manifold are thy works! In wisdom hast thou made them all. The earth is full of thy riches" (Psalms, 104:24).

Chapter 2. On the beholding of God in His footsteps in this sensible world.

But since, as regards the mirror of sensible things, we may contemplate God, not only through them, as through footprints, but also in them, in so far as he is in them by essence, power, and presence, and this consideration is loftier than the preceding; wherefore this kind of consideration occupies the second place, as the second grade of contemplation, whereby we must be guided to the contemplation of God in all created things, which enter our minds through the bodily senses.

We must observe, therefore, that this sensible world, which is called the macrocosm—that is, the long world—enters into our soul, which is called the microcosm—that is, the little world—through the gates of the five senses, as regards the apprehension, delectation, and distinction of these sensible things; which is manifest in this way: In the sensible world some things are generant, others are generated, and others direct both these. Generant are the simple bodies; that is, the celestial bodies and the four elements. For out of the elements, through the power of light, reconciling the contrariety of elements in things mixed, are generated and produced whatever things are generated and produced by the operation of natural power. Generated are the bodies composed of the elements, as minerals, vegetables, sensible things, and human bodies. Directing both these and those are the spiritual substances, whether altogether conjunct, like the souls of the brutes, or separably conjunct, like rational souls, or altogether separate, like the celestial spirits, which the philosophers call Intelligences, we Angels. On these, according to the philosophers, it devolves to move the heavenly bodies, and for this reason the administration of the universe is ascribed to them, as receiving from the First Cause—that is, God—that inflow of virtue which they pour forth again in relation to the work of government, which has reference to the natural consistence of things. But, according to the theologians, the direction of the universe is ascribed to these same beings, as regards the works of redemption, with respect to which they are called "ministering spirits sent forth to do service for the sake of them that shall inherit salvation."

Man, therefore, who is called the lesser world, has five senses, like five gates, through which the knowledge of all the things that are in the sensible world enters into his soul. For through sight there enter the sublime and luminous bodies and all other colored things; through touch, solid and terrestrial bodies; through the three intermediate senses, the intermediate bodies; through taste, the aqueous; through hearing, the aërial; through smell, the vaporable, which have something of the humid, something of the aerial, and something of the fiery or hot, as is clear from the fumes that are liberated from spices. There enter, therefore, through these doors not only the simple bodies, but also the mixed bodies compounded of these. Seeing, then, that with sense we perceive not only these particular sensibles—light, sound, odor, savor, and the four primary qualities which touch apprehends—but also the common sensibles—number, magnitude, figure, rest, and motion; and seeing that everything which moves is moved by something else, and certain things move and rest of themselves, as do the animals, in apprehending through these five senses the motions of bodies, we are guided to the knowledge of spiritual motions, as by an effect to the knowledge of causes.

In the three classes of things, therefore, the whole of this sensible world enters the human soul through apprehension. These external sensible things are those which first enter into the soul through the gates of the five senses. They enter, I say, not through their substances, but through their similitudes, generated first in the medium, and from the medium in the external organ, and from the external organ in the internal organ, and from this in the apprehensive power; and thus generation in the medium, and from the medium in the organ, and the direction of the apprehensive power upon it, produce the apprehension of all those things which the soul apprehends externally.

This apprehension, if it is directed to a proper object, is followed by delight. The sense delights in the object perceived through its abstract similitude, either by reason of its beauty, as in vision, or by reason of its sweetness, as in smell and hearing, or by reason of its healthfulness, as in taste and touch, properly speaking. . . .

After this apprehension and delight there comes discernment, by which we not only discern whether this thing be white or black (because this alone belongs to the outer sense), and whether this thing be wholesome or hurtful (because this belongs to the inner sense), but also discern why this delights and give a reason therefor. And in this act we inquire into the reason of the delight which is derived by the sense from the object. This happens when we inquire into the reason of the beautiful, the sweet, and the wholesome, and discover that it is a proportion of equality. . . .

All these things are footprints, in which we may behold our God. For, since an apprehended species is a similitude generated in a medium and them impressed upon the organ, and through that impression leads to the knowledge of its principle—that is, of its object—it manifestly implies that that eternal light generates from itself a similitude, or splendor, coequal, consubstantial, and coeternal, and that He who is the image and similitude of the invisible God, and the splendor of the glory, and the figure of the substance which is everywhere, generates, by his first generation of himself, his own similitude, in the form of an object in the entire medium, unites himself, by the grace of union, to the individual of rational nature, as a species to a bodily organ, so that by this union he may lead us back to the Father as the fontal principle and object. If, therefore, all cognizable things generate species of themselves, they clearly proclaim that in them, as in mirrors, may be seen the eternal generation of the Word, the Image, and the Son, eternally emanating from God the Father. . . .

Chapter 3. On the beholding of God through His image impressed upon the natural powers.

But, since the two grades above described, leading us to God by his footprints, whereby he is reflected in all created things, have guided us to the point where we entered into ourselves—that is, into our minds, in which the divine image is reflected—we must now, in the third place, enter into ourselves, and leaving, as it were, the forecourt outside, endeavor, through a mirror, to see God in the Holy Place—that is, in the forepart of the Tabernacle—wherein, as from a candlestick, the light of truth is reflected on the faces of our minds, in which, indeed, is resplendent the image of the most blessed Trinity.

Enter, therefore, into thyself and see that thy mind loves itself most fervently, and could not love itself if it did not know itself, or know itself if it did not remember itself, since we seize nothing through intelligence that is not present in our memory. And hereby thou perceivest, not with the eye of flesh, but with the eye of reason, that thy soul has a threefold power. Consider, therefore, the operations and habits of these three powers, and thou wilt be able to see God through thyself, as through a likeness, and this is seeing him through a glass and in a riddle.

But the operation of memory is retention and re-presentation, not only of things present, corporeal, and temporal, but also of things successive, simple, and sempiterna. For the memory retains past things through recollection, present things through susception, future things through foresight. It retains also simple things; for example, the principles of continuous and discreet quantities, as point, instant, unity, without which it is impossible to remember or to think the things which have these for their principles. No less does it retain, as sempiternal and sempiternally, the principles and dignities of the sciences, because it can never so forget them, while it uses reason, that it will not accept them and assent to them, as soon as it hears them, and this not as if it perceived them afresh, but as recognizing them to be innate in itself and familiar. . . . And thus, through the operations of the memory, it appears that the mind itself is an image of God, and a similitude so present to him, and having him so present to it, that it actually grasps him, is potentially capable of holding him, and may become a partaker in him.

Again, the operation of the intellective power consists in the perception of the meaning of terms, propositions, and inferences. But the intellect seizes the meanings of terms when it comprehends, by definition, what any particular thing is. But a definition can be made only through higher notions, and these have to be defined by still higher ones, until we arrive at the highest and most general, without a knowledge of which the lower ones cannot be definitely under-understood. Unless, therefore, we know what being-in-itself is, we cannot know the definition of any special substance. . . .

The action of the power of choice is observed in counsel, judgment, desire. Counsel consists in inquiring which is better—this or that. By "better" we mean approaching more closely to the best, But approach implies greater assimilation. No one, therefore, knows whether this is better than that, unless he knows that it more closely resembles the best. And no one knows that one thing more closely resembles another, unless he knows that other. For I do not know that this man resembles Peter, unless I know or am acquainted with Peter. Every one, therefore, who takes counsel is impressed with the knowledge of the highest good. But any certain judgment with respect to things about which counsel can be taken must follow some law. And no one judges with certainty according to a law, unless he is certain that that law is right, and that he must not judge it. But our minds judge with regard to themselves. Since, then, they may not judge the law according to which they judge, that law is superior to our minds, and by this they judge according as it has been impressed upon thim. And nothing is superior to the human mind save him alone who made it. Therefore, in judging, our deliberative power ascends to the divine laws, if it analyze with complete analysis. Desire, again, is chiefly directed to that which most deeply moves it. But that moves it most deeply which is most deeply loved; and that which is most deeply loved is happiness. Again, happiness is not posssessed except through the highest and ultimate end. But human desire craves nothing save the highest good, or what is co-ordinated with it, or what has some resemblance to it. Such is the power of the highest good that nothing can be loved by the creature save through the desire of that good. The creature is deceived and errs, when it accepts the semblance and image for the truth.

Behold, therefore, how near the soul is to God, and how memory leads to eternity, intelligence to truth, and power of choice to the highest goodness, according to their operations. Again, according to the order, origin, and habit of these powers, it leads up to the Blessed Trinity itself; for from memory arises intelligence, as its offspring; because then we understand, when a similitude which is in the memory, results in clearness of intellect, which is nothing else than the Word. From memory and intelligence is breathed forth love, as the bond between the two. These three—the generant mind, the word, and love—are in the soul as memory, intelligence, and love, which are consubstantial, coequal, and coeval, reciprocally passing in each other. If, therefore, God is perfect spirit, he has memory, intelligence, and will; he has the begotten Word and the breathed Love. These are necessarily distinguished, since the one is produced by the other, not essentially, not accidentally; therefore, personally. When, therefore, the mind considers itself, it rises through itself, as through a mirror, to behold the blessed Trinity of Father, Word, and Love—three persons coeternal, coequal, and consubstantial—so that each of the three is in each of the other two, whereas one is not the other, but these three are one God. . . .

Chapter 4. On the beholding of God in His image, as reformed by the gifts of grace.

But since, not only by passing through ourselves, but also within ourselves, we may behold the First Principle, and this vision is superior to the preceding, this mode of consideration occupies the fourth grade of contemplation. Strange it seems, when it has been shown that God is so near to our minds, that so few are able to behold the First Principle in themselves. But the reason is not far to seek. The human mind, distracted by cares, does not enter into itself through memory; beclouded with phantasms, it does not return to itself through intelligence; allured by appetites, it does not revert to itself through desire for internal sweetness and spiritual joy. Wherefore, being totally prostrate among these sensible things, it cannot enter in into itself, as into the image of God.

And since a man must lie in the spot where he falls, unless some one sets to work and helps him to rise, our souls could not be perfectly raised from these sensible things to the intuition of itself, and of eternal truth in itself, had not Truth, taking on human form in Christ, become a stair for it, repairing the former stair, which in Adam had been broken down. Hence, however far a man may be illuminated by the light of nature and acquired science, he cannot enter into himself, to enjoy himself in the Lord, save through the mediation of Christ, who says: "I am the door; by me if any man enter in, he shall be saved, and shall go in and out and shall find pasture" (John, 10:9). But we do not approach this door unless we believe in him, hope for him, love him. If, therefore, we wish to re-enter to the fruition of truth, as into Paradise, we must go in through faith, hope, and love toward the mediator between God and man, Jesus Christ, who is, as it were, the tree of life in the midst of Paradise.

The image of our mind, therefore, must be clothed with the three theological virtues, whereby the soul is purified, illuminated, and perfected, and thus the image is reformed, repaired, and made suitable for the heavenly Jerusalem, and a part of the Church militant, which, according to the Apostle, is the offspring of the heavenly Jerusalem. For he says: "The Jerusalem that is above is free, which is our mother" (Gal. 4:26). The soul, therefore, that believes in, hopes for, and loves Jesus Christ, who is the Word of the Father, incarnate, uncreated, inspired—that is, the way, the truth, and the life—does three things. In believing, through faith, in Christ as the uncreated Word, which is the word and glory of the Father, it recovers spiritual hearing and sight—hearing to receive the sayings of Christ, sight to behold the glories of his light. In longing with hope to receive the inspired word, through desire and affection it recovers its spiritual scent. In embracing with love the incarnate Word, as deriving delight from it, and in passing over into it through ecstatic love, it recovers spiritual taste and touch. Having recovered these senses, and seeing, hearing, smelling, tasting, and embracing its spouse, it is able to sing, like a bride, the Song of Songs, which was composed for the exercise of contemplation in this fourth grade, which no one comprehends save him who receives it, because it consists rather of affectional experience than of rational reflection. For in this grade, having recovered its interior senses, so as to see that which is supremely beautiful, to hear that which is supremely harmonious, to smell that which is supremely odoriferous, to taste that which is supremely sweet, to apprehend that which is supremely delightful, the mind is disposed to mental ecstasies—that is, through devotion, admiration, and exultation, according to the three exclaimations uttered in the Song of Songs. Of these, the first is uttered through superabundance of devotion, whereby the soul becomes like a rod of smoke from the perfumes of myrrh and frankincense. The second is uttered through excellence of admiration, whereby the soul becomes as the dawn, the moon, and the sun, according to that process of illuminations which lift up the soul to consider and admire its spouse. The third takes place through superabundance of exultation, whereby the soul becomes rich in the joys of the sweetest delight, resting wholly upon its Beloved. Having acquired these things, our spirits become hierarchic to ascend aloft, through conformity to that supernal Jerusalem into which none enters, unless it first descend into his heart through grace, as John saw in his Apocalypse. But it descends into the heart when, through reformation of the image, through the theologic virtues, and through delights of the spiritual senses and upliftings of ecstasies, our spirits become hierarchic—that is, purged, illuminated, and perfected. Thus, likewise, it is marked by the grades of the nine orders, inasmuch as within it are disposed, in due order, annunciation, dictation, guidance, ordination, invigoration, command, acceptance, revelation, unification, which, in their grades, correspond to the nine orders of the Angels, so that the grades of the three first named have regard to the nature of the human soul; the three following grades, to its industry; the last three to grace. Possessing these, the soul, when it enters into itself, enters the supernal Jerusalem, where, considering the orders of the Angels, it sees in them God, who, dwelling in them, performs all their actions. Whence Bernard says to Eugenius that God in the Seraphim loves as charity; in the Cherubim knows as truth; in the Thrones sits as equity; in the Dominions rules as majesty; in the Principalities guides as principle; in the Powers preserves as health; in the Virtues acts as virtue; in the Archangels reveals as light; in the Angels assists as piety. From all these God is seen as all in all, through contemplation of him in those minds in which he dwells through gifts of the most abounding charity. . . .

From these two middle steps, over which we pass to the contemplation of God within us, as in mirrors of created images, and, as it were, after the manner of wings outstretched for flight—wings holding the middle place—we may understand that we are led to divine things through the natural powers of the rational soul, in accordance with their operations, habitudes, and scientific habits, as appears from the third grade. We are led, in the same manner, through the hierarchic acts of human minds—viz., purgation, illumination, and perfection; by the hierarchic revelations of the Holy Scriptures, given to us through the Angels, according to the saying of the Apostle, that "the law was ordained through angels by the hand of a mediator" (Gal. 3:19) and, finally, we are led through the hierarchies and hierarchic orders, which in our minds have to be disposed after the manner of the heavenly Jerusalem. Our minds, filled full with all these lights, are inhabited by the divine Wisdom, like houses of God, being made daughters, spouses, and friends of God, members, sisters, and co-heirs of Christ the head, and, likewise, temples of the Holy Spirit, founded by faith, reared by hope, and dedicated to God by sanctity of mind and body. All this is accomplished by the perfectly sincere love of Christ, "shed abroad in our hearts through the Holy Ghost which was given to us," (Rom. 5:5) and without which we cannot know the secret things of God. For, as no one can know the things of a man save the spirit of man which is in him, even so the things of God none knoweth, save the Spirit of God. Let us, therefore, be rooted and grounded in love, that we may be strong to apprehend, with all the saints, what is the length of eternity, the breadth of liberality, the height of majesty, and the depth of judging wisdom.

Chapter 5. On the beholding of the Divine Unity, through its primary name, which is Being.

But, inasmuch as we may contemplate God, not only without us and within us, but also above us—without us, by his footsteps, within us, by his image, and above us, by the light which is impressed upon our minds (which is the light of eternal truth, since these minds of ours are formed directly by the truth itself)—those who are exercised in the first have entered the court in front of the tabernacle; those who are exercised in the second have entered the Holy Place; while those who are exercised in the third enter with the High Priest into the Holy of Holies, where above the ark are the cherubim of glory, overshadowing the mercy-seat. These we understand to mean two modes or grades of contemplating the invisible and eternal things of God. One of these relates to the essential attributes of God; the other to the special attributes of the (three) persons. The first mode first and chiefly fixes our vision upon Being itself, Telling us that *That which Is* is the first name of God. The second mode fixes our vision upon *The Good* itself, telling us that this is the first name of God. The first looks specially toward the Old Testament, which chiefly proclaims the unity of the Divine Essence; whence it was said to Moses: "I am that am" (Exod. 3:14). The second looks to the New Testament, which determines the plurality of the (divine) persons, baptizing in the name of the Father, the Son, and the Holy Spirit. Wherefore, our master, Christ, wishing to lift up to the perfection of the gospel the young man who had observed the law, ascribed to God chiefly and alone the attribute of goodness. He says: "None is good save one, even God" (Mark, 10:18). Damascenas, therefore, following Moses, says that *He who Is* is the first name of God; Dionysius, following Christ, says the *The Good* is the first name of God.

Let him, therefore, who desires to contemplate the invisible things of God, as regards unity of essence, first fix his eyes upon being itself, and see that it is so absolutely certain in itself that it cannot be thought not to be; because, being absolutely pure, it presents itself in the complete absence of non-being, just as naught presents itself in the complete absence of being. Even, therefore, as pure naught contains naught of being or of its conditions, so, on the contrary, being contains naught of non-being, either actually, or potentially, either according to the real truth, or to our estimate. But since non-being is a privation of being, it enters our intelligence only through being. Being, on the other hand, does not enter our intelligence through anything but itself, because everything that is understood, is understood either as not-being, or as being potentially, or as being actually. If, therefore, non-being can be understood only through being, and potential being only through actual being, and being designates the pure act of that which is, it follows that being is what first enters the intellect, and this being it is that is pure act. But this is not particular being, which is limited being, because it is mixed with potentiality; nor is it analogous being, because this has least of actuality, being that which in the smallest degree is. It remains, therefore, that this being is the divine being. . . .

The being, therefore, which is pure being, being simply, and being absolute is being primary, eternal, superlatively simple, actual, perfect, and one. And these things are so certain that the opposite of them cannot be thought by him who understands being. From one of them, likewise, the rest may be inferred. For, since being is being simple, it is simply first; because it is simply first, it is not made by aught else, nor could it be made by itself; therefore, it is eternal. In like manner, since it is first and eternal, it is not composed of other things; therefore it is perfectly simple, Again, since it is first, eternal, and perfectly simple, it contains no possibility intermingled with its actuality; therefore it is perfectly actual. Since it is first eternal, perfectly simple, and perfectly actual, therefore it is altogether perfect; such a thing neither lacks aught, nor can aught be added to it. Since it is first, eternal, perfectly simple, perfectly actual, and altogehter perfect, therefore it is in the highest degree one; for that which is called omnifarious superabundance is so called with respect to all things. Also, that which is called superabundance simply cannot possibly belong save to one being. Hence, if God is the name for being, primary, eternal, altogether simple, altogether actual, altogether perfect, it is impossible that he should be thought not to be, or not to be one, and no more. "Hear, therefore, O Israel! the Lord our God is one God." (Deut. 6:4). If thou beholdest this in pure simplicity of mind, thou art in some sort suffused with the illumination of the eternal light. But thou hast wherewithal to be uplifted into admiration; for being is first and last; it is eternal and altogether present; it is most simple and greatest; it is altogether actual and altogether immutable; it is altogether perfect and infinite; it is in the highest degree one, and yet in all modes. If thou admirest these things with a pure mind, thou art suffused with a greater light, because thou seest, further, that it is last because it is first. For, because it is first, it performs all things by reason of itself, whence it must be the ultimate end, the beginning and consummation, Alpha and Omega. It is most excellent, because it is eternal. For, because it is eternal, it is not limited by another; it does fail from itself; it does not pass from one thing to another. Therefore, it has neither past nor future, but is solely present. It is greatest, because it is altogether simple. Because it is altogether simple in essence, it is greatest in virtue; inasmuch as virtue is the more nearly infinite, the more it is united. It is altogether immutable, because it is altogether actual. For, because it is altogether actual, it is pure act, and, because it is such, it acquires nothing new, and loses nothing which it has; hence it cannot be changed. It is infinite, because it is altogether perfect. For, because it is altogether perfect, nothing better, nobler, or worthier than it can be thought; hence, nothing greater. And every such thing is infinite. It is in all modes, because it is in the highest degree one. For, because it is in the highest degree one, it is the universal principle of all multipliciy, and, for the same reason, it is the universal cause of all things—efficient, formal, and final—as likewise the cause of being, the ground of understanding, the order of living. It is, therefore, in all modes, not as the essence of all things, but as the altogether superexcellent, altogether universal, and altogether sufficient cause of all essences. Its virtue, because in the highest degree united in essence, is in the highest degree infinite and manifold in efficacy.

Chapter 6. On the beholding of the Most Blessed Trinity in its name which is Good.

After the consideration of essentials, the eye of the intelligence must be raised to the contemplation of the Most Blessed Trinity, so that the second Cherub may be set up beside the first. For, as being is the principle of the vision of essentials and the name whereby other things are known, so the good is the chief foundation for the contemplation of emanations. Behold, therefore, and observe how the Best—which simply is, than which nothing better can be thought, and which is such that it cannot be thought not to be, because to be is altogether better than not to be—is in such a way that it cannot be rightly thought unless it be thought as three and one; for by the good is meant that which is self-diffusive. Therefore the Supreme Good is supremely self-diffusive. But the highest diffusion cannot be unless it be actual and intrinsic, substantial and hypostatic, natural and voluntary, free and necessary, indeficient and perfect. Unless, therefore, there were eternally in the Highest Good an actual, consubstantial, and hypostatic production, as noble as that which produces, in the form of generation and spiration, so as to produce an eternal principle eternally acting as co-principle, and which shall be beloved and beloved in company, that is, begotten and breathed forth—that is, Father, Son, and Holy Spirit—it would in no way be the Highest Good, because it would not be in the highest degree diffused; for temporal diffusion in created things is only as a centre or point in comparison with the infinity of eternal goodness. Hence no diffusion can be thought greater than this, in which the diffuser communicates to another his whole substance and nature. It would not be the Highest Good, if it could lack reality or intellect. If, therefore, with thy mind's eye, thou canst behold the purity of goodness—which is the pure act of a principle, in charity loving with a love that is gratuitous, due, and compounded of grace and duty; which is the most complete diffusion, in the manner of nature and of will; which is a diffusion after the manner of the Word, in which all things are said, and after the manner of a gift, in which all other gifts are given—thou mayest see, through the supreme communicability, and through the highest communicabilty the highest consubstantiality, and through the highest consubstantiality the highest configurality, and through theses the highest co-equality, and through this the highest co-eternity, and through all the aforesaid the highest co-intimity, whereby one is necessarily in the other through the higest circumincession, and one acts along with the other through the omnifarious indivision of the substance, the virtue, and the action of the Most Blessed Trinity. . . .

Chapter 7. On mental and mystic ecstasy, wherein rest is given to the intellect, the affection passing wholly over, through ecstasy, into God.

After our mind has passed through these six considerations, which are like the six steps to the throne of the true Solomon, whereby there is an ascent to peace, wherein the true man of peace rests in a peaceful mind, as in an inner Jerusalem; like the six wings of the Cherub, by which the mind of the true man of contemplation, full of the enlightement of supernal wisdom, may be able to rise aloft; like the first six days, in which the mind is exercised, that finally it may attain to the Sabbath of rest—after our mind has beheld God outside of itself, by his footsteps and in his footsteps; within itself, through his image and in his image; above itself, by the similitude of the divine light reflected above as, and in that light, as far as is possible, according to the stage of progress and the exercise of our mind, when at last, on the sixth day, it shall have reached such a point as to behold in the first and highest principle and in Jesus Christ, the mediator between God and man, those things the like of which can in no degree be found in created things, and which go beyond all perspicacity of the human intellect, it remains that, beholding these things, it shall transcend and pass beyond, not only this sensible world, but also itself; in which transition Christ is the way and the door, Christ is the stair and vehicle, as the mercy-seat placed above the ark of God, and the sacrament hidden from before the ages. He who looks at this mercy-seat, gazing with his face fully turned at Him who hangs on the cross, through faith, hope, and charity, through devotion, admiration, praise, and jubilation, makes the passover, that is, the transition, with him, so that through the rod of the cross he passes over the Red Sea from Egypt into the desert, where he tastes the hidden manna, and rests with Christ as in the tomb, being, as it were, outwardly dead, nevertheless feeling, as far as is possible in the condition of pilgrimage, what was said on the cross to the robber who clung to Christ: "This day shalt thou be with me in Paradise" (Luke, 23:43). This also was shown to the Blessed Francis, when, in the ecstasy of contemplation of the lofty mountain (where I thought out these things which are written), there appeared to him a six-winged Seraph, fastened to a cross, as I and many others heard from a companion of his, who was with him at the time when he passed over into God through ecstasy of contemplation, and was set forth as an example of perfect contemplation, as formerly he had been of perfect action, like a second Jacob changed into Israel, that through him God might invite all truly spiritual men to this kind of trance and mental ecstasy, more by example than by word. But in this transition, if it is to be perfect, all intellectual operations must be left behind, and the whole apex of affection transferred and transformed into God. But this is a mystical and most secret thing, which no one knows save him who receives it; and no one receives it save him who desires it; and no one desires it save him whom the fire of the Holy Spirit, sent upon earth by Christ, inflames to the very marrow; and therefore, in this, nature can do nothing, and industry but little, little heed must be paid to inquiry and much to unction; little to language and very much to internal joy; little to words and writing and the whole to the gift of God—that is, to the Holy Spirit; little to created things and all to the creative essence, the Father, Son, and Holy Spirit, while we say with Dionysius to God the Trinity: "Superessential Trintiy and Over-God, better than best overseer of Christian theosophy, direct us to the more than unknown, the superlucent and super-sublime apex of mystical utterances, where the new and absolute and inconvertible and unchangeable mysteries of theology are hid in the superlucent darkness of occult-teaching science, which is super-splendent in the perfect, supermanifest gloom, in which all things are reflected, and which overfills the invisible intellects with the splendors of the invisible overblest." So much to God. But to the friend, to whom these things are written, let us say with the same: Do thou, O friend, proceeding boldly on the way to mystic visions, abandon the senses and the operations of the intellect; abandon things sensible and things invisible, and all non-being and being; and, as far as possible, unknowingly restore thyself to the unity of Him who is above all essence and science. For in rising, by an immeasurable and absolute ecstasy of pure mind, above thyself and all things, thou shalt ascend, abandoning all things and freed from all things, to the superessential ray of divine darkness. But if thou wouldst know how these things are done, ask grace, not learning; desire, not intellect; the groaning of prayer, not the diligence of reading; the spouse, not the master; God, not man; darkness, not clearness; not light, but fire totally inflaming and transporting into God by excessive unctions and most ardent affections. This fire, indeed, is God, and his way is toward Jerusalem, and it was kindled by the man Christ, in the fervor of his most ardent passion—a fervor of which he alone truly partakes who says: "My soul hath chosen strangling and my bones death" (Job, 8:15). He who chooseth this death may see God, because it is true beyond doubt: "Man shall not see me and live" (Exod. 23:22). Let us die, therefore, and enter into darkness. Let us impose silence on our anxieties, our appetites, and our imaginings. Let us pass with Christ crucified from this world to the Father, that when the Father is shown to us we may say with Philip: "It sufficeth us" (John, 14:8). Let us hear Paul: "My grace is sufficient for thee" (2 Cor. 12:9). Let us exult with David, saying: "My flesh and my heart faileth; but God is the strength of my heart and my portion forever" (Psalms, 73:26). "Blessed be the Lord for evermore: and let all the people say: Amen and Amen" (Psalms, 89:52).

Notes